Frank Modell Stop trying to cheer me up!

DODD, MEAD & COMPANY
New York

Copyright © 1978 by Frank Modell
All rights reserved
No part of this book may be reproduced in any form
without permission in writing from the publisher
Printed in the United States of America

1   2   3   4   5   6   7   8   9   10

Of the 160 drawings in this book, 156 appeared originally in *The New Yorker* and were copyrighted © in the years 1948 through 1978, inclusive, by the New Yorker Magazine, Inc.

Library of Congress Cataloging in Publication Data

Modell, Frank.
    Stop trying to cheer me up!

    1. American wit and humor, Pictorial.
I. Title.
NC1429.M67A4 1978   741.5'973   78-17557
ISBN 0-396-07627-0

Stop trying to cheer me up!

*For Daisy and Irving,
and for Jim Geraghty*

Introduction

I can remember way back, long before I could draw or knew what funny was, my father getting angry. He would lean his face close to mine, raise an index finger and shout, "Pay attention to me when I'm speaking to you." He was an excitable man, who could without warning burst into laughter or fly into a temper. Whenever his rage happened to be focussed on me, he needn't have worried that I wasn't paying attention. I was. No longer to his message—he had already got that across. I was watching the way anger worked on the topography of his face just inches away from mine: the narrowed eyes, the vertical furrow between the brows, the inflated nostrils. Then my mother would speak. "There's nothing to get so excited about," she would say, trying to mollify him. Her expressions were like a code to me. She contrived a smile I could read as "This is awful, but we know that in a moment it will pass." She was right. It always did.

Sometimes their roles would be reversed. My mother never went into a rage, but she could be disturbingly silent when she was peeved about something. My father's playful attempts to cheer her and relieve the tension were never immediately effective.

These family dramas seldom called for much participation from me. I was being talked about a lot, and sometimes talked at, but not very often talked to. I didn't even know what provoked the laughter or rage half the time, so I would concentrate on faces and expressions, hoping to figure out what all the excitement was about.

This small cast of characters expanded when guests came over for an evening of cards. I would be introduced and receive a handshake and a broad smile. My parents would be told how I'd grown or who I was the spitting image of. Then I was sent off to bed while the men settled around one card table and the women round another. Lying there in the dark, I could hear their good-natured chatter, the clatter of poker chips, the cards being shuffled and slapped against each other. Conversation at each table had its own special character. From the contract bridge table came "I bid no trump. By the way, did you ever find a pair of shoes to go with your blue coat? Daisy, I think it's your bid." Talk at the men's table was usually about cronies who had gotten sick, failed in business, been seen the week before looking terrible, or had just plain died. Then there'd be a roar and "You son of a gun, I have three aces!"

My father loved telling funny stories and put everything he had into their delivery. Thoroughly enjoying himself every step of the way, he would build them, slowly at first, to a resounding crescendo and end them with the explosive punch line, bringing himself and his audience to tears and screams of laughter. It became clear to me that where funny stories are concerned, giving is a lot more fun than receiving. By the time they broke for coffee and cake, I was asleep.

I didn't want to be an artist in those days. I thought it would be great to be a street cleaner. I liked the white uniforms, the big brushes, and the sound of fallen leaves being brushed down the wet gutters of our small Philadelphia street. Then one day when I was sick in bed, I was given pencils, crayons, and a sheaf of hotel stationary (my father was a traveling salesman) to keep me amused, so I started to draw. To my surprise, my mother, my father, the family doctor, and the lady who came to clean, all thought my work was wonderful: my Abraham Lincoln copied from a penny drew raves. It wasn't so much the art I enjoyed, it was the visibility I was getting.

In school there were certain subjects I could not seem to ever master, such as arithmetic, English, science, geography and music and history, and on the playing field I was always the last one chosen for softball or touch; so I decided to hang on to drawing pictures. Only years later did I discover that I was a cartoonist.

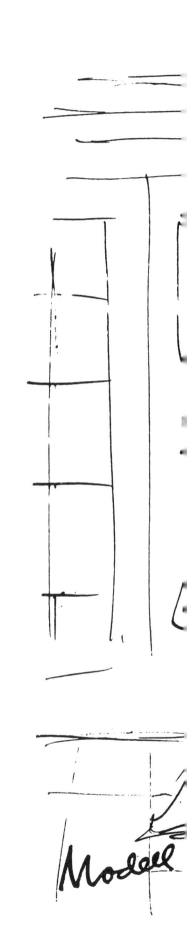

"It says, 'I'm smart, yes, but not trendy.'"

"He's not happy unless he's in the great outdoors killing something."

"Bad news! The frost is on the punkin."

"Look where you're going!"

"I've been dying to get you two together. You're the two most amusing men I've ever met."

"You never like the cut of anybody's jib."

"You call that hung by the chimney with care?"

"Oh, fine! The one time we're invited on a boat it has to rain!"

"I suppose you know you're spoiling that dog."

"And when did it first occur to you that perhaps life is _not_ a cabaret?"

"Now, don't *you* start complaining."

"Never mind the 'You're not going to believe this.' Just answer the question, yes or no."

"Excuse me, but I believe you're sitting on my tuffet."

"All right, all right! Knock it off!"

"What a coincidence! I'm left-handed, too."

"Actually, I'm not off duty. I'm just having some fun."

"Oh, for heaven's sake! If you're just going to lie there and sulk, take _my_ chair."

"*Are you two married or anything?*"

"Hot as all getout, isn't it?"

"You know the type. Remembers only what he wants to remember."

"Here come the representatives from the overdeveloped countries."

"Guess what! Mr. Corbett's going to be our lord and master."

"Oh, shut up!"

"That really kills you, doesn't it?"

"We're through, do you hear? Through! Washed up! Kaput!"

"Goodness! You startled me for a moment!"

"Making a mess. What are _you_ doing?"

"Not ŏ, dummy, o͞o."

"Well, what's eating you? I got your chair or something?"

"Yuk!"

"I'm Melanie Burdick. I understand you're the extra man."

"I'll say one thing for you, Marvin. You're all snake."

"Oh, I'm so glad you both could come! Everyone else here terrifies me."

"Lillian, I want you to meet one of my oldest and dearest friends."

"Can I change it if she thinks it's too icky?"

"As the days dwindle down to a precious few, why shouldn't you order what you want?"

"Boy, am I glad to see you!"

"Do you think you can manage a smile? It's only for a fiftieth of a second."

"And I'll have the sole amandine, but hold the nuts."

"If you think it's so amusing, _you_ send it, but I'm not signing _my_ name to it."

"Is that Miss Ms or Mrs. Ms?"

"You have to admit that the kitty was adorable, even if you can't stand cat-food commercials."

"The ad said, 'Money back if not delighted.' Look at me. Do I look delighted?"

"Oh, come off it!"

"I will not talk to myself, I will not talk to myself."

"Stick to local papers and you won't get so depressed."

"Mother, am I poisonous?"

"It's the flight that's supposed to be non-stop, not the Martinis."

"Well, Mr. Decision Maker! We're waiting."

"Will you kindly remove that bird when I'm talking to you?"

"Excuse me. If you were my husband, what would you like for dinner tonight?"

"Never mind the 'I frequently ask myself the same question.' Just answer yes or no."

"Do you know what the doctor said? He said you are a _very_ bad patient."

"*First let me introduce myself. I'm Craig Claiborne, and this is Julia Child.*"

"I didn't say I wasn't _serious_. I just said I don't want to get involved."

"Mirror, mirror on the door, whom do all the boys adore?"

"I don't recall anyone asking me where _I_ might prefer to sit."

"*A conversation piece is the <u>last</u> thing she needs.*"

"*Oh, come on, Harry! It can't be as bad as all that!*"

"Your fresh orange juice, is it canned or frozen?"

"And stop trying to cheer me up!"

"*Big deal!*"

"*And no teaching toys.*"

"I've decided to call myself Drake. Duck is so common."

"Nonsense! I think it's refreshing to see a T-shirt that doesn't say anything."

"Why do you insist upon finding something good to say about everyone who infuriates me?"

"You know what you have? You have awfully good taste, Marvin. I really mean it!"

"Let's watch the sudden stops, Mac!"

"It needs additives."

"Oh, I still think you're a great clown, Olaf. You're just no fun anymore."

"I've been putting off getting them a wedding gift. Somehow I didn't think it would last."

"If he wanted _me_ to let him out, he'd ask _me_."

"Poor Emily! The years have not been kind to her."

"And how much is this bit of nonsense?"

"Now you two keep quiet and let me do the talking."

"Now watch this. Sit!"

"Eat!"

"It's nothing, dear. A man just wants my opinion."

"Who the hell do you think you're kidding?"

"You're no trouper!"

"His will reads as follows: 'Being of sound mind and disposition, I blew it all.'"

"Bugs! What about bugs?"

"*Double, double toil and trouble . . .*"

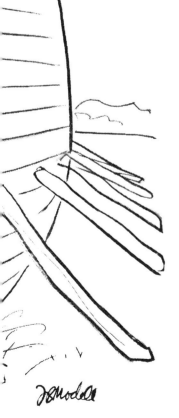

"You have a son in college? I don't believe it."

"Three ships is a lot of ships. Why can't you prove the world is round with _one_ ship."

"Miss Kent, who took my candy bar?"

"If it please Your Honor, I would like to point out again that I am <u>not</u> the defendant but the defendant's counsel."

"That's Harry Krance.
He knows whereof he speaks."

"I see your tennis elbow doesn't seem to be bothering you anymore."

"Look, if I'm boring you, say so."

"Could you please take this back? My boss just invited me to Benihana."

"He doesn't want dog food. He wants *people* food."

"Just because the painting doesn't happen to appeal to Marvin doesn't necessarily mean it stinks."

"Don't tell me you have bad news, too."

"Just who the hell do you think you're fooling?"

"If it's up there, I'll be there."

"I didn't say I liked her. I merely said 'Wow!'"

"Look! I happen to be <u>very</u> busy. Do you mind?"

"What makes you think you're so hot?"

"Do you want a fat one that's too short or a tall one that's too scrawny?"

"He just heard about stuffing."

"Moping is not relaxing!"

"What a coincidence! I couldn't help noticing you're reading a book I was thinking of reading myself."

"Oh, my goodness! Look who died I didn't even know was still alive!"

"What a day! Now she wants an asp!"

"I believe you're right. It *is* a Chagall."

"You're darn right I'm a bigot, and with good reason, too."

"I do adore you. I keep moving away because I'm farsighted."

"You should watch this. You might learn something."

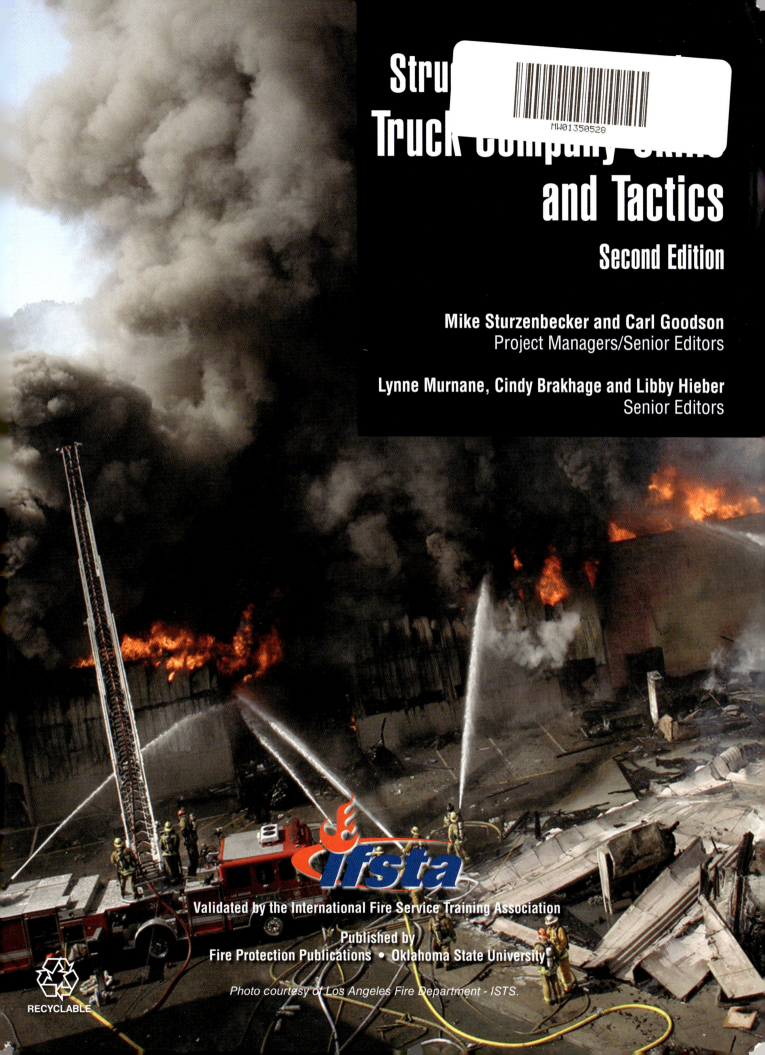

Structural Truck Company Skills and Tactics

Second Edition

Mike Sturzenbecker and Carl Goodson
Project Managers/Senior Editors

Lynne Murnane, Cindy Brakhage and Libby Hieber
Senior Editors

Validated by the International Fire Service Training Association

Published by
Fire Protection Publications • Oklahoma State University

Photo courtesy of Los Angeles Fire Department - ISTS.

The International Fire Service Training Association

The International Fire Service Training Association (IFSTA) was established in 1934 as a *nonprofit educational association of fire fighting personnel who are dedicated to upgrading fire fighting techniques and safety through training*. To carry out the mission of IFSTA, Fire Protection Publications was established as an entity of Oklahoma State University. Fire Protection Publications' primary function is to publish and disseminate training texts as proposed and validated by IFSTA. As a secondary function, Fire Protection Publications researches, acquires, produces, and markets high-quality learning and teaching aids as consistent with IFSTA's mission.

The IFSTA Validation Conference is held the second full week in July. Committees of technical experts meet and work at the conference addressing the current standards of the National Fire Protection Association® and other standard-making groups as applicable. The Validation Conference brings together individuals from several related and allied fields, such as:

- Key fire department executives and training officers
- Educators from colleges and universities
- Representatives from governmental agencies
- Delegates of firefighter associations and industrial organizations

Committee members are not paid nor are they reimbursed for their expenses by IFSTA or Fire Protection Publications. They participate because of commitment to the fire service and its future through training. Being on a committee is prestigious in the fire service community, and committee members are acknowledged leaders in their fields. This unique feature provides a close relationship between the International Fire Service Training Association and fire protection agencies, which helps to correlate the efforts of all concerned.

IFSTA manuals are now the official teaching texts of most of the states and provinces of North America. Additionally, numerous U.S. and Canadian government agencies as well as other English-speaking countries have officially accepted the IFSTA manuals.

Copyright © 2010 by the Board of Regents, Oklahoma State University

All rights reserved. No part of this publication may be reproduced in any form without prior written permission from the publisher.

ISBN 978-0-87939-387-8   Library of Congress Control Number: 2010931186

Second Edition, First Printing, August 2010   *Printed in the United States of America*

10   9   8   7   6   5   4   3   2

If you need additional information concerning the International Fire Service Training Association (IFSTA) or Fire Protection Publications, contact:

Customer Service, Fire Protection Publications, Oklahoma State University
930 North Willis, Stillwater, OK 74078-8045
800-654-4055   Fax: 405-744-8204

For assistance with training materials, to recommend material for inclusion in an IFSTA manual, or to ask questions or comment on manual content, contact:

Editorial Department, Fire Protection Publications, Oklahoma State University
930 North Willis, Stillwater, OK 74078-8045
405-744-4111   Fax: 405-744-4112   E-mail: editors@osufpp.org

---

Oklahoma State University in compliance with Title VI of the Civil Rights Act of 1964 and Title IX of the Educational Amendments of 1972 (Higher Education Act) does not discriminate on the basis of race, color, national origin or sex in any of its policies, practices or procedures. This provision includes but is not limited to admissions, employment, financial aid and educational services.

Chapter Summary

Chapters

1	Introduction to Truck Company Operations	4
2	Enhanced Fire Behavior	16
3	Firefighter Safety and Survival	58
4	Loss Control	90
5	Ground Ladders	120
6	Size-Up for Truck Company Operations	146
7	Controlling Utilities and Building Systems	174
8	Access to Structures	200
9	Access into Structures	216
10	Fireground Search and Rescue	250
11	Ventilation Size-Up	282
12	Horizontal Ventilation	308
13	Vertical Ventilation	342
14	Special Ventilation Operations	406

Appendix

A	Coordinated Fireground Operations	435

Glossary 443

Index 451

Table of Contents

List of Tables x
Preface xi
Introduction 1

1 Introduction to Truck Company Operations 4
Case History 7
Truck Company Operations Defined 8
   Enhanced Fire Behavior 9
   Firefighter Safety and Survival 10
   Loss Control 10
   Ground Ladders 10
   Size-Up for Truck Company Operations 11
   Controlling Utilities and Building Systems 11
   Access to Structures 12
   Access into Structures 12
   Fireground Search and Rescue 12
   Ventilation Size-Up 12
   Horizontal Ventilation 13
   Vertical Ventilation 14
   Special Ventilation Operations 14
Summary 14
Review Questions 15

2 Enhanced Fire Behavior 16
Case History 19
Fire Science 20
   Combustion 20
   Heat and Temperature 21
   Heat of Combustion and Heat Release Rate 23
      Heat of Combustion 23
      Heat Release Rate 24
Fire Development in a Compartment 24
   Stages of Fire Development 24
      Incipient Stage 26
      Growth Stage 26
      Fully Developed Stage 29
      Decay Stage 29
   Factors That Affect Fire Development 30
      Fuel Type 31
      Availability and Location of Additional Fuel 31
      Compartment Geometry 32
      Ventilation 34
      Thermal Properties of the Enclosure 35
      Ambient Conditions 35
      Impact of Changing Conditions 35
      The Modern Fire Environment 36
Analyzing the Fire: Fire Behavior Indicators 36
   Building Features 37
   Smoke 38
      Smoke Color 38
      Optical Density and Opacity 40
      Physical Density 40
      Hot Gas Layer 40
   Airflow 40
   Heat 42
   Flame 43
   Analyzing the Fire 43
Extreme Fire Behavior 46
   Flashover 46
      Radiation-Induced Flashover 47
      Ventilation-Induced Flashover 48
      Misconceptions about Flashover 50
   Backdraft 51
      The Gray Area: Flashover or Backdraft? 53
   Smoke Explosion 54
   Other Fire Gas Ignitions 54
   Factors Influencing Extreme Fire Behavior 55
Summary 56
Review Questions 56

3 Firefighter Safety and Survival 58
Case History 61
Standard Safety Behaviors 62
   IFSTA Risk Management Model 63
   Other Risk Management Models 63
      Dynamic Risk Assessment 63
      Crew Resource Management 64
   Key Safety Behaviors 65
Fireground Safety 66
   "Routine" Calls 66
   "Self-Vented" Fires 67
   Structural Collapse 68
   Elements of Fireground Safety 71
      Working within an Incident Management System 71
      Working within the Incident Action Plan (IAP) 72
      Working within the Personnel Accountability System 72
      Wearing Appropriate PPE and Respiratory Protection 74

　　　　Adequately Sizing-up the Situation.............. 74
　　　　*Performing a Risk/Benefit Analysis
　　　　　　for Every Action* 75
　　　　*Making Sure that Orders are
　　　　　　Understood* 75
　　　　Maintaining Situational Awareness............ 75
　　　　*Maintaining Company Discipline
　　　　　　and Team Integrity*............................... 77
　　　　Maintaining Communications..................... 78
　　　　*Reporting Identified Hazards
　　　　　　Immediately* 79
　　　　*Knowing and Following Departmental
　　　　　　SOPs*.. 79
　　　　*Employing Safe and Effective Strategy
　　　　　　and Tactics*.. 79
　　　　*Having a Rapid Intervention Crew
　　　　　　Standing By* 79
　　　　*Setting Up a Rehab Unit on All Working
　　　　　　Fires*... 80
　　　　*Using Emergency Escape Techniques
　　　　　　When Needed* 82
　　　Emergency Egress 82
　　　　Firefighter Lost 82
　　　　Firefighter Trapped....................................... 82
　　　　Locating Windows and Doors 83
　　　　Window Egress.. 84
　　　　Door Egress 85
　　　　Wall Breach... 86
Summary... 87
Review Questions... 88

4　Loss Control.. 90
Case History 93
Preincident Loss Control Planning 94
　　Risk Identification 95
　　Risk Evaluation 96
　　Plans Development.. 97
Incident Loss Control Operations.......................... 98
Primary Loss Control 98
　　Proper Size-Up 98
　　Effective Strategy 99
　　Adequate On-Scene Resources............................. 99
　　Effective Method of Attack 99
　　Effective Ventilation 100
　　Thorough Overhaul... 100
　　　　Evidence Preservation 101
　　　　Firefighter Safety... 102
　　　　Hidden Fire 103
　　　　Toxic Products of Combustion 103
Secondary Loss Control 104
　　Assisting the Fire Attack...................................... 105
　　　　Forcible Entry... 105
　　　　Pulling Ceilings.. 106
　　　　Opening Walls 107
　　Ventilation 107
　　　　Smoke Control 107
　　　　Heat Removal 108
　　Salvage 109
　　　　Protecting Floors and Floor Coverings........ 110
　　　　Protecting Exposed Contents 110
　　　　Water Control 112
　　　　Water Removal 113
Post-Incident Loss Control Operations 114
　　Economic Loss Control... 114
　　Psychological Loss Control 116
Summary... 117
Review Questions... 118

5　Ground Ladders 120
Case History 123
Ground Ladder Selection and Handling 124
　　Ladder Selection 125
　　Ladder Handling 126
　　　　Fitness... 126
　　　　Technique... 127
　　　　Practice 127
　　Ladder Raises 127
　　　　Pole Ladder Raises...................................... 128
　　Positioning Ground Ladders 135
　　　　*Factors Affecting Ground
　　　　　　Ladder Placement*................................. 135
Tactical Use of Ground Ladders 136
　　Access.. 136
　　　　Access to Buildings...................................... 136
　　　　Access into Structures................................. 137
　　　　Roof Access.. 137
　　　　Secondary Egress 138
　　Rescue 138
　　　　Above-Grade Ladder Rescues 138
　　　　Below-Grade Ladder Rescues..................... 138
　　Ventilation 138
　　　　Horizontal Ventilation 138
　　　　Vertical Ventilation 139
Nonstandard Uses for Ground Ladders............. 139
　　Mechanical Advantage Systems......................... 140
　　Positioning Intake Strainers 140
　　Water Removal 141
　　Bridging 142
Summary... 144
Review Questions... 144

6 Size-Up for Truck Company Operations ... 146
Case History ... 149
Size-Up for Truck Companies ... 150
- Preincident Size-Up ... 150
- Size-Up During Dispatch and Response ... 152
  - *Time of Day* ... 152
  - *Day of Week* ... 153
  - *Season of the Year* ... 153
  - *Weather* ... 154
- Size-Up on Arrival ... 155
- Ongoing Size-Up ... 155

NIOSH Model ... 156
Fire Behavior ... 157
- Smoke ... 158
- Analyzing Smoke ... 158
  - *Volume* ... 158
  - *Color and Density* ... 158
  - *Air Flow (Pressure)* ... 159

Building Construction ... 160
- Age of Building ... 160
- Type of Construction ... 161
- Building Modifications ... 162
- Fire Characteristics ... 164
  - *Attics* ... 164
  - *Basements* ... 165
  - *Townhouses* ... 165
  - *Victorians* ... 166
  - *Large Dwellings* ... 167
  - *Warehouses* ... 167
  - *Office Buildings* ... 168

Structural Collapse ... 168
- Collapse Potential ... 169

Occupancy Type ... 170
- Life Safety ... 170
- Hazardous Materials ... 171

Summary ... 171
Review Questions ... 172

7 Controlling Utilities and Building Systems ... 174
Case History ... 177
Fuel Control ... 178
- Situational Differences ... 179
  - *Controlling Natural Gas in Structure Fires* ... 179
  - *Controlling LPG in Structure Fires* ... 181
  - *Controlling Fuel Oil in Structure Fires* ... 183

Gas Leaks without Fire ... 185
- Approach ... 185
- Perimeter Control ... 185
- Hazard Assessment ... 186
- Hazard Mitigation ... 187
  - *Control of Natural Gas and LPG Leaks* ... 187

Electricity Control ... 188
- Controlling Electricity in Structure Fires ... 188
  - *Residential Occupancies* ... 188
  - *Commercial Occupancies* ... 190
  - *Industrial Occupancies* ... 190
- Downed Electrical Wires ... 191
  - *Perimeter Control* ... 192
  - *Hazard Identification* ... 194

Water Control ... 195
- Water Control in Structure Fires ... 196
  - *Sprinklered Buildings* ... 196
  - *Unsprinklered Buildings* ... 197
- Water Leaks without Fire ... 198
  - *Buildings with Basements or Cellars* ... 198

Summary ... 199
Review Questions ... 199

8 Access to Structures ... 200
Case History ... 203
Topography and Landscaping ... 203
- Overcoming Site Obstacles ... 206

Gates ... 206
- Manually Operated Gates ... 207
- Automated Gates ... 207
- Lockboxes ... 208

Fences ... 209
- Wire Fences ... 209
- Chain-Link Fences ... 209
- Wooden Fences ... 211
- Vinyl Fences ... 211
- Decorative Metal Fences ... 211
- Masonry Walls ... 211

Security Measures ... 212
- Barbed Wire ... 212
- Razor Ribbon ... 212
- Fence Spikes ... 213
- Wall Tops ... 213
- Guard Dogs ... 214
- Booby Traps ... 214

Summary ... 215
Review Questions ... 215

9 Access into Structures ... 216
Case History ... 219
Forcible Entry Tools ... 220
Doors ... 222

Door Size-Up	222
Residential/Commercial Doors	224
Forcing Residential/Commercial Doors	*224*
Industrial/Institutional Doors	228
Forcing Industrial/Institutional Doors	*230*
Door Security Systems	234
Overcoming Door Security Systems	*235*
Windows	**235**
Window Size-Up	237
Types of Windows	237
Breaking Windows	237
Residential/Commercial Windows	*238*
Industrial/Institutional Windows	*238*
Window Security Systems	238
Overcoming Window Security Systems	*239*
Walls	**242**
Types of Exterior Walls	243
Breaching Wood-Frame Walls	*243*
Breaching Masonry Walls	*245*
Breaching Concrete Walls	*246*
Breaching Metal Walls	*248*
Summary	**248**
Review Questions	**249**

10 Fireground Search and Rescue 250

Case History	**253**
Search and Rescue	**253**
Search Size-Up	254
Building Type	*255*
Time Period	*255*
Fire Situation	*256*
Conducting a Search	**258**
Building Search Safety	258
Primary Search	259
Primary Search Priorities	*259*
Primary Search Tools	*260*
Primary Search Methods	*263*
Vent, Enter, Search (VES)	266
Marking Systems	266
Large-Area Search	268
Rescue	270
Sheltering in Place	*271*
Evacuation	*272*
Secondary Search	272
Searching Multistory Buildings	**273**
Multistory Search Methods	273
Rapid Intervention	**274**
RIC Formation	275

Tools and Equipment	275
Full PPE and SCBA	*276*
Appropriate Communications Equipment	*276*
Thermal Imaging Cameras	*276*
Personal Illumination Equipment	*277*
Forcible Entry Tools	*277*
Rescue Air Supply	*277*
Rescue Ropes	*278*
Rescue Litters	*278*
Operational Modes	279
Stand-by Mode	*279*
Entry or Deployment Mode	*280*
Summary	**281**
Review Questions	**281**

11 Ventilation Size-Up 282

Case History	**285**
Ventilation Overview	**285**
Natural Ventilation	286
Tactical Ventilation	286
Life Safety	*286*
Incident Stabilization	*287*
Property Conservation	*287*
Ventilation Size-Up	**287**
Review of Fire Behavior	**289**
The Burning Regime and Extreme Fire Behavior	289
Analyzing the Fire	290
Smoke Behavior	290
Smoke Volume	*290*
Smoke Color and Density	*291*
Air Flow (Pressure)	*292*
Building Construction	**292**
Age and Type of Building	293
Older Buildings	*293*
Newer Buildings	*295*
Positive Construction Features	295
Steel Framing Members	*296*
Self-Closing Fire Doors	*296*
Automatic Sprinkler Systems	*296*
Built-In Fire Suppression Systems	*296*
Elevator Shafts	*298*
Automatic Smoke Vents	*298*
Negative Construction Features	298
Elevator Shafts	*298*
Synthetic Materials	*299*
Planters and other Landscape Features	*299*
Security Measures	*299*
Occupancy-Related Features	*299*

Coordination with Rescue and Fire Attack 299
    Timing of Ventilation 300
    Location of Ventilation Opening....................... 300
    Method of Ventilation.. 302
        Horizontal vs. Vertical Ventilation 302
        Natural vs. Mechanical Ventilation 302
        Situations Requiring Mechanical
          Ventilation 303
Other Ventilation Size-Up Considerations........ 303
    Exposures.. 303
    Weather... 304
        Wind 304
        Temperature.. 305
Summary.. 306
Review Questions... 306

12 Horizontal Ventilation............................... 308
Case History 311
Use of Horizontal Ventilation Tools
    and Equipment 312
    Ventilation Tools 312
    Ventilation Equipment 312
        Fans.. 313
        Flexible Ducts.. 313
Building Construction Related to
    Horizontal Ventilation..................................... 316
    Windows 316
        Fixed Windows 317
        Single- and Double-Hung Windows........... 317
        Casement Windows..................................... 318
        Horizontal-Sliding Windows 318
        Awning Windows 318
        Jalousie Windows 319
        Projected Windows...................................... 319
        Hopper Windows 319
        Energy-Efficient Windows.......................... 319
    Doors 320
        Swinging Doors 321
        Sliding Doors 321
        Overhead-Type Doors 323
        Roll-Up Doors... 323
        Telescoping Doors....................................... 323
    Walls 324
        Stem Walls 325
        Interior Firewalls 325
        Exterior Walls 325
Establishing and Supporting Horizontal
    Ventilation... 329
    Location of Fire 329
    Wind Direction and Speed 329

    Location of Ventilation Openings 329
Natural Horizontal Ventilation 330
    Doors... 331
    Windows 332
        Breaking Windows 332
Mechanical Horizontal Ventilation 333
    Using Smoke Ejectors 333
    Using Blowers 333
    Using Nozzles (Hydraulic Ventilation) 334
Precautions against Upsetting Established
    Horizontal Ventilation..................................... 337
    Improper Implementation 337
    Inadequate Control of Exit Openings 337
    Improperly Located Exit Opening 338
    Improperly Directed Fire Streams 338
    Improper Placement of Salvaged Contents 338
    Building Construction 338
    Wind 339
Summary.. 340
Review Questions... 340

13 Vertical Ventilation 342
Case History 345
Establishing and Supporting Vertical
    Ventilation... 346
    Vertical Ventilation Safety................................. 347
        Identifying Vertical Ventilation
          Hazards 347
        Getting Firefighters to the Roof 348
        Reading a Roof.. 348
        Sounding a Roof 350
        Working on a Roof...................................... 351
        Working with Protective Hoselines 351
    Opening a Roof... 352
Vertical Ventilation Tools 355
    Cutting Tools.. 355
        Rotary Saw... 356
        Chain Saw... 357
        Pick-Head Axe 358
    Stripping Tools 359
        Pick-Head Axe 359
        Pike Pole.. 360
        Rubbish Hook 360
        Sledgehammer... 361
Roof Construction... 361
    Pitched Roofs... 361
        Types of Pitched Roofs 363
        Hazards of Pitched Roofs 367
        Venting Pitched Roofs................................. 368

Flat Roofs 368
    Types of Flat Roofs *370*
    Hazards of Flat Roofs *375*
    Venting Flat Roofs *377*
Arched Roofs 379
    Types of Arched Roofs *380*
    Hazards of Arched Roofs *382*
    Venting Arched Roofs *382*

Lightweight Roof Construction **383**
Panelized Roofs 383
Trussed Roofs 385
    Parallel Chord Trusses *385*
    Pitched Roof Trusses *387*
Wooden I-Beams 388

Roof Coverings **389**
Wooden Shakes and Shingles 390
Composition Roofing and Shingles 391
Tar and Gravel 392
Urethane/Isocyanate Foam 392
Single-Ply/Synthetic Membrane 393
Tile and Slate 393
Light-Gauge Metal or Fiberglass 394
Steel Clad 394

Existing Roof Openings **396**
Scuttle Hatches 396
Penthouses (Bulkheads) 396
Skylights 396
Monitors 397
Turbine (Rotary Vane) Vents 397
Light and Ventilation Shafts 398
Ridge Vents 398
Clerestory Windows 399

Cutting the Ventilation Exit Opening **399**
Louver Vents 401
    Center-Rafter Cut *401*
    Dicing *402*
Rolling Back Panelized Roofs 402
Trench (Strip) Ventilation 403

Summary **405**
Review Questions **405**

Chapter 14 Special Ventilation
    Operations **406**
Case History **409**
High-Rise Fire Operations **410**
Staffing 410
Fire Attack 410
Elevators 411
Fire Behavior in High-Rise Buildings 412
    Stack Effect *412*
    Mushrooming *413*

High-Rise Ventilation **414**
Vertical (Top) Ventilation 415
    Getting Firefighters to the Roof *415*
Channeling Smoke 417
    Pressure Transfer *418*
    Neutral Pressure Plane *418*
    Effects of Wind *420*
Ventilating Below the Fire 422
Ventilating the Fire Floor 422
Ventilating Above the Fire 423

HVAC and Smoke-Control Systems **424**
Built-In Ventilation Devices 425
    Automatic Roof Vents *425*
    Atrium Vents *425*
    Monitor Vents *426*
    Skylights *426*
    Curtain Boards *427*

Underground Structures **428**
Windowless Buildings **429**
Highly Secure Buildings **429**
Remodeled Buildings **430**
Summary **431**
Review Questions **431**

Appendix **433**
A   Coordinated Fireground Operations 435

Glossary **443**

Index **451**

List of Tables

Table 2.1	Fire Behavior Indicators	44
Table 2.2	Flashover Indicators	50
Table 2.3	Backdraft Indicators	53
Table 3.1	Common Products of Combustion	74
Table 9.1	Rotary Saw Blades	222

Preface

This second edition has undergone a title change from **Fireground Support Operations** to **Structural Fire Fighting: Truck Company Skills and Tactics** in order to better reflect the subject matter contained in the manual. This manual is intended to build on the information contained in IFSTA's **Essentials of Fire Fighting** text.

A manual of this size and scope could not have been created without the expertise, dedication, and hard work of the members of the validation committee.

IFSTA Structural Fire Fighting: Truck Company Skills and Tactics Second Edition Validation Committee

Chair
Wes Kitchell
Santa Rosa (CA) Fire Department

Secretary
Tim Kreis
Phoenix (AZ) Fire Department

Committee Members

Mark Butterfield
Hutchinson Community College – Fire Science
Hutchinson, KS

Michael Donovan
Bridgeport (CT) Fire Department

Edward Hadfield
Firetown Training Specialists
Corona, CA

Edward Hartin
Gresham (OR) Fire & Emergency Services

Rick Karasaki
Honolulu (HI) Fire Department

Jeffrey Lara
Yukon (OK) Fire Department

Lavarn Lucas
Hilton Head Island (SC) Fire & Rescue

Robert Madden
Bend (OR) Fire & Rescue

Richard Merrell
Farifax County (VA) Fire Rescue Department

Darren Olguin
San Ramon Valley (CA) Fire Protection District

Shan Raffel
Institution of Fire Engineers – Australia

Harold Richardson
Yarmouth Fire Department
Nova Scotia, Canada

Clifford Thompson
Rogers (AR) Fire Department

Bob Waldron
Mead, WA

Derek Williams
Mesa (AZ) Fire Department

The following organizations and individuals have also contributed information, photographs, or other assistance that made final completion of this manual possible:

Allen (TX) Fire Department
Division Chief Jonathan Boyd

Bilco Company
New Haven, CT

Bullard Company
Cynthiana, KY

Cedar Rapids (IA) Fire Department

Dave Coombs
Columbia River (OR) Fire and Rescue

Matt Daly
Bronxville, NY

Bob Esposito
Pennsburg, PA

Keith Flood
Santa Rosa (CA) Fire Department

Florida State Fire College
Charlie Brush

Dick Giles
Stillwater, OK

Federal Emergency Management Agency (FEMA)

Gresham (OR) Fire and Rescue

Ingalls (OK) Fire District
Capt. Tom Hughes

Ron Jeffers
Union City, NJ

Las Vegas (NV) Fire Department
Capt. Brian Gray
FF Darell Aronson and The Las Vegas Fire Explorers

Los Angeles (CA) Fire Department – In Service Training Section
Capt. Richard Fields

Dr. George McClary
Santa Rosa, CA

McKinney (TX) Fire Department
Ron Moore

District Chief Chris Mickal
New Orleans (LA) Fire Department Photo Unit

Rick Montemorra
Mesa (AZ) Fire Department

Montezuma-Rimrock (AZ) Fire Department

National Institute for Standards and Technology (NIST)

North Las Vegas (NV) Fire Department
Assistant Chief Bruce Evans
Capt. Aric Neuharth
Capt. Travis Anderson and the Staff of Station 52
Capt. John Wright and the Staff of Station 54
Capt. Chuck Williams and Family
FF Jake Levesque

Oklahoma State Fire Marshal's Office

Mark Pare

Ed Prendergast
Chicago, IL

Ramfan Corporation
Spring Valley, CA

Razor Wire International
Phoenix, AZ

Jeff Seaton
San Jose (CA) Fire Department

Stillwater (OK) Fire Department

Super Vacuum Manufacturing Co., Inc.
Loveland, CO

Tempest Technology Corp.
Fresno, CA

Chris Wagers
Topeka (KS) Fire Department

Structural Fire Fighting: Truck Company Skills and Tactics Project Team

Senior Editors/Project Managers
Mike Sturzenbecker
Carl Goodson

Senior Editors
Cindy Brakhage
Libby Heber
Lynne Murnane

Technical Reviewer
Fred Stowell

Production Coordinator
Ann Moffat

Illustrators and Layout Designers
Errick Braggs
Ben Brock

Missy Hannan
Ruth Mudroch
Clint Parker

Photographers
Jeff Fortney
Brett Noakes

Editorial Assistant
Tara Gladden

Research Technicians
Elkie Burnside
Gabriel Ramirez

The IFSTA Executive Board at the time of validation of the **Structural Fire Fighting: Truck Company Skills and Tactics** manual was as follows:

IFSTA Executive Board

Chair
Jeffrey Morrissette
State Fire Administrator
Commission on Fire Prevention and Control
Windsor Locks, CT

Vice Chair
Paul Valentine
Fire Marshal
Village of Mount Prospect
Mount Prospect, IL

Board Members

Stephen Ashbrock
Fire Chief
Madeira & Indian Hill Fire Department
Cincinnati, OH

Roxanne Bercik
Assistant Chief
Los Angeles Fire Department
Los Angeles, CA

Mary Cameli
Assistant Chief
Mesa Fire Department
Mesa, AZ

Bradd Clark
Fire Chief
Owasso Fire Department
Owasso, OK

Dennis Compton
Chairman
National Fallen Firefighters Foundation
Mesa, AZ

Frank Cotton
Battalion Chief
Memphis Fire Department
Memphis, TN

George Dunkel
Consultant
Scappoose, OR

John W. Hoglund
Director Emeritus
Maryland Fire and Rescue Institute
College Park, MD

John Judd
Chairman, Board of Directors
Institution of Fire Engineers
Moreton in Marsh, UK

Wes Kitchell
Santa Rosa Fire Department
Santa Rosa, CA

Dr. Lori Moore-Merrell
Assistant to the General President
International Association of Fire Fighters
Washington, DC

Executive Director
Chris Neal
Director
Fire Protection Publications
Oklahoma State University
Stillwater, OK

Introduction

Introduction Contents

Purpose/Scope 1
Key Information 2

Introduction

Of all activities performed on the fireground, truck company operations are some of the most critical and the most dangerous. Truck company operations refers to fireground activities that include but are not limited to forcible entry, ventilation, utility control and search and rescue. These activities are often called truck company operations because truck companies typically perform these duties. When these operations are needed, however, they must be performed quickly and safely whether there is a truck company on scene or not – even if the department does not have a ladder truck. Because of the critical aspect of truck company operations, all firefighters should be properly trained and proficient in these tasks.

While tasks assigned to truck companies are often different than those given to suppression crews, the actions of both complement one another and must be performed in a coordinated manner to ensure safety. For example, if suppression crews begin an interior attack before the structure is ventilated, or if ventilation is performed in the wrong location, conditions inside the structure may become untenable. Therefore, it is critical that all truck company operations be coordinated with suppression activities by the incident commander to have a successful outcome.

This manual builds on the information contained in **Fireground Support Operations** 1st Edition and has a special focus on safe fireground operations. Each chapter has a Safety Points section following the learning objectives that highlights specific safety information for the truck company activities that are addressed in the chapter. More specifically, safe operations are discussed in detail in the text where appropriate. For example, safety information is provided for types of roofs that a firefighter may encounter, including the safest and most stable locations for firefighters on each type of roof. In addition, a brief scenario is placed at the end of each chapter to encourage the reader to think about lessons learned in the chapter in more of a real-world application.

Purpose and Scope

This manual is intended to serve as a reference in formal training courses on fireground support operations and in self-study by individual firefighters. The material in this manual combines and updates information previously contained in the IFSTA **Fireground Support Operations**, **Fire Service Ground Ladders**, and **Fire Service Loss Control** manuals. The knowledge, skills, and abilities discussed in this manual are critical to safe and efficient structural fire fighting.

It is assumed that the readers of this manual will have read the IFSTA **Essentials of Fire Fighting** manual, and will have successfully completed a recognized training course in basic fire fighting theory and practice. Therefore, this manual focuses on fireground support operations in greater depth than presented in Essentials.

Key Information

Various types of information in this manual are given in shaded boxes marked by symbols or icons. See the following definitions:

Safety Alert
Provides additional emphasis on matters of safety.

Case History
A case history analyzes an event. It can describe its development, action taken, investigation results, and lessons learned. Illustrations can be included.

Information
Information sidebars give additional relevant information that is more detailed, descriptive or explanatory than that given in the text.

Louver Cut — Rectangular exit opening cut in a roof, allowing a section of roof deck (still nailed to a center rafter) to be tilted, thus creating an opening similar to a louver. Also called center rafter cut.

A key term is designed to emphasize key concepts, technical terms, or ideas that firefighters need to know. They are listed at the beginning of each chapter and the definition is placed in the margin for easy reference.

Three key signal words are found in the text: **WARNING, CAUTION,** and **NOTE.** Definitions and examples of each are as follows:

- **WARNING** indicates information that could result in death or serious injury to fire and emergency services personnel. See the following example:

> **WARNING!**
> Because roof supports almost always run perpendicular to the outside walls, firefighters should never walk diagonally across the roof of a burning building.

- **CAUTION** indicates important information or data that fire and emergency service responders need to be aware of in order to perform their duties safely. See the following example:

> **CAUTION**
> Whenever firefighters ascend to a roof, a secondary means of egress from the roof must be provided. This can be accomplished by placing ladders on two or more sides of the building.

- **NOTE** indicates important operational information that helps explain why a particular recommendation is given or describes optional methods for certain procedures. See the following example:

NOTE: If conditions require, plank sheathing can be stripped away with pike poles or rubbish hooks instead of being tilted into a louver vent.

Introduction to Truck Company Operations

Chapter Contents

CASE HISTORY 7	Access into Structures 12
Truck Company Operations Defined 8	Fireground Search and Rescue 12
Enhanced Fire Behavior 9	Ventilation Size-Up 12
Firefighter Safety and Survival 10	Horizontal Ventilation 13
Loss Control 10	Vertical Ventilation 14
Ground Ladders 10	Special Ventilation Operations 14
Size-Up for Truck Company Operations 11	**Summary** **14**
Controlling Utilities and Building Systems ... 11	**Review Questions** **15**
Access to Structures 12	

Divider page photo courtesy of the Los Angeles Fire Department —ISTS.

chapter 1

Key Terms

Truck Company..8

Introduction to Truck Company Operations

Learning Objectives

After reading this chapter, students will be able to:

1. Define the term truck company.
2. Summarize the tasks commonly included in truck company operations.

Chapter 1
Introduction to Truck Company Operations

Case History

According to NIOSH investigative report F2002-40, Iowa firefighters were called to a fire in a 2½-story wood-frame dwelling in September 2002. On arrival, firefighters saw smoke showing under the eaves of the roof. When an interior crew could not locate the seat of the fire, vertical ventilation was ordered. Two firefighters accessed the roof from an aerial platform. One of the firefighters masked up because of heavy smoke on the roof, but the other did not. The firefighter wearing SCBA used a chain saw to make cuts in the roof while the other firefighter acted as backup or spotter. Lacking SCBA, the second firefighter covered his face with his hands because of the smoke and heat. After the cuts had been made, but before the roof decking could be removed, the second firefighter indicated to the first that they needed to exit the roof immediately. Both firefighters retreated back toward the aerial platform, but before they could reach it, the second firefighter fell to his knees saying that he could not continue. Seconds later, the roof under the second firefighter collapsed and flames erupted from the hole in the roof. The firefighter who had fallen from the roof into the fire below was quickly located by an interior attack crew. With help from a rapid intervention crew (RIC), the interior crew was able to extricate the victim. The victim was pronounced dead at a local hospital. An autopsy found that the victim died of smoke inhalation, intra-alveolar hemorrhage, and carbon monoxide intoxication.

As this case history clearly shows, even though tactical ventilation and other truck company operations are critically important to the overall fire suppression effort, they are potentially very dangerous — even fatal. Regardless of how demanding and dangerous these operations may be, they must be performed quickly and efficiently when needed — whether a ladder truck is on scene or not. Nonetheless, no matter how demanding and dangerous these operations are, they must be performed quickly and efficiently when needed.

When a fire starts inside a structure, certain predictable things occur. Given an adequate supply of oxygen, the fire will continue to burn until one of two things happens: the fire is extinguished by some external intervention (fire attack or extinguishing system activation), or it goes out when all the available fuel has been consumed. While the fire burns, it produces heat that helps to sustain the process. The fire also produces varying amounts of smoke and other toxic and flammable products of combustion that may fill the building.

A burning building filled with smoke and superheated gases is a hostile and potentially life-threatening environment for both occupants and firefighters. To survive this environment, firefighters must learn to accurately assess the situation and then calculate the risks involved compared to the potential benefits to be gained from each action being considered.

Firefighters have been and continue to be injured or killed in so-called *routine* fires or those that have *self-vented* by breaking a window or burning through the roof. In addition, any number of non-fire hazards may be present on the fireground, such as energized downed electrical wires, gaseous or liquid fuel leaks, or toxic or explosive materials. Firefighters must learn how to recognize the potentially lethal conditions in these seemingly innocuous situations and know how to mitigate those conditions.

In fires where the oxygen supply is limited, potentially explosive backdraft conditions can develop. If these conditions are not recognized by the first-arriving fire crews and if effective ventilation is not performed before entry is attempted, the results could be catastrophic.

If firefighters are to quickly but safely enter a burning building to search for trapped occupants and extinguish a fire, a number of other things need to happen — sometimes sequentially, sometimes simultaneously. These things include sizing up the building and the fire, gaining access to the building and its interior, ventilating the building, and controlling the utilities. As they perform these tasks, the firefighters should keep loss control in mind. As soon as the situation and available resources allow, firefighters should spread salvage covers and take other steps to control collateral damage.

Truck Company Operations Defined

Tasks performed at structure fires other than fire suppression are commonly known as **truck company operations** because they are typically the responsibility of truck companies. In this context, truck company operations refer to all of the various tasks and evolutions that are required to assist or support a structure fire suppression operation without necessarily being directly involved in it **(Figure 1.1)**. In other words, truck company operations include what has traditionally been called *truck work*, with or without a ladder truck on scene. Properly performed truck company operations can and often do prevent or reduce loss of life in structure fires.

Many fire departments throughout North America have dedicated their truck companies to perform tasks needed to assist in the fire attack. However, when these operations are needed, they must be performed quickly and safely whether there is a truck company on scene or not — even if the department doesn't have a ladder truck **(Figure 1.2)**.

All firefighters, regardless of their regular assignment, should have a working knowledge of truck company operations. Therefore, this manual focuses on tasks that need to be performed without specifying who performs them. In many structure fires, fire attack crews and truck personnel work side by side. While their goals are the same — saving lives and protecting property — their respective roles and functions are different. This manual addresses those differences.

> **Truck Company (Ladder Company)** — Group of firefighters assigned to a fire department aerial apparatus who are primarily responsible for search and rescue, ventilation, salvage and overhaul, forcible entry, and other fireground support functions.

Figure 1.1 Firefighters performing truck company operations must work closely with suppression crews. *Courtesy of the Los Angeles Fire Department – ISTS.*

Figure 1.2 Truck company skills and tactics must be implemented on the fireground even if a truck company is not on scene.

Many of the tools and techniques discussed in this manual are the same as those in the IFSTA **Essentials of Fire Fighting** manual, but they are addressed at a more enhanced level in this text.

Each chapter begins with a review of the relevant safety issues. The skills chapters begin with a review of the construction issues involved, move to the tools needed to safely and effectively apply the techniques discussed, and conclude with a company-level scenario relevant to the topic of the chapter. The following text explains the chapters of this manual and provides the detail necessary to understand and perform each aspect of truck company operations.

Enhanced Fire Behavior

Chapter 2 reviews the fire behavior principles discussed in **Essentials**, especially those principles related to fire development in a compartment. New information has been added that deals with reading fire behavior indicators and extreme fire behavior **(Figure 1.3, p. 10)**.

Figure 1.3 Conditions on the fireground can change instantly. Therefore, it is critical that firefighters be able to recognize fire behavior indicators. *Courtesy of the Los Angeles Fire Department – ISTS.*

Firefighter Safety and Survival

Chapter 3 addresses the vitally important topic of firefighter safety and survival. The focus of the information is on individual actions that firefighters can take to avoid getting into trouble and how to get out trouble if necessary. The following topics are discussed:

- Maintaining situational awareness
- Crew integrity
- Rapid intervention
- Communications
- Accountability
- Air management
- Emergency escape techniques **(Figure 1.4)**

Loss Control

Chapter 4 discusses all aspects of loss control in structure fires **(Figure 1.5)**. Loss control is considered from preincident planning, through operations during incidents, to operations after the incident is terminated.

Ground Ladders

Chapter 5 addresses the use of ground ladders in truck company operations **(Figure 1.6)**. Ground ladders have a number of applications on the fireground from gaining access to a building, gaining access into it, and accessing windows and the roof. The use of aerial devices is discussed in various chapters as appropriate.

Figure 1.4 Firefighters must be cognizant of their surroundings and should maintain situational awareness.

Figure 1.6 Truck company crews must be able to quickly and efficiently deploy ground ladders on the fireground. *Courtesy of the Los Angeles Fire Department – ISTS.*

Figure 1.5 Thermal imaging cameras (TICs) can be used during overhaul to locate hidden fires.

Size-Up for Truck Company Operations

Chapter 6 discusses the critically important topic of size-up as applied to emergency incidents in general and to tactical truck company operations in particular **(Figure 1.7, p. 12)**. In addition to the safety issues pertaining to those making the size-up, the safety of those who will enter the hazard zone is also addressed. Size-up is considered from approaching the scene, assessing the building profile using thermal imaging cameras and infrared heat sensors, and deciding what initial actions are needed.

Controlling Utilities and Building Systems

Chapter 7 discusses controlling utilities in a structure **(Figure 1.8, p. 12)**. Controlling fuels such as natural gas and liquefied petroleum gas (LPG), electrical power, and water supply are addressed. When to shut off utilities is discussed because arbitrarily shutting off some services can create additional problems, including serious safety issues.

Figure 1.8 Properly coordinated utility control is critical for the life safety of both firefighters and victims.

Figure 1.7 A proper size-up sets the tone for the entire incident.

Access to Structures

Chapter 8 discusses the various natural and man-made obstacles that can hinder fire department access to an involved structure **(Figure 1.9)**. Ways of overcoming topographical features, gates, fences, and other security measures are considered.

Access into Structures

Chapter 9 addresses the various aspects of gaining access into a burning building **(Figure 1.10)**. Included are safety and tactical considerations, as well as tools and techniques beyond those discussed in **Essentials**.

Fireground Search and Rescue

Chapter 10 discusses the critically important topic of fireground search and rescue **(Figure 1.11)**. In addition to the safety and tactical considerations involved in the primary and secondary searches, rapid intervention practices and the use of thermal imaging cameras are addressed.

Ventilation Size-Up

Chapter 11 discusses ventilation size-up; that is, conducting a secondary size-up that focuses specifically on tactical ventilation **(Figure 1.12)**. A ventilation size-up assesses how the fire is behaving, the volume of smoke and what it looks like, and how the smoke is behaving. Also considered are building construction and other features that affect ventilation favorably or unfavorably. The effects of tactical ventilation on the fire attack are also discussed.

Figure 1.9 Weather conditions can pose a challenge for responding crews.

Figure 1.11 Proper personnel accountability is critical when deploying search teams in a hazardous area.

Figure 1.10 Truck company personnel must be prepared to gain access to the structure by any means necessary.

Figure 1.12 Any ventilation efforts on the fireground affect the ventilation profile of the structure. *Courtesy of the Los Angeles Fire Department –ISTS.*

Horizontal Ventilation

Chapter 12 addresses all forms of horizontal ventilation **(Figure 1.13, p. 14)**. How various construction features affect horizontal ventilation is considered. Also discussed are the tools and equipment needed to perform horizontal ventilation in a safe and effective manner. Both natural and forced horizontal ventilation are discussed.

Figure 1.13 Positive pressure ventilation is a form of horizontal ventilation.

Figure 1.14 Firefighters performing vertical ventilation must be able to perform their task and exit the roof quickly.

Vertical Ventilation

Chapter 13 discusses all forms of vertical ventilation **(Figure 1.14)**. Various types and styles of roofs and roof coverings, their effect on the safety of vent crews on these roofs, and their effects on vertical ventilation are addressed. Also considered are the tools and techniques needed to conduct safe and effective vertical ventilation operations.

Special Ventilation Operations

Chapter 14 addresses ventilating extraordinary structures such as high-rise buildings **(Figure 1.15)**, underground structures, windowless buildings, highly secure buildings, and those that have been extensively remodeled. The tools and techniques needed to conduct safe and effective ventilation operations in these unusual structures are also discussed.

Summary

The success of any structure fire suppression operation may depend on the support given by other personnel on the fireground. In many cases, the other personnel are members of ladder companies who are trained and equipped for truck company operations. In other cases, there may not be a ladder truck on scene – or even in the department – so these operations must be carried out by engine company personnel or firefighters assigned to other units.

Figure 1.15 High–rise fires pose a unique challenge for ventilation efforts. *Courtesy of Matt Daly.*

The types of support provided to fire suppression crews consist of gaining access to a burning structure by breaching walls or fences, forcing entry through doors and windows, laddering the building, and performing a variety of other functions. These other functions include fireground search and rescue and interior operations such as heat removal and salvage. One of the most important functions performed by truck company personnel involves tactical ventilation — either horizontal or vertical. Another important function performed by truck company personnel is loss control — before, during, and after an incident.

The balance of this manual presents information that expands on all of the above and ties it together. When that information is combined with the necessary training and experience, firefighters should be able to perform their duties safely and effectively.

Review Questions

1. What is a truck company?
2. What are the fireground tasks commonly performed by a truck company?

Enhanced Fire Behavior

Chapter Contents

CASE HISTORY **19**	Airflow 40
Fire Science **20**	Heat 42
Combustion 20	Flame 43
Heat and Temperature 21	Analyzing the Fire 43
Heat of Combustion and Heat Release Rate ... 23	**Extreme Fire Behavior** **46**
Fire Development in a Compartment ... **24**	Flashover 46
Stages of Fire Development 24	Backdraft 51
Factors That Affect Fire Development ... 30	Smoke Explosion 54
Impact of Changing Conditions 35	Other Fire Gas Ignitions 54
The Modern Fire Environment 36	Factors Influencing Extreme Fire Behavior ... 55
Analyzing the Fire: Fire Behavior Indicators **36**	**Summary** **56**
Building Features 37	**Review Questions** **56**
Smoke 38	

Divider page photo courtesy of Gresham (OR) Fire and Rescue.

chapter 2

Key Terms

Autoignition 23
Autoignition Temperature (AIT) 23
Backdraft 51
British Thermal Unit (Btu) 22
Celsius Scale 22
Combustion 20
Conduction 24
Convection 24
Fahrenheit Scale 22
Fire Tetrahedron 21
Fire Triangle 20
Flashover 28

Heat Flux 28
Heat of Combustion 23
Heat Release Rate (HRR) 23
Incipient Stage Fire 26
Joule 22
Kinetic Energy 21
Potential Energy 21
Pyrolysis 23
Radiation 24
Rollover 28
Thermal Layering 26
Vaporization 23

Enhanced Fire Behavior

Learning Objectives

After reading this chapter, students will be able to:

1. Define combustion.
2. Describe the process of pyrolysis.
3. Describe the four stages of fire development.
4. Explain the process of fire development in a structural compartment.
5. Describe the factors that affect fire development in a compartment.
6. Describe the five categories of fire behavior indicators.
7. Summarize the various fire behavior indicators associated with smoke.
8. Differentiate between radiation-induced and ventilation-induced flashover.
9. Summarize the indications of a potential backdraft.
10. Differentiate between a backdraft and a smoke explosion.
11. Summarize the factors influencing extreme fire behavior.

Safety Points

While reading this chapter, keep the following safety points in mind:

- Firefighters must understand how fires develop in compartments.
- Firefighters must know how to read fire behavior and smoke movement.
- Firefighters must know the indicators of extreme fire behavior such as flashover, backdraft, and other fire gas ignitions – and how to deal with them.

Chapter 2
Enhanced Fire Behavior

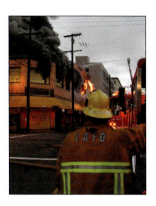

Case History

According to NIOSH Report 98F-06, Ohio firefighters responded to a basement fire in a one-story, single-family dwelling in 1998. Upon arrival, they observed light smoke rising from the roof and the resident reported that there was heavier smoke in the basement near the electrical panel. Advancing a hoseline into the basement, the fire attack team encountered moderate smoke and broke out a basement window to provide a second means of egress. While trying to locate the fire, firefighters observed pulsing smoke and lazy orange flames at the ceiling. They extinguished flames near a light fixture on the ceiling but observed the fire reignite and travel across the ceiling. When a firefighter lifted a ceiling tile with an axe to check fire conditions above the suspended ceiling, he introduced air into this void space triggering a backdraft. The suspended ceiling crashed down onto the firefighters because of the overpressure created by the backdraft, and the basement filled with black smoke. Although disoriented by the thick smoke and ceiling collapse, firefighters attempted to escape from the basement. Several firefighters made it out, but two others did not. They died from smoke inhalation, burns, and blunt force trauma.

As the foregoing case history shows, even when firefighters attempt to do the right thing while fighting interior structure fires, the results can sometimes be catastrophic. Firefighters' knowledge of fire behavior serves as a foundation for understanding the strategies, tactics, and specific task assignments required in fire fighting operations. Developing expertise in the application of this knowledge requires an understanding of the science of fire dynamics *and* practical fireground experience. Neither one alone is sufficient.

IFSTA's **Essentials of Fire Fighting** provides a solid foundation for developing knowledge of basic fire science and fire dynamics – commonly referred to as *fire behavior*. However, there is more to understanding practical fire dynamics related to fire fighting tactical operations. This chapter examines fire behavior in structure fires with an emphasis on reading key indicators to anticipate fire development, and understanding the influence of changes in ventilation. Firefighters must be able to anticipate fire development and spread and take appropriate tactical action to mitigate the risk. An example of this is properly ventilating the structure in order to prevent extreme fire conditions. In addition, firefighters must understand the impact and influence of their actions on fire behavior and the importance of controlling the fire environment to increase firefighter and occupant safety. These connections are clearly shown in the following case history.

> According to NIOSH Report F2000-23, Utah firefighters responded to a fire in the attached garage of a tri-level, single-family dwelling in March of 2000. On arrival, firefighters observed flames and smoke issuing from a garage window and from around the garage door. The first-arriving engine crew attacked the fire from the exterior and quickly darkened the fire in the garage. Believing that the fire in the garage was mostly out, the Incident Commander then tasked the same crew with primary search. When they took their hoseline to the third level (above the garage) to conduct a search, the firefighters encountered heavy black smoke down to the floor. A crew from the next-arriving engine was ordered to assist with primary search and ventilation and they followed the hoseline in. They began their search on the second level and when they also encountered heavy black smoke, they broke out a dining room window. A third crew set up a positive pressure fan at the front door. Shortly after breaking the window, the second engine crew reported a rapid rise in temperature. Fire extended rapidly from the garage on the first level to the second and third levels and the first engine crew searching above the garage was cut off from their means of egress. They were unable to control the fire and two members of that crew later reported that the heat was so intense that they were "unable to think." Two members of that crew and the second crew conducting search and ventilation operations were able to escape. However, one member of the crew working above the garage was unable to make it down the stairs and was trapped on the upper level. After being extricated by a Rapid Intervention Crew, he later died from smoke inhalation.

Fire Science

Basic fire science is familiar to most firefighters and provides a good starting point for improving understanding of fire dynamics and structural fire behavior. Most of what follows reviews the highlights of the fire behavior chapter in **Essentials**.

Combustion

Combustion — An exothermic chemical reaction that is a self-sustaining process of rapid oxidation of a fuel, that produces heat and light.

Fire Triangle — Plane geometric figure of an equilateral triangle that is used to explain the conditions necessary for fire. The sides of the triangle represent heat, oxygen, and fuel.

In this context, **combustion** is termed as a rapid and self-sustaining chemical process that yields heat and usually light. In flaming combustion, oxidation involves fuel in the gas phase. This requires solid fuels to be converted to the gas phase or liquid fuels to be vaporized. When heated, both solid and liquid fuels give off vapors that mix with oxygen in the air and can burn, producing flames. Some solid fuels, particularly those that are porous and can char, undergo oxidation at the surface of the fuel. This is known as nonflaming or smoldering combustion.

In the study of fire behavior, models provide a simplified way of looking at a complex phenomenon such as combustion. The **fire triangle** is a simple model that explains nonflaming or surface combustion (smoldering) such as glowing charcoal **(Figure 2.1)**. Heat, fuel, and oxygen are required for this **chemical** reaction to occur. If you sufficiently remove or reduce any one of these, the reaction stops.

Flaming combustion is more accurately explained using another model, the **fire tetrahedron**, which is comprised of the following four elements: heat, fuel, oxygen, and a self-sustained chemical reaction **(Figure 2.2)**. Each component of the tetrahedron must be in place for flaming combustion to occur. As with the fire triangle, the reaction stops if any of these components is removed or sufficiently reduced.

NOTE: Even when flaming combustion ceases, there may be sufficient heat, fuel, and oxygen for nonflaming or smoldering combustion to continue.

Fire Tetrahedron — Model of the four elements/conditions required to have a fire. The four sides of the tetrahedron represent fuel, heat, oxygen, and chemical chain reaction.

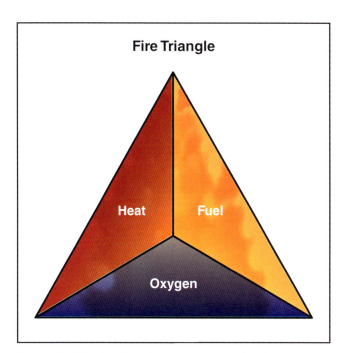

Figure 2.1 The fire triangle represents nonflaming combustion.

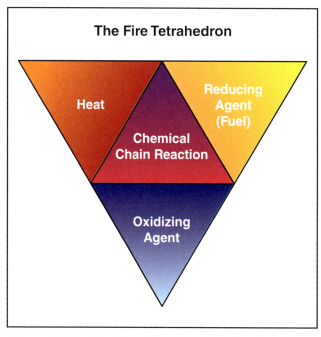

Figure 2.2 The fire tetrahedron represents flaming combustion.

Heat and Temperature

Most people have a basic understanding of heat and temperature. However, these terms are often incorrectly used interchangeably. As discussed in *Essentials*, heat is a form of energy, and energy exists in two states: potential and kinetic. **Potential energy** is the energy contained in an object that may be released in the future. **Kinetic energy** is often defined informally as energy of motion. Thermal energy (often referred to as *heat energy*) is kinetic energy associated with the movement of the atoms and molecules that comprise matter.

Before ignition, a fuel has potential chemical energy. When that fuel burns, the chemical energy is converted to kinetic energy in the form of thermal energy (heat) and light. Temperature is a measurement of kinetic energy. Heat is the movement of thermal energy from objects of higher temperature to those of lower temperature **(Figure 2.3, p. 22)**. This concept is particularly important in understanding both fire development and fire control tactics.

By definition, *energy* is the capacity to perform work. Work occurs and energy is expended when a force is applied to an object over a distance or when a chemical, biological, or physical transformation is made in a substance. Energy cannot be measured directly. Instead, it is necessary to measure the

Potential Energy — Stored energy possessed by an object that can be released in the future to perform work once released.

Kinetic Energy — The energy possessed by a moving object.

Celsius Scale — Temperature scale on which the freezing point is 0 degrees and the boiling point at sea level is 100 degrees. Also known as Centigrade scale.

Fahrenheit Scale — Temperature scale on which the freezing point is 32°F (0°C) and the boiling point at sea level is 212°F (100°C) at normal atmospheric pressure.

Joule (J) — Unit of work or energy in the International System of Units; the energy (or work) when unit force (1 newton) moves a body through a unit distance (1 meter); takes the place of calorie for heat measurement (1 calorie = 4.19 J).

British Thermal Unit (Btu) — Amount of heat energy required to raise the temperature of one pound of water one degree Fahrenheit. One Btu = 1.055 kilo joules (kJ).

work that it does. In the case of heat, work means increasing temperature – causing the average level of kinetic energy within the molecules of a substance to increase.

Several different scales can be used to measure temperature, however, the most common are **Celsius** and **Fahrenheit**. Celsius is the temperature scale used in the metric system while Fahrenheit is the scale used in the customary system. The freezing and boiling points of water provide a simple way to compare these two scales **(Figure 2.4)**.

In the metric system used in technical literature, the Canadian fire service, and most of the rest of the world, **joules** are the unit of measure for heat energy. While a joule is defined as being equal to one newton over a distance of one meter, in relation to fire behavior it is more relevant to think of joules in terms of heat. It takes 4 186 joules to raise the temperature of one kilogram (kg) of water one degree Celsius. The U.S. fire service uses the customary system in which the unit of measure for heat energy is the **British thermal unit (Btu)**. One Btu is the amount of heat required to raise the temperature of one pound of water one degree Fahrenheit. By comparison, 1 Btu equals approximately 1 100 joules.

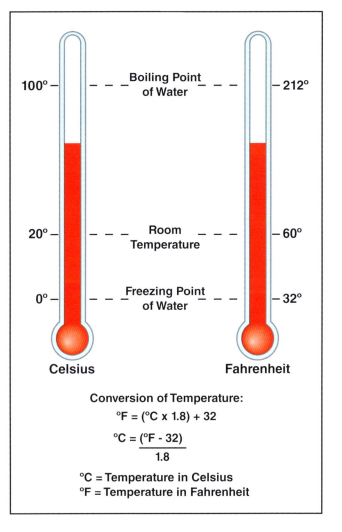

Figure 2.4 Celsius and Fahrenheit scales.

Conversion of Temperature:
$$°F = (°C \times 1.8) + 32$$
$$°C = \frac{(°F - 32)}{1.8}$$
°C = Temperature in Celsius
°F = Temperature in Fahrenheit

Figure 2.3 Heat is the movement of thermal energy from objects of higher temperature to those of lower temperature.

Energy exists in many forms and can change from one form to another. In the study of fire behavior, the conversion of energy into heat is particularly important because heat is the energy component of the fire tetrahedron. When a fuel is heated, its temperature increases. Applying additional heat causes **pyrolysis** (the chemical decomposition of a substance through the action of heat) in solid fuels and **vaporization** of liquid fuels, releasing ignitable vapors or gases. A spark or other external source can provide the energy necessary for ignition, or the fuel can be heated until it ignites without a spark or other source. Once ignited, the process continues the production and ignition of fuel vapors or gases so that the combustion reaction is sustained.

There are two forms of ignition – piloted ignition and autoignition. Piloted ignition occurs when a mixture of fuel and oxygen encounters an ignition source with sufficient heat energy to start the combustion reaction **(Figure 2.5)**. **Autoignition** occurs without any external flame or spark to ignite the fuel gases or vapors. In this case, the fuel surface is chemically heated to the point at which the combustion reaction occurs. **Autoignition temperature (AIT)** is the temperature to which the surface of a substance must be heated for ignition and self-sustained combustion to occur. The autoignition temperature of a substance is always higher than its piloted ignition temperature. While both piloted and autoignition occur under fire conditions, piloted ignition is the most common.

> **Pyrolysis** — Thermal or chemical decomposition of fuel (matter) because of heat that generally results in the lowered ignition temperature of the material.
>
> **Vaporization** — Process that changes a liquid into a gaseous state. The rate of vaporization depends on the substance involved, heat, and pressure.
>
> **Autoignition** — Ignition that occurs when a substance in air, whether solid, liquid, or gaseous, is heated sufficiently to initiate or cause self-sustained combustion without an external ignition source.
>
> **Autoignition Temperature (AIT)** — The temperature at which autoignition occurs through the spontaneous ignition of the gases or vapor given off by a heated material.

Figure 2.5 A spark plug provides the piloted ignition in an internal combustion engine.

Heat of Combustion and Heat Release Rate

The chemical content of any fuel determines its **heat of combustion** and has a significant influence on its energy or **heat release rate (HRR)**. Firefighters often talk about how *hot* a fire was, usually referring to temperature. While temperature is significant, HRR is a critical aspect of fire dynamics that is often overlooked by firefighters.

Heat of Combustion

The heat of combustion of a given fuel is the total amount of energy released when a specific amount of that fuel is oxidized (burned). In other words, some materials release more heat energy than others depending on their chemical makeup. Heat of combustion is usually expressed in either kilojoules/gram (kJ/g) or megajoules/kilogram (MJ/kg). Many plastics, flammable liquids,

> **Heat of Combustion** — Total amount of thermal energy (heat) that could be generated by the combustion (oxidation) reaction if a fuel were completely burned. The heat of combustion is measured in British Thermal Units (Btu) per pound or calories per gram.
>
> **Heat Release Rate (HRR)** — Total amount of heat produced or released to the atmosphere from the convective-lift fire phase of a fire per unit mass of fuel consumed per unit time.

and flammable gases contain more potential heat energy than wood. This is particularly significant to firefighters given the widespread use of synthetics as structural materials and finishes and in building contents.

Heat Release Rate

Heat release rate (HRR) has a direct impact on the flow rate necessary for fire control and on whether a compartment fire will reach flashover. Even though it is not quite as easy to measure as temperature, recognizing the fuel types and configurations that will result in high HHR is an important element in understanding the fire environment and anticipating fire behavior.

HRR is the energy released per unit of time as a given fuel burns. This is usually expressed in kilowatts (kW) or megawatts (MW). HRR is dependent on the type, quantity, and orientation of the fuel. The characteristics of the compartment in which a fire is burning can also affect the heat release rate. In most fires, HRR varies over time — increasing as more fuel becomes involved and then falling as fuel is consumed.

Fire Development in a Compartment

Being able to visualize how a fire develops and spreads within and beyond a single enclosed room or space (compartment) is essential to firefighter safety and effective tactical operations. When a fire occurs in an unconfined area such as outdoors, much of the heat energy released by the burning fuel is dissipated, with only a small amount radiating back to the fuel to continue the combustion process. The interaction between the fire and its environment changes considerably when a fire occurs within a compartment inside a building.

In addition to the heat of combustion and heat release rates discussed earlier, recognizing the influence of heat transfer is important to understanding fire development within a compartment and its possible spread beyond that enclosure. As discussed in **Essentials**, **conduction** is the transfer of heat energy by direct contact. **Radiation** is the transfer of heat energy as an electromagnetic wave without an intervening medium. **Convection** is the transfer of heat energy by a fluid or gas.

In the early stages of a fire in an enclosed fire environment, heat is transferred through all of these mediums, but mainly through convection in the movement of hot smoke and fire gases. Flames heat air within the compartment and the radiated heat may release more flammable vapors of gases from nearby objects. The heated air and other gases then circulate (mostly upward) and heat is transferred to objects within the compartment by conduction. As with all heat transfer, the flow of heat is from the hot fire gases to the cooler structural surfaces, building contents, and air. Convection is the dominant method of heat transfer in the early stages of fire development **(Figure 2.6)**. However, as the room approaches full involvement, radiation from flames and the hot gas layer becomes the more dominant method of heat transfer.

Stages of Fire Development

Following ignition, fire development in a compartment may be described in terms of several stages: incipient, growth, fully developed, and decay. However, the boundaries between these stages are not always clearly defined, particularly

---

Conduction — Physical flow or transfer of heat energy from one body to another through direct contact or an intervening medium from the point where the heat is produced to another location or from a region of high temperature to a region of low temperature.

Radiation — The transmission or transfer of heat energy from one body to another body at a lower temperature through intervening space by electromagnetic waves such as infrared thermal waves, radio waves, or X-rays.

Convection — Transfer of heat by the movement of heated fluids or gases, usually in an upward direction.

outside the laboratory. Despite this limitation, the stages of fire development provide a good framework for firefighters to understand fire development in a compartment **(Figure 2.7)**.

The stages illustrated are an attempt to describe the complex reaction that occurs as a fire develops in a space with no suppression action being taken. The ignition and development of a fire in a compartment is very complex and

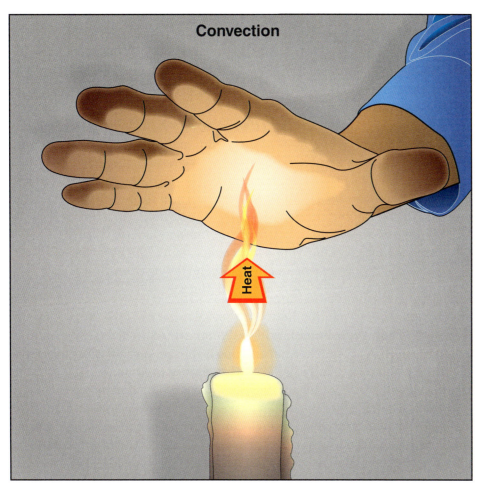

Figure 2.6 Heat rises through convection.

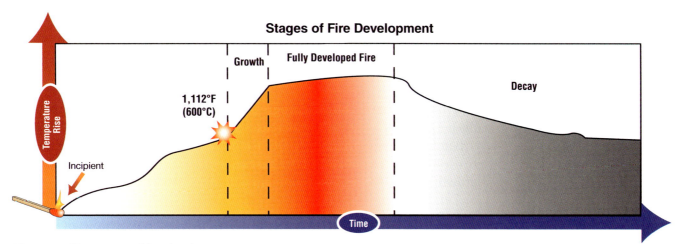

Figure 2.7 The stages of fire development.

influenced by many variables. As a result, not all fires develop through all of the stages described. This information is intended to show fire as a dynamic process that is dependent on many factors for its growth and development.

Incipient Stage

The **incipient stage** starts with ignition – the point where the three elements of the fire triangle come together and combustion begins. The following example describes the development of a typical incipient-stage fire within a compartment.

> *In a typical living room, a discarded cigarette ignites the fabric covering on a polyurethane chair cushion. Initially, combustion occurs at the surface of the fuel with no visible flames. A small amount of smoke rises from the chair cushion. A short time later, flames become visible and the fire begins to grow more quickly as radiant heat begins to pyrolyze the area of the chair adjacent to the point of ignition. The heat release rate and smoke production increase, resulting in development of a plume of smoke and hot air rising from the chair to the ceiling. Upon reaching the ceiling, the hot gases spread horizontally as a ceiling jet. The rate of combustion increases with flames reaching several feet (meters) above the chair and a layer of hot smoke and gases forms at the ceiling. The room remains near ambient temperature and oxygen concentration is still close to a normal 21 percent.*

> **Incipient Stage Fire** — Fire that is in the initial or beginning stage and that can be controlled or extinguished by portable fire extinguishers or small hoselines.

> **Thermal Layering** — Outcome of combustion in a confined space in which gases tend to form into layers, according to temperature, with the hottest gases found at the ceiling and the coolest gases at floor level. Also called Thermal Balance or Heat Stratification.

As smoke begins to accumulate in the compartment, it does so in a manner called **thermal layering**. Thermal layering is the tendency of gases to stratify according to temperature. Other terms sometimes used to describe this tendency are *heat stratification* and *thermal balance*. The hottest gases tend to be in the top layer, while the cooler gases form the lower layers. In addition to the effects of heat transfer through conduction and convection described earlier, radiation from the hot gas layer also acts to heat the exposed surfaces of the compartment and its contents.

While thermal layering is often pictured as smoke staying at the ceiling level and clear air below, the distinction is not always this sharply defined. As smoke moves away from the fire, it will cool and drop lower toward the floor. Additionally, as smoke production increases, the volume of smoke may simply fill the compartment, leaving no clear air below. However, ceiling temperatures will generally be higher than those at the floor.

Growth Stage

As a fire continues to burn, it progresses to the growth stage. The thickness of the hot gas layer at the ceiling increases and flames reach the ceiling and begin to bend and move horizontally. Occasionally, isolated flames can be observed in the hot layer of smoke and fire gases overhead. As the fire continues in the growth stage, its rate of development will increase as long as it has sufficient fuel and oxygen.

When sufficient oxygen is available, fire development is controlled by the characteristics and configuration of the fuel. A significant factor influencing the rate of development is how the burning fuel is oriented relative to horizontal

(**Figure 2.8**). Under these conditions, the fire is said to be *fuel controlled*. But as the fire continues to grow and requires more oxygen, the neutral plane in any open doorway also drops due to increased smoke production. This further reduces the area available for air intake, restricting the oxygen supply. When fire development is limited by a lack of oxygen, the fire is said to be *ventilation controlled*.

The controlling factor is important to firefighters because it determines how the fire will change when ventilation is increased. When the fire is fuel controlled, increased ventilation will generally reduce temperatures within the compartment and thereby slow or prevent its progression to flashover. On the other hand, increasing the air supplied to a ventilation-controlled fire will increase the rate of heat release and may result in extreme fire behavior.

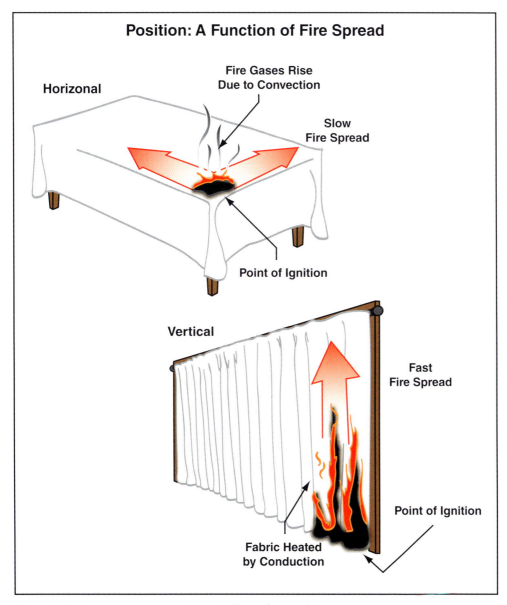

Figure 2.8 How a material is positioned affects the way it burns.

Chapter 2 • Enhanced Fire Behavior 27

⚠️ It is critical that tactical ventilation be performed in a planned and systematic manner to maximize the positive effects while minimizing the potential for intensifying the fire.

Rollover — Condition in which the unburned combustible gases released in a confined space (such as a room or aircraft cabin) during the incipient or early steady-state phase accumulate at the ceiling level. These superheated gases are pushed, under pressure, away from the fire area and into uninvolved areas where they mix with oxygen. When their flammable range is reached and additional oxygen is supplied by opening doors and/or applying fog streams, they ignite and a fire front develops, expanding very rapidly in a rolling action across the ceiling.

Heat Flux — Scientific measurement of how much heat is available for transfer to human skin (or any other surface).

Flashover — Stage of a fire at which all surfaces and objects within a space have been heated to their ignition temperature and flame breaks out almost at once over the surface of all objects in the space.

As the fire progresses, the chance for a condition called **rollover** increases. During a rollover, flames begin to move intermittently through the hot gas layer **(Figure 2.9)**. While a rollover can sometimes be dramatic, it is not the same as flashover (discussed later in this chapter). The ceiling temperature approaches 1,100°F (600°C) during a rollover and the heat being radiated to the floor may be sufficient to ignite ordinary materials such as newspaper. If there is an open doorway, hot smoke will push through the opening into any adjacent compartment while cooler air is drawn inward at the bottom (below the neutral plane), providing the oxygen required for continued fire development. As the temperature of fuels within the compartment continues to increase, so does the rate of pyrolysis, with unburned decomposition products accumulating in the hot layer of smoke. As temperature and **heat flux** (heat being absorbed) continue to increase, the compartment may rapidly transition to full involvement – with or without **flashover**.

If flashover occurs – and it does not in every case – it will occur as the fire transitions from the growth stage to the fully developed stage. Flashover is discussed in detail later in this chapter in the Extreme Fire Behavior section.

Figure 2.9 Flames can be seen in the hot gas layer during a rollover. *Courtesy of NIST.*

Fully Developed Stage

In the incipient and early growth stages of many compartment fires, heat transfer is largely dependent on convection. Hot smoke and gases rise from the fire and spread laterally across the ceiling to the walls, heating those surfaces in the process. However, as the fire progresses toward the fully developed stage, the temperature of the hot gas layer increases. When this happens, radiant heat from flames and the hot gas layer transfer heat to fuel (furniture, carpet, etc.) within the compartment and becomes an increasingly significant influence on fire development.

An Alternative Path — As mentioned earlier, flashover does not occur in every compartment fire. The availability of both fuel and oxygen determine whether a fire within a compartment will progress to flashover. First, the available fuel must have sufficient energy (heat of combustion), and this energy must be released quickly enough (heat release rate) to develop flashover conditions. The second factor is ventilation. A developing fire must have enough available oxygen to reach flashover, and a sealed room may not contain a sufficient volume of air. In that case, heat release will be limited by the available air supply. If there is insufficient ventilation, the fire may not reach the peak heat release of a fully developed fire **(Figure 2.10)**.

Returning to the example of the fire ignited in the upholstered chair, if the ventilation conditions were changed by closing the door to the adjacent room, ignition and fire development through the incipient stage and into the growth stage would be quite similar to that described earlier. However, this is where the path changes course and the fire enters the decay stage due to limited oxygen supply.

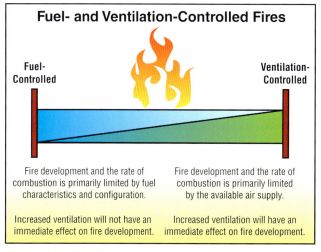

Figure 2.10 Fire development may be limited by fuel characteristics or the availability of an air supply.

Decay Stage

A fire may enter the decay stage due to consumption of available fuel or due to limited oxygen supply. Of these two conditions, decay due to limited oxygen supply is of much greater concern to firefighters. As the fire develops through the growth stage and into the fully developed stage, hot gases that cannot escape from the compartment cause the smoke layer to thicken and expand downward from the ceiling toward the floor. While the fire continues to burn, the oxygen concentration in the room drops, flaming combustion decreases, the heat release rate is reduced, and the fire enters the decay stage.

Despite the reduction in heat release rate, the temperature within the compartment continues to rise because the fire is still burning. If the compartment remains intact (the door remains closed, the windows do not fail, and the fire does not burn through the compartment lining into a structural void) the fire may actually reduce the oxygen concentration to the point that it self-extinguishes due to insufficient oxygen. This is one possibility, and is the safest of potential outcomes.

When a fire is controlled or limited in heat release rate by the available oxygen, firefighters must be concerned about what may happen if the air supply to the fire is increased by the failure of a window or someone opening a door.

Two potential consequences of the introduction of air to the compartment in the decay stage are ventilation-induced flashover and backdraft.

Ventilation-Induced Flashover — If a fire is ventilation-controlled, it can be thought of as being similar to a gasoline engine running with the choke closed. With the choke closed, the engine runs sluggishly, but if the choke is opened the engine increases speed and power output. In a ventilation-controlled fire, increasing the air supply increases the HRR. If this increase is sufficient it may cause the involved compartment or compartments to flash over.

Backdraft — If ventilation is increased, the heat release rate will also increase. If the concentration of flammable combustion and pyrolysis products is above the upper flammable limit, the temperature is above 1,100°F (600°C) or another source of ignition is available, and ventilation is increased, a backdraft may occur.

Flashover and backdraft are discussed in greater detail in the section of this chapter on Extreme Fire Behavior.

It is important to recognize that most compartment fires that grow beyond the incipient stage become ventilation controlled. Even when doors and/or windows are open, there is often insufficient air to allow the fire to continue to develop based on the available fuel. When windows are intact and doors are closed, the fire may move into a ventilation-controlled state even more quickly. While this reduces the heat release rate, fuel will continue to pyrolize, creating extremely fuel-rich smoke.

> The following discussion of fire development examines fire behavior in a single compartment to illustrate fire progression. Actual conditions within a building composed of multiple compartments can vary widely. The compartment of origin may be in the fully developed stage while adjacent compartments may be in the growth stage. In addition, an attic or void space may be in a severely underventilated decay stage while adjacent compartments are in the growth or fully developed stage. This makes reading the fire and assessing the hazards presented by fire conditions a critical task for everyone working inside the burning building.

Factors That Affect Fire Development

A number of factors influence fire development within a compartment. These factors include the following:

- Fuel type
- Availability and location of additional fuel
- Compartment geometry (volume and ceiling height)
- Ventilation (and changes in ventilation)
- Thermal properties of the enclosure
- Ambient conditions (wind, temperature, humidity, etc.)

Fuel Type

As discussed earlier in the section addressing fuel, the type of fuel involved in combustion impacts both the amount of heat released and the time over which that release occurs. In a compartment fire, the most fundamental fuel characteristics influencing fire development are mass and surface area. Combustible materials with high surface-to-mass ratios are much more easily ignited and will burn more quickly than the same substance with less surface area. In addition, many ordinary combustibles such as wood and paper are significantly influenced by fuel moisture. Water absorbs heat that would otherwise contribute to the process of pyrolysis.

Firefighters should be able to recognize potential fuels in a building or compartment and use that information to estimate the fire growth potential for the building or space. Materials with high heat release rates, such as polyurethane foam-padded furniture, would be expected to burn rapidly once ignition occurs.

Availability and Location of Additional Fuel

A number of factors influence the availability and location of additional fuels. These include the configuration of the building, contents and interior finish (non-structural fire load), construction (structural fuel load), and location of the fire in relation to fuel that has not yet become involved.

Figure 2.11 Compartmentalized occupancies can slow the spread of fire.

Building configuration is the layout of the structure including the number of stories, avenues for fire spread, compartmentation, and barriers to fire spread. A building may have a high fire load, but be highly compartmentalized with fire doors blocking the spread of hot smoke and fire gases **(Figure 2.11)**. On the other hand, buildings with open floor plans or unprotected vertical shafts may provide the fire with access to fuel throughout the building **(Figure 2.12)**.

The contents of a structure are often the most readily available fuel source in a compartment fire. The quantity and nature of building contents significantly influence fire development **(Figure 2.13, p. 32)**. When contents have a high heat of combustion and heat release rate, both the intensity of the fire and rate of development will be greater. For example, synthetic furnishings such as polyurethane foam will begin to pyrolize rapidly under fire conditions (even when located some distance from the seat of the fire), accelerating the process of fire development.

Figure 2.12 Open floor plans allow fire to spread rapidly.

The type of construction influences fuel load as some types of building materials are more combustible than others. For example, in wood-frame buildings, the structure itself is a source of fuel. In addition to structural members, combustible interior finishes, such as wood paneling, can be a significant factor influencing fire spread **(Figure 2.14, p. 32)**.

Figure 2.13 The contents of occupancies such as furniture showrooms can significantly influence fire development.

Figure 2.14 Interior finishes can greatly contribute to fire spread.

> It is important to distinguish between a contents fire involving furnishings and compartment linings (interior finish) and one that has begun to involve structural elements. In other words, is it a fire in a building or a burning building? Firefighters should continually assess conditions and maintain an awareness of whether they are dealing with a contents fire or a structure fire.

The proximity (in relation to the fire) and the continuity of contents and structural fuels also influence fire development. Fuels in the upper level of adjacent compartments will be more quickly pyrolized by the hot gas layer, and continuous fuels (such as combustible interior finishes) will rapidly spread the fire from compartment to compartment. Similarly, the location of the fire within the building will influence fire development. When the fire is located low in the building, such as in the basement or on the first floor, convected heat will cause vertical extension through unprotected stairways and vertical shafts. Fires originating on upper levels generally extend downward much more slowly **(Figure 2.15)**.

> According to NIOSH Report F2005-13, Wyoming firefighters were called to a fire in a tri-level townhouse in April of 2005. On arrival, firefighters saw smoke issuing from the top floor of the structure which consisted of a basement and two stories above ground. Following a report of children trapped on the top floor, two firefighters took a charged attack line up the interior stairway. Shortly after they entered, a smoke explosion occurred. After the explosion, the fire intensified in the stairway trapping the two firefighters on the top floor. Even though they were wearing full PPE and SCBA, both firefighters succumbed to smoke inhalation and thermal injuries.

Compartment Geometry

All other things being equal, a fire in a large compartment will develop more slowly than one in a small compartment due to the greater volume of air and

Figure 2.15 Fires originating on the upper levels of a structure tend to extend downward more slowly. *Courtesy of Ron Jeffers.*

structural material that must be heated. However, this large volume of air will support the development of a larger fire before ventilation becomes the limiting factor.

As in the following case history, a high ceiling may also mask the extent of fire development by allowing a large volume of hot smoke and other fire gases to accumulate at upper levels. This can occur even while conditions at floor level remain relatively unchanged. These situations are particularly hazardous because conditions can change rapidly if this hot gas layer ignites.

> According to NIOSH Report F2007-18, in June of 2007 South Carolina firefighters were called to a fire in a single-story furniture store. On arrival, firefighters saw heavy black smoke rising from the rear loading dock area of the unsprinklered metal building. However, firefighters entering through the front of the store saw little smoke inside the expansive showroom. When a rear door was opened, the fire above the suspended ceiling greatly intensified and rolled through the showroom. Interior crews were ordered out of the building, but approximately three minutes later the interior flashed over and the truss-supported roof collapsed. Nine firefighters failed to escape the flames.

Ventilation

As discussed earlier in this chapter, for a fire to develop, sufficient oxygen must be available to support burning beyond the incipient stage. The available air supply in a compartment significantly influences how the fire develops within the space. Existing ventilation is the actual and potential ventilation of a structure based on structural openings, construction type, and building ventilation systems. For the most part, all buildings exchange air inside the structure with air outside the structure. In some cases, this is due to leakage through cracks and other gaps in construction. In other cases, air exchange occurs through the heating, ventilating, and air conditioning (HVAC) system **(Figure 2.16)**. In general, these existing ventilation openings are fixed and do not change, even under fire conditions. However, the status of other potential ventilation openings, such as windows and doors, can change during fire development and alter the ventilation profile. Under fire conditions, windows can fail and doors can be left open, increasing ventilation **(Figure 2.17)**.

When a fire develops to the point where it becomes ventilation controlled, the available air supply will determine the speed and extent of fire development and sometimes the direction of fire spread. When a fire starts, existing ventilation conditions dictate the actual exchange of products of combustion inside the building or compartment with outside air. It is critical to recognize the potential for changing ventilation conditions during fire fighting operations. When firefighters make additional ventilation openings by opening doors or windows to enter a building or create other openings

Figure 2.16 Air exchange in a structure can occur through the HVAC system.

Figure 2.17 The failure of windows in a structure fire can increase the amount of oxygen available to the fire. *Courtesy of the Los Angeles Fire Department – ISTS.*

to vent the structure, they change the ventilation profile. Taking tactical action to limit air reaching the fire can also influence fire behavior. Before taking any of these actions, firefighters should consider the potential effect on the behavior of the fire.

Thermal Properties of the Enclosure

Thermal properties include insulation, heat reflectivity, retention, and conductivity. When a compartment is well insulated, less heat is lost and more heat remains available to increase temperature and speed the combustion reaction. Similarly, surfaces that reflect heat direct the heat back to the combustion reaction, increasing its speed. Materials such as masonry act as a heat sink and will retain heat energy, sustaining high temperatures for a long period of time. Other structural materials, such as metal, conduct heat readily. While not retaining heat to the same degree as masonry, these materials can transfer heat to other combustibles through conduction, spreading the fire beyond the compartment or compartments already involved. Thermal windows (those with multiple layers separated by inert gas) can also act to contain heat in a developing fire **(Figure 2.18)**. Many modern buildings have thermal windows and other energy-saving features that also serve to contain any fires burning inside.

Figure 2.18 Thermal windows can contain heat in a developing fire.

Ambient Conditions

While ambient temperature and relative humidity can have an impact on the ignitability of many fuels, these weather phenomena are less significant factors inside a structure which is designed to minimize their impact on the occupants. However, high humidity and cold temperatures can impede the natural movement of smoke, and wind can accelerate fire development. Some buildings, such as cold-storage facilities, maintain extremely low temperatures inside. Other buildings, such as foundries and other industrial facilities, commonly have higher internal temperatures.

Strong winds can significantly influence fire behavior, particularly when ventilation changes produce unintended consequences. If a window fails or a door is opened on the windward side of the building, fire intensity and spread can increase significantly. Some winds, such as those associated with normal weather patterns, are predictable; others, such as those associated with approaching storms, are less predictable and can have dramatic effects on structural fire behavior.

Impact of Changing Conditions

Structure fires can be dynamic and ever-changing phenomena. Factors influencing fire development can change as the fire extends from one compartment to another. Extension of the fire can provide additional fuel or high temperatures that cause windows to break and fall out, thus changing the ventilation profile. Considering that most fires beyond the incipient stage are or will quickly become ventilation controlled, changes in ventilation are likely to be one of the most significant factors in changing fire behavior. In some cases, these changes are caused by the fire acting on building materials; while in other cases fire behavior is influenced (positively or negatively) by tactical operations. Firefighters must recognize that opening a door to make entry for fire attack or search can have as much impact on ventilation as opening a window to purposefully vent smoke and products of combustion.

The Modern Fire Environment

The chemical composition of fuel influences its heat of combustion (the amount of heat released by a given mass of fuel) and the heat release rate (the rate at which that heat is released). Oxidation of a specific amount of fuel releases a given amount of heat energy. As discussed earlier in this chapter, kilojoules per kilogram (kJ/kg) is a standard unit of measure for heat of combustion. A fuel's heat of combustion is dependent on its chemical content and the heat of combustion for hydrocarbon fuels such as plastics, gasoline, propane, and methane can be considerably higher than that of cellulose fuels such as wood.

Figure 2.19 This synthetic lumber looks like real wood but will behave like plastic under fire conditions. *Courtesy of Donny Howard.*

In many older cities, the types of materials of which residential, commercial, institutional, and industrial buildings are constructed varies greatly from those used in more modern structures. While some relatively new communities are constructed of modern building materials, the majority of cities and towns in North America are a mixture of every type of building material available. Regardless of the age of a community, any particular building may contain materials that burn with intensity and liberate highly toxic and flammable combustion products **(Figure 2.19)**. Many modern materials such as synthetic paints, floor coverings, and upholstery materials burn with an intensity uncharacteristic of natural materials such as wood and cotton. Newer buildings are designed with efficient insulating systems that help maintain interior climate control. These buildings and their finishes and furnishings can promote the development of extreme fire behavior by producing very intense fires with highly flammable products of combustion.

Analyzing the Fire: Fire Behavior Indicators

Responsibility for size-up and risk assessment is not limited to fire officers. Everyone on the fireground needs to develop and maintain a high level of *situational awareness* (see Chapter 3). One element of situational awareness is recognition of key fire behavior indicators. This includes not only recognizing what the fire is doing at the moment, but anticipating changes in behavior as the fire is influenced by fire control actions and tactical ventilation. This section provides a simple overview of key fire behavior indicators. However, developing the ability to analyze a fire requires both training and experience.

Fire behavior indicators can be divided into the following five major categories:

- Building features
- Smoke
- Air flow
- Heat
- Flame

Building Features

Building features are indicators of potential fire behavior prior to ignition. During pre-incident planning surveys, firefighters should practice reading the building under nonfire conditions to identify critical characteristics that are likely to influence fire behavior and structural stability under fire conditions.

The first of the critical building features is construction type. The type of building involved influences both fire behavior and structural stability under fire conditions. Combustible construction such as wood frame (Type V), masonry and wood (ordinary or Type III), and heavy timber (Type IV) construction contribute to the fuel load, while non-combustible (Type II) and fire-resistive (Type I) construction do not. However, it is important to note that construction classification refers to structurally supporting materials, not interior finish and roofing materials. These items may contribute substantially to the fire load, even in a noncombustible or fire-resistive structure. For this reason, items such as interior finishes and roofing materials are considered to be building factors, even while not technically part of the building itself.

As discussed earlier in this chapter, the existing ventilation in a structure is the actual and potential air flow based on natural air currents, structural openings, construction types, and building ventilation systems. Under fire conditions, firefighters must consider the exchange of smoke with fresh air from the involved compartments and other smoke-filled areas of the building and from the exterior or other parts of the building or the outside atmosphere. It is also critical to assess the impact on fire behavior from potential changes to the existing ventilation.

In addition to ventilation and fire load, the size of the building is a major factor in heat release rate and total heat released by the fire **(Figure 2.20)**. These factors are central to determining the flow rate and total volume of water that will be required to control and extinguish a fire in a particular building. In addition to influencing fire flow, the size of the building can also influence other fire behavior indicators. For example, if the building is large and has a high ceiling, a large volume of smoke (unburned fuel) may be produced before smoke indicators are visible from the exterior. Other buildings have large plenum spaces or cocklofts that can conceal a significant volume of smoke and fire without them being visible even inside the building.

As discussed in the section on factors influencing fire development, the insulation and energy efficiency of the structure can also influence fire behavior. However, like many other building factors, thermal characteristics of the structure may not be visible during fire fighting operations. Evaluating building factors from a fire behavior perspective is a critical element in pre-incident planning. Many newer energy-efficient buildings can contain the heat and smoke from an interior fire longer than many older buildings. For example, windows in

Figure 2.20 The size of a building can affect heat release rate.

Figure 2.21 Reflective film can delay the discovery of a fire from the outside.

some buildings are coated with reflective film that is designed to reduce heating from the sun **(Figure 2.21)**. But this film can also keep an interior fire from being seen from the outside, thus allowing for greater fire development before discovery. Anything that delays discovery increases the chances of flashover and backdraft conditions developing.

Smoke

Smoke is a result of incomplete combustion. As such, it must be considered as *unburned fuel*. Under the right conditions, smoke can ignite in a flashover, backdraft, or smoke explosion and present a significant threat to firefighter safety.

The volume and location of smoke discharge from a burning building can provide some indication of fire location and extent, but these indicators need to be verified. Smoke color, density, pressure, and movement are other indicators of fire behavior. It is important to consider smoke volume and location in addition to other fire behavior indicators to get a clear picture of actual fire conditions. Fires that are ventilation-controlled tend to produce a greater volume of smoke than those that are fuel-controlled; however, where smoke is discharged from a building may be some distance from the seat of the fire.

Smoke Color

Smoke color can vary considerably depending on the nature of the fuel that is burning, the conditions under which it is burning, and other factors in the fire environment. In addition to observing smoke color as part of an initial size-up, it is also important to notice changes in color as the fire progresses. The most common variations in smoke color are as follows:

- Petroleum products, rubber, and many plastics produce black smoke **(Figure 2.22)**.
- Wood and other ordinary combustibles produce smoke ranging from light gray to yellowish or dark brown **(Figure 2.23)**, but may produce black smoke when the fire has a limited air supply.
- Lighter-colored smoke frequently contains a substantial concentration of toxic and flammable pyrolysis products **(Figure 2.24)**.
- Dark smoke generally results from an underventilated fire or combustion of petroleum products **(Figure 2.25)**.

Figure 2.22 This tire fire is producing thick, black smoke. *Courtesy of District Chief Chris E. Mickal, NOFD Photo Unit.*

Figure 2.23 Wood and other ordinary combustibles produce various shades of gray smoke. *Courtesy of District Chief Chris E. Mickal, NOFD Photo Unit.*

Figure 2.24 Even light-colored smoke may be highly toxic. *Courtesy of Dick Giles.*

Figure 2.25 This dark smoke is the result of the combustion of petroleum products. *Courtesy of District Chief Chris E. Mickal, NOFD Photo Unit.*

Temperature and humidity in the fire environment can affect the volume of smoke produced and how it behaves. Smoke color is only one of a number of indicators used to assess fire behavior, and it must be considered along with all the others.

Optical Density and Opacity

The terms *optical density* and *opacity* are used to describe how difficult it is to see through the smoke. Optically dense or thick smoke contains a high concentration of particulates and is difficult to see through. Like color, optical density is related to fuel type and ventilation. The burning of hydrocarbons and many synthetic fuels as well as underventilated conditions will result in increased optical density of the smoke.

Physical Density

The term *physical density* refers to the buoyancy of the smoke. Smoke that is buoyant will rise quickly and smoke that is not will hang low to the floor. In general, buoyancy is related to the temperature of the smoke — the higher the temperature, the greater the buoyancy. Smoke produced shortly after ignition in the early stages of fire development may not be very buoyant due to limited heat release. In addition, buoyancy may be affected by humidity, the operation of automatic sprinklers (or application of water from hoselines), or the smoke may simply cool as it moves away from the fire.

Hot Gas Layer

Firefighters often gauge the thickness of the hot gas layer in a compartment by the height of the smoke above the floor. However, the ceiling height must also be considered in this assessment. Compartments with very high ceilings can contain huge volumes of unburned and highly flammable smoke and other fire gases.

Early in fire development, the hot gas layer may be poorly defined, with warm smoke diffusing into the slightly cooler air in the compartment. As the fire develops, the increased temperature differential between the smoke and the cooler air below will more sharply define the hot gas layer and it will become lower **(Figure 2.26)**. If the fire continues to burn in a ventilation-controlled state, the smoke and hot gases can lower completely to the floor.

Even more important than the height of the hot gas layer are *changes* in its height. A sudden rise could indicate that some type of ventilation has occurred – either tactically by firefighters or caused by the fire breaking a window. Gradual lowering of the hot gas layer could indicate deteriorating conditions and increased potential for flashover. However, inappropriate or excessive application of water can also cause lowering of the hot gas layer. Sudden lowering could indicate deteriorating conditions caused by flashover in an adjacent compartment. Firefighters should report these changes to Command whenever they are seen.

Airflow

Airflow refers to the movement of air toward burning fuel and the movement of smoke out of the compartment. Airflow is caused by pressure differentials inside and outside the compartment and by gravity current (differences in

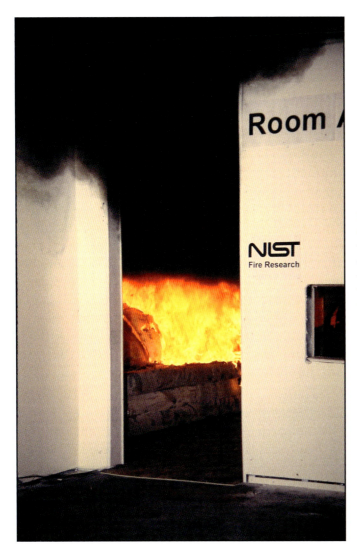

Figure 2.26 The increased temperature differential between the smoke and the cooler air below helps to define the hot gas layer. *Courtesy of NIST.*

density between the hot smoke and cooler air). Mixing of the smoke and air occurs at the interface between the hot gas layer and the cooler air below. This is a critical factor in creating the conditions required for backdraft and many types of fire gas ignitions.

Airflow indicators include pressure and velocity, turbulence, direction, and movement of the hot gas layer. High velocity smoke discharge and turbulent movement are caused by pressure and are generally indicative of high temperature within the compartment. However, the size and shape of the opening from which the smoke is being discharged must be considered. For a given volume of smoke, velocity and turbulence will be greater through smaller openings.

As a fire produces hot smoke and other gases within a compartment or building, these gases expand and increase the internal pressure. As the fire develops, more pressure is created. Pressure causes the smoke to move, and the greater the pressure, the greater the movement. When the entire space within a compartment or building has been filled with smoke, the smoke will be forced out of any available opening. As mentioned earlier, where the smoke is discharged from the building may be some distance from the seat of the fire **(Figure 2.27, p. 42)**. When firefighters see a large volume of very dense smoke billowing out under great pressure, there can be little doubt that a large and

Figure 2.27 Smoke discharged from the building may be some distance from the seat of the fire. *Courtesy of Gresham (OR) Fire and Emergency Services.*

very intense fire is burning within. However, if firefighters see light smoke moving lazily on the top floor of a building, it does not always mean that a fire is not burning in the plenum or attic space above them. Once again, firefighters should not base their assessment of fire conditions on any single observation. Each observation must be considered in relation to the overall situation.

The direction of the airflow can also provide valuable information about the fire behavior. When air moves into an opening (inlet) without any smoke discharge, it is likely that smoke is building within the space or being discharged from another opening (exhaust). When this condition is reversed and smoke comes out with no inward movement of air, it is likely that another opening is serving as an inlet. When the movement is bidirectional and air moves in at the bottom and smoke moves out at the top, this may be the only opening into the compartment or that other exhaust openings may be inadequate. Smoke discharge without inward movement of air or bidirectional air flow both indicate that the fire is likely to be moving toward the opening.

Pulsing airflow (alternate outward movement of smoke followed by an inward movement of air) is indicative of an underventilated fire with potential backdraft conditions. If the compartment is not full of smoke, this may appear as rising and lowering of the hot gas layer. Consider other indicators in determining if backdraft conditions are likely to exist. It is critical to remember that these pulsations can vary in duration and that backdraft does not always occur immediately after an opening is made. The time between making an opening and occurrence of a backdraft is dependent on many factors including distance of the compartment with backdraft conditions from the opening. Airflow is an extremely useful indicator, but it must be viewed as one part of an overall evaluation of critical fire behavior indicators.

Heat

Visual indicators of heat include observed effects such as blistering paint, bubbling roofing tar, crazing glass, and blackened windows. Fire stream effects such as evaporation of water from hot surfaces or lack of return from a temperature check (brief application of water fog into the hot gas layer to check for heat overhead) also provide an indication of elevated temperature. Thermal imaging cameras or infrared heat sensors also provide highly effective means of locating interior fires from the outside by scanning buildings for heat.

Tactile effects (perceptible by touch) include sensing temperature or temperature changes. Firefighters may sense temperature and changes in temperature, but this is limited by the thermal protection provided by their protective clothing and their focus on the task at hand. In addition, self-contained breathing apparatus may be equipped with a temperature-sensing device that provides a warning at a specified level of heat exposure. Because of the limitations of the sensors, it is unlikely that they will provide sufficient early warning to permit egress during rapid increases in temperature such as those associated with flashover and other forms of rapid fire development. While firefighters must be attentive to heat levels and temperature changes, it is often difficult to perceive these changes quickly enough to react to rapidly developing fire conditions. This reinforces the importance of firefighters maintaining their situational awareness and integrating all the observed fire behavior indicators into their ongoing size-up and risk assessment.

Flame

In a working fire, firefighters' attention is sometimes drawn to the flame like a moth to a candle. However, flame is only one of many fire behavior indicators. Visible flames may provide an indication of the size of the fire — fire showing from one window or fire showing from all windows on the fire floor **(Figure 2.28)**. The size and extent of the fire may also be indicated by the effect (or lack thereof) of fire streams on flaming combustion.

Figure 2.28 Flames may provide an indication of the size of the fire. *Courtesy of Gresham (OR) Fire and Emergency Services.*

The location of the flames may also provide important information. If the flames are visible from outside the structure, it allows firefighters to assess flame indicators along with ventilation and air flow. If visibility inside a burning building allows, firefighters should try to observe flame height, and whether the flames are impinging on the ceiling or are bending to spread horizontally. Even when flames cannot be seen, the sounds that are produced as flames consume some materials can give an indication of the location of the fire. If firefighters can see flames in the hot gas layer it may indicate *ghosting* (pockets of flame seen intermittently in the smoke) and impending rollover. Flame color is largely dependent on the type of fuel involved, but if flames go from light yellow to reddish orange, it may also indicate reduced oxygen concentration. A bright white flame usually indicates high temperature such as that generated by burning magnesium and other combustible metals.

Analyzing the Fire

While firefighters' attention is frequently drawn to visible flame and smoke, it is essential that they consider information provided by all of the fire behavior indicators. As conditions change, different information will become relevant in predicting fire behavior.

Table 2.1, p. 44, lists some of the more important fire behavior indicators for each of the four stages of fire development: incipient, growth, fully developed, and decay. For the decay stage, the indicators listed are for decay due to limited ventilation. Decay due to fuel consumption can occur at both ends of the spectrum. First, if there is insufficient fuel for the fire to extend beyond the object or room of origin it may decay due to lack of fuel. On the other hand, the fire may progress through the growth and fully developed stages and subsequently run out of fuel, often resulting in a loss of structural integrity. In both of these cases, fire behavior indicators are likely to be self-evident. The process of reading the fire begins well before ignition with consideration of building factors in both typical occupancies and target hazards. On scene, this process continues with assessment of the current building condition,

Table 2.1
Fire Behavior Indicators

	Incipient	Growth	Fully Developed	Decay
Building	Not a major issue in recognition of incipient stage fires. These factors significantly influence potential for development beyond the incipient phase. Building factors (such as size and ventilation profile) also influence how other fire behavior indicators will present.	Size, construction, fire load and ventilation profile influence ongoing fire development.	As with the growth stage, size, construction, and fire load influence fire development. Fire effects on the building can change the ventilation profile.	The influence of these factors during the decay stage depends largely on fire effects on the building. Confinement of the fire (note that this may apply to a single compartment or void space and not the entire building). The hazard of ventilation-induced extreme fire behavior (such as backdraft) is increased when building contents have a high heat of combustion.
Smoke	Limited smoke and lack of a well-defined layer of hot gases in the upper area of the compartment. If smoke is visible from the exterior, volume will generally be light in color with little buoyancy.	Smoke may be visible from the exterior. If visible, volume and velocity will be greater than in an incipient stage fire (see air flow indicators). A well-defined layer of hot smoke in the upper level of the compartment will be present. If smoke is not confined to the compartment it will be spreading into adjacent compartments.	Smoke will darken to darker gray, brown, or black. Smoke color is influenced to a substantial extent by what is burning and color may vary. Volume, optical density, and volume of smoke will increase. The height of the hot gas layer (and neutral plane at openings) is influenced by the ventilation profile, but if the compartment is not well ventilated, the hot gas layer will drop close to the floor as the fire progresses through this stage.	Smoke will change to darker gray, brown, or black. Smoke color is influenced to a substantial extent by what is burning and color may vary. Light color smoke or black smoke can become dense gray/yellow. Yellow smoke is often associated with decay due to limited ventilation (and backdraft conditions). However, color alone is not a reliable indicator as smoke may also be gray, black, or brown. Smoke that is optically dense and has the appearance of texture is a more significant indicator. Optical density and volume of smoke will increase. The height of the neutral plane is influenced by the ventilation profile, but if the compartment is not well ventilated, it will drop close to the floor as the fire progresses through this stage. Under ventilation-controlled decay conditions, the hot gas layer will generally (but not always) fill the compartment with pressurized smoke exiting small openings.

Table 2.1 *Courtesy of Ed Hartin.*

	Incipient	Growth	Fully Developed	Decay
Air Flow	Air flow is generally not a major factor in recognition of incipient stage fires. However, some light smoke discharge and inward air movement may be observed from openings close to the seat of the fire.	Air flow is dependent on the ventilation profile. If a compartment has a single opening (such as a door), there will be a bi-directional air flow (smoke out the top and air in the bottom). As the fire grows, the velocity of smoke discharge and air intake will increase. Velocity is likely to be greater at openings close to the fire. However, air flow at exterior openings is significantly influenced by wind and ambient weather conditions.	Air flow is dependent on the ventilation profile. However, given a single opening such as a door, smoke will exit out the top while air moves in the bottom. A fully developed fire will generally produce a strong and well-defined air flow. The velocity of smoke and air movement will commonly be quite high and smoke discharge will be turbulent.	Air flow is dependent on the ventilation profile. However, given a single opening such as a door, smoke will exit out the top while air moves in the bottom. A fully developed fire will generally develop a strong and well-defined air flow. The velocity of smoke and air movement will commonly be quite high and smoke discharge will be turbulent. However, air flow is significantly influenced by the size of the opening and proximity to the fire.
Heat	Low (near ambient) temperature within the compartment. Depending on the degree of insulation, a heat signature may or may not be visible from the exterior using a thermal imaging camera (TIC).	Temperature inside the fire compartment and adjacent spaces will be above ambient, but will be lower in compartments located further away from the fire. Condensation disappears from windows in or near the fire compartment, brownish staining on window glazing from pyrolysis products may become visible, heat indicators may be visible from the exterior of the compartment, particularly cracking window glass or heat at the upper level of doors. An increasing overall temperature within the compartment. It is likely that a heat signature will be observed in the area of the fire compartment using a thermal imaging camera (TIC) from the exterior. Inside the building, convection gases will be visible using the TIC.	In this stage of development, the fire is producing substantial heat. There are likely to be visual indicators of high temperature such as blackened windows, crazing window glazing. Hot surfaces (i.e., doors) may be detected using a fire stream or thermal imager. Firefighters can feel the heat even through their structural turnout clothing.	Temperature during the decay stage can initially be quite high, and continue to rise for some time. There are likely to be visual indicators of high temperature such as blackened windows, crazing window glazing. Hot surfaces (i.e., doors) may be detected using a fire stream or thermal imager. Firefighters can feel the heat even through their structural turnout clothing.
Flame	Fire confined to a small area (i.e., the object of origin) and flames lower than ceiling height.	Fire extending beyond the object of origin and flames may reach ceiling height, bend and begin to travel horizontally across the ceiling or through the hot gas layer. Flame may also be visible from the exterior. Later in the growth stage, isolated flames may be observed in the hot gas layer away from the immediate fire area (one indicator of ventilation-controlled conditions).	Flames may be visible from the exterior, indicating the area and extent of involvement to some degree. Fire will involve the entire compartment in this post-flashover stage of fire development. Flames may be readily visible, but also may be obscured by smoke as the fire becomes ventilation controlled.	In ventilation-controlled decay, flaming combustion is reduced. However, flames may be present. Ignition of fire gases escaping from the compartment (as they mix with air) can provide a strong indication of fuel rich, oxygen-deficient decay conditions. Conditions can vary considerably in different parts of the structure. Backdraft conditions can exist in a compartment or void space while a fully developed fire exists with flames showing from several windows.

smoke, air flow, heat, and flame indicators. Firefighters must evaluate fire conditions from the exterior as part of their individual and crew-based tactical size-up and continue the process as long as they are working around, on top of, or inside the structure.

As part of their size-up process, firefighters develop a mental image of what they think is going on. For example, the indicators they have observed may suggest that this is a room and contents fire; or this is a deep-seated fire that is likely to be burning in structural void spaces. When observed conditions prove to be inconsistent with their previous mental image, it is important for firefighters to reconsider their earlier conclusions and not simply dismiss the conflicting information as irrelevant. Conditions are always changing and the size-up process is always based on incomplete information. Fire behavior indicators that conflict with their expectations should cause firefighters to question what is really going on.

Extreme Fire Behavior

When firefighters die of traumatic causes (non-heart attack or stress related) in structure fires, it is often because they are overwhelmed by sudden and extreme changes in fire behavior. Firefighters who become lost or disoriented while working on a hoseline often do so after experiencing a structural collapse or some form of extreme fire behavior.

Wildland firefighters refer to high rates of fire spread and heat output that preclude offensive suppression methods as extreme fire behavior **(Figure 2.29)**. The same term can be applied to rapid and often catastrophic fire behavior such as flashover, backdraft, smoke explosion, and other fire gas ignitions. While each of these phenomena has a different mechanism, each has the potential for great harm due to the rapid release of tremendous amounts of energy.

In structure fires, fire behavior is often a sequential phenomenon. For example, a fire progressing from the growth stage through flashover to the fully developed stage is a sequence of events. Extreme fire behavior is the result of rapid fire development leading to flashover, which is followed by a sustained increase in heat output. On the other hand, rapid combustion or an explosion of accumulated fire gases is an example of a transient event and is more characteristic of backdraft and other fire gas ignitions. These transient events release a tremendous amount of energy, which may or may not be followed by a sustained increase in heat release rate.

Flashover

As mentioned earlier in this chapter, when flashover occurs it is the sudden transition from the growth stage to the fully developed stage of a fire in a compartment. However, flashover does not occur in every interior fire. Fires often transition slowly from the growth stage to the fully developed stage without flashing over. If flashover does occur, the thickness of the hot gas layer will increase dramatically and flames will exit through any openings in the compartment **(Figure 2.30)**. As flames and smoke fill more of the doorway opening, the area available for intake of air (below the hot gas layer) is reduced and the fire becomes ventilation controlled. The fire will continue to develop but is limited by the available oxygen.

Figure 2.29 Wildfires often exhibit high rates of fire spread. *Courtesy of the Los Angeles Fire Department – ISTS.*

Figure 2.30 Flashover can occur almost instantly. *Courtesy of NIST.*

As this occurs, the smoke that pushes out of the open doorway will start to heat the adjacent compartment. As the temperature of the smoke and hot gases in the adjacent compartment increases, pyrolysis increases as well. When flashover occurs in the first compartment, fire easily extends into the second compartment.

Flashover can occur almost instantaneously, and flame spread can move faster than firefighters attempting to escape. The heat flux created by a flashover is not survivable for more than a few seconds – even when wearing full PPE and SCBA – and can result in disorientation as well as thermal burns. The most effective way for firefighters to manage this risk is by maintaining an awareness of developing fire conditions and controlling the fire environment through effective fire control and ventilation tactics.

In general, there are two mechanisms that can induce flashover – radiation and ventilation. The following are descriptions of these mechanisms.

Radiation-Induced Flashover

Flashover is a heat-driven phenomenon. As a compartment fire develops, a plume of hot fire gases rise to the ceiling and begin to raise the temperature of the compartment and its contents. Moving from incipient to growth stage, radiant heat from the fire and hot gas layer increases, further heating other fuel packages in the compartment (heat flux). Nearing flashover, radiant heat becomes the dominant method of heat transfer, and the heat flux is sufficient to quickly raise the temperature of the fuel packages in the compartment to their ignition temperature. As previously discussed, developing sufficient heat flux release to reach flashover is dependent on ventilation as well as the availability of sufficient fuel.

Ventilation-Induced Flashover

When the existing air supply within a compartment does not provide sufficient oxygen, the fire becomes ventilation-controlled. If additional ventilation is provided, it increases the heat release rate which may lead to flashover. If this occurs, the fire suddenly transitions to the fully developed stage.

Additional ventilation can be provided by occupants opening doors to escape the fire or by firefighters forcing entry. As shown in the following case history, a failure to recognize the potential for ventilation-induced flashover can have disastrous consequences.

According to NIOSH Report F2002-34, two Florida firefighters perished while participating in live-fire training in an acquired structure in July of 2002. The building was a single-story, concrete block structure with a wood frame roof. The fire was located in a bedroom (converted garage) on the north side of the structure. Fuel for the fire consisted of approximately five wooden pallets, a bale of straw, and a twin-size urethane mattress. Other fuel in the burn room included carpeting, urethane foam carpet pad, and combustible interior finish – doors, wooden molding, wall-mounted headboards, and painted gypsum drywall on the walls and ceiling.

During this fire training evolution, flashover occurred shortly after ventilation was increased by the opening of a large window in the room where the fire was located. The rapid fire development trapped and severely burned the two firefighters who subsequently died from their injuries.

The fire investigation report by the State Fire Marshal's Office said:

*"All of the participants stated that from the beginning of the exercise they did not have any concerns regarding the conditions of the fire inside the structure and that it appeared to them as **normal** fire behavior. The only fire condition changes of concern occurred when steam filled the hallway during application of water…There was no evidence that any of the participants could foresee that a flashover would occur during the exercise."*

Engineers at the National Institute of Standards and Technology (NIST) performed a series of five full-scale tests based on the conditions involved in this incident. Researchers varied the fuel load for each test. Flashover occurred within seconds after increased ventilation in each of the experiments. NIST fire analysis indicated that the gases were so fuel-rich in the burn room that some time was required for mixing to occur with a resulting flashover.

A number of factors contributed to this tragic event. NFPA® 1403 prohibits the use of fuel such as polyurethane mattresses and requires removal of synthetic carpeting and pad due to the high heat of combustion and heat release rate of these types of materials. The fuel load and ventilation profile in this incident were both contributing factors in these fatalities.

A variety of factors determine whether flashover will occur in any particular compartment fire. The factors involved are as follows:

- Surrounding temperature when the fire started
- Inside dimensions of the compartment
- Where the fire is located in the compartment
- Dimensions and shapes of wall openings (windows, doors)
- Characteristics of interior wall coverings
- Heat loss from the compartment
- Heat release rate of the materials involved
- Rate of fire growth
- Effects of any HVAC systems

A fire starting in a large unheated building will grow more slowly than one in a compartment that is smaller and warmer to begin with. A fire that starts in the middle of a large open compartment will grow at a different rate than one starting against a wall or in a corner **(Figure 2.31)**. Compartments with numerous window and doorway openings allow heat to escape more readily, which slows fire growth. In addition, fire growth is also affected by the nature of fuels involved and the amount of heat that wall and ceiling coverings absorb. Operating HVAC systems can increase the rate of fire growth and the intensity with which it burns by providing abundant oxygen. All of these factors can work together to slow or accelerate fire growth, and the faster the fire grows, the more likely it is for flashover to occur.

Recognizing flashover potential and understanding the mechanisms that cause this extreme fire behavior phenomenon is critically important. However, the ability to recognize key indicators and predict the probability of flashover is even more important. Indicators of potential or impending flashover are listed in **Table 2.2, p. 50**.

Firefighters must remember not to focus on one indicator to the exclusion of the others; reading fire conditions requires that they see the big picture. The section of this chapter dealing with fire behavior indicators provides additional information on assessment of fire conditions.

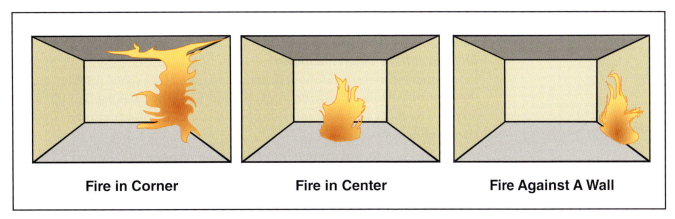

Figure 2.31 Where a fire is located in a compartment can affect its rate of growth.

Table 2.2
Flashover Indicators

Building	Flashover can occur in all types of buildings. Building factors can influence how quickly a fire will reach flashover (i.e., fire load, ventilation profile, thermal properties) and should be considered an integral part of ongoing risk assessment.
Smoke	Smoke indicators may or may not be visible from the exterior of the structure. However, smoke conditions indicating a developing fire are a warning sign of potential flashover conditions. After making entry, the presence of hot gases overhead and lowering of the hot gas layer are key indicators.
Air Flow	A strong bidirectional air flow (air in and smoke out) can be a significant indicator of flashover that will move in the direction of the opening. However, any air movement toward the fire can result in flashover. Increasing velocity of the air flow when combined with other indicators can be a strong flashover indicator. Use of a thermal imaging camera (TIC) can allow more effective observation of convective heat currents within the building.
Heat	Outside the fire compartment, perception of increasing temperature may not provide reliable warning of impending flashover. However, perception of increasing temperature and observation of heat indictors such as pyrolysis of fuel packages some distance from the fire should be considered as a strong indicator of worsening fire conditions and potential for flashover. Use of a TIC allows observation of increased temperature potentially flaming combustion within the hot gas layer. Observation of the opening to the fire compartment will indicate high temperature at the top of the opening. From the exterior, increasing velocity of smoke discharge also indicates increasing temperature within the building. A TIC may allow observation of a pronounced heat signature in the area of the fire compartment.
Flame	Isolated flames traveling in the hot gas layer (ghosting) or more substantially through the gas layer or across the ceiling (rollover). These flames may or may not be visible without a thermal imaging camera. A later (potentially too late) indicator of impending flashover is rollover moving along the ceiling of the fire compartment and into adjacent spaces.

Courtesy of Ed Hartin.

Misconceptions about Flashover

Common misconceptions about flashover are often translated into inaccurate descriptions of what occurred in particular fires when reported to the news media. The most common misconceptions about flashover can be summarized as follows:

- If a room is fully involved, it must have flashed over.
- If a room fire burns intensely, it must have flashed over.
- Full room involvement is synonymous with flashover.

While flashover does involve an intensely burning compartment fire that rapidly progresses to full involvement, these elements do not define it. Research has shown that many compartment fires burn intensely and slowly progress to full involvement without flashing over. Flashover is defined by its characteristics — progressing rapidly (almost instantaneously) from intense burning to full involvement.

Backdraft

A ventilation-controlled compartment fire in the decay stage can produce a large volume of flammable smoke and other gases due to incomplete combustion. This mixture of flammable products can be well above its upper flammable limit. While the rate of heat release from a ventilation-controlled fire is limited in the decay stage, high temperatures are usually still present within the compartment. An increase in ventilation (such as opening a door or window) can result in a deflagration (explosively rapid combustion) called a **backdraft**.

When potential backdraft conditions exist in a compartment, the space is filled with unburned fuel (smoke) that is at or above its ignition temperature and only lacks sufficient oxygen to burn. Making a horizontal opening provides the missing component (oxygen) and backdraft results **(Figure 2.32)**.

However, backdraft can occur with the creation of either a horizontal or vertical opening. All that is required is mixing hot, fuel-rich smoke with air. Backdraft conditions can develop within a room, a void (such as an attic or a small room within a larger structure), or within an entire building. Any time a compartment or space contains extremely hot combustion products,

> **Backdraft** — Instantaneous explosion or rapid burning of superheated gases that occurs when oxygen is introduced into an oxygen-depleted confined space. The stalled combustion resumes with explosive force. It may occur because of inadequate or improper ventilation procedures. Very rapid, often explosive burning of hot gases that occurs when oxygen is introduced into an oxygen-depleted confined space. It may occur because of inadequate or improper ventilation procedures.

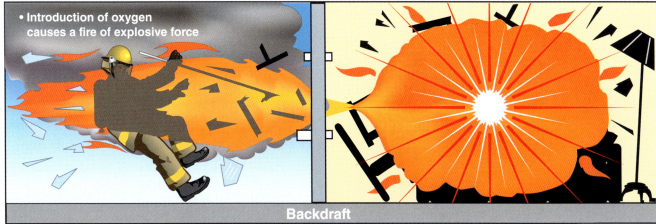

Figure 2.32 Improper ventilation for the conditions may result in a backdraft.

potential for backdraft must be considered before creating any openings into the compartment. To some degree, the violence of backdraft is dependent on the extent to which the fuel/air mixture is confined. The more confined the deflagration, the more violent it will be. If circumstances in a given situation *require* that the compartment be vented, and the involved compartment is located where vertical ventilation is possible, venting vertically reduces the risks involved as the flames and overpressure from the backdraft are allowed to discharge harmlessly into the atmosphere. However, as is evident in the following case history, vertical ventilation will not always prevent a backdraft from occurring inside a burning building.

> According to NIOSH Report 98-F05, Illinois firefighters were called to a fire in a tire shop in February of 1998. On arrival, firefighters found no smoke showing from the exterior of this large commercial building of masonry construction with a bowstring truss roof. Entering the building, firefighters encountered some smoke in the showroom located at the front of the building and heavy smoke in the upper area of the service bays. A truck company performing roof ventilation reported that shortly after they vented the roof, heavy smoke and fire issued from the vent opening. When an overhead door was opened in the service area, the inflow of air mixed with the hot gas layer resulting in a backdraft. Two firefighters perished, three were seriously injured, and five others barely escaped.

Fire conditions in the foregoing case history were somewhat atypical. Backdraft conditions developed because of fire involvement of the polystyrene insulation on the underside of the truss roof and combustion above a stable hot gas layer. Fires do not always follow typical patterns – firefighters must expect the unexpected.

While backdraft conditions are usually associated with enclosed spaces that are completely filled with hot products of combustion, this does not preclude the possibility of a backdraft in a compartment that is not filled with smoke (particularly in large-volume compartments with high ceilings). A fire burning above the hot gas layer may develop backdraft conditions in the upper level of the compartment, even when conditions at floor level are only moderately affected.

As with flashover, it is critical to recognize the potential warning signs of backdraft conditions. The indicators of the potential for a possible backdraft are listed in **Table 2.3**.

While pulsing smoke movement is commonly recognized as a backdraft indicator, raising and lowering of the bottom of the hot gas layer is not. However, when the compartment or structure is not full of smoke, changes in pressure and volume of smoke can raise or lower the bottom of the hot gas layer – rather than pulsing discharge of smoke from compartment or building openings.

It is often assumed (incorrectly) that a backdraft will always occur immediately or soon after making an opening into the building or involved compartment. Mixing of hot flammable products of combustion with air through the action of gravity current, pressure differential, and wind effects sometimes takes time.

Table 2.3
Backdraft Indicators

Building	Confinement of the fire. This may involve the entire building or a single compartment or void space. The potential for a backdraft is increased when building contents have a high heat of combustion.
Smoke	Pressurized smoke exiting small openings may ignite briefly in open air. Light-colored smoke or black smoke becoming dense gray-yellow. NOTE: Smoke color alone is not a reliable indicator. Smoke that is optically dense is a more significant indicator. Rising and lowering of the neutral plane (similar to pulsing air flow when the compartment is not full) is also a significant indicator.
Airflow	Smoke leaving the building from small openings in puffs or at intervals and having the appearance of "breathing" (pulsing air flow) may ignite briefly in open air. High-velocity turbulent smoke discharge from larger openings.
Heat	High heat. Smoke-stained windows, high velocity smoke discharge from small openings.
Flame	Little or no visible flame, but conditions can vary widely in different parts of the structure. Backdraft conditions can exist in a compartment or void space while a fully developed fire is burning with flames showing from several windows.

Courtesy of Ed Hartin.

> When backdraft potential is observed, firefighters should delay entry until tactical ventilation has changed conditions inside the building or compartment.

The effects of a backdraft can vary considerably depending on a number of factors. These variables include the following:

- Volume of flammable products of combustion
- Degree of confinement
- Speed with which fuel and air mix
- Where ignition occurs

The Gray Area: Flashover or Backdraft?

Ventilation-induced flashover and backdraft can both result from increased air supply to a ventilation-controlled fire. The major difference is that a flashover occurs when an already actively burning fire is greatly intensified by a relatively sudden increase in available oxygen. On the other hand, a backdraft occurs when an under-ventilated fire that has continued to produce significant amounts of extremely hot unburned fuels (dense smoke) is suddenly infused with the oxygen it needs to burn explosively. In the field it is not always possible to determine which of these phenomena may have occurred. While somewhat different, both present similar indicators and are significant threats to firefighters.

Smoke Explosion

While the term *smoke explosion* has often been used to describe a backdraft, it is actually a quite different phenomenon. A smoke explosion is a form of fire gas ignition — that is, the ignition of accumulated flammable products of combustion. It is possible for this event to occur in smoke that has accumulated some distance from the seat of the fire. Unlike ghosting or rollover, a smoke explosion involves ignition of a mixture of air and flammable combustion products that are already within the flammable range.

The key differences between a backdraft and a smoke explosion are the temperature of the fire gases and the oxygen concentration. In a backdraft, the fire gases are hot and the oxygen concentration is low. A smoke explosion does not require additional oxygen because the combustible fire gases are already within their flammable range. When fire gases are within their flammable range and a source of ignition is present, they will ignite and burn with great intensity. Fire gases can accumulate far from the seat of the fire (in an adjacent compartment or in some cases even an adjacent building) and be ignited by an ignition source unrelated to the fire. In other cases, flammable products can accumulate at the ceiling level or in a void and be ignited by a burning ember disturbed during overhaul.

Unlike flashover and backdraft, there are no specific indicators of smoke explosion because the fire gases may not be visible. The key is recognizing the potential for the accumulation of products of combustion and to use mitigation techniques such as effective ventilation or the application of water fog (gas cooling) to reduce the potential hazard.

Flashover, backdraft, and smoke explosion are all forms of extreme fire behavior, but they are quite different phenomena. In some cases it will be difficult to differentiate between the outcomes of these events under fireground conditions – all result in rapidly deteriorating conditions that can be very hazardous for any firefighters in the immediate area. The importance of understanding these three extreme fire behavior phenomena is in recognizing the conditions that may result in extreme fire behavior and how they might be mitigated.

Other Fire Gas Ignitions

As previously discussed, fire gas ignition is simply ignition of accumulated flammable products of combustion (smoke). In addition to the extreme fire behavior phenomena just discussed, one other form of fire gas ignition is worth examining.

When hot, fuel-rich smoke vents from a compartment it frequently ignites when mixed with the outside air. This is often seen when windows are vented or entry is made through a door. Observation of these conditions generally indicates high temperature and an under-ventilated fire in a compartment.

While flames burning outside the structure at a ventilation opening are releasing their heat energy to the outside environment rather than inside the building, the fire can spread back inside as the oxygen concentration in the compartment increases. Good door entry procedures such as having a charged hoseline present when making the opening, controlling the door, and using the hoseline to cool hot gases overhead can minimize the hazards **(Figure 2.33)**.

Factors Influencing Extreme Fire Behavior

It is important to understand the *initiating events* related to extreme fire behavior such as flashover, backdraft, and smoke explosions. Because any of them can trigger (initiate) extreme fire behavior, the order of the following factors is of no particular significance. The most common factors influencing extreme fire behavior are as follows:

- *Increased heat* — An increase in heat promotes additional pyrolysis, which increases the volume of available fuel. The heat also keeps the gaseous fuels ready to ignite as soon as sufficient oxygen is added.

- *Increased ventilation* — An increase in ventilation to an under-ventilated fire increases heat release rate, and if backdraft conditions exist, adds the missing oxygen to the superheated fuels. A sudden increase in available oxygen under ventilation-controlled conditions can and will initiate extreme fire behavior.

- *Ignition source* — Gaseous fuels that are within their flammable or explosive ranges – having sufficient fuel and oxygen to ignite and burn – need only a source of ignition to trigger an event. Such an event would most likely be classified as a smoke explosion. Sources of ignition can be introduced by firefighters opening or closing electrical switches or using cutting torches or other flame-producing devices during forcible entry or rescue operations. Firefighters can also expose hot embers or coals during fire control or overhaul operations.

Figure 2.33 Making entry with a charged hoseline can help lessen the hazards for firefighters.

> *Fire Behavior Scenario:*
>
> On a July evening, you and your truck company are first to arrive at a fire in a single-story tire recapping business housed in a Type III building. The few windows in the building are dark and you cannot see inside. The metal-clad front door feels hot and tiny puffs of smoke light up when they emerge from the crack at the bottom of the door.
>
> Heavy black smoke billows from vents on the arched roof.
>
> - How would you characterize the conditions in your initial radio report?
> - What would you do before making entry for fire attack?
> - What tools would you use to help locate the seat of the fire?

Summary

To perform safely and effectively as a member of a truck company in structure fires, firefighters must have a solid understanding of fire behavior. To accurately size up a structure fire and make reasonable decisions based on that assessment, firefighters and their officers must be able to read a fire and anticipate its most likely behavior. Knowing the basic fire behavior indicators as well as those related to flashover, backdraft, smoke explosion, and other extreme fire behavior phenomena allows firefighters to take positive steps to prevent these events from occurring or to minimize their effects.

Review Questions

1. What is combustion?
2. What occurs during pyrolysis?
3. What are the four stages of fire development? What occurs during each stage?
4. Beginning with ignition, how does a fire develop in a compartment?
5. What factors affect fire development in a compartment?
6. What are the five categories of fire behavior indicators? What key information about the fire is provided by each indicator?
7. What information about the fire is provided by smoke?
8. What is the difference between radiation-induced and ventilation-induced flashover?
9. What are the indications of a potential backdraft?
10. What is the difference between a backdraft and a smoke explosion?
11. What are the factors which influence extreme fire behavior?

Firefighter Safety and Survival

Chapter Contents

CASE HISTORY 61	Structural Collapse 68
Standard Safety Behaviors 62	Elements of Fireground Safety 71
IFSTA Risk Management Model 63	Emergency Egress 82
Other Risk Management Models 63	**Summary** 87
Key Safety Behaviors 65	**Review Questions** 88
Fireground Safety 66	
"Routine" Calls 66	
"Self-Vented" Fires 67	

chapter 3

Key Terms

Emergency Escape Breathing Support System (EEBSS) 83
Immediately Dangerous to Life and Health (IDLH) 72
Incident Action Plan (IAP) 72
Incident Command System (ICS) 71
Incident Management System 71
Personnel Accountability Report (PAR) 72
Rapid Intervention Crew (RIC) 71
Rehab 80

Firefighter Safety and Survival

Learning Objectives

After reading this chapter, students will be able to:

1. Explain the IFSTA Principles of Risk Management as they apply to fireground operations.
2. Explain the safe person element of the British Dynamic Risk Assessment model.
3. Describe the four critical leadership skills in the Crew Resource Management program.
4. Explain the importance of a safety first mindset.
5. Describe the dangers associated with routine and self-vented fires.
6. Summarize the indicators of a potential structural collapse.
7. Summarize the benefits to firefighter safety from each of the elements of fireground safety.
8. Define rapid intervention crew (RIC).
9. Define personnel accountability report (PAR).
10. Describe the concept of situational awareness.
11. Describe the procedures for a firefighter's emergency egress from a building.

Safety Points

Firefighter safety and survival on the fireground are the focus of this chapter. Other critically important safety considerations that are not addressed in this chapter include the following:

- Physical conditioning
- Adequate training
- Adequate equipment
- Emergency vehicle operation

Chapter 3
Firefighter Safety and Survival

Case History

According to NIOSH Report F2006-26, Wisconsin firefighters were called to a possible fire in a single-family residence in August of 2006. When the first units arrived, only light smoke was seen coming from the house. When a neighbor said that there might be someone inside, two firefighters were assigned to conduct a primary search. As other firefighters searched for the seat of the fire — which was in the unfinished basement — the two firefighters masked up and entered the front door. By that time the entire first floor was filled with smoke, so the two firefighters decided to conduct their search crawling on their hands and knees. Just inside the front door, they heard a loud crack and the floor beneath them suddenly collapsed. The two firefighters were dropped into the basement, but one (the victim) landed in the room where the fire was raging, and the other landed behind a masonry fireplace foundation and was protected from the fire by collapse debris. The injured firefighter was rescued by a rapid intervention crew sent in following the floor collapse. The remains of the other firefighter, who died of smoke inhalation and thermal burns, were not recovered until the next day.

This incident and many others clearly show that there are no *routine* fires or other emergency calls. Every call is potentially lethal for responding firefighters **(Figure 3.1, p. 62)**. Fighting fires and performing search and rescue operations in burning buildings can be very dangerous work. Other truck company tasks involve risk as well.

> If firefighters are to safely and effectively carry out their duties inside and outside of burning buildings, they must keep safety and survival in mind at all times.

Even though the interior of a burning building can sometimes be a hostile and even lethal environment, firefighters are expected to function efficiently when necessary. It is therefore vitally important for firefighters to learn to survive in these environments. The case histories cited in this chapter and throughout the manual are clear examples of how hazardous the fireground can be and how firefighters' actions directly impact their level of safety.

Figure 3.1 Every emergency call is potentially lethal for firefighters.

This chapter begins with a discussion of standard safety behaviors that have proven successful in many incidents. A discussion follows on the safety and survival techniques that have been developed and widely adopted due to negative experiences during fires in the past. Finally, specific techniques that firefighters can use to escape if they are trapped in a burning building are discussed.

Standard Safety Behaviors

It is vitally important for all firefighters and other emergency responders to understand incident priorities because they translate into how personnel and other resources are deployed on scene. As discussed in **Essentials**, certain universal priorities apply on every emergency response. In order of importance, these universal priorities are as follows:

- Life safety
- Incident stabilization
- Property conservation

In every emergency incident, life safety is always the highest priority. Firefighters need to understand that life safety includes *their* lives as well as those of any other people, pets, or livestock that are at risk in the situation. This aspect of the life safety priority can be stated as follows:

> ***Firefighters did not start the fire, nor did they put the victims in that situation, and they are not obligated to sacrifice themselves in a heroic attempt to extinguish a fire or save a victim — and certainly not to recover a body.***

In fact, it can be argued that protecting the lives of the firefighters is the *highest* fireground priority. The logic behind this position is simple — if a firefighter suffers a disabling injury while attempting to extinguish a fire or save a victim, the following could result:

- He or she may be unable to help others who are in danger.
- Additional firefighters may have to be taken away from other critical duties to aid the injured firefighter.
- The additional firefighters may be exposed to the same hazard faced by the injured firefighter.

> For their own safety and survival, firefighters must learn to recognize hazards and how to mitigate or avoid them.

IFSTA Risk Management Model

The IFSTA *Principles of Risk Management* were developed after reviewing a number of risk management models currently being used in the fire service. The three most prominent models considered were those developed by the Phoenix (AZ) Fire Department, NFPA® 1500, and the *Ten Rules of Engagement for Structural Fire Fighting* developed by the International Association of Fire Chiefs (IAFC). The IFSTA *Principles of Risk Management* are as follows:

- Activities that present a significant risk to the safety of members shall be limited to situations where there is a potential to save endangered lives.
- Activities that are routinely employed to protect property shall be recognized as inherent risks to the safety of members, and actions shall be taken to avoid these risks.
- No risk to the safety of members shall be acceptable when there is no possibility to save lives or property.

To be effective during emergency incidents, these principles must be used as part of the size-up process and when creating the Incident Action Plan. There are three key points to keep in mind when applying these principles:

- Team integrity is vital to safety and must always be emphasized **(Figure 3.2)**.
- No property is worth the life of a firefighter.
- Firefighters should not be committed to interior offensive fire fighting operations in abandoned or derelict buildings that are known or reasonably believed to be unoccupied.

Figure 3.2 It is crucial that team integrity be maintained at all times.

Other Risk Management Models

Other risk management models are used in the fire service. Two of the most prominent models are *Dynamic Risk Assessment* and *Crew Resource Management*.

Dynamic Risk Assessment

Adapted from the British fire service, Dynamic Risk Assessment can be defined as: A continuous process of identifying hazards and risks and taking steps to eliminate or reduce them in the rapidly changing circumstances of an operational incident. The term *dynamic* is used to describe the ongoing assessment of an ever-changing situation. While the British model includes both *safe place* and *safe person* elements, only the safe person element is discussed here. This is because a safe place cannot be assured on the fireground.

The safe person element of the Dynamic Risk Assessment model has two equally important components: *organizational responsibilities* and *individual responsibilities*.

Organizational responsibilities. In this component of the safe person element, the organization is responsible for selecting the right personnel for each assignment, and for providing them with the following:

- Adequate information.
- Appropriate personal protective equipment (PPE).
- Needed tools and equipment.
- A safe Incident Action Plan.
- Necessary instruction and training.
- Effective supervision.

Individual responsibilities. In this component of the safe person element, the individuals involved are responsible for the following:

- Being competent to perform the assigned task.
- Working as an effective member of a team.
- Working within the Incident Action Plan.
- Adapting to changing circumstances.
- Watching out for themselves and other members of the team.
- Recognizing their own capabilities and limitations.

Crew Resource Management

A blue-ribbon committee of the International Association of Fire Chiefs studied a safety system that has been adopted by several industries and the U.S. military. The committee concluded that if the system were adopted by the fire service, the number of firefighter injuries and fatalities could be reduced. This comprehensive program is called *Crew Resource Management* (CRM). The CRM program provides better teamwork, improved communication and problem solving, promotes team member input while preserving legal authority, and provides for proactive accident prevention. While there are many facets to the program, in general it addresses leadership and followership.

Those in leadership positions are obligated to acquire and develop four critical leadership skills: authority, mentoring, conflict resolution, and mission analysis.

- ***Authority*** — involves the leader ensuring mission safety, fostering an environment of respectful communication, establishing tasks with clearly defined goals, and considering crew input.

- ***Mentoring*** — involves the leader demonstrating skills and techniques, demonstrating professional standards and best practices, verbalizing errors and limitations promptly, recommending solutions, monitoring and assessing crew performance, and motivating crew members.

- ***Conflict resolution*** — involves the leader identifying core conflict issues, encouraging diplomatic questioning of the actions/decisions of others, acknowledging differences of opinion, and accepting constructive criticism.

- ***Mission analysis*** — involves the leader evaluating risk versus gain, identifying objectives, developing strategies and tactics to meet the identified objectives, implementing an action plan, expecting the unexpected, evaluating the effectiveness of the action plan, and devising alternative strategies.

Goal attainment and teamwork require people who can think and follow directions. In this context, followers are not to be viewed in a negative manner. To function safely and effectively, CRM requires team members (followers) to do the following:

- Respect authority.
- Be safe.
- Keep their fellow workers and leaders safe.
- Accept that authority goes with responsibility.
- Know the limits of their own authority.
- Desire to make the leader succeed.
- Possess good communication skills.
- Develop and maintain a positive learning attitude.
- Keep their egos in check.
- Demand clear assignments.
- Establish an assertiveness/authority balance.
- Accept direction and information as needed.
- Publicly acknowledge mistakes.
- Report status of work.
- Be flexible.

A paper describing the CRM program in detail is available from the International Association of Fire Chiefs. It is also available through their web site (www.iafc.org).

Key Safety Behaviors

To help firefighters function safely and effectively during emergency incidents, the following list of key safety behaviors has been developed. All firefighters should attempt to apply these behaviors whenever they are on duty. Key safety behaviors are as follows:

- Maintain situational awareness.
- Walk, don't run when preparing to board apparatus.
- Use handrails when mounting or dismounting apparatus.
- Always use seat belts **(Figure 3.3)**.
- Drive apparatus defensively and only as fast as conditions allow.
- Stop apparatus at any intersection where vision is obstructed.
- Wear appropriate PPE and respiratory protection.
- *Never* breathe smoke.
- Work safely and with an appropriate level of aggressiveness.

Figure 3.3 Seatbelts should be used *without exception* when riding in the fire apparatus.

- Always work according to the Incident Action Plan — no freelancing.
- Maintain crew integrity.
- Maintain communications with Command.
- Always have an escape route (hoseline/lifeline).
- Evaluate every hazard — know the risks involved.
- Maintain awareness of air supply and withdraw before low-air alarm sounds.
- Match hoselines, nozzles, and extinguishing agents to the fire.
- Coordinate ventilation and fire control operations.
- Look and listen for signs of impending collapse.
- Report anything unusual immediately.
- Only breathe supplied air during overhaul.
- Illuminate and ventilate the work area as necessary.
- Get help when moving or lifting heavy or bulky items.
- Rotate fatigued companies through Rehab.
- Everyone takes care of everyone else.

While some of the foregoing points may apply to non-fireground activities, even these help to foster and maintain a *safety first* mindset. This attitude is crucial if firefighters are to end their fire service careers with a service retirement and not a disability retirement.

In addition, one of the most important ways that these safety behaviors become a part of the departmental culture and of individual behavior is through training. When the department develops SOPs that reflect these safety behaviors, personnel must then be trained to function according to those SOPs instinctively and without having to consciously consider the safest course of action in any given situation. In other words, functioning safely must become second nature.

Fireground Safety

The history of firefighter fatalities in structure fires shows that these incidents often involve certain false assumptions by firefighters. Some of these false assumptions relate to so-called *routine* calls and so-called *self-vented* fires.

"Routine" Calls

In this context, routine refers to fires and other emergency calls that appear to be innocuous and relatively easy to handle **(Figure 3.4)**. Routine fires range from a small cooking fire or a typical room-and-contents fire to fires that are beyond the point where an offensive interior operation is reasonable. The following case history is a tragic example of such a *routine* call.

In the majority of relatively small fires in structures, everything is as it first appears and all goes according to plan. Entry is made and the fire is located and extinguished as a primary search is being conducted. Any residual smoke is exhausted from the building, the origin and cause are determined and documented, and any needed salvage and overhaul operations are conducted. When all responsibilities are completed, the crews gather their gear and return to quarters.

According to NIOSH Report F2005-07, California firefighters were called to a fire in a two-story residential structure in February of 2005. On arrival, firefighters saw that the top floor was almost totally involved in fire. A second alarm was called and on-scene units prepared to attack the fire in a defensive mode. An overhead power line had burned through and fallen into a tree and onto the ground in the yard of the burning residence. Firefighters marked the downed wire with caution tape. However, approximately one hour after the first units arrived on scene, an engine company officer walked under the tree and was electrocuted when he made contact with the downed wire. Despite emergency medical efforts on scene, he was pronounced dead at a local hospital.

Figure 3.4 Firefighters must be vigilant for hazards, even on *routine* calls. *Courtesy of Bob Esposito.*

When firefighters have been involved in a series of these fires where nothing unusual happens and there are no serious firefighter injuries, it is easy for them to become complacent and begin to think of such fires as *routine*. However, in all too many of these *routine* fires, all is not as it first appears. If firefighters fail to recognize the signs that something is seriously wrong, the results can be catastrophic.

"Self-Vented" Fires

When firefighters approach a working structure fire and smoke and flames are rising from the roof, they may assume that the interior will be relatively free of heat and smoke because the fire has *self-vented* **(Figure 3.5, p. 68)**. Unfortunately, this is not always true. Fires may continue to burn vigorously inside of structures even after they have broken a window or burned through the roof. When a fire burns through to the outside, it is an uncontrolled process and is *not* the same as planned and coordinated tactical ventilation by firefighters.

Chapter 3 • Firefighter Safety and Survival **67**

Figure 3.5 Just because a fire has *self-vented* does not mean it is any less hazardous. *Courtesy of District Chief Chris Mickal, NOFD Photo Unit.*

> According to NIOSH Report F2005-09, Texas firefighters were called to a fire in an abandoned single-family dwelling in February of 2005. First-arriving crews saw smoke and flames venting from the roof at the rear of the structure. A fast-attack crew entered through the front door and found visibility good inside. However, just as they started to apply water on the fire, conditions deteriorated rapidly and the roof collapsed, trapping one firefighter under burning debris and sending a fireball rolling through the house. Five firefighters on interior attack lines were burned by the fireball, and they followed hoselines to find their way out. When it was determined that a firefighter was missing, rapid intervention crews followed the hoselines to the victim. According to the autopsy report, the firefighter died of smoke inhalation and thermal injuries.

From a firefighter safety and survival standpoint, the preceding case history raises the question of why firefighters were sent inside a structure that was known to be abandoned. This case also involved another cause of firefighter fatalities in structure fires — structural collapse.

Structural Collapse

As the following case history shows, firefighters can be in danger from structural collapse even when they are *outside* a burning building. Therefore, important elements of firefighter safety and survival include an ongoing assessment of the building's collapse potential and the establishment of collapse zones in these incidents. Firefighters can also reduce the hazards of structural collapse by positioning their apparatus and hoselines near the corners of the buildings where they are strongest.

According to NIOSH Report F2004-37, Tennessee firefighters were called to a working fire in a single-story church in April of 2004. The victim was the IC on the fire and he had just completed a 360-degree size-up of the involved structure. As he was calling for all interior crews to withdraw from the building because of structural instability, the brick facade collapsed outward and buried him under the rubble. The victim was so badly injured that he never recovered and he succumbed to his injuries several weeks later.

In many departments, the policy is to cordon off an area equal to one and one-half times the height of the structure (**Figure 3.6**). Obviously, if the structure is as tall or taller than the width of the adjacent street, the collapse zone would, in effect, close the street completely. However, many departments routinely close the street in front of a burning building to improve access for emergency vehicles and to prevent pedestrians from entering the hazardous area (**Figure 3.7**). With extremely tall structures, such as high-rises, establishing an adequate collapse zone may not be feasible.

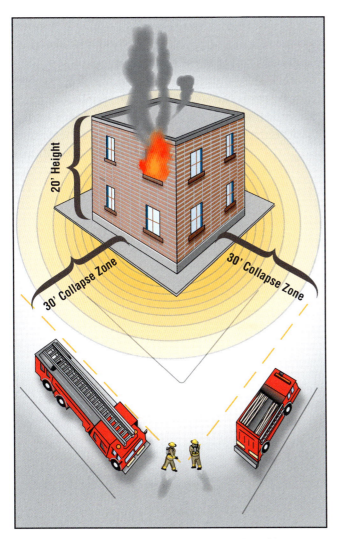

Figure 3.6 The established collapse zone should be 1½ times the height of the structure.

Figure 3.7 Closing the street in front of the involved structure allows for emergency vehicle access. *Courtesy of the Los Angeles Fire Department – ISTS.*

Chapter 3 • Firefighter Safety and Survival

Once inside the building, firefighters must continue to be vigilant for signs of impending structural collapse. The longer a fire burns inside a building, the more likely fire-weakened structural members are to suddenly and unexpectedly fail. To protect themselves in these situations, firefighters need to be aware of the impending collapse indicators. According to a National Fire Academy course entitled *Firefighter Safety and Survival*, these indicators include the following:

- Heavy fire — no progress after 10-12 minutes in wood or ordinary construction
- Walls/floors bowing or sagging
- Distortion of doors/windows
- Beams pulling away from supports
- Little or no runoff while using heavy streams
- New cracks developing or moving
- Walls disassemble under stream impact

Other possible indicators should be considered as well. For example, if firefighters working inside or outside of the building hear structural creaks, cracks, or groans not normally associated with this type of fire, or if they see smoke coming from mortar joints in a masonry wall, they should inform their supervisor immediately. If a crew is working independently when members see or hear any of these indicators, they should inform Command of the situation and immediately withdraw until the integrity of the structure can be evaluated. In addition, if the building contains significant live loads (stock, furniture, boxes of water-absorbent materials, etc.) or dead loads (heavy machinery, HVAC units, or fluid tanks), the added weight increases the collapse potential **(Figure 3.8)**.

CAUTION
Because the fire may have been burning for some time before it was discovered and reported, and because lightweight roof/floor assemblies can fail quickly when exposed to the heat of a fire, the time between arrival and impending collapse may be shorter than anticipated.

> As one very experienced fire officer put it, "The building is your enemy – know your enemy!"

Figure 3.8 Dead loads greatly increase the potential for structural collapse.

To help reduce the risk of firefighters being inside a burning building when it collapses, it is standard operating procedure in many departments to keep track of the elapsed time after the beginning of the initial attack. For example, in some departments the IC notifies dispatch when the initial attack begins, and dispatch announces the elapsed time at specified intervals — perhaps every 5 minutes. If significant progress toward control and extinguishment has not been achieved after a specified number minutes, all interior crews are ordered out, the attack mode is changed from offensive to defensive, and a **personnel accountability report (PAR)** is ordered. Some departments that had previously established 20 minutes as the SOP for ordering all interior crews out have reduced that time significantly based on past experiences.

The case histories already cited are ample reminders that burning buildings do collapse, and when they do, the results can be tragic. Departments need to be prepared to deal with this type of incident, which requires developing a structural collapse SOP and training on its implementation.

Elements of Fireground Safety

As mentioned earlier in this chapter, performing emergency work inside burning buildings can be extremely dangerous. Experience in a great number of structure fires has produced a list of behaviors that can help to reduce these risks. Firefighter safety and survival on the fireground is dependent upon a number of equally important elements:

- Working within an **Incident Management System**
- Working according to the Incident Action Plan (IAP)
- Working within the personnel accountability system
- Wearing appropriate PPE and respiratory protection
- Adequately sizing-up the situation
- Performing a risk/benefit analysis for every action.
- Making sure that orders are understood
- Maintaining situational awareness
- Maintaining company discipline and team integrity
- Maintaining communications
- Reporting identified hazards immediately
- Knowing and following departmental SOPs
- Employing safe and effective strategies and tactics
- Having a **rapid intervention crew (RIC)** standing by
- Setting up a Rehab Unit on all working fires
- Using effective emergency escape techniques when needed

Working within an Incident Management System

Because a National Incident Management System (NIMS)-compliant incident management system provides a coherent organizational structure and common communications on the fireground, it is easier for fire units and their members to remain oriented and focused on the job at hand. Orientation and focus promote safe and effective fireground operations. Many departments have adopted the **Incident Command System (ICS)** as their incident management system; others have chosen different systems.

Incident Management System — System described in NFPA® 1561, *Standard on Fire Department Incident Management System*, that defines the roles, responsibilities, and standard operating procedures used to manage emergency operations. Such systems may also be referred to as Incident Command Systems (ICS).

Rapid Intervention Crew (RIC) — Two or more fully equipped and immediately available firefighters designated to stand by outside the hazard zone to enter and effect rescue of firefighters inside, if necessary. Also known as Rapid Intervention Team.

Incident Command System (ICS) — System by which facilities, equipment, personnel, procedures, and communications are organized to operate within a common organizational structure designed to aid in the management of resources at emergency incidents.

Working within the Incident Action Plan (IAP)

All firefighters on scene should be familiar with the contents of the **Incident Action Plan (IAP)**, whether written or not. This ensures that everyone is aware of potential safety issues, the overall strategy, and the tactical objectives that have been established. Each company and its members should have a clear understanding of what they are responsible for accomplishing. This prevents freelancing and promotes coordinated effort, both of which enhance the safety of everyone involved.

Working within the Personnel Accountability System

As described in **Essentials**, the purpose of using an accountability system on the fireground is to ensure that only those who are authorized and properly equipped to enter an **immediately dangerous to life and health (IDLH)** environment – such as a burning building – are allowed to do so. A number of different accountability systems are used in North America; however, they all have the same purpose — to control movement into and out of a hazardous environment. With a proper personnel accountability system, every entrant's location and status can be tracked as long as that person remains in the hazard zone.

In a typical accountability system, a designated person (*persons* in the case of multiple entry points) verifies that each entrant's PASS device is turned on and records each entrant's name, company, SCBA pressure, assignment, and estimated safe working time in the hazardous environment. In some systems, the identification part of the record keeping is done automatically through the use of a name tag (sometimes called a *passport*) carried by each firefighter **(Figure 3.9)**. Identification can also be obtained by the use of a bar code reader that scans each entrant's code as the person passes through the accountability checkpoint. Other items, such as SCBA pressure and assignment, must still be recorded manually. This process can also be expedited and simplified by using a laptop or notebook computer at each entry point.

Another critically important part of any accountability system is the **personnel accountability report (PAR)**. By definition, a PAR is an organized roll call in which each on-scene supervisor reports the status of his or her crew when requested **(Figure 3.10)**. PARs may be requested at the Incident Commander's (IC) or Incident Safety Officer's (ISO) discretion, at specified intervals, or due

Figure 3.9 Passports should be given to the designated accountability officer prior to entering the hazardous area.

> **Incident Action Plan (IAP)** — Written or unwritten plan for the disposition of an incident. The IAP contains the overall strategic goals, tactical objectives, and support requirements for a given operational period during an incident.

> **Immediately Dangerous to Life and Health (IDLH)** — Any atmosphere that poses an immediate hazard to life or produces immediate irreversible, debilitating effects on health.

> **Personnel Accountability Report (PAR)** — A roll call of all units (crews, teams, groups, companies, sectors) assigned to an incident. Usually by radio, the supervisor of each unit reports the status of the personnel within the unit at that time. A PAR may be required by SOP at specific intervals during an incident, or may be requested at any time by the IC or the ISO.

Figure 3.10 Personnel accountability reports are crucial for maintaining firefighter accountability on the fireground.

to the occurrence of a benchmark event. Benchmark events on the fireground include the following:

- Changing attack modes from offensive to defensive
- Significant change in conditions (unexpected or catastrophic events such as flashover, backdraft, structural collapse, report of a missing or distressed firefighter, or PASS device activation)
- Fire control or extinguishment

The use of an accountability system is required by NFPA® 1500, *Fire Department Occupational Safety and Health Program*, and NFPA® 1561, *Standard on Emergency Services Incident Management System*. Using such a system requires the following:

- Development of a departmental SOP describing the system to be used (including when and how)
- Training all personnel in the use of the designated system
- Strict enforcement of the SOP during emergency incidents

If an accountability system is incorporated into departmental culture, fireground command and control will be improved, firefighter safety/survival will be enhanced, and the chances of the department having to defend itself in court will be reduced.

> One of the most fundamental rules of firefighter safety and survival is: everyone looks out for everyone else.

Wearing Appropriate PPE and Respiratory Protection

Because the environments inside burning buildings are potentially hostile – even lethal – it is imperative that firefighters wear the protective clothing and respiratory protection provided them. As shown in the NIOSH Reports cited earlier, firefighters are at risk even when working outside the structure. Even though the use of PPE and SCBA does not guarantee safety, wearing them conscientiously will reduce the chances of serious injury or death.

At structure fires, one of the times when firefighters need to be especially conscientious about wearing the appropriate PPE – respiratory protection in particular – is also when they are least likely to do so. During overhaul operations, firefighters can be exposed to a variety of hazards including numerous toxic gases. **Table 3.1** shows a few common hazardous products of combustion. Because the health effects of some of these gases are delayed – sometimes for years – it is easy for firefighters to be lulled into a false sense of security. Departments should adopt and strictly enforce SOPs requiring the use of appropriate PPE and respiratory protection during overhaul **(Figure 3.11)**.

Adequately Sizing-up the Situation

A timely and accurate initial size-up, followed by a succession of subsequent assessments of the fireground situation, are critical safety elements. These practices are sometimes called *Dynamic Risk Assessment*. Size-up is how the problem at hand is defined. The size-up must include not only what is hap-

**Table 3.1
Common Products of Combustion and Their Toxic Effects**

Asbestos	A magnesium silicate mineral that occurs as slender, strong flexible fibers. Breathing of asbestos dust causes asbestosis and lung cancer.
Carbon Monoxide	Colorless, odorless gas. Inhalation of carbon monoxide causes headache, dizziness, weakness, confusion, nausea, unconsciousness, and death. Exposure to as little as 0.2% carbon monoxide can result in unconsciousness within 30 minutes. Inhalation of high concentration can result in immediate collapse and unconsciousness.
Formaldehyde	Colorless gas with a pungent irritating odor that is highly irritating to the nose. 50-100 ppm can cause severe irritation to the respiratory track and serious injury. Exposure to high concentrations can cause injury to the skin. Formaldehyde is a suspected carcinogen.
Nitrogen Dioxide	Reddish brown gas or yellowish-brown liquid, which is highly toxic and corrosive.
Particulates	Small particles that can be inhaled and be deposited in the mouth, trachea, or the lungs. Exposure to particulates can cause eye irritation, respiratory distress (in addition to health hazards specifically related to the particular substances involved).
Sulfur Dioxide	Colorless gas with a choking or suffocating odor. Sulfur dioxide is toxic and corrosive and can irritate the eyes and mucous membranes.

Source: *Computer Aided Management of Emergency Operations (CAMEO) and Toxicological Profile for Polycyclic Aromatic Hydrocarbons.*

pening at the moment, but what the fire is likely to do as time passes, what may happen if certain conditions are allowed to develop, and what will be needed to mitigate the problem. With the problem defined, safe and effective strategy and tactics can be employed to mitigate the risk.

Performing a Risk/Benefit Analysis for Every Action

Anyone issuing or receiving an order should weigh the risk involved against the potential benefit to be gained by any course of action *before* it is carried out. Keeping the IFSTA *Principles of Risk Management* in mind, he or she should quickly determine the degree of risk that is acceptable for the assignment — *high* risk for lifesaving potential, *moderate* risk for property-saving potential, and *no* acceptable risk where neither lives nor property can be saved. Consciously choosing to avoid unnecessary risk during an incident can sometimes be quite difficult. For example, if friends or relatives of a trapped victim are at the scene and pleading for someone to do something, making the appropriate decision not to take unwarranted risks can be very stressful for the IC and the other firefighters on scene. Civilians are often not aware of the principles of risk management, and they lack the training and experience to make the necessary judgments about when it is prudent to take risks and when it is not. As described in NIOSH Report 99F-47, cited in Chapter 1, firefighters — especially fire officers — *must* make those judgments as the situation dictates.

Figure 3.11 The use of proper PPE and SCBA is critical to firefighter safety, even during overhaul.

Making Sure that Orders Are Understood

Proper understanding of orders on the fireground is critical to safety and effective operations. This applies equally to orders that are *received* from a supervisor as well as orders *issued* to a subordinate. When issuing an order face-to-face, officers should look for signs of understanding or a lack thereof, and ask the recipient to verify what was said **(Figure 3.12)**. When given an order, officers and firefighters should make sure they understand what terms mean *in that context*, and should repeat them back or paraphrase them. They should also verify how successful completion of the assignment is defined, what resources are available, and the amount of time allowed. They should mentally carry out the assignment to make sure they understand it. Any doubts should be addressed *before* starting to carry out the assignment.

Figure 3.12 Officers should look for signs of understanding when issuing an order.

Maintaining Situational Awareness

When carrying out orders on the fireground, maintaining *situational awareness* means knowing what is going on in the immediate surroundings. Firefighters must be able to recognize threats to their safety, understand the nature and extent of those threats, and know how to avoid or mitigate them. Wildland firefighters are taught to "look up, look down, look around" as a way of maintaining awareness of their situation. Likewise, structural firefighters must avoid developing *tunnel vision* when confronted with a fire or other problem. They must continue to *look* for changes in the situation and in how the fire and smoke are behaving, *listen* for sounds such as creaks and squeaks that might indicate deteriorating structural integrity, and *feel* for vibrations and structural movements.

Any firefighter who detects something unusual for that situation – from a sudden build-up of heat or smoke density to structural movement – must communicate this information to the other members of the company and to the company officer or Command. In an often-studied case history from Washington state, four firefighters (an entire crew) perished in a warehouse fire when the floor beneath them suddenly collapsed, dropping them into a fire raging in the basement below. A contributing factor was that one of the crew members failed to report that he noticed the floor being extremely hot even though there was no fire in the compartment where they were operating.

Air management. Another critical aspect of maintaining situational awareness is *air management*. In any environment that requires the use of supplied air – oxygen-deficient atmospheres or those contaminated with smoke or other toxic gases – firefighters must constantly monitor the status of their air supply. As always, they must know and follow their departmental SOPs regarding air management and the directions of their supervisors. However, in the absence of an air management SOP, and if crews or teams are working independently from their immediate supervisor, they should *not* wait until their low-air alarm sounds to begin their withdrawal from a contaminated atmosphere. Instead, unless they are using an air line system with an extensive air supply, they should track both their air supply and their elapsed time on air.

Knowing that the actual service time is shorter than the rated capacity of open-circuit SCBA, firefighters should make a conscious decision when they have used half of their air supply. If they were able to enter the hazard zone and proceed directly to their current location, it should take them approximately the same amount of time to get back to a clear atmosphere – assuming that the contamination hasn't expanded and spread. On the other hand, if they reached their current location only after a slow and methodical search in zero- or near-zero visibility, they may be able to withdraw in less time than it took to get where they are. In that case, depending upon the priority of the assignment (life safety, incident stabilization, property conservation), they may be able to remain in the contaminated atmosphere somewhat longer. But, as mentioned before, this should be a *conscious* decision based on the facts of the situation.

Effects of fire on the building. Yet another critical aspect of maintaining situational awareness inside a burning building is frequently assessing the effects that the fire may have had on the structural stability of the building. When a fire is burning inside a building, the more time that has elapsed since the fire started, the greater the chances are that the fire has spread from the building contents to the building itself. When this occurs, structural integrity begins to deteriorate **(Figure 3.13)**. While decisions regarding the attack mode (offensive/defensive) are made at the Command level, firefighters inside a burning building can provide the IC with information about the fire and the structural integrity of the building that may not be visible from the outside.

For example, if a fire is raging inside a building but the drywall is still intact, the integrity of the building is not yet threatened. But if drywall is not protecting the structure, either because it was never installed or has burned through, the structural components of the building itself are likely to be involved and deteriorating. However, if the building is filled with smoke and visibility inside is zero or near zero, it may be impossible to assess the degree of structural involvement visually. In that case, firefighters have only their knowledge of the building – gained through preincident planning surveys – combined with the elapsed time the fire has been burning to make a dynamic assessment of its structural integrity. In the absence of factual information about the structural integrity of the building, firefighters and Command should err on the side of caution.

Figure 3.13 Firefighters need to be able to recognize signs of structural instability. *Courtesy of District Chief Chris E. Mickal, NOFD Photo Unit.*

Maintaining Company Discipline and Team Integrity

Keeping a fire company or crew together in the sometimes chaotic atmosphere of a working structure fire can be vitally important to their safety and survival. Firefighters who become separated from their companies or companies that stray from their designated location or assignment are at increased risk. Numerous firefighter fatalities have been attributed, at least in part, to a breakdown in crew integrity.

Company discipline is also an important part of the ICS and may prevent the need for rapid intervention at an incident. It is important that firefighters follow the direction of their company officers and maintain contact with other team members.

> According to NIOSH Report F2003-12, Ohio firefighters were called to a fire in a two-story residence in March of 2003. Firefighters entered through the front door with an uncharged hoseline, and they encountered high heat and heavy smoke. When water failed to reach the nozzle, the company officer left his crew and went back outside where he started to untangle the hose in the yard. Shortly thereafter, the interior of the house flashed over. Interior firefighters escaped the structure with their turnouts smoking. It was soon determined that one firefighter was missing, and a rapid intervention crew was sent in to search for him. He was found within 10 minutes but was pronounced dead of thermal burns on arrival at the hospital. Other firefighters reported having seen the victim running through the house after it flashed over. Had the crew exited with the officer, the result may have been different.

Maintaining Communications

Communication is one of the most important safety factors on any emergency scene. One of the reasons for keeping a crew intact is to maintain communication between individual crew members and between crew members and their supervisor. The company officer must be able to communicate with other operating units and Command. Command must be able to communicate with all operating units and other involved agencies such as law enforcement, public works, and local political leadership. This level of interoperability requires radios and other equipment with the necessary capability and flexibility to allow communication between agencies.

The communication most directly involved in firefighter safety and survival is that which takes place on the fireground. One aspect of fireground communication related to safety is the use of appropriate terminology. For example, it is important to differentiate between *a fire in a structure* and a *structure fire*. In the first case, the contents of the structure are on fire; in the second, the structure itself is burning.

Maintaining communication in a hazardous environment is a constant challenge for firefighters. In an IDLH environment, the OSHA two-in/two-out rule requires that crews entering such an environment stay together and remain in visual, voice, or physical contact at all times. According to an OSHA interpretation of the rule, radio contact does *not* meet the requirement for voice contact — crew members must be able to hear each other's voices without amplification. The crew must also be in visual, voice, or radio contact with the *rapid intervention crew* (RIC) standing by outside of the hazard zone.

What makes the two-in/two-out rule work is *communication* — between crew members, between crews, and between operational units (Divisions, Groups) and Command. If one firefighter sees a threat to the crew's safety and communicates it to the other crew members and the supervisor, the crew can either avoid the hazard or mitigate it. In addition, the information can be passed on to other personnel working at the incident. This increases everyone's safety.

> ⚠ All firefighters must maintain their situational awareness and communicate anything that seems unusual.

In terms of firefighter safety and survival, one of the most critical aspects of fireground communications is for every firefighter to know his or her department's protocol for calling for help. It is SOP in many departments for firefighters in distress to call, "Mayday, Mayday, Mayday!" on every available channel — provided they have a radio. Other departments use, "Emergency traffic — firefighter in distress!" This terminology is perhaps most consistent with the NIMS-ICS requirement to use *clear text*. Regardless of what term is used, it is critically important that it be part of the departmental SOP and is the term used by all likely mutual aid companies.

If firefighters in distress make radio contact, they can then describe their situation and location and give the status of their air supply. If firefighters become separated from their company and trapped in a burning building, they need to call for help *immediately*! While they may find it embarrassing to call a Mayday, it is better to be embarrassed than dead!

Reporting Identified Hazards Immediately

Another critically important action that fire crews can take is to notify other nearby firefighters or crews and Command of any safety hazard they encounter on the fireground **(Figure 3.14)**. Regardless of the nature of the hazard, the sooner it is reported, the sooner mitigation measures can be started. As in the case history from Washington state mentioned earlier, entire fire companies have been killed because one member failed to communicate critical information about the fire environment to other members of the team.

Knowing and Following Departmental SOPs

Adopting SOPs does not automatically increase firefighter safety and survival on the fireground. Firefighters must know and adhere to these SOPs. Compliance with departmental SOPs can be accomplished in two ways: voluntary compliance and enforcement. Of these, voluntary compliance (self-discipline) is by far the most desirable. Enforcement is necessary when there is a lack of voluntary compliance with safety SOPs on the fireground.

Enforcement of departmental SOPs regarding firefighter safety and survival on the fireground also has two aspects: education and coercive action. If firefighters are educated about what the SOPs require and reasons for the requirements they will usually comply out of self-interest. But given that fire departments and their officers can be held liable for damages if existing SOPs are not enforced, they have considerable incentive to enforce them.

Figure 3.14 Firefighters working inside the structure should notify Command of any hazards encountered.

Employing Safe and Effective Strategy and Tactics

While the overall strategy for an incident is established at the Command level, the tactical objectives used to implement the strategy are determined at lower levels in the fireground organization. In some cases, this even occurs at the company level. Regardless of who makes the determination, every tactic employed must be *both* safe and effective. A tactic that is safe but ineffective does little or nothing to solve the problem for which firefighters were called to the scene. Likewise, a tactic that is effective but unsafe is equally unacceptable. These decisions are the basis of the dynamic risk assessment discussed earlier in this chapter.

Having a Rapid Intervention Crew Standing By

As mentioned earlier, a rapid intervention crew is required by both NFPA® 1500 and OSHA regulations whenever firefighters are in the hazard zone inside a burning building. If there is more than one entry point into the hazard zone, more than one RIC will be required. In every case, at least two fully equipped firefighters must be standing by outside the hazard zone to rescue the interior

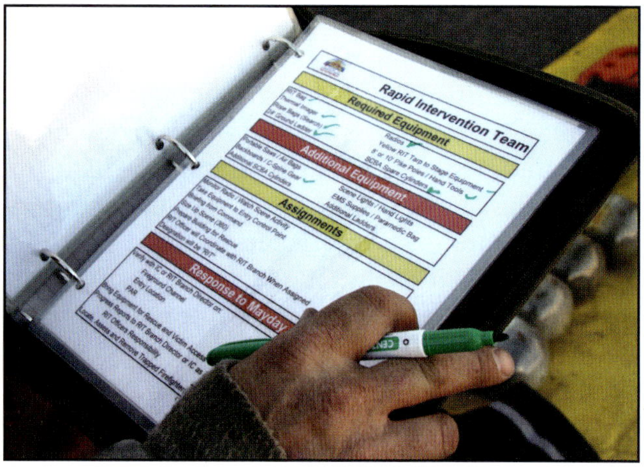

Figure 3.15 Rapid intervention crews must be well-organized and ready to enter the hazard zone immediately if needed.

crew, if necessary **(Figure 3.15)**. Firefighter safety/survival may depend on rapid intervention following a partial building collapse, a lost or disoriented firefighter running low on air, or a firefighter suffering a medical emergency in the hazard zone. Rapid intervention is discussed in greater detail in Chapter 10, Fireground Search and Rescue.

> ⚠ While two firefighters may be sufficient to locate a firefighter in distress, it may take a dozen or more firefighters to effect the rescue.

Setting Up a Rehab Unit on All Working Fires

Rehabilitation units, or **Rehab**, are essential to the safety and survival of firefighters involved in strenuous fire fighting activities. Rehab units are set up to provide shelter from the elements, relief from the effects of extreme heat or cold, water to maintain hydration, and medical evaluation, treatment, and transportation if needed **(Figure 3.16)**. For extended incidents, food is often provided to maintain nutrition levels. The following are the most common reasons why Rehab units are needed for all firefighters participating in an operation:

- The work must be performed in all types of weather.
- The work is often physically demanding.
- The work is sometimes extremely stressful.
- PPE is very effective at trapping internal heat.
- Exhausted firefighters are prone to injury.
- Incidents may last for extended periods of time.

Structure fires occur at all hours of the day and night and in all seasons of the year. Therefore, the tasks involved in truck company operations may have to be performed in the blazing sun of a summer day or in the frigid cold of a winter night. If a Rehab unit has been established, firefighters can be rotated through it to cool down or warm up as the case may be.

Rehab — Term for a rehabilitation station at a fire or other incident where personnel can rest, rehydrate, and recover from the stresses of the incident.

Figure 3.16 Rehab units are a place for firefighters to relax, rehydrate, and obtain medical treatment if needed.

Figure 3.17 Medical treatment can be initiated in the rehab unit if necessary. *Courtesy of Ron Jeffers*.

The numerous tasks required of firefighters on the fireground are physically challenging. If a Rehab unit has been set up, fatigued firefighters can be rotated through to rest, rehydrate, and have their temperature, pulse rate, and blood pressure checked. If necessary, emergency medical treatment can be started before affected firefighters are transported to a medical facility **(Figure 3.17)**. Others can recover sufficiently to take on other assignments.

Conducting search and rescue operations in the extreme heat and heavy smoke of a structure fire can be both physically and psychologically stressful for those involved. Just being told that someone is still inside a burning building is enough to increase the heart rate of even the most seasoned firefighter. Knowing that a trapped victim – even another firefighter – can survive only for a limited time in the oxygen-deficient atmosphere of a smoky fire places those assigned to search and rescue under tremendous pressure. If a Rehab unit has been established, psychologically exhausted firefighters can be rotated through to allow them to calm down and decompress before being reassigned.

The PPE that firefighters wear in structure fires today is excellent at keeping the heat of a fire away from them. However, the very qualities that make the turnouts effective at keeping heat out make them equally effective at keeping heat in. When the heat of a fire engulfs the outside of a firefighter's protective clothing and the heat generated by his or her physical activity fills the inside of the protective envelope, the temperature and humidity inside the turnouts can become extreme.

When on-scene resources are limited, the same firefighters who performed search and rescue operations and suppressed the fire may also have to perform overhaul. Given the physical and psychological demands of these activities, it is understandable why firefighters become fatigued. Even when on-scene resources are adequate, the nature of truck company operations places tremendous physical demands on the firefighters involved. Regardless of how or why firefighters become fatigued on the fireground, the results are the same — decreased productivity and increased risk of injury. Exhausted firefighters take longer to complete assigned tasks, and they are more likely to be injured in the process.

The Rehab unit should be located far enough from the scene that firefighters can safely remove their turnout clothing and SCBA. The unit should be large enough to accommodate multiple crews, based on the size of the incident, and should provide suitable protection from the elements. During hot weather, it should be cool and provide shade. During cold weather, it should be warm and dry. The location should be free of exhaust fumes from apparatus or equipment. Firefighters should enter and exit the Rehab area as a crew.

Using Emergency Escape Techniques When Needed

As the case histories cited earlier in this chapter show, structure fires are uncontrolled environments in which conditions can change with astounding speed. When truck company personnel are conducting search and rescue operations in burning buildings, things can suddenly go wrong and they can find themselves isolated from the rest of their crew, sometimes in life-threatening conditions. In these circumstances, their best chance for survival is if they communicate their situation to Command, if possible, and follow their departmental SOPs on firefighters in distress. Some of the most widely used techniques are discussed in the following section.

Emergency Egress

Being lost or trapped in a burning building is a very stressful experience — for those in distress as well as those trying to come to their aid. However, if firefighters in this situation have been trained in emergency escape techniques (sometimes called by the misnomer *self-rescue*) and apply them quickly and calmly, their chances of survival are greatly enhanced.

Firefighter Lost

Assuming that a firefighter does not have a disabling injury and is not trapped in a burning building but merely separated from fellow firefighters and lost or disoriented, there are a number of things he or she can do to find a way out. First, the firefighter should call a Mayday and activate the PASS device. Then the firefighter should listen for sounds of activity by other firefighters and try to retrace the steps that got him or her there. However, the route taken into the location may now be blocked by fire or collapse rubble. If the lost firefighter cannot hear other firefighters or has no way of contacting them, he or she should attempt to use the emergency egress techniques described in **Essentials**. Because of their potential importance to firefighter safety and survival, those techniques are repeated here:

- Locate a hoseline and follow it out **(Figure 3.18)**.
- Crawl in a straight line with hands on floor, moving knee to hand.
- Crawl in one direction (all left turns or all right turns) once in contact with a wall.
- Call out or make noise that other firefighters might hear.

Firefighter Trapped

When firefighters are trapped in a burning building, their first priority is to survive. Their first actions should be to initiate a Mayday (if possible), activate their PASS devices, and seek safe refuge. To increase their chances of survival, they must try to stay calm because panic can decrease their ability to think clearly and increase their rate of respiration, which will deplete the air supply in their SCBA sooner. Given that they are trapped, they should move to the safest area available and alert Command of their situation and approximate or last known location — provided that they have a radio.

Because the sound of a PASS device can make transmitting and receiving radio messages difficult or impossible, trapped firefighters will have to mute them or turn them off to use their radios. To use their radios, trapped firefighters may have to alternately turn their PASS devices on and off for one-minute intervals to allow them to hear transmissions from the RIC or other emergency traffic. If they do not have a radio, they should activate their PASS devices, shine a flashlight toward the ceiling, and wait for rescuers to locate them.

Knowing that a firefighter trapped in a burning building is almost certainly using his or her SCBA in order to breathe, rescuers should take a spare air supply for each missing firefighter with them as they search. The spare air supply may consist of SCBA cylinders, complete SCBA units, or dedicated RIC packs (see Chapter 10).

Figure 3.18 Following a hoseline can be helpful for emergency egress.

> According to NIOSH, so-called *buddy breathing* techniques are unreliable and more likely to produce two victims instead of one. NIOSH recommends providing respiratory assistance and quickly removing the victim to a clear atmosphere.

If a firefighter is trapped under or entangled in rubble or debris, it may not be possible to immediately extricate them. If his or her SCBA is equipped with an **Emergency Escape Breathing Support System (EEBSS)** — a fitting designed to allow the cylinder to be refilled in the harness instead of being exchanged — the cylinder can be filled from one brought in by the RIC **(Figure 3.19, p. 84)**. In this situation, the trapped firefighter's air supply can be maintained by using as many spare cylinders as necessary until he or she can be freed from entrapment.

The foregoing are all proven techniques that have worked in actual fireground situations. However, if the situation makes them ineffective at getting firefighters out of the building, they should use the escape techniques described in the following sections.

Locating Windows and Doors

When firefighters are lost or disoriented in a dark and/or smoke-filled part of a building, they should call a Mayday and exit the building as quickly as possible. They should try to locate a window or door that might provide an exit route. To do so they should move to the nearest wall, and staying low to avoid

Emergency Escape Breathing Support System (EEBSS) — Safety system on an SCBA that allows two units to be hooked together in the event that one fails.

WARNING!
Never remove your facepiece or compromise the proper operation of your SCBA in any way to share your air supply with anyone — not even another firefighter.

Figure 3.19 Emergency Escape Breathing Support Systems (EEBSS) allow supplemental breathing air to be provided to a downed firefighter.

Figure 3.20 Wiping the wall with a gloved hand can help in locating a window or door.

the heat in the upper part of the room, they should crawl along the wall *wiping* it with one gloved hand from the floor to as high as they can reach without standing up **(Figure 3.20)**. This technique should help them quickly locate any window that is within about 4 feet (1.2 m) of the floor. If no windows are found, they will eventually find a door unless it is buried by collapse debris.

Window Egress

Once a window has been located, firefighters should break out the window pane using a tool, a piece of furniture or debris, or any other means available. The point is to quickly make the window opening large enough for them to pass through without having to remove any part of their protective ensemble other than their SCBA. If circumstances allow, it is best to remove the entire window. Even though there is some risk of injury to other firefighters who may be working directly below the window, the sounds of the window glass hitting the sidewalk or ground may attract someone's attention. Once the window has been removed, firefighters can escape by crawling out of the window — provided it is close to the ground. Even in some upper-story windows, firefighters may be able to lower themselves using an emergency escape rope if they are so equipped **(Figure 3.21)**. Otherwise, from a second-story they may be able to crawl out of the window opening and hang by their hands before pushing away from the wall and dropping to the ground **(Figure 3.22)**.

If they aren't equipped with an emergency escape rope and the window is too high for them to safely jump or drop from it, firefighters can straddle the windowsill and attempt to attract the attention of someone on the ground **(Figure 3.23)**. They can activate their PASS devices, yell, and/or shine a flashlight to alert those on the ground of their situation.

NOTE: Firefighters should *not* drop their helmets or any other part of their protective ensemble in an attempt to attract attention.

If heat escaping from the window opening makes it impossible for them to continue sitting there, they may hook one leg over the windowsill and let their bodies hang below the opening. Obviously, this technique can only be done for a very short time while a ladder is being placed beneath them to climb down.

> **WARNING!**
> Jumping or dropping from any height while wearing SCBA may pull you over backwards and lead to serious injury. If possible, remove the SCBA unit first.

Figure 3.21 Firefighters should be proficient with emergency escape techniques. *Courtesy of the Florida State Fire College.*

Figure 3.22 The drop distance can be reduced by hanging from the windowsill.

Figure 3.23 Straddling a window and activating the PASS device may gain the attention of personnel on the ground.

When a ladder is in place, the firefighter should swing onto the ladder and climb down in the normal way. Techniques that require firefighters to dive head-first onto a ladder and then swing their legs around and slide down the ladder beams have proven to be very dangerous. At least one firefighter has been killed and several have been seriously injured practicing these techniques. In a life-or-death situation, firefighters must do whatever is necessary to save themselves, but these high-risk techniques are *not* recommended.

Door Egress

When lost or disoriented firefighters have crawled along a wall and found a door, they should check it for heat before opening it. If the door is cool to the touch, firefighters should attempt to open it. Once the door is open, they should look or feel around inside the room to try to identify its contents. The items found inside may tell them whether the room is a closet, storeroom, or some other type of space. In a residential occupancy, if the room contains shoes, clothing, etc., it is not likely to be the best way out. If it is another type of room, they should enter the room, close the door behind them, and begin to crawl along a wall as in the first room. This exploration should lead them either to a window or another door. If it is a window, they should follow the foregoing instructions. If it is another door, they should again check it for heat, and proceed as with the first one. This should eventually lead them to a window or door that will provide an exit path. If they are in a room without windows and the only door they can find is hot to the touch, they must consider breaching a wall to escape.

Wall Breach

Before firefighters attempt to breach a wall to escape, they should feel it for heat just as before opening a door. If the wall is cool to the touch, they can begin to create an opening large enough for them to pass through without having to remove their SCBA or any other part of their protective ensemble. Interior walls of either gypsum wallboard or lath and plaster over wood or metal studs are relatively easy to breach. This can be done with almost any forcible entry tool, a piece of furniture, or if necessary, a turnout boot **(Figure 3.24)**. Removing the wall between any two adjacent studs will only create an opening approximately 14 inches (350 mm) wide. It may be necessary to remove the wall sections on both sides of a stud and remove the stud as well.

> **CAUTION**
> If the wall is load-bearing, removing a stud could initiate structural collapse.

> **CAUTION**
> Before breaching any wall, firefighters should check it for heat. Once the wall is breached, they should make sure there is a floor or other solid surface on the other side before proceeding through the opening.

Breaching interior walls with heavy wooden paneling or exterior walls of almost any material can be more difficult than breaching interior walls covered with gypsum drywall or lath and plaster. However, given the urgency of this situation, it is certainly worth the effort. The trapped firefighters may have to use whatever forcible entry tool they may have with them or whatever else they can find in the room that might help them breach the wall. It may require every bit of their ingenuity and skill to break or pry wooden siding from wall studs or to chip the mortar from between bricks in a wall.

Figure 3.24 Interior gypsum walls are relatively easy to breach.

Figure 3.25 Exterior wall breaches can be performed by personnel outside the structure to assist in rescue.

In the process, other firefighters outside may hear the commotion inside and realize what it means. The firefighters outside can then begin to help breach the wall. Given that they have a wider variety of tools available, if they can reach the point that needs to be breached, firefighters outside are likely to be able to breach the wall in short order **(Figure 3.25)**.

> **Safety Scenario:**
>
> As an engine company officer, you and your four-member company arrive at a working fire in a three-story wood frame apartment house on a sunny Sunday afternoon. Heavy fire and smoke are visible on the second floor of the building. Other engines have been on scene for more than 10 minutes. Your department doesn't have a ladder truck and the nearest mutual-aid truck is miles away. You are ordered to conduct a primary search of the building.
>
> - What are the safety considerations for your company?
> - What questions would you ask before starting to carry out your orders?
> - Where would you start your search?
> - Would you divide your crew?

Summary

Firefighters are frequently required to work in the often hostile and potentially lethal environment inside burning buildings. Because firefighters can be injured or killed by any of several contingencies common to these fires, they must learn to recognize the signs of these phenomena before they develop. They must learn to recognize the dangers inherent in so-called *routine* calls and fires that have *self-vented*. Firefighters must also learn to recognize the signs of imminent flashover, backdraft, and structural collapse — as well as how to mitigate or avoid them. Finally, if they become lost or trapped in a burning building, they must know how to initiate a Mayday call and wait for a RIC, or escape if possible.

Review Questions

1. What are the IFSTA *Principles of Risk Management*? How are they intended to increase firefighter safety during fireground operations?
2. What is the safe person element of the *Dynamic Risk Assessment* model?
3. How do the four leadership skills in the *Crew Resource Management* program enhance firefighter safety during fireground operations?
4. Why is it important for every firefighter to have a 'safety first' mindset?
5. What are the dangers of the routine fire and a fire that has self-vented?
6. What are the indicators of a potential structural collapse?
7. How do the elements of fireground safety increase firefighter safety?
8. What is a rapid intervention crew?
9. What is a personnel accountability report?
10. What is situational awareness?
11. What are the various procedures a firefighter might use for emergency egress from a building?

Loss Control

Chapter Contents

CASE HISTORY 93
Preincident Loss Control Planning 94
    Risk Identification 95
    Risk Evaluation 96
    Plans Development 97
Incident Loss Control Operations 98
Primary Loss Control 98
    Proper Size-Up 98
    Effective Strategy 99
    Adequate On-Scene Resources 99
    Effective Method of Attack 99
    Effective Ventilation 100
    Thorough Overhaul 100

Secondary Loss Control 104
    Assisting the Fire Attack 105
    Ventilation 107
    Salvage 109
Post-Incident Loss Control Operations 114
    Economic Loss Control 114
    Psychological Loss Control 116
Summary 117
Review Questions 118

chapter 4

Key Terms

Compressed Air Foam
  System (CAFS) 112
Lapping 108
Loss Control 93
Overhaul 100
Piercing Nozzle 109

Primary Damage 93
Rekindle 101
Salvage 109
Secondary Damage 93
Size-Up 98

Loss Control

Learning Objectives

After reading this chapter, students will be able to:

1. Describe the fireground function of loss control.
2. Distinguish between primary and secondary damage.
3. Describe the three purposes of a preincident planning survey.
4. Describe the procedures used to control primary damage.
5. Describe the procedures used to control secondary damage.
6. Describe the procedures used to remove heat from the interior of a building.
7. Summarize the salvage procedures which are used to assist in fire attack.
8. Summarize the procedures used to protect exposed contents in a building.

Safety Points

While reading this chapter, keep the following safety points in mind:

- During preincident planning, firefighters should identify and document the presence of toxic or explosive hazardous materials and items, such as heavy dead loads, highly absorbent contents not on pallets, or inadequate drainage from upper floors, that might increase the potential for structural collapse. Potential loss control problems should be communicated to all affected response units.

- During salvage and overhaul operations, firefighters should wear appropriate protective clothing and breathe air only from their SCBA until the atmosphere has been tested and found to be within safe limits.

Chapter 4
Loss Control

Case History

According to a report by the Boston Sparks Association, Massachusetts firefighters were called to a fire in a 100-year-old hotel in 1972. The hotel was undergoing extensive renovation at the time. The fire department responded with sufficient resources to control the fire in a timely manner. During overhaul operations approximately three hours after the fire was reported, the building suddenly collapsed, killing nine firefighters and injuring nine others. While the structure may have been weakened by the fire, the most serious weakness was created by unauthorized structural changes made during the renovation. The collapse appeared to have been triggered by the weight of the firefighters and the water used to extinguish the fire.

Historically, the work that has come to be known as **loss control** at structure fires was originally done by civilian salvage crews hired by fire insurance companies. The goal of these crews was to save as much as possible of the policyholders' properties during a fire, thereby reducing the amount of money the insurance companies would have to pay **(Figure 4.1, p. 94)**. Over time, public fire departments began to add this responsibility to the services they were already providing. Salvage functions were still seen as less important than fighting the fire, and in many departments, they were often performed almost as an afterthought. Today, salvage is recognized as a very important fire department function that is a part of the broader category called loss control.

The purpose of loss control is to reduce damage from fire, smoke, water, inclement weather, or other contingencies before, during, and after a fire. In other words, armed with knowledge about the involved occupancy gathered during preincident planning surveys, loss control operations consist of those actions that aid in reducing primary and secondary damage during and after the fire. **Primary damage** is damage produced by the fire and smoke. **Secondary damage** is damage that results from fighting the fire and/or leaving the property unsecured. Secondary damage can result from forcible entry, ventilation, and overhaul operations as well as from leaving a structure vulnerable to further damage from the weather and vandalism or theft.

Firefighters should consider loss control when conducting preincident planning surveys, while fighting structure fires, and during post-fire operations. This chapter discusses these three phases of loss control related to structure fires.

Loss Control — The practice of minimizing damage and providing customer service through effective mitigation and recovery efforts before, during, and after an incident.

Primary Damage — Damage caused by a fire itself and not by actions taken to fight the fire.

Secondary Damage — Damage caused by or resulting from those actions taken to fight a fire and leaving the property unprotected.

Figure 4.1 A historic fire insurance patrol station.

Preincident Loss Control Planning

The purpose of all preincident planning, including that for loss control, is to increase incident safety, efficiency, and effectiveness. These ends are achieved by raising the firefighter's familiarity with a particular building and its contents, and by reducing the number of decisions that must be made during a fire in that building. Until acted upon by some outside intervention, all structure fires are uncontrolled emergencies.

> By definition, emergencies are events that are emerging — they are dynamic and changing events.

Unless someone or something acts to stop the progress of a fire, it will continue to burn until all the available fuel and/or oxidizing agent have been consumed. For the firefighters assigned to control and extinguish a structure fire, preincident loss control information helps them make faster and more informed on-scene decisions. This information also allows them to focus on protecting themselves and others, stabilizing the situation, and conserving property. Before a fire ever starts, preincident planning can answer many questions about the building, its contents, and many fire-related problems to be expected.

Using a systematic preincident planning process can increase the likelihood of a successful outcome on the fireground. As in all other aspects of truck company operations, preincident planning helps firefighters prepare to perform loss control operations in a given building more safely and more effectively. By becoming familiar with a structure and its contents, firefighters can develop plans that can help them reduce the overall loss resulting from a fire in that occupancy.

Typically, preincident loss control planning is done in conjunction with other preincident planning. This ensures that loss control is considered at each step in the process of developing an overall preincident plan — sometimes called an *operational plan* or *contingency plan*. Some departments use very sophisticated risk analysis and management systems as the basis for their preincident planning related to loss control. Other departments take a less structured approach to assessing loss control risks and developing strategies for mitigating those risks. In this context, a loss control risk is any aspect of a building or its contents that has the potential for producing primary or secondary loss if there is a fire in that building. Regardless of what system is used to assess and manage loss control risks, all such systems involve the same basic steps — risk identification, risk evaluation, and plans development.

Risk Identification

Risk identification is usually accomplished through an ongoing program of preincident planning surveys. As discussed in **Essentials**, these site visits are commonly called *surveys* to differentiate them from code enforcement inspections. Regardless of what these visits are called, they have the same three purposes:

1. To allow firefighters to become familiar with the building and its contents
2. To gather information for plans development
3. To inform building owners/occupants of anything that they can do to reduce the risk of loss

During preincident planning surveys, firefighters should look for and document any condition that might increase primary or secondary loss. Firefighters should note such items as the following:

- Life safety hazards
- Means of primary and secondary access or egress
- Repositories of vital information that *must* be protected, if possible
- Vital processes that should be shut down only if absolutely necessary
- Biohazards and highly flammable or reactive materials or processes
- Structural designs that increase loss potential
- Highly absorbent contents that need to be protected from water

Firefighters should also identify the locations of Safety Data Sheets (SDS), emergency contact lists, areas of restricted access, and items or areas of extremely high value. In addition, they should discuss with the property owner/occupant the need to keep absorbent stock on pallets and to keep it stable by not piling or stacking it too high **(Figure 4.2, p. 96)**. Firefighters should also point out the benefits of general good housekeeping.

In addition, firefighters should note any of the following features or systems that might reduce the risk of loss:

- Fire escapes, smoke towers, and areas of refuge **(Figure 4.3, p. 96)**
- Automatic fire doors
- Built-in fire detection/suppression systems
- Automatic smoke vents **(Figure 4.4, p.96)**

Figure 4.2 Property owners should be instructed in the proper storage of absorbent material to prevent damage.

Figure 4.4 Automatic smoke vents aid in the ventilation of the structure.

Figure 4.3 Areas of refuge are often found in large structures.

Additionally, residential neighborhoods as well as those in which large commercial, industrial, and institutional occupancies are located should be surveyed and the results documented. Many neighborhoods consist of structures of approximately the same age, type of construction, and use. Other neighborhoods include structures that are significantly different from adjacent buildings. All these commonalities and differences should be identified and documented so that appropriate preincident plans can be developed and distributed.

Risk Evaluation

When all the information from the planning survey has been gathered, it must be evaluated. This evaluation involves using judgment and experience to assess how any particular item will increase or decrease the potential for primary or secondary loss. For example, automatic fire doors may help to reduce primary loss by limiting the spread of a fire, but they may also impede the occupants' escape from the building. Automatic sprinklers may help to reduce primary loss by controlling or extinguishing a fire while it is still relatively small. However, automatic sprinklers may also add to secondary loss by reducing the building's structural integrity because of the weight of a possibly large quantity of water added to upper floors. The water discharged by automatic sprinklers may also damage or destroy building contents not involved in the fire. Therefore, every item of information must be evaluated for its positive and/or negative loss control potential. This information can also be used to identify additional fire department tools and equipment that might be needed in the event of a fire in that occupancy.

Plans Development

Once a building has been surveyed and the loss control risks have been identified and evaluated, the information and conclusions should be translated into operational or contingency plans. In terms of structure fires, the initial response level should be determined and documented so that the appropriate number and types of resources are dispatched whenever a fire is reported there. Mitigation plans should be devised for the most likely hazards to be encountered if a fire starts in the building. The mitigation plans may necessitate the acquisition of additional equipment and training on the implementation of the plans. In addition, any plans that are developed should include a loss control element. The loss control element of the plans may specify or indicate the following:

- Most effective and least destructive means of gaining entry into the building such as lock boxes, etc. (**Figure 4.5**)
- Most effective means of evacuating or protecting building occupants during a fire such as exits, fire escapes, areas of refuge, etc.
- Where vital business records, such as data storage devices and filing cabinets, are located and how best to protect them during a fire (**Figure 4.6**)
- When and how built-in fire suppression systems, such as automatic sprinklers and standpipes, are to be supported and used (**Figure 4.7**)
- How building contents are to be protected from smoke and water damage such as with salvage covers, plastic sheeting, etc.

Figure 4.5 Property owners should be encouraged to install lock boxes at the entrances to their buildings to prevent unnecessary damage from forcible entry.

Figure 4.6 Vital business records should be identified during preincident planning and their preservation made a priority in loss control efforts.

Figure 4.7 Fire department connections (FDCs) should be identified during the preincident visit.

Another important aspect of preincident planning in any building is confidentiality. Any designs, materials, processes, or other proprietary information that firefighters observe during preincident planning surveys *must* be kept confidential. In fact, some business owners may require visiting firefighters to sign a confidentiality agreement before they are allowed to tour the premises. Likewise, information about building security measures and techniques to overcome them must be protected.

Incident Loss Control Operations

Once a fire has started within a building, the flames, heat, and smoke can cause an enormous amount of damage to the structure and its contents. This primary damage was once seen as outside the control of the firefighters. However, with advancements in fire detection and suppression system technology and fire fighting tools and techniques, firefighters are more capable of rapid fire extinguishment and primary damage reduction than ever before.

During a structure fire, secondary damage can result from forcible entry, fire attack, ventilation and smoke removal, water use and removal, and overhaul. However, given the proper training and equipment, firefighters can minimize secondary damage. An important part of minimizing secondary damage is conducting an adequate dynamic risk assessment (size-up) so that an accurate picture of the problem is developed. In addition to being a safety hazard for those fighting the fire, an inaccurate size-up can sometimes cause a delay in appropriate actions being taken, resulting in unnecessary loss.

Primary Loss Control

One of the most important ways that firefighters can limit primary damage in a structure fire is to extinguish the fire as quickly and as efficiently as possible. In general, the most important factors in limiting primary damage are as follows:

- Proper size-up
- Effective strategy
- Adequate on-scene resources
- Effective method of attack
- Effective ventilation
- Thorough overhaul

While other firefighters carry out direct fire attack, truck company personnel can gain entry, conduct search and rescue operations, and support all of these efforts by performing horizontal or vertical ventilation and controlling building utilities. Effective ventilation can have a positive effect on fire behavior. It clears the atmosphere inside the burning building and makes fire control, search and rescue, and overhaul operations easier and safer.

Proper Size-Up

To paraphrase the definition given in **Essentials**, **size-up** is the ongoing (dynamic) mental evaluation process performed by the officer in charge of an incident to evaluate all influencing factors and to develop strategic goals and tactical objectives before committing personnel and equipment to a course

> **CAUTION**
> Inappropriate or poorly executed ventilation can accelerate fire growth and increase primary damage. In some cases, anti-ventilation or compartmentalization (isolating involved sections until sufficient resources are in place to attack the fire) can assist in limiting fire spread and smoke damage.

Size-Up — Ongoing mental evaluation process performed by the operational officer in charge of an incident that enables him or her to determine and evaluate all existing influencing factors that are used to develop objectives, strategy, and tactics for fire suppression before committing personnel and equipment to a course of action.

of action **(Figure 4.8)**. Size-up results in a plan of action (IAP) that may need to be adjusted as the situation changes. It includes such factors as life safety, the nature and scope of the incident, time (day/week), weather, location, property involved, occupancy, exposures, and available fire fighting resources.

Even though the overall size-up is the responsibility of the officer in charge (IC), every firefighter on scene should continuously assess the incident and his or her situation — in other words, maintain their situational awareness throughout the incident.

Effective Strategy

Figure 4.8 A good size-up helps in the determination of needed resources.

The responsibility for determining the strategy for any incident rests with Command. However, it is the responsibility of every firefighter on scene to know what that strategy is and to do his or her utmost to implement it. Individual firefighters can help to implement the designated strategy by listening carefully to orders as they are given, and working conscientiously as a member of the company, crew, or team to carry them out.

Adequate On-Scene Resources

Amassing sufficient numbers and types of resources on-scene can greatly enhance the efficiency, effectiveness, and safety of fire attack and truck company operations. Thorough preincident planning can help ensure that these resources are part of the initial alarm response. If they are not part of the initial response, the IC may have to call for additional resources after sizing-up the situation and developing an IAP. The delay involved in having to wait for additional resources to arrive at the scene may slow the fire attack and result in increased primary damage.

Effective Method of Attack

The method of attack can certainly affect the amount of primary and secondary damage from a fire. If the number and size of the attack lines are insufficient to deliver enough water onto the fire to absorb the heat being produced, the fire will continue to grow and damage or destroy more of the building and/or its contents. Also, if water is applied to the outside of a building while the fire is burning inside, the fire is more likely to destroy the entire building. To limit both primary and secondary damage, there must be a sufficient number of firefighters properly trained and equipped to deliver the required amount of water onto the fire. The sooner they can do this, the better the result will be.

Some tactics are more effective than others. For example, indiscriminately applying water onto a fire in a building can disrupt the thermal balance, increase steam production (perhaps injuring interior firefighters), decrease visibility, and possibly spread the fire. On the other hand, where the contents of a structure and not the building itself are involved, gas-cooling techniques can be very effective. Intermittent application of water fog to the hot-gas layer will help cool walls and ceilings without disrupting the thermal balance. When the smoke level rises as a result of gas cooling, water can then be applied to the burning materials. Also, the application of Class A foam can be effective under the right circumstances.

Effective Ventilation

As mentioned earlier, truck company personnel can help to limit primary damage by performing timely horizontal or vertical ventilation in a planned and coordinated manner **(Figure 4.9)**. Until an interior structure fire is ventilated, the dense smoke and heat inside the building may prevent firefighters from finding trapped occupants or the seat of the fire, and even prevent them from approaching the fire close enough to deliver their water effectively. Trapped heat and smoke can cause further fire spread and seriously damage building contents. Under the right conditions, trapped heat and smoke can lead to other dangerous conditions such as flashover or backdraft. Ill-timed or incorrect ventilation can also increase fire intensity and spread, resulting in additional fire damage. Timely and effective (coordinated) ventilation can reduce primary loss by limiting the spread of the fire and by helping hose crews to locate and extinguish the fire as quickly as possible.

Figure 4.9 Ventilation efforts should be done in a planned and coordinated manner. *Courtesy of Bob Esposito.*

> **Overhaul** — Those operations conducted once the main body of fire has been extinguished that consist of searching for and extinguishing hidden or remaining fire, placing the building and its contents in a safe condition, determining the cause of the fire, and recognizing and preserving evidence of arson.

Thorough Overhaul

Another way to limit primary damage in a structure fire is by performing a thorough **overhaul**. Even though overhaul normally takes place after a fire has been knocked down, the damage done by hidden fire is still primary damage. Finding and extinguishing all remaining fire completes the fire suppression phase of the operation and can prevent a costly rekindle that could destroy all that remains of the building and even spread to uninvolved buildings nearby. A thorough overhaul can be a very important part of primary loss control at structure fires **(Figure 4.10)**. However, in this context *thorough* does not mean indiscriminately soaking the entire building and its contents with water. As in the fire attack phase of the operation, firefighters need to apply water judiciously during overhaul. In some cases, smoldering material can be removed from the building before being wet down or immersed in water outside **(Figure 4.11)**.

To reduce the chances of a **rekindle** and to eliminate the need to post a fire watch when engine crews leave the scene, some departments set up portable electronic rekindle detectors after a working structure fire **(Figure 4.12)**. These units normally operate from battery power but can operate on AC power if available. When smoke or heat is detected, the unit automatically transmits an alarm by radio signal to the fire department communications/dispatch center.

Rekindle — Reignition of a fire because of latent heat, sparks, or smoldering embers; can be prevented by proper overhaul.

Figure 4.10 Thorough overhaul is necessary to ensure the fire is completely extinguished.

Figure 4.11 Smoldering items can be brought outside for extinguishment to prevent water damage.

Figure 4.12 Rekindle detectors transmit an alarm to the appropriate location if reignition occurs. *Courtesy of Rick Montemorra.*

Evidence Preservation

Before the IC allows firefighters to begin the overhaul of any structure fire, he or she must consult with the investigator or whoever is responsible for determining the origin and cause of the fire. This allows the investigator an opportunity to collect or protect critical evidence before overhaul begins. It also helps to ensure that the evidence is not disturbed or destroyed by the firefighters during overhaul.

Firefighter Safety

As in every other phase of fireground operations, firefighter safety is a major consideration during overhaul. A number of factors can make the overhaul process very hazardous for the firefighters assigned to it.

> In 2002, Mark Noble, a nineteen-year veteran of the Olympia (WA) Fire Department was diagnosed with brain cancer. After surgery to remove the tumor, Mark began a regimen of chemotherapy and radiation. During his treatment, Mark started researching the connection between firefighters and cancer. What he found was that firefighters are exposed to highly toxic substances in virtually every fire — especially during overhaul. These toxic substances include asbestos, benzene, polycyclic aromatic hydrocarbons (PAH), and polychlorinated biphenyls (PCB) in addition to carbon monoxide (CO) and other well-known products of combustion. The toxic effects can accumulate with repeated exposures.
>
> In his research, Mark found that when compared to the general adult population, firefighters are twice as likely to develop intestinal cancer, liver cancer, prostate cancer and non-Hodgkin's lymphoma; 2.25 times as likely to develop malignant melanoma and three times as likely to develop other skin cancers; 2.5 times as likely to develop testicular cancer; three times as likely to develop bladder cancer and leukemia; 3.5 times as likely to develop brain cancer; and four times as likely to develop kidney cancer.
>
> In 2005, at age 47, Mark Noble lost his battle with the brain cancer that he almost certainly developed because of the toxins to which he was exposed as a firefighter. Mark loved being a firefighter, but he said that if he had it to do over, he would wear his SCBA more and would be more conscientious about hooking up apparatus exhaust collection hoses.
>
> *Permission granted by Mrs. Rebecca Noble and ERGOMETRICS & Applied Personnel Research, Inc., who produced a video interview with Mark during his final months. The video is available at www.ergometrics.org.*

Firefighters should not be allowed to work in areas with elevated levels of carbon monoxide (CO) and other toxic products of combustion without SCBA because their judgment can be seriously impaired, which can lead to poor decisions that could place them or others in danger. As described in the foregoing case history, firefighters may be exposed to carcinogens and a host of other life-threatening substances. If the same firefighters who extinguished the fire and performed other associated tasks are assigned to perform overhaul, as is often the case, then firefighter fatigue must be considered. When firefighters experience the physical and psychological drain that often follows the knockdown of a difficult and dangerous fire, their level of concentration may not be as high as when they were fresh and rested. Mental exhaustion can make firefighters more likely to miss subtle danger signs in the damaged structure such as creaking, cracking, or other sounds that might otherwise alert them to an impending structural collapse. Physical exhaustion reduces strength and coordination and slows reflexes — all of which increase the likelihood of injury while operating tools and equipment. Fatigue could make the firefighters less capable of reacting to and escaping from any dangerous situation that might suddenly develop.

Supervisors must closely monitor their crews to ensure that they wear their gloves and use appropriate respiratory protection to help limit their exposure to long-term health hazards. Providing adequate resources for long-duration incidents and setting up one or more Rehab units — and rotating crews through them — will help to prevent accidents due to physical exhaustion. When the overhaul operation is completed, firefighters must thoroughly clean their turnouts, gloves, helmets, and any other contaminated gear to prevent residual exposure **(Figure 4.13)**.

Hidden Fire

Obviously, finding all remaining fire can be a significant problem if the fire has done major damage to the building. This is especially true when there are layers of rubble and debris because glowing embers can remain hidden. Finding hidden fires can also be difficult where structural damage was less severe. For example, embers can smolder inside walls and other structural voids that appear normal from the outside. Infrared heat detectors and thermal imaging equipment can make locating these and other hidden fires much easier, thereby reducing the chances of missing a hot spot **(Figure 4.14)**.

After fire control has been achieved, some departments withdraw all interior personnel and use blowers to help locate hot spots. The increased airflow through the damaged portion of the structure will sometimes fan glowing embers enough for them to start producing smoke, allowing firefighters to locate them. Obviously, this procedure must be done carefully and with charged hoselines ready to extinguish any fire that is discovered. If this technique is used, the additional airflow can also help to reduce the level of CO and other toxic products of combustion in the areas where firefighters must work during overhaul. However, the time-tested methods of looking for wisps of smoke, feeling for hot spots, and listening for the crackle of fire can still be used effectively. Regardless of what method is used to find hidden fires, applying Class A foam can help to extinguish hot spots more effectively.

Toxic Products of Combustion

Even after all visible smoke has been cleared from a compartment in which a fire has been burning, invisible but highly toxic products of combustion can continue to be present in dangerous concentrations. In addition to the CO that is always present after a fire, any of several other toxic gases may be present, depending upon the types of materials that were involved and the conditions under

Figure 4.13 Cleaning turnout gear after a structure fire helps to prevent residual exposure.

Figure 4.14 Thermal imaging cameras can help in locating areas of hidden fire.

Figure 4.15 The fireground atmosphere should be constantly monitored for toxic products of combustion.

which they burned. If a broad-spectrum gas analyzer is available, the atmosphere within the damaged area should be checked for all known or suspected gases that may be present **(Figure 4.15)**. If not, firefighters should breathe air only from their SCBA or other supplied-air respirator until overhaul is completed or they are allowed to leave the contaminated area.

As discussed in Chapter 2, Enhanced Fire Behavior, structure fires can produce or release a variety of toxic gases in addition to CO, depending upon the types of materials that are involved. Other common fire gases and their sources are as follows:

- ***Acrolein*** **(CH_2=CHCHO)** — a strong respiratory irritant produced when polyethylene is heated and when items containing cellulose, such as wood and other natural materials smolder. It is used in the manufacture of pharmaceuticals, herbicides, and tear gas.

- ***Hydrogen chloride*** **(HCl)** — a colorless but very pungent and irritating gas given off in the thermal decomposition of materials containing chlorine such as polyvinyl chloride (PVC) and other plastics.

- ***Hydrogen cyanide*** **(HCN)** — a colorless gas with a characteristic almond odor. Twenty times more toxic than CO, it is an asphyxiant and can be absorbed through the skin. HCN is produced in the combustion of natural materials, such as wool and silk, which contain nitrogen. It is also produced when polyurethane foam and other plastics that contain urea burn. The concentrated bulk chemical is also used in electroplating.

- ***Carbon dioxide*** **(CO_2)** — a colorless, odorless, and nonflammable gas produced in free-burning fires. While it is nontoxic, CO_2 can asphyxiate by excluding the oxygen from a confined space. It is also a respiratory accelerant that can increase the intake of other toxic gases.

- ***Nitrogen oxides*** **(NO and NO_2)** — two toxic and dangerous gases liberated in the combustion of pyroxylin plastics. Because nitric oxide (NO) readily converts to nitrogen dioxide (NO_2) in the presence of oxygen and moisture, nitrogen dioxide is the substance of most concern to firefighters. Nitrogen dioxide is a pulmonary irritant that can also have a delayed systemic effect. The vapors and smoke from the oxides of nitrogen have a reddish brown or copper color.

- ***Phosgene*** **(CCl_2O)** — a highly toxic, colorless gas with a disagreeable odor of musty hay. It may be produced when refrigerants, such as Freon, contact flame. Phosgene can be expected in fires in cold-storage facilities or in fires involving heavy-duty HVAC systems. It is a strong pulmonary irritant, the full harmful effect of which is not evident for several hours after exposure.

Secondary Loss Control

While other firefighters are limiting primary loss by attacking a structure fire, truck company personnel can make significant contributions to the secondary loss control effort. Secondary loss control considerations may involve assisting the fire attack, ventilation, and salvage.

Assisting the Fire Attack

There several ways in which truck company personnel can assist in the attack on interior structure fires. The first is by creating exterior and interior openings in the structure by forcible entry for entry or attack by hose crews. The second is by pulling ceilings and opening walls to allow water to be applied more directly.

Forcible Entry

One of the most effective means of secondary loss control is performing forcible entry in a professional manner **(Figure 4.16)**. While quick and efficient access into the building can reduce primary damage by helping the direct interior fire attack to begin sooner, it can also reduce secondary loss if unnecessary damage is avoided by using the least destructive tools and techniques to gain access to the interior of the building.

Opening Exterior Doors and Windows. Property damage can be minimized without impeding the fire suppression operation if a door can be opened with a key or security code obtained from a lockbox. Likewise, loss can be reduced if a door can be taken off by removing the hinge pins. Also, loss is minimized if a window can be opened instead of being broken out **(Figure 4.17)**. Finally, when doors and windows are not damaged while gaining entry, it makes it easier to secure the building after the incident.

Figure 4.16 Performing forcible entry efficiently and with as little damage as possible is a sign of professionalism.

Figure 4.17 Windows can sometimes be opened manually without having to be broken. It is always important to 'try before you pry'.

Figure 4.18 Forcible entry can be performed by truck company personnel to provide access for suppression crews.

Opening Interior Doors. When on-scene resources allow, truck company personnel are assigned to accompany each interior fire attack crew. These personnel wear the same level and types of PPE as the attack crews, and they carry a set of irons or other forcible entry tools with them. When the attack crew needs a door to be opened, truck company personnel use the tools and techniques described in **Essentials** and Chapter 9 of this manual to open the door **(Figure 4.18)**.

Pulling Ceilings

One of the most critical elements in the rapid control and extinguishment of a fire is for the direct application of water by attack crews. In many cases, an intact ceiling separates attack crews from a fire in the attic. This requires the use of penetrating nozzles or most likely the pulling of the ceiling material with pike poles or ceiling hooks **(Figure 4.19)**. If the fire situation and on-scene resources allow, pulling the ceilings should be done only after the contents of the room directly below the attic have been properly protected. In some cases, it may be advantageous to pull the ceilings over hallways and other areas with little or no contents to protect. This may only require rolling out hall runners instead of having to spread salvage covers.

While pulling ceilings for access to a fire is effective, it is not without its risks. If the ceiling is suspended from open-web trusses that have been weakened by the fire, the entire roof assembly may suddenly collapse. Of course, the rapid suppression of an attic fire also helps to maintain the structural integrity of the roof assembly. If roof assemblies and the dead loads they support are identified and evaluated during preincident planning, firefighters will be able to make a more informed assessment of the risks and benefits of pulling the ceilings in these buildings during a fire.

In some attics, the insulation is sealed under a sheet of plastic. This additional layer of material can make opening the attic much more difficult. When ceilings are pulled, large amounts of insulation and other debris — some of which may be on fire — can drop down into the room below. Therefore, as mentioned earlier, firefighters may delay pulling the ceiling until the contents of the room below have been removed or protected.

Figure 4.19 Pike poles are very effective in pulling ceiling material.

Once an attic fire has been controlled, the initial opening in the ceiling can be enlarged for further extinguishment. This, however, should not occur until the contents of the room have been removed or fully protected. When all rooms under the area of fire involvement have been protected, the rest of the ceiling may be pulled down as necessary until the attic fire is completely extinguished and overhaul is completed. If available, a TIC can be used effectively to help locate any hidden fire.

Opening Walls

Many older structures were built with balloon-frame construction. Because a fire originating in the basement or cellar of this type of building has an unimpeded pathway to the attic, extinguishing fire inside the walls is a high priority. For attack crews to have access inside these walls, truck company personnel must open them up. Whether finished with gypsum drywall or lath and plaster, the interior side of most exterior walls can be cut open using an axe or power saw, or they can be broken open with a Halligan tool **(Figure 4.20)**.

Ventilation

Like forcible entry, ventilation performed in a professional manner can contribute to both primary and secondary loss control. As discussed earlier, effective and coordinated tactical ventilation can limit the spread of fire, heat, and smoke within a building, which can reduce primary damage. However, poorly timed or placed ventilation can increase both primary and secondary loss significantly. For example, if the initial ventilation opening cut in a roof is too small or is in the wrong location, having to enlarge the original opening or cut additional holes can delay fire extinguishment and greatly increase the costs of post-fire repairs. Also, if rafters, joists, or trusses are cut unnecessarily, the structural integrity of the roof assembly is reduced and the costs of repairs can be much greater. As in forcible entry, if windows are broken out for horizontal ventilation instead of being opened, firefighters will be unable to close the openings if necessary for ventilation control, and the cost of replacing the broken glass and window frames increases the secondary loss.

Figure 4.20 Opening walls is often necessary to locate areas of hidden fire.

Smoke Control

Firefighters should confine smoke to the smallest area possible in any way that is consistent with the IAP. For example, ventilating as close as possible to the seat of the fire helps to limit fire spread and channels smoke and heat to the outside **(Figure 4.21)**. Also, if a hallway is to be used to channel smoke to a window, the doors to the rooms that open onto the hallway should be closed first, if possible. Archways and other large wall openings without doors

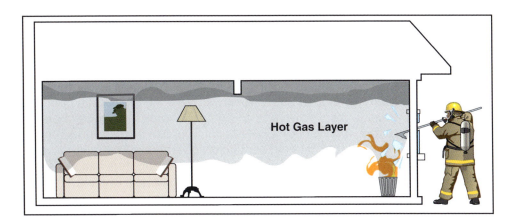

Figure 4.21 Ventilation should be performed as close as possible to the seat of the fire.

can be sealed with salvage covers or plastic sheeting. Closing interior doors and pressurizing uninvolved rooms with blowers are also effective ways to confine smoke.

Heat Removal

Another important function that truck company personnel can perform once they are inside a burning building is that of heat removal. In this context, heat removal is not done to influence fire behavior but is done to release heat from areas away from the fire and channel it to another portion of the building or to the outside.

Removing the heat from the interior of the structure as soon as possible can have several positive effects. It allows heat to escape to the outside and thereby reduces the interior temperature and makes it more tenable for both firefighters and any remaining occupants. Along with the heat, residual smoke can also be removed, which makes the atmosphere inside the building clearer and more breathable. It can also reduce the amount of heat and smoke damage to the building and its contents. The application of water-fog discharged in controlled bursts (pulses) can be used to reduce the temperature of the area. A light spray of water onto linings can also help to reduce the compartment boundary temperatures.

Once a fire has been controlled, firefighters inside the building can sometimes remove heat by placing smoke ejectors in open windows and doors or by discharging hose streams through open windows. These techniques are discussed in greater detail in the ventilation chapters. The other way that heat is removed from the interior of a building is by firefighters opening exterior windows and doors. This technique is sometimes called *vent-as-you-go*.

CAUTION
Indiscriminately opening windows throughout a building can change the ventilation profile and adversely affect fire behavior.

Lapping — Means by which fire spreads vertically from floor to floor in a multistory building. Fire issuing from a window laps up the outside of the building and enters the floor(s) above, usually through the windows.

Vent-As-You-Go

When a fire has burned for some time inside a building, especially a fire that has smoldered for hours, parts of the building well away from the seat of the fire may be charged with heat and smoke. During this time, heat and smoke were forced up open stairwells and through connecting hallways, spreading the products into adjacent areas. The products from a smoldering fire may have also been spread throughout the building by the HVAC system. In that case, virtually every room in the building may be charged with heat and smoke – even those with their hallway doors closed. Vent-as-you-go techniques can be used effectively to clear these smoke and heat-filled spaces.

To remove heat and smoke from a room with one or more exterior windows, the windows in that room can be opened to allow the heat and contaminants out after the door to the room has been shut **(Figure 4.22)**. However, heat and smoke from a fire on a lower floor could enter through the open window by a phenomenon known as **lapping**. This possibility should be ruled out before windows are opened or left open.

Removing heat and smoke from a room will facilitate the search of the room by allowing it to cool down and air out. As long as the hallway door remains closed, the open windows will not compromise positive-pressure ventilation (PPV) or other tactical ventilation operations that may be in progress. Once the room has been searched, the firefighters inside can exit the room leaving the windows open. They must close and mark the hallway door to indicate that the room has been searched.

Figure 4.22 Windows should be opened from the inside by firefighters when performing vent-as-you-go.

Salvage

One of the most effective means of reducing secondary loss in a structure fire is by performing rapid and effective **salvage** operations. Firefighters help to limit secondary loss whenever they initiate any salvage effort — simple or complex. For example, firefighters can reduce secondary loss simply by not allowing their protective clothing and equipment to soil upholstered furniture, draperies, and similar items that they handle or come in contact with inside the occupant's home or business.

If there are sufficient on-scene resources, firefighters should start salvage operations on the floor below the fire as soon it is safe to do so. In some cases, it may even be prudent to delay the fire attack long enough to allow a certain amount of salvage work to be done first. For example, if there is an attic fire above an office containing computers and associated data storage devices, files, technical illustrations, or other papers vital to the survival of the business, it may be cost-effective to delay the attack long enough for salvage covers to be spread over computer workstations, desks, drafting tables, or filing cabinets. The value of the contents in the room below can easily exceed the cost of repairing or replacing the ceiling and roof assembly. In this case, delaying the fire attack while covering the high-value contents may slightly increase the primary damage, but it can *greatly* decrease the secondary damage. Of course, any decision to delay fire attack must include consideration of the effects the fire may have on structural integrity, especially if the roof assembly incorporates trusses or other lightweight components.

In the same scenario, if the initial attack were made with **piercing nozzles** pushed up through the ceiling, the fire attack and salvage operations could be performed simultaneously **(Figure 4.23, p. 110)**. However, if this tactic were to be used from the exterior — down through the roof — the suppression effort could drive smoke and flame downward onto the firefighters performing salvage operations below. Therefore, such tactics must be used with discretion.

In structure fires, a variety of salvage operations may be required to meet secondary loss control objectives. Some of the more common loss control objectives are explained in the following text.

Salvage — Methods and operating procedures associated with fire fighting by which firefighters attempt to save property and reduce further damage from water, smoke, heat, and exposure during or immediately after a fire by removing property from a fire area, by covering it, or other means.

Piercing Nozzle — Nozzle with an angled, case-hardened steel tip that can be driven through a wall, roof, or ceiling to extinguish hidden fire.

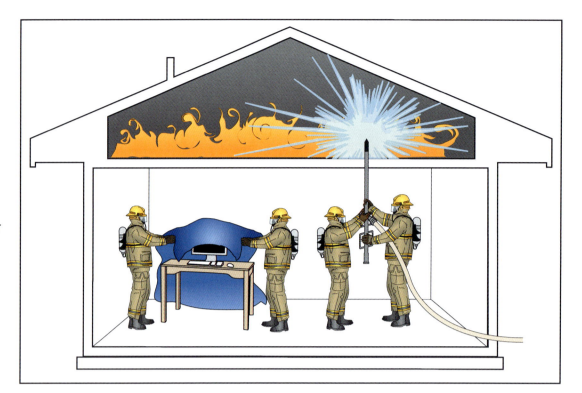

Figure 4.23 The use of piercing nozzles can allow suppression and salvage operations to occur simultaneously.

Protecting Floors and Floor Coverings

Whenever possible, firefighters should protect the floors and floor coverings between their point of entry into the structure and the fire-involved area. They can do so by using narrow canvas or plastic floor runners — sometimes called *hall runners* — in hallways and other high-traffic areas **(Figure 4.24)**. In rooms where firefighters are likely to pull the ceilings, the floors can be protected with salvage covers or plastic sheeting.

Protecting Exposed Contents

In some incidents, protecting exposed contents can be more beneficial to an occupant than extinguishing the fire. For example, if the contents are in a business office that contains vital records on computers/servers, protecting them from water, smoke, and other damage can mean the difference between the business surviving financially or going bankrupt. Such records may be contained in filing cabinets or in computer hard drives or servers **(Figure 4.25)**. In other cases, family photos and other possibly irreplaceable memorabilia should be protected if possible. The exposed contents of burning buildings can be protected in two general ways: being removed and being covered.

Removing contents. In some situations, perhaps the most effective way to protect the contents of a burning building is to remove them from danger. If the situation dictates and on-scene resources allow, firefighters wearing full PPE and SCBA can begin removing exposed contents even before the fire attack begins. The priorities for content removal are similar to those for search and rescue. Exposed property should be removed in the following order:

- That nearest the seat of the fire
- That in the most likely path of fire spread
- That on the floor above the fire

Figure 4.24 Hall runners protect floors and floor coverings in high-traffic areas.

Figure 4.25 Business hard drives and servers should be identified as a salvage priority during preincident planning.

Figure 4.26 Passing items from one firefighter to another in succession is an efficient way to remove building contents.

Obviously, combustible contents nearest the fire are the most threatened and should be removed before becoming involved. When the contents to be moved consist of many small items, firefighters can form a line similar to a bucket brigade and simply pass each item from one firefighter to the next **(Figure 4.26)**. In most cases, it will be reasonable to move contents outside of the burning building, although that may not always be possible or necessary. Similar to the areas of safe refuge to which building occupants can be moved to protect them from a fire, combustible building contents can be moved to areas unlikely to be threatened by the fire. These areas are most likely to be on a floor below the fire floor.

Based on the configuration of the fire floor, and on current and expected fire behavior, firefighters can forecast where the fire is most likely to spread. With that in mind, they can remove combustible contents to an area of safety within the building or to the outside.

Once the portable contents of the fire floor have been removed, firefighters can concentrate on saving the contents of the floor above because fires tend to spread upward. Firefighters must do everything necessary to protect their means of egress while they work because the floor above the fire is a potentially dangerous place. If possible, there should always be two widely separated

Figure 4.27 Salvage covers are a good way to protect furniture and other items.

Figure 4.28 Water flow from sprinklers should be stopped as soon as the fire is extinguished to reduce the amount of secondary damage.

Compressed Air Foam System (CAFS) — Generic term used to describe a high-energy foam-generation system consisting of an air compressor (or other air source), a water pump, and foam solution that injects air into the foam solution before it enters a hoseline.

exit locations. In addition, because firefighters will be focused on their assignments, a crew with a charged hoseline should be assigned to monitor and protect the primary exit.

Covering contents. In many cases, it may neither be practical nor even possible to remove some building contents. Some exposed contents will be too numerous, too bulky, or too heavy for the available firefighters to move. In fact, contents such as industrial machinery may be bolted down. In these cases, the best option for firefighters may be to cover the items to protect them from water and smoke damage.

The most common way for firefighters to protect furniture and other items is with salvage covers **(Figure 4.27)**. Firefighters can use the techniques described in **Essentials** to cover these contents. In offices, retail shops, and similar occupancies, rows of desks or tables can be covered with plastic film. With the film contained on a roll and a pike pole handle inserted through the roll, two firefighters can quickly cover rows of desks or tables by walking down parallel aisles.

Water Control

Another means of reducing secondary loss is by training hose crews to apply water judiciously, namely, they should use only as much water as necessary to extinguish the fire and no more. As mentioned earlier, stopping the flow of water from open sprinklers as soon as the fire is controlled also reduces secondary damage **(Figure 4.28)**. In addition, some departments use only 100 foot (30 m) lengths of hose inside of buildings to reduce the number of couplings from which water may leak.

After a fire has been knocked down, placing a leaking nozzle out a window can also reduce water damage. Class A foam applied with **compressed air foam systems (CAFS)** or with conventional attack lines can also reduce secondary loss. When properly applied, Class A foam reduces the amount of water needed for extinguishment. This in turn results in decreased water damage.

Some materials can absorb moisture from the air in the humid environment created when the heat of a fire turns the water from hoselines or sprinklers to steam. Absorbing water from the floor or the air can cause some materials to expand enough to crack the walls of the room in which they are confined. This can potentially lead to structural collapse if structural members such as load-bearing walls are damaged by this expansion. In other situations, water absorbed by materials at the bottom of a tall stack can cause the entire stack to lose stability and topple over. If the stacked materials happen to be rolls of newsprint that can weigh more than 2,500 pounds (1.58 t) each, such a collapse could be lethal for firefighters nearby **(Figure 4.29)**.

Figure 4.29 Newsprint and other absorbent stacked materials pose a serious danger to firefighters.

Water Removal

Water used to extinguish an interior structure fire can do significant damage if it is absorbed by building contents packaged in cardboard boxes or other absorbent material. Absorbed water, and that accumulating on the floor, can add a tremendous amount of weight to a structure. For example, a building measuring 50×100 feet (15 m by 30 m) with an accumulation of water 6 inches (150 mm) deep on an upper floor requires the structure to support an additional 78 tons (71 t) of weight. If that water is not removed through floor drains and scuppers or is not channeled down stairways, it can threaten the structural integrity of the building. Therefore, another important salvage-related function of truck company personnel inside a burning building is to remove the accumulated water as quickly and efficiently as possible. There are a number of proven techniques for this purpose that may involve the following:

- Wiping water from horizontal surfaces
- Constructing water chutes and catch basins
- Using mops, squeegees, scoop shovels, or water vacuums to remove water from floors
- Using portable pumps to evacuate water from basements and other low areas
- Breaching exterior walls to create improvised scuppers
- Removing toilets to allow water to drain into the sewer system

Figure 4.30 Squeegees are a good tool to use when removing excess water.

Assuming that no more water is being added, water that has accumulated on the floor of a burning building can sometimes be removed by simply using brooms or squeegees to push the water toward open floor drains or open stairways **(Figure 4.30)**. In other cases, toilets can be removed from the floor to allow water to drain down the sanitary sewer. If these techniques are not successful, it may be necessary to build a chute on the floor below and drill or cut a large hole in the ceiling to drain the water into the chute and out an exterior window. For more information on the construction of water chutes, refer to Chapter 5, Ground Ladders.

A situation in which an accumulation of water may not threaten the structural integrity of the building, but is no less intolerable, is when a basement or other subsurface area has been flooded. These situations can render a building untenable by shorting out electrical service to the entire building, by extinguishing pilot lights in central heating units, or by becoming contaminated with untreated sewage. As long as the water accumulation has not become contaminated with sewage, ignitable liquids, or other hazardous materials, truck company personnel may be assigned to remove the accumulation. The usual means of removing this water is by using a portable auxiliary pump to direct the water into the nearest storm drain.

While removal of water from the structure is important, firefighters must be careful not to discharge water that is contaminated with toxins or other hazardous materials into public sewers, storm drains, or bodies of water. The runoff water from virtually every structure fire may be contaminated to some degree, but seriously contaminated water must be contained until it can be decontaminated or removed for proper disposal. Contaminated water can be temporarily contained in catch basins, ditches, or other low areas that have been properly dammed or diked.

The potential for contaminated runoff from a fire in a particular occupancy should be determined during preincident planning surveys and appropriate mitigation plans developed. The state or provincial Environmental Protection Agency (EPA) and local health departments should be consulted when developing these plans. The plans should also include benchmarks for when these agencies should be called to a fire scene.

Post-Incident Loss Control Operations

Loss control operations should continue after a structure fire has been extinguished. These post-fire operations may take two forms — *economic* loss control and *psychological* loss control. It is important for firefighters to deal with both forms of loss.

Economic Loss Control

To reduce economic losses from fires, firefighters should salvage as much of the occupant's property as possible while overhauling the fire. Before they leave the scene, firefighters should properly secure the building to prevent possible looting, vandalism, or damage from inclement weather.

During overhaul, any cash or other valuables such as checkbooks, credit cards, stock certificates, professional credentials, jewelry, computers, or firearms that are found should be turned over to the IC or law enforcement. Photo albums, videotapes, personal collections, trophies, awards, and other items that may have sentimental value to the owner/occupant should be placed in a protected area. Some departments provide the owner/occupant with cardboard boxes and packing material to make protecting salvaged items easier. Some also make a videotape of the scene after overhaul is completed to record damage to the building's contents, which can greatly assist the owner/occupant in filing insurance claims.

After salvage and overhaul operations have been completed, but before firefighters leave the scene, the fire-damaged building should be properly secured. Securing a building may involve covering ventilation holes in the roof with plywood or oriented strand board (OSB), salvage covers, or plastic sheeting to prevent additional damage from the elements **(Figure 4.31)**. Securing the building may also involve boarding up open doorways and window openings to discourage trespassers **(Figure 4.32)**. In some areas, commercial post-fire restoration companies will secure fire-damaged properties. Firefighters may also set up a rekindle detector as described earlier or post a fire watch.

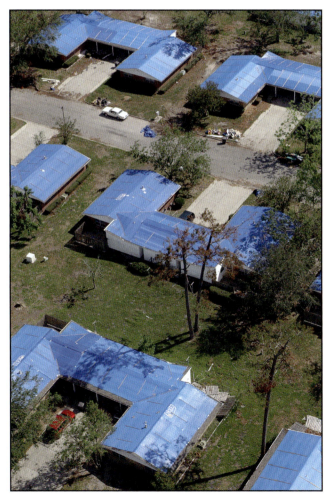

Figure 4.31 Tarps are often used after fires and in disaster areas to provide temporary protection. *Courtesy of FEMA.*

Figure 4.32 Boarding up open windows and doors helps to deter theft.

Chapter 4 • Loss Control **115**

Figure 4.33 Temporary chain link fences are often necessary at fire scenes to prevent unauthorized access.

The building owner/occupant may be required to secure the entire property if there are potential hazards in or around the building, such as downed electrical wires, fire-weakened structural components that could collapse, or holes in floors into which someone could fall. Securing the property may involve installing a temporary chain link fence, posting a security guard, or both **(Figure 4.33)**. If hazardous conditions exist, firefighters should make the owner/occupant aware of them by conducting a tour of the property if safety allows, or by providing the owner/occupant with a written description of the hazardous conditions. The property should not be released to the owner/occupant until he or she has signed a receipt or other form of documentation. The release document should include any instructions to the owner/occupant covering safety guidelines as appropriate.

Psychological Loss Control

As a result of the fire, the property owner/occupant may have lost irreplaceable mementos, important records and documents, a family pet, or — worst of all — a family member, friend, employee, or coworker. Firefighters need to be sensitive to the psychological trauma that property owner/occupants may have suffered, even if it is not apparent from their demeanor. With a departmental commitment to support customer service and loss control, firefighters can reduce the psychological impact of the fire on the occupant.

One of the first things firefighters can do to reduce psychological fire loss is to use discretion about where they deposit debris during overhaul. If possible, firefighters should place burned materials in a location that is not in full view of the owner/occupant or spectators. Another thing firefighters can do is refer the victims to individuals and agencies (Red Cross, Salvation Army, etc.) providing counseling and other services to help fire victims get their lives back to normal.

Recognizing the importance of these services, some departments have formalized the process in various ways. For example, a number of fire departments have developed booklets that serve as after-the-fire guides for those who have experienced a structure fire. These guides contain the telephone numbers of local relief agencies and a brief description of the types of services each provides. The guides can help the owner/occupants arrange for temporary housing, if that is needed, or any of a wide variety of other services. While the guides contain local information, most are based upon the FEMA booklet entitled *After the Fire! Returning to Normal*, published by the U.S. Fire Administration **(Figure 4.34)**.

Fire departments can also reduce psychological losses by taking an active role in helping fire victims cope with this significant disruption of their lives and/or livelihoods. This assistance can be as basic as providing shelter and security at the scene. It can also involve notifying friends or family of the situation, providing a cell phone with which the victims can contact sources of support, and/or transporting them to temporary housing. Some departments have on-call chaplains who can come to the scene and assist fire victims in coping with their losses.

Figure 4.34 *After the Fire! Returning to Normal* is a free publication from the U.S. Fire Administration and is a good resource for those who have suffered a fire loss.

> **Loss Control Scenario:**
>
> A fire is burning vigorously in the cockloft above a small two-story office building of Type III construction. The top floor is occupied by an architectural firm and the ground floor by a retail office supply store. As other firefighters set up lines for an interior attack, you and your company are ordered to salvage the interior.
>
> - When would you begin salvage operations?
> - Where would you start?
> - What would be the highest priority?
> - What tools and equipment would you use?
> - What methods could be used to remove accumulated water?

Summary

For both humanitarian and political reasons, a fire department should do anything reasonable to reduce the amount of loss suffered by the victims of a fire. Publicly funded fire departments have a legal and moral responsibility to protect their citizens from preventable fire losses. This means that fire departments should develop preincident plans for fireground loss control and train and equip their firefighters to conduct fireground operations in the most efficient and least destructive ways possible. Forcible entry, fire attack, ventilation, salvage, and overhaul operations should all be performed with both safety and loss control in mind. Politically, reducing both primary and secondary losses from structure fires can result in increased public support for the fire department. Public support can translate into increased funding for the department.

Regardless of what forms of loss control and victim support the department provides, the reductions in economic and psychological losses and the resulting increase in public goodwill toward the department make these efforts critically important.

Review Questions

1. What is the purpose of fireground loss control?
2. What is the difference between primary and secondary damage?
3. What are the three purposes of a preincident planning survey?
4. What are the various procedures that can be used to control primary damage?
5. What are the various procedures that can be used to control secondary damage?
6. What procedures are used to remove heat from the interior of a building?
7. What salvage procedures are used to assist fire attack?
8. What procedures are used to protect exposed contents in a building during fireground operations?

Ground Ladders

Chapter Contents

CASE HISTORY 123	**Nonstandard Uses for Ground Ladders**....139
Ground Ladder Selection and Handling ...124	Mechanical Advantage Systems................140
Ladder Selection......................................125	Positioning Intake Strainers.....................140
Ladder Handling......................................126	Water Removal..141
Ladder Raises..127	Bridging...142
Positioning Ground Ladders....................135	**Summary**..144
Tactical Use of Ground Ladders............136	**Review Questions**............................144
Access..136	
Rescue..138	
Ventilation..138	

chapter 5

Key Terms

Butt	126
Fly Section	128
Pole Ladder	128
Spurs	129
Staypoles	128

Ground Ladders

Learning Objectives

After reading this chapter, students will be able to:

1. Describe the critical factors considered when selecting a ground ladder for fireground operations.
2. Describe the procedure for raising a pole ladder using four (4) firefighters.
3. Summarize the factors affecting the placement of ground ladders during fireground operations.
4. Describe the tactical uses for ground ladders during fireground operations.
5. Describe nonstandard uses for ground ladders.

Safety Points

While reading this chapter, keep the following safety points in mind:

- Use enough personnel to safely handle the ladder selected.
- Use proper body mechanics and ladder handling techniques.
- Check for electrical wires and other overhead obstructions before raising any ladder.
- Watch for falling glass and other debris when positioning ladders.
- Ensure that the base is stable before starting to raise a ladder.
- Ensure that the ladder can be leaned against a stable surface.
- Ensure that ladders are tied in or otherwise secured before climbing them.
- Extend ladders 3 to 5 rungs above parapet walls and roof eaves.
- Extend ladders a maximum of one foot above metal railings.
- Tie ladders to secure anchor points to prevent unwanted movement.
- Maintain adequate spacing between firefighters to avoid overloading ladders.
- Always sound the roof before stepping off a ladder.
- DO NOT use ground ladders to break windows.
- DO NOT position ground ladders over window or doorway openings where flames could impinge on the ladder.

Chapter 5
Ground Ladders

In 1999, a California firefighter was seriously injured when the unsecured base of a ladder he was on slid away from the wall of a burning building. The 24-foot (7.3 m) straight ladder had originally been leaned against the top of an 18-foot (5.5 m) wall but was later moved to a wall section that was only about 13 feet (4 m) high. In the second location, nearly half of the ladder's length was above the point of contact with the wall. When the firefighter climbed the ladder and leaned forward to place a chain saw onto the roof, the base of the ladder slipped and skidded away from the building. The spurs of the ladder caught in a crack in the pavement and abruptly stopped the skid. The abrupt stop threw the firefighter off the ladder onto the pavement below.

As this case history shows, a situational change on the fireground may necessitate a change in the tools and equipment used. It also shows how important it is that ground ladders be properly secured when firefighters are on them. This chapter discusses these and other critical factors in the safe and effective use of fire service ground ladders.

Many truck company activities involve the use of ground ladders. In a structure fire incident, ground ladders may be needed for any or all of the following:

- Gaining access to the outside of a burning building
- Reaching lockboxes to facilitate rapid and nondestructive entry
- Reaching windows to facilitate entry, horizontal ventilation, or rescues
- Accessing the roofs of some structures for vertical ventilation

In many cases, the use of ground ladders on the fireground can be made much more efficient during an incident if the ladders that might be needed for a given building are identified during preincident planning **(Figure 5.1, p. 124)**. Knowing in advance which ground ladders will be needed in a given location allows firefighters to remove those ladders from the apparatus and take them to the point of application initially. This saves the time that would be needed to determine the ladder requirements and then return to the apparatus to obtain the ladders needed.

Figure 5.1 Knowing which ladders are needed for a particular structure can make fireground operations much more efficient. *Courtesy of Bob Esposito.*

To be fully functional when needed, fire service ground ladders must be properly maintained and tested regularly. For firefighters to function both safely and effectively in truck company operations where ladders are used, they must master all of the individual ladder skills described in **Essentials**. They must also master various ladder skills as a member of a team, including the techniques specified in their departmental SOPs on ground ladders. To perform these ladder evolutions when needed, firefighters must be physically fit — with special emphasis on upper body strength — and employ proper body mechanics and ladder handling techniques.

Ground Ladder Selection and Handling

A wide variety of ground ladders are used by the fire service in North America. The following are the most common types of ground ladders currently in use:

- Single (straight) ladders
- Roof ladders **(Figure 5.2)**
- Folding (attic) ladders
- Extension ladders
- Combination ladders

Figure 5.2 Roof ladders have hooks that can be deployed for stability.

To be of maximum usefulness on the fireground, ladders must be fully functional and in good repair. To ensure that ladders are safe to use when needed, firefighters must follow the maintenance procedures recommended by the ladder manufacturer, as prescribed in departmental SOPs, and as specified in NFPA® 1932, *Standard on Use, Maintenance, and Service Testing of In-Service Fire Department Ground Ladders*.

Ladder Selection

Selecting and using ground ladders in a safe, timely, and effective manner is an integral part of a coordinated attack on a structure fire. Unless the situation dictates otherwise, the longest ground ladder on scene should be deployed first, then the next longest, etc. Prior to selecting and positioning ground ladders, a number of factors should be considered. The most critical factors are:

- Primary objective (rescue, window, or roof access)
- Fire size and location
- Current and expected fire behavior

As mentioned earlier, selecting the most appropriate ladder for a given building can be made much easier if all of the ladders that might be needed for a fire in that building have been identified ahead of time during pre-incident planning. Ladder selection on the fireground may be limited by the inventory of ladders carried on department apparatus. Even in the best-equipped department, newer apparatus with a full complement of the latest ladders may be temporarily out-of-service and older units with smaller or older ladder inventories may be all that are on scene at a given incident. To operate with maximum safety and effectiveness, firefighters need to be proficient with *all* the ground ladders carried on all apparatus in their departments. In addition, if they regularly or even occasionally operate with mutual aid units, they need to be proficient with the ladders carried on the mutual aid apparatus as well.

Through a combination of training and experience, it is also important for firefighters to develop a sense of the *effective length* of various ground ladders. The effective length of a ladder is always shorter than its actual length because of the safe climbing and working angle. Firefighters should develop an awareness of how many vertical feet (meters) each size of ladder will reach when positioned at the ideal climbing angle. As discussed in **Essentials**, the ideal climbing angle for ground ladders is 75 degrees from horizontal **(Figure 5.3)** There may be situations in which overhangs or other obstructions force firefighters to position ground ladders at less than the ideal climbing angle. At these angles, ladders are put under extraordinary stress and firefighters must be especially careful not to overload them. A lower climbing angle also increases the potential for the ladder spurs to slide away from the building when positioned on concrete or other hard surfaces. At angles less than 75 degrees, the distance between personnel on the ladder

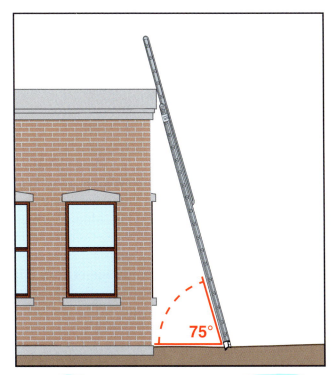

Figure 5.3 The ideal climbing angle for ground ladders is 75 degrees from horizontal.

should be increased. In other situations, such as in narrow alleys or separations between buildings, firefighters may be forced to position ground ladders at angles steeper than ideal. At these angles, ladders are less stable and are more likely to pull away from the point of contact.

> ⚠ To prevent unwanted movement of ladders set at steep angles, firefighters must tie or otherwise secure them in place.

Likewise, it is important for firefighters to develop a sense of how far from a building the **butt** or base of the ladder must be placed to create the ideal climbing angle. As also discussed in **Essentials**, the proper distance can be determined by dividing the used length of the ladder by four. The used length of a ladder in position is the vertical distance above the ground where the ladder contacts the building — not the full length of the ladder.

Butt —Heel (lower end) of a ladder.

> ⚠ The ladder selected must not only be long enough to reach the objective at a safe climbing angle, but must also extend three to five rungs above any parapet or roof eave.

Ladder Handling

To avoid or limit injuries when handling ground ladders, firefighters must have sufficient upper body strength and flexibility, and use proper body mechanics and ladder handling techniques. On ladders requiring more than one firefighter, working together as a team is critical to firefighter safety. While most fire service ground ladders require similar handling techniques, each type and size has certain unique handling characteristics. Therefore, the keys to safe and effective ladder handling are fitness, technique, and practice – both individually and as a team.

Fitness

The time that firefighters invest in weight training and practicing ladder handling techniques will pay dividends on the fireground in terms of injury avoidance and ladder handling efficiency. Firefighters are trained to lift with their legs instead of their backs, and it is important that they do so when lifting ladders from apparatus or the ground. However, while it is important for firefighters to develop and maintain their overall physical fitness, most of the physical strength required when handling fire service ground ladders is in the upper body **(Figure 5.4)**. To develop and maintain sufficient upper body strength, firefighters must participate in a weight training program with elements for the following:

- Hands (grip strength)
- Arms (lifting, pushing/pulling)
- Shoulders (overhead lifting, pushing/pulling)
- Upper and lower back (overall stability)

While physical strength is imperative, it is equally important that personnel handling ground ladders have good hand/eye coordination and good depth perception. Hand/eye coordination is needed when raising and extending ladders. Depth perception is critical when calculating required ladder length and when positioning ladders.

Any firefighter fitness program should meet the requirements of the applicable NFPA® standards. The most relevant fitness-related standards are NFPA® 1500, *Standard on Fire Department Occupational Safety and Health Program* and NFPA® 1583, *Standard on Health-Related Fitness Programs for Fire Department Members.*

Technique

The specific techniques that firefighters use to lift, carry, raise, and position fire service ground ladders should be consistent with those discussed and illustrated in **Essentials**. However, based on local conditions, some departments may choose to develop different techniques for handling certain types of ladders in particular situations. Firefighters should always follow their departmental SOPs.

Figure 5.4 Adequate upper body strength is needed to properly handle ground ladders.

If a fire department chooses to use a nonstandard technique for handling ladders, the technique should be thoroughly tested under controlled circumstances before being used on the fireground. If the technique proves to be both safe and effective in testing, it should be included in an SOP and everyone who is affected by it trained on its use. Those most directly affected should be given a sufficient amount of hands-on training to become proficient in deployment during emergency operations.

Practice

Regardless of whether firefighters are using new ladder handling techniques or recognized techniques, they should be given thorough initial training and frequent refresher training so that mastery is achieved and individual and team skills are maintained. Experience has shown that firefighters need relatively frequent practice on those skills at which a high level of mastery in required, but are needed infrequently in the field **(Figure 5.5, p. 128)**. Likewise, they need less practice on the skills that they use frequently on actual incidents.

Ladder Raises

To be both safe and effective when handling fire service ground ladders, firefighters must master all of the raises described in **Essentials** and any others that may be used locally. Some of these raises are intended to be used by individual firefighters, but others are team operations requiring two or more firefighters. The following single-ladder and extension-ladder raises are described and illustrated in **Essentials**:

- Single firefighter raises
- Two-firefighter raises
- Three-firefighter raises
- Four-firefighter raises

Figure 5.5 Frequent practice with ground ladder deployment will make the task easier under stressful conditions on scene. *Courtesy of Dave Coombs.*

Firefighters should refer to **Essentials** for the techniques involved in handling the listed ground ladders. However, the four-firefighter raises do not include pole ladders. Therefore, these techniques are included here.

Pole Ladder Raises

Pole ladders are equipped with **staypoles** (sometimes called *tormentor poles*) for added stability **(Figure 5.6)**. The staypoles are used to assist in lifting the ladder vertically and in leaning the ladder into the building. When the ladder is in the vertical position and the **fly section** is being extended or retracted, the staypoles

Figure 5.6 Staypoles give added stability to pole ladders.

also provide lateral stability. Because of their length and weight, closely coordinated teamwork is required to raise pole ladders safely and efficiently.

When five or six firefighters are available to raise a pole ladder, it may be performed either perpendicular (at a right angle) or parallel to the building. When only four firefighters are available to raise a pole ladder, the operation must be performed perpendicular to the building. The perpendicular technique is preferred because it eliminates the need for a 90-degree pivot of the

> **Pole Ladder** — Large extension ladder that requires tormentor poles to steady the ladder as it is raised and lowered. Also called Bangor Ladder.
>
> **Staypoles** — Poles attached to long extension ladders to assist in raising and steadying the ladder. Some poles are permanently attached, and some are removable. Also called Tormentor Poles.
>
> **Fly Section** — Extendable section of ground extension or aerial ladder.

ladder that is required when it is raised parallel to a building. As the ladder is being pivoted, the staypoles must be repositioned and stability is somewhat reduced during this maneuver.

A minimum of four firefighters are required to raise a pole ladder, but adding a fifth or sixth firefighter to the team increases both safety and efficiency. However, on any given incident there may only be four firefighters available. Therefore, because the number of firefighters involved does not change the steps in the procedure, only the four-fighter raise is detailed here.

Unattached staypoles. Current NFPA® requirements for pole ladder design dictate that staypoles be permanently attached to the beams of the ladder. However, pole ladders with detachable poles may still be in service. In these instances, follow departmental SOPs with regard to pole attachment.

Four-firefighter pole ladder raise. Most pole ladders currently in service have the poles permanently attached to the ladder beams. The following procedure assumes that to be the case:

Step 1: The ladder is placed flat on the pavement (fly up) with the butt spurs nearly touching the building **(Figure 5.7)**.

(**NOTE:** If the ladder needs to be turned over to position the fly out, it should be done at this point.)

Step 2: Place the butt of the ladder against the building.

Step 3: The firefighters at the tip walk about 10 feet (3 m) away from the ladder tip and turn toward the building to receive the poles.

Step 4: The firefighters at the butt unlatch the **spur** end of the staypoles and pick them up **(Figure 5.8)**.

Spurs — Metal points at the end of a ladder or staypoles.

Step 5: The firefighters with the poles walk toward the tip of the ladder, raising the poles hand-over-hand as they go **(Figure 5.9)** and continually check for overhead obstructions.

Step 6: The staypoles are brought to the vertical and then lowered toward the two waiting firefighters **(Figure 5.10)**.

Step 7: When the firefighters assigned to the poles have control of them, the other firefighters turn around, estimate the height where the ladder will contact the building, and calculate how far the butt of the ladder will need to be from the building. They then position themselves at the tip of the ladder **(Figure 5.11)**.

Step 8: The firefighters at the tip of the ladder simultaneously lift it, pivot under the nearest beam, and face the building **(Figure 5.12)**.

Step 9: The firefighters lift the ladder hand-over-hand as they walk toward the building, and as soon as the angle permits, the firefighters on the staypoles assist by pushing the ladder tip upward **(Figure 5.13)**.

Step 10: The raise is continued until the ladder is vertical against the building **(Figure 5.14)**.

Step 11: The firefighters at the butt grasp a low rung (palm up), and with the other hand, grasp a rung above their heads (palm down).

Chapter 5 • Ground Ladders 131

Step 12: The firefighters lift the ladder and move the butt the required distance away from the base of the building **(Figure 5.15)**.

Step 13: With the firefighters at the butt footing the ladder, the firefighters on the staypoles pull the tip of the ladder into a vertical position away from the building **(Figure 5.16)**.

Step 14: The firefighters on the staypoles reposition themselves at right angles to the ladder for increased lateral stability **(Figure 5.17)**. They call out to each other to either push or pull on their poles to maintain the ladder in a vertical position.

Step 15: One of the two firefighters moves into position to foot the ladder.

Step 16: One firefighter foots the ladder while the other pulls on the halyard to extend the fly. The firefighter on the staypole in front of the ladder determines when the ladder tip is at the desired height **(Figure 5.18)**.

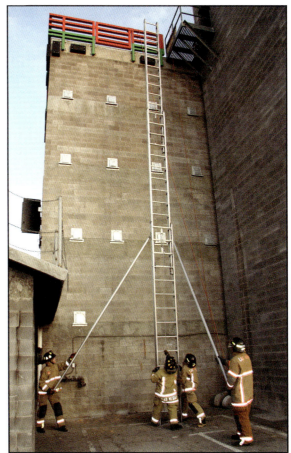

Chapter 5 • Ground Ladders **133**

Step 17: The firefighters on the staypoles reposition themselves on either side of the ladder and it is gently lowered into position **(Figure 5.19)**.

Step 18: The firefighters on the staypoles walk the ends of the poles to the base of the building **(Figure 5.20)**.

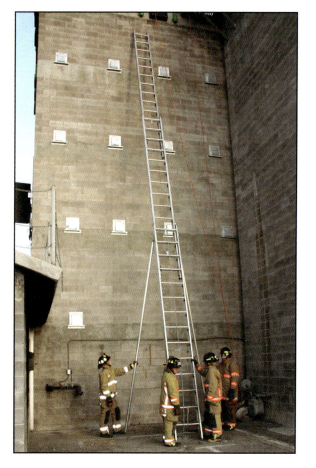

CAUTION

The staypoles must not be wedged into place. They are not designed to support the weight of the ladder and occupants, but merely to increase lateral stability.

134 Chapter 5 • Ground Ladders

Positioning Ground Ladders

Deciding where to place a ground ladder during a fire fighting operation is usually, but not always, the responsibility of the officer in charge. Under some circumstances, the senior firefighter on the ladder team may make that decision. To help with that decision, the following guidelines are provided.

Factors Affecting Ground Ladder Placement

Numerous factors dictate where to position a ladder. If a ladder is to be used for positioning a firefighter to break a window for ventilation, it should be placed alongside the window to the windward (upwind) side **(Figure 5.21)**. The tip should be even with the upper portion of the window. The same position can be used when firefighters need to climb in or out of narrow windows or direct hose streams into them.

If a ladder is to be used for entry or rescue through a window, the ladder tip is usually placed on the mid-line of the window slightly below the sill **(Figure 5.22)**. If the sill projects out from the wall, the tip of the ladder can sometimes be wedged under it for additional stability. If the window opening is wide enough to permit the ladder tip to project into it and still allow room beside it to facilitate entry/exit and rescue, the ladder can be placed so that it extends two or three rungs into the window opening **(Figure 5.23)**.

Figure 5.22 Ladders positioned for rescue should be placed mid-line with the window and slightly below the sill.

These are not the only ladder placement considerations, however. Other ladder placement guidelines include the following:

- Ladder at least two points on different sides of a building for roof access/egress.
- Avoid placing ladders over door or window openings where they may be exposed to flames or excessive heat.
- Place ladders at building strong points (such as the corners) when possible.

Figure 5.21 Ladders positioned for ventilation should be placed on the windward side of the window.

Figure 5.23 The ladder tip can extend a few rungs into the window if the window is wide enough to allow entry and exit.

- Place the ladder directly in front of the window when it is to be used as a support for a smoke ejector removing cold smoke after a fire has been extinguished. Place the ladder tip on the wall above the window opening.
- Avoid placing ladders where they may come into contact with overhead obstructions such as wires, tree limbs, or signs.
- Avoid placing ladders on uneven or soft surfaces.
- Avoid placing ladders in front of doors or other paths of travel that firefighters or evacuees will need to use.
- Avoid placing ladders on icy sidewalks or over trapdoors or deadlights.
- Do not place ladders against unstable walls or surfaces.
- Communicate ladder locations to interior crews so they can be used for emergency egress if necessary.

Tactical Use of Ground Ladders

As mentioned earlier in this chapter, ground ladders have a variety of uses on the fireground. The following sections discuss some of those applications.

Access

There are a number of ways in which ground ladders can be used for access on the fireground. The following are brief descriptions of ways to gain access.

Access to Buildings

Ground ladders are sometimes needed to gain access to the outside of burning buildings. Many residential and industrial occupancies are surrounded by fences. These fences are often topped with barbed wire or razor ribbon to discourage trespassers **(Figure 5.24)**. A growing number of residential communities and even individual residences are surrounded by stone or masonry walls, wrought iron fences, or combinations thereof **(Figure 5.25)**.

In most cases, access can be gained by opening gates in fences or walls. However, when gate openings are not sufficiently large or when access is needed from a number of directions, firefighters must either breach the barriers or

Figure 5.24 Security measures can make access to a structure difficult.

Figure 5.25 Masonry perimeter walls are common features of larger residences and gated communities.

Figure 5.26 A-frame ladders can be deployed over some fences to allow access.

Figure 5.27 Straight ladders can be lashed together at the top of a fence or wall.

find ways to get over them. When it would be faster and easier to cross over the barriers than breach them, which is usually the case, ground ladders are often the most effective means of doing so. In some cases, A-frame or combination ladders can be used **(Figure 5.26)**. In other cases, two straight ladders can be used — one on either side — lashed together where they intersect at the top of the fence or wall **(Figure 5.27)**.

Access into Structures

As will be discussed in Chapter 9, gaining access to the interior of an unoccupied building can sometimes be difficult, time-consuming, and destructive to the property that firefighters are trying to protect. Using a ladder to reach a lockbox and obtain a key or access code to the door of the building saves time, is easier than forcing entry, and is nondestructive **(Figure 5.28)**. Ground ladders are often the best means of reaching windows that must be opened or broken out to gain entry into the building or for rescue or horizontal ventilation.

Roof Access

While vertical ventilation is not the only reason for using ladders to access the roof of a burning building, it is the most frequent. Other reasons for using ladders to access roofs are the following:

- Performing rescues from rooftops
- Checking for spot fires started by embers carried aloft from another fire

Figure 5.28 The use of a ground ladder may be necessary to gain access to a lockbox.

- Protecting the structure from fire in an adjacent building
- Gaining a height advantage when applying water to a fire in an adjacent building

Secondary Egress

In addition to providing a means for access, ladders can also serve as a means of secondary egress from a building involved in fire. Ladders should be placed to upper floors and the roof not only to provide access, but also to provide a secondary means of egress if the primary egress route is blocked by rapid fire progress or collapse.

Rescue

Ground ladders can be used in a variety of ways to facilitate rescue operations on the fireground. When occupants are trapped inside burning buildings, they may need to be assisted or carried up or down a ladder. As described and illustrated in **Essentials**, a number of ladder-based rescue techniques can be used. In general, ladders are used to rescue victims who are located above or below grade.

Above-Grade Ladder Rescues

Rescuing people trapped on floors above the ground floor, or in other elevated locations, are the most common situations in which ground ladders are used for rescue. As described and illustrated in **Essentials**, there are one-, two-, and three-firefighter methods of assisting conscious victims and carrying unconscious victims down fire service ground ladders **(Figure 5.29)**.

Below-Grade Ladder Rescues

Fireground rescues of people trapped below grade are far fewer in number than those above grade. Because these incidents occur infrequently, firefighters need to train for them more often to maintain their skills. Below-grade rescues can be even more challenging than those above grade because of the added dangers associated with possible atmospheres that will not support life. Among these possibilities are oxygen deficiencies, which are not uncommon below grade, as well as accumulations of toxic gases that are heavier than air. Any of these situations may change a rescue to a recovery operation.

Ventilation

As mentioned earlier, some of the most frequent uses for ladders on the fireground are to help firefighters reach locations where ventilation openings are needed. Ground ladders may be needed for both horizontal and vertical ventilation.

Horizontal Ventilation

Because the majority of windows in buildings are above ground level, firefighters usually need ladders to reach windows that need to be opened for horizontal ventilation **(Figure 5.30)**. As will be discussed in Chapter 12, the tools and techniques described in

Figure 5.29 There are numerous techniques for using ground ladders to rescue victims.

Figure 5.30 Ladders are typically needed for horizontal ventilation on upper floors. *Courtesy of District Chief Chris Mickal, NOFD Photo Unit.*

Figure 5.31 Below-grade window wells that do not have protective barriers will need ground ladders deployed to prevent injuries to personnel.

Essentials should be used when firefighters need to open windows for horizontal ventilation. Even with ground-level windows, ladders must often be placed across window openings as a safety barrier to prevent people from falling into the window openings **(Figure 5.31)**.

Vertical Ventilation

Ground ladders will often be needed to reach the roof of a burning building to create openings for vertical ventilation. In the absence of an aerial device, ground ladders are the primary means of gaining access to the roof of structures up to four stories in height **(Figure 5.32)**. As will be discussed in Chapter 13, vertical ventilation is one of the major tasks of truck companies. Creating a ventilation opening in the roof of a burning building is often the safest way to mitigate potential backdraft conditions and may prevent a flashover from occurring. Allowing products of combustion to vent to the atmosphere through a roof opening can greatly reduce the amount of heat and smoke with which interior crews must contend. The tools and techniques described in ***Essentials*** should be used when creating ventilation openings in roofs.

Nonstandard Uses for Ground Ladders

Fires and other emergencies are initially *uncontrolled situations* and it is virtually impossible to anticipate and plan for every possible contingency in every incident. Therefore, firefighters and their officers must sometimes handle situations that are not addressed in any departmental SOP. In short, they must analyze the situation at hand and devise a unique but safe and

Figure 5.32 Ground ladders are commonly used for roof access and egress if an aerial device is not available.

effective way of dealing with it. This often requires using standard tools and equipment in nonstandard ways. Nonstandard uses of ladders are those that do not involve climbing up or down the ladder.

NOTE: Firefighters should be aware that using any tool or piece of equipment in a way other than that for which it was designed may void any warranties by the manufacturer. Firefighters must always follow any departmental SOPs on nonstandard uses of tools and equipment.

While not preferable, after performing a risk/benefit analysis of the situation, using a ladder in a nonstandard way may be justified if a life could be saved or significant property protected. Some nonstandard uses for fire service ground ladders include mechanical advantage systems, positioning intake strainers, water removal, and bridging.

Mechanical Advantage Systems

While there are other possible uses of ladders in mechanical advantage systems, the most common application is in lowering injured victims from points above grade **(Figure 5.33)**. The steps involved in setting up and using a system through a window are as follows:

Step 1: Raise a ground ladder to a point just above the window as if a hoseline were to be operated from the ladder.

Step 2: A full turn in the haul rope is taken around the bottom rung of the ladder and the working end is passed up the underside of the ladder.

Step 3: Near the window sill level, the working end of the haul rope is passed back through the rungs and over the rung nearest the top of the window opening.

Step 5: The working end of the haul rope is passed through the window opening and tied to the litter harness.

Step 6: Two guidelines are attached to opposite ends of the litter and dropped from the window opening to the ground.

Step 8: With firefighters on the ground tending the guidelines and the haul rope, the litter is lifted through the window opening and is slowly lowered to the ground.

Positioning Intake Strainers

When drafting water from a static (nonpressurized) source such as a pond or lake, it is important to maintain 24 inches (600 mm) between the intake strainer and the bottom of the water source. A roof ladder or other single ladder can be used for this purpose.

With an intake hose connected to the pump, the intake strainer can be positioned using the following steps:

Step 1: Select a ladder that will reach from the drafting site to the bottom of the water source (keeping in mind the angle of the ladder and where it can be placed to meet the 2-foot (.6 m) requirement).

Step 2: Slip the free end of the intake hose (with strainer attached) between two lower rungs of the ladder.

Step 3: Lower the butt of the ladder into the water until it rests on the bottom. This tilts the strainer toward the horizontal and keeps it off the bottom **(Figure 5.34, p. 142)**.

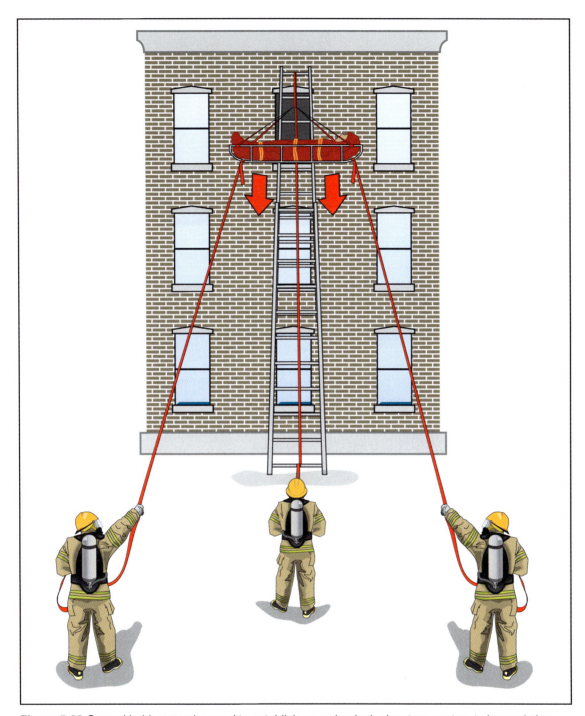

Figure 5.33 Ground ladders can be used to establish a mechanical advantage system to lower victims from upper stories.

Water Removal

Ladders can also be used to aid in the removal of accumulated water from buildings. The water may be from hoselines used during both fire attack and overhaul operations. It may also be from open sprinklers or leaking pipes. Regardless of the source of the water, as discussed in the chapter on loss control, the weight of accumulated water can significantly increase the likelihood of structural collapse. While ladders can be used to construct a variety of water removal contrivances, they are most often used to construct water chutes.

Figure 5.34 Intake strainers can be kept off the bottom of a water source during drafting using ground ladders.

Figure 5.35 Water chutes are constructed using A-frame ladders to channel water from upper floors out of the structure.

Water chutes are constructed on the floor below the one on which the water has accumulated. They are positioned directly beneath holes cut in the upper floor to allow the water to be drained. To construct a water chute, use the following steps:

Step 1: Open a window in an outside wall.

Step 2: Position a step ladder or A-frame directly below the drain hole (or where the drain hole will be created).

Step 3: Place pike poles at the edges of a salvage cover with the pike extending off the end of the cover.

Step 4: Roll the edges over the pike poles toward the middle until there is a 3-foot (1m) width between the rolls.

Step 5: Hook the pike ends to the ladder and extend the poles out the window to create the chute.

The water chute is now ready to direct water from the upper floor through the open window to the outside (**Figure 5.35**).

Bridging

When necessary to save lives, ladders can be used to bridge the gap between two points. While this technique may be used to span any relatively narrow gap – natural or constructed – the following discussion describes bridging between two adjacent buildings.

If the gap between the buildings is not more than one-third its length, a single ladder can be laid on the roof of one building and the tip simply slid over to the other building. The same technique can be used from window to window, roof to window, or vice versa between buildings.

However, if the width of the gap is more than one-third the length of the available ladder, a different technique must be used. Because of the physical forces involved, it may be impossible to slide the ladder across the gap but it must be lowered into position from the vertical. In this technique, the butt of the ladder is positioned close to the gap to be spanned. Guide ropes are tied to the top of each beam, and the ladder is raised to the vertical. Then, with one or two firefighters heeling the ladder, firefighters holding each of the ropes control the movement of the ladder and slowly lower it across the gap **(Figure 5.36)**.

Once the ladder is in place, firefighters can crawl across the gap if necessary. Obviously, anyone crawling across *must* have a belay line attached. If circumstances allow, a wooden plank can be laid between the ladder beams to create a walking surface. If the gap is narrow enough, the handle of a pike pole can be used as a handrail. If not, firefighters can stretch a rope across the gap to provide a handhold.

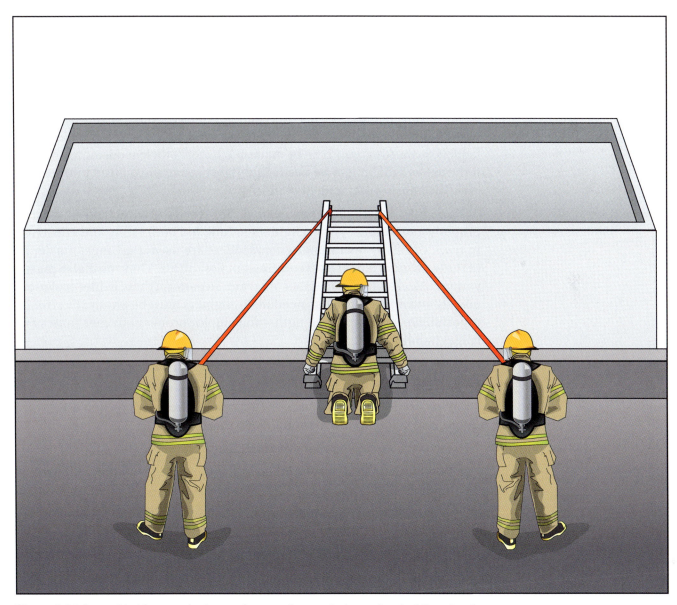

Figure 5.36 Ground ladders can be lowered across the gap between two buildings to allow access.

> **Ground Ladder Scenario:**
>
> A fully developed fire is burning on the top floor of a two-story wood-frame apartment building with a pitched roof. Your engine company is ordered to ladder the roof for ventilation.
>
> - As a minimum, how many ladders would you raise?
> - What types of ladders would you select?
> - What length of ladders would be required to access the roof?
> - Where would you position the ladders?
> - Where would you be sure NOT to position them?

Summary

Many truck company tasks involve the use of ground ladders. Ground ladders may be needed to gain access to the outside of a burning building or to reach lockboxes to facilitate rapid and nondestructive entry. Ground ladders may be used for window access to facilitate entry, horizontal ventilation, and rescues. They may also be needed to access roofs for vertical ventilation and in nonstandard applications in unusual situations. In many cases, the use of ladders on the fireground can be made much more efficient during an incident if the ladders that might be needed for fighting a fire in a given building are identified during preincident planning.

To be fully functional when needed, fire service ground ladders must be properly maintained. For firefighters to function both safely and effectively in truck company operations where ladders are used, they must master all of the individual ladder skills outlined in **Essentials**. They must also master various ladder skills as a member of a team. To perform these ladder evolutions quickly and efficiently when needed, firefighters must be physically strong – especially in upper body strength – and employ proper body mechanics and ladder handling techniques.

Review Questions

1. What are the critical factors considered by firefighters when selecting a ground ladder for a fireground operation?
2. What is the procedure for a four-firefighter raise of a pole ladder?
3. What factors affect the placement of a ground ladder during a fireground placement?
4. What are the tactical uses for ground ladders during a fireground operation?
5. How can ground ladders be used for emergency situations not addressed in SOPs?

Size-Up for Truck Company Operations

Chapter Contents

CASE HISTORY 149	**Building Construction** 160
Size-Up for Truck Companies 150	Age of Building 160
Preincident Size-Up 150	Type of Construction 161
Size-Up During Dispatch and Response 152	Building Modifications 162
Size-Up on Arrival 155	Fire Characteristics 164
Ongoing Size-Up 155	**Structural Collapse** 168
NIOSH Model 156	Collapse Potential 169
Fire Behavior 157	**Occupancy Type** 170
Smoke 157	Life Safety 170
Reading Smoke 158	Hazardous Materials 171
	Summary 171
	Review Questions 172

Divider page photo courtesy of Ron Jeffers.

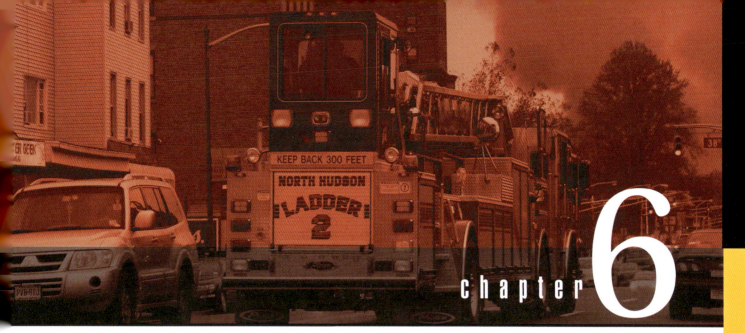

chapter 6

Key Terms

Balloon-Frame Construction 160	Fire Wall 165
Bowstring Truss 161	Rain Roof 162
Cockloft 164	

Size-Up for Truck Company Operations

Learning Objectives

After reading this chapter, students will be able to:

1. Define size-up.
2. Describe the information gathered during preincident size-up.
3. Describe the size-up information gathered during all stages of an operation.
4. Summarize the NIOSH model for initial size-up of a fire.
5. Describe the various characteristics of smoke and the size-up information provided by those characteristics.
6. Explain the relationship between building construction features and fire behavior.
7. Describe the fire characteristics of attics, basements, and various building types.

Safety Points

When reading this chapter, keep the following safety points in mind:

- Initial size-up sets the tone for the entire incident.
- Effects of delayed response on fire development must be considered.
- An accurate assessment of the situation is directly related to incident safety.
- If the ongoing size-up indicates a changing situation, operational plans should be changed to meet the new conditions.
- Maintaining situational awareness is the individual firefighter's ongoing size-up.

Chapter 6
Size-Up for Truck Company Operations

Case History

According to an NFPA® investigative report, firefighters in New York State were called to a fire on the second floor of a three-story, wood-frame building in 1978. The fire had spread into a wall of this partially sprinklered apartment house and before the fire was extinguished the following morning, four firefighters were dead and several more were injured.

According to the post-fire analysis, the deaths were the result of a combination of two factors: (1) how the building was constructed, and (2) delayed ventilation. The building was of balloon frame construction that allowed the fire to spread inside the wall from the second floor into the attic space above the third floor. Ventilation was delayed, apparently because the fire situation was not accurately assessed by those first on the scene. The results were that water from the attic sprinklers turned to steam and forced fire and superheated gases from the unvented attic down into the third floor rooms. Water from the attic sprinklers – heated to scalding temperatures – was cascading down into the rooms on the third floor. The scalding water cut off the means of egress for the firefighters trapped on the third floor.

This tragic incident is just one example of firefighters being injured or killed, at least in part due to an improper size-up upon arrival. While the size-up of interior structure fires is an inexact science, there are things can be done to increase their accuracy. Proper size-up greatly reduces the chances of firefighter fatalities like those described in this case history. In addition to understanding fire behavior as presented in **Essentials** and this manual, firefighters need to have a thorough knowledge of the structures within their response districts and how fires inside these buildings may be affected by the age of the building, type of construction, construction materials used, and other factors.

In some cases, firefighters may fail to understand how a fire inside a structure is behaving because they are unfamiliar with the type of construction and its characteristics or with renovations that the structure has undergone over the years. Both of these problems can be mitigated by firefighters observing the types of construction common to their response districts and by an ongoing program of preincident planning inspections. This helps to keep firefighters current on any new construction or renovations taking place in their districts.

This chapter begins with a discussion of the general characteristics of the size-up process and how the process applies to truck company operations. Also discussed are some general descriptions of fires that have all too often resulted in firefighters being injured or killed. The chapter continues with discussions of various fire conditions that are potentially lethal for firefighters. Finally, various types of building construction are discussed along with how fires may behave in each type.

Size-Up for Truck Companies

Although it can be described in many different ways, size-up is simply the process of making careful observations and drawing reasonable conclusions from those observations. Just because the process is simple, however, does not mean that it is always easy. In fact, from a life-safety standpoint, accurately sizing-up a fire situation is sometimes one of the most difficult functions. Regardless of the difficulty, proper size-up is critical in every incident.

The size-up of a structure fire typically has the same elements regardless of who in the emergency response organization is assessing the situation and what their fireground responsibilities are. What differs, however, is how their observations are interpreted and translated within the Incident Action Plan (IAP). In general, the size-up of a structure fire begins with preincident familiarization and planning long before the fire is reported. It continues once units are dispatched and when they respond to the scene. Once on scene, the size-up continues as conditions are assessed and resources deployed. Size-up is an ongoing process on the fireground until the incident is terminated.

Preincident Size-Up

Before an incident is reported, firefighters begin the size-up process by becoming familiar with all structures in their response area in general and with identified target hazards in particular. When doing preincident planning on a particular building, firefighters should consider the following:

- Building factors
  - Size (Dimensions)
  - Construction (Materials)
  - Age (Condition) **(Figure 6.1)**
  - Access (To/into)
- Water supply
  - Availability (Piped system/water shuttle)
  - Capability (Adequate/needing to be supplemented)
- Occupancy information
  - Life safety (Occupants/firefighters)
  - Hazards (Normal/extraordinary) **(Figure 6.2)**
- Resources
  - Needed (Normal/extraordinary)
  - Availability (Immediately/special call)
  - Capability (Adequate/need to be supplemented)

Figure 6.1 Consideration of the age of a structure is an important factor during size-up.

Figure 6.2 Some common fireground hazards.

Chapter 6 • Size-Up for Truck Company Operations **151**

Size-Up During Dispatch and Response

Size-up for a structure fire incident typically starts with the initial dispatch. Firefighters begin to develop a mental image of the problem with which they are confronted based on the information received in the initial dispatch and what can be observed around them. Factors to be considered when responding are as follows:

- Type of incident
  - Structure fire (Residential/commercial)
  - Other (Target hazard/threatened structure)
- Location of incident
  - Address (If known) (**Figure 6.3**)
  - Intersection (If specific address unknown)
  - Landmarks (In undeveloped areas)
- Time
  - Time of day (Sleep time, work time, school time)
  - Day of week (Weekday, weekend)
  - Season (Holidays, major sports)
- Weather
  - Winter (Delayed response)
  - Summer (Crowds/traffic congestion)

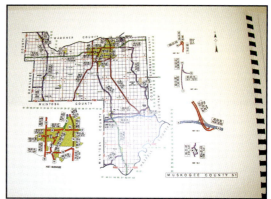

Figure 6.3 Map books are found on most emergency vehicles and provide information on the best response route.

Of these factors, the time of day, day of week, season of the year, and weather are especially critical.

Time of Day

The time of day has a number of possible effects on the size-up of a structure fire. This factor may increase or decrease the likelihood of the building being occupied or of a fire being discovered and reported. For example, during the late night and early morning hours, a residential structure is more likely to be occupied, and the occupants may be asleep. On the other hand, a small business office or retail store is unlikely to be occupied at that time unless there is an apartment above it. The time of day can also affect the volume of vehicular and pedestrian traffic, such as children walking to or from school, crowds gathering at sports venues or places of entertainment, or rush hour traffic obstructing response routes. Such traffic can adversely affect the response times of additional resources (**Figure 6.4**).

The time of day when a fire occurs can increase the challenges in some occupancies. For example, a fire in a fully occupied elementary school may result in large numbers of faculty and students exiting the buildings and large numbers of parents converging on the school at the same time. Likewise, because elderly patients in a nursing home may be confused and disoriented by a fire at night, protecting them can be a challenge.

Figure 6.4 Traffic congestion often slows the response of emergency vehicles. *Courtesy of Ron Jeffers.*

Figure 6.5 Large retail stores are often crowded during business hours.

Day of Week

The day of the week can also affect the size-up of a structure fire. School buildings are often (but not always) vacant in the evenings and on weekends. However, movie theaters and other public buildings, health clubs and sports facilities, and places of worship are often occupied on weekends — sometimes by large numbers of people. Many retail businesses are very crowded during business hours on weekends but may be closed on Sundays **(Figure 6.5)**. Daylight hours on weekdays may involve heavy traffic congestion in business and commercial districts. Because of differences in response times and differences in occupant loads, the need for laddering buildings and conducting search and rescue operations may increase or decrease because of the day of the week.

Season of the Year

There can also be significant seasonal differences that affect the size-up of a structure fire. For example, the fireworks associated with the 4th of July and certain other holidays can add to the danger and difficulties faced by fire-

Chapter 6 • Size-Up for Truck Company Operations

Figure 6.6 Fireworks are a common hazard encountered around the 4th of July holiday.

fighters **(Figure 6.6)**. Likewise, added decorations and increases in merchandise inventories at Christmas and certain other holidays increase fire loads. In addition, the increased traffic congestion caused by seasonal shoppers and those attending major sporting events can slow emergency responses and increase the likelihood of traffic accidents involving fire apparatus.

Weather

Weather doesn't usually have as much influence on interior structure fires as it does on wildland fires. However, as shown in the following case history, extreme weather can affect structure fire behavior and therefore makes a difference in the size-up of these incidents.

> According to NIOSH Report F2007-12, Virginia firefighters were called to a fire in a two-story residence in April of 2007. Because the person who woke the occupants and escorted them to a nearby home failed to inform the firefighters that the building was no longer occupied, the IC ordered a search of the burning building. While a two-man crew wearing full protective clothing and SCBA was conducting a primary search of the upper story, 48 mph (77 km/hr) winds suddenly intensified a fire burning on the second floor and forced fire and smoke throughout the living area. Both firefighters attempted to exit the building, but only one escaped.

Even if the wind is not strong enough to affect the behavior of an interior structure fire, high ambient temperature and humidity take a toll on firefighters operating at the scene. This may require more frequent crew relief and may increase the need for medical monitoring, establishing a Rehab Unit, and calling in additional companies for crew rotations. Likewise, it is sometimes more difficult for firefighters to function in extremely cold conditions, and the weight of protective clothing can add to firefighter fatigue. Winter weather can slow the response of emergency vehicles because of wet, snowy, or icy streets and roads. Access to buildings may be more difficult in winter if sidewalks and driveways are covered with ice and snow. In addition, roof operations may be more difficult and dangerous because of slippery conditions on pitched roofs **(Figure 6.7)**. Firefighters working outside may be vulnerable to frostbite or hypothermia on prolonged incidents.

Figure 6.7 Snow on pitched roofs often makes ventilation efforts difficult.

Those assigned to perform truck company tasks must continually evaluate how each of the factors involved in sizing-up a structure fire may apply in a given situation. They must carefully observe the situation at hand and decide which of the factors apply, in what way, and to what extent.

> ⚠ While it may be difficult to observe every critical factor or anticipate every possible contingency, the skill and diligence with which these observations and decisions are made will determine how successful the operation is likely to be and, more important, how safe it is likely to be.

All of the foregoing items are important assessments at structure fires. From the standpoint of size-up and incident safety, one of the most critical factors to evaluate in a structure fire is how the fire is behaving.

Size-Up on Arrival

Once on scene, firefighters continue their size-up. The size-up on arrival includes certain basic factors that need to be addressed and questions that need to be answered. Factors that need to be considered on arrival at a structure fire are as follows:

- What happened? (fire, explosion, lightning?)
- What is happening now? (Read the fire and the building)
- What is likely to happen? (Extreme fire behavior or structural collapse likely?)
- Are the resources on scene or en route sufficient? (If not, what else is needed?)

Ongoing Size-Up

After a report on conditions has been transmitted, an IAP developed, and on-scene resources deployed, firefighters must continue to monitor fire and building conditions and evaluate the effectiveness of control efforts throughout the incident. The factors that need to be considered during the suppression of a structure fire are as follows:

- What effect have the initial resources had on the fire? (Minimal/control or extinguishment achieved?)
- Are still more resources needed? (If so, what type, how many?)
- Are different tactics needed? (If so, what type?)

All fireground personnel, including those assigned to truck companies, must consider the foregoing and make appropriate decisions based upon the answers to those questions. However, the Incident Commander (IC) must also consider the following during initial size-up:

- Is immediate intervention needed to save lives? (Persons seen/reported?)
- What are the risks to firefighters and other emergency responders? (Extreme fire behavior, structural collapse, downed wires, vehicular traffic, hazardous materials?)
- Are the needed resources immediately available or will their responses be delayed? (Distance, weather, traffic congestion?)

One reason that an accurate size-up is so important is that the initial report on conditions and the IAP are based on it. The size-up is also the basis for the initial tactical decisions and for one of the most critical decisions facing the first-arriving officer: "Are the resources that are on scene or en route sufficient to handle this incident?" If the answer is "no," or even "maybe," then additional resources must be requested *immediately*. If the request for additional resources is delayed, by the time they arrive at the scene the fire may have progressed to the point where even more resources are needed. Therefore, the initial size-up often sets the tone for the entire incident. If the initial size-up is accurate, the incident is more likely to be handled in a safe and efficient manner. If the initial size-up is inaccurate, the incident is more likely to deteriorate and the chances of firefighter injuries or fatalities are increased.

Making an accurate initial size-up of a structure fire is difficult because it requires a knowledge of fire behavior, building construction, and resource availability and capability. In addition, an accurate size-up requires enough experience and judgment to understand how all of those factors relate to the situation at hand. The more that is known about each of these factors and of the particular building involved, the more likely an accurate size-up will be made. Therefore, it is not only necessary for the first-in officer to be knowledgeable with regard to fire behavior and building construction, but it is also very important for him or her to be familiar with the particular building involved. The officer performing the size-up needs to know whether the building is likely to be occupied at the time of the incident, whether the building is equipped with any fire suppression systems, and whether the building has been remodeled (how and to what extent). The first-in officer also needs to know the type of construction, the era in which the building was constructed, and what the building contains.

NIOSH Model

As previously mentioned, the initial size-up of a structure fire can be described in a number of different ways. From the standpoint of truck company operations, the size-up recommended by the National Institute for Occupational Safety and Health (NIOSH) is a reasonably good model. NIOSH recommends that the initial size-up of a structure fire include the following information:

- Fire size and location (room/contents, fully involved, floor(s), front/rear)
- Length of time the fire has been burning (estimated)
- Conditions on arrival (nothing showing, light smoke, heavy involvement)
- Size of the building (single/multistory, floor area, and height)
- Age of building (obvious weathering or other deterioration, modern construction materials)
- Presence of combustible materials (wooden structure, wooden roof assembly)
- Occupancy (residential, commercial, high hazard)
- Renovations or modifications (facades, false ceilings, additions)
- Previous fires (if known)
- Dead loads that might affect structural integrity (HVAC, water tank on roof)
- Adjacent exposures (fire extension, smoke contamination)
- Resources at scene or available (mutual aid)

In addition to the items on the NIOSH list, some jurisdictions have come to realize that the availability of a reliable water supply is a critical factor that must be considered during size-up. Some rural areas may depend partially or entirely on mobile water supply (**Figure 6.8**). The time it takes to establish the needed water supply under these conditions must be factored into the IAP.

Fire Behavior

To fight interior structure fires effectively and increase their chances of surviving these fires unscathed, firefighters must apply all the knowledge of fire behavior they gained from training and experience when sizing up specific situations. Interior structure fires have and continue to injure and kill firefighters. It is likely that at least some of these casualties can be attributed to a lack of the knowledge and skills necessary to function safely in these hostile environments.

Figure 6.8 Mobile water supply may be the only means of water in some rural areas. *Courtesy of Montezuma-Rimrock (AZ) Fire Department.*

Among the specific situations that often lead to firefighter injuries or deaths are fires that flashover unexpectedly, fires in which backdraft potential is not handled correctly, and fires in which the burning building collapses. Because smoke may be visible a considerable distance from the fire scene, it can sometimes be the first and most obvious sign of how a fire is behaving.

Smoke

As was discussed in Chapter 2, smoke is a result of incomplete combustion, and as such, it must be considered as *unburned fuel*. Under the right conditions, smoke can ignite in a flashover, backdraft, or smoke explosion; any of which could significantly threaten firefighter safety.

From a size-up standpoint, smoke color and density, velocity and direction, turbulence, pulsations, and sounds can all provide some indication of fire behavior, but these indicators need to be verified. It is also important to consider smoke volume and location in addition to other fire behavior indicators to get a clear picture of actual fire conditions. Fires that are ventilation-controlled tend to produce a greater volume of smoke than those that are fuel-controlled; however, the location where smoke is discharged from a building may be some distance from the seat of the fire.

For their own safety, firefighters should remember that smoke contains a host of different toxic substances, perhaps even airborne asbestos particles (a known carcinogen). Therefore, when firefighters must enter a smoke-filled building, they should follow the safety behaviors listed in Chapter 3, Firefighter Safety and Survival, especially the one that says — *never* breathe smoke **(Figure 6.9, p.158)**.

Remember that smoke is unburned fuel that could be ready to ignite!

Figure 6.9 Firefighters should always wear SCBA in the hazardous area until told to discontinue its use by the Incident Commander.

Analyzing Smoke

For their own safety and for the effectiveness of fireground operations, firefighters must learn to accurately *analyze smoke*. This includes observing its characteristics and drawing reasonable conclusions from them. When analyzing smoke, firefighters should look for certain common characteristics. The most common characteristics of smoke are:

- Volume
- Color and Density
- Air Flow (Pressure)

Volume

Although there are differences in the volume of smoke produced by various materials when they burn and by the conditions in which they burn, the volume of smoke is still a good indicator of the fire situation. In general, the greater the volume of smoke, the bigger and more intense the fire **(Figure 6.10)**. While it is possible for a large fire to produce little smoke, these conditions rarely exist outside of the laboratory or in certain industrial processes. It is far more likely that a large fire will produce a large volume of smoke, depending upon what is burning and under what conditions. Some petroleum products produce huge volumes of smoke from relatively small fires. However, in most structure fires, firefighters should assume — until proven otherwise — that a lot of smoke means a lot of fire.

Color and Density

The color and density of smoke can often give firefighters some idea of the type of products involved. Black smoke typically indicates that petroleum products, rubber, or plastics are involved. Wood and other combustibles produce smoke that ranges from light gray to yellow or dark brown **(Figure 6.11)**. To review information related to the color and density of smoke, refer to Chapter 2.

Figure 6.10 Large volumes of smoke often indicate a large and intense fire. *Courtesy of the Los Angeles Fire Department – ISTS.*

Figure 6.11 Greyish yellow smoke is often an indicator of the combustion of wood or other common combustibles. *Courtesy of Ron Jeffers.*

Air Flow (Pressure)

As a fire burns within a structure, convection causes the smoke and other gases to expand and rise. If the smoke and gases are confined, they begin to build up pressure. As the confined fire gets bigger and more intense, more pressure is created. When the entire space within a compartment has been filled with smoke, the smoke will be forced out under pressure through every available opening. The higher the pressure, the greater the movement **(Figure 6.12)**.

Figure 6.12 The higher the pressure in the involved compartment, the greater the movement of smoke from the compartment. *Courtesy of Bob Esposito.*

When firefighters see a large volume of optically dense smoke billowing out under great pressure, there can be little doubt that a large and intense fire is burning inside the building. However, if firefighters see light smoke moving lazily on the top floor of a building, it may be from an incipient-stage fire in the compartment or a fire burning very intensely in the attic or cockloft above them. Once again, each observation must be considered in relation to the overall situation.

However, smoke is merely one of several fire behavior indicators that firefighters should also assess during their initial and ongoing size-ups of an interior structure fire. Heat and flame are other important indicators as well. For more information on indicators for extreme fire behavior such as flashover and backdraft, refer to Chapter 2.

Firefighters must not base their entire size-up on any single observation.

Building Construction

It is vitally important for firefighters to understand the relationship between building construction and fire behavior. They must understand that, as in the fire described at the beginning of this chapter, an operating fire sprinkler can reduce the effectiveness of a ventilation opening cut directly above the sprinkler. They must also be aware of how various building designs — such as those that are tightly sealed for energy conservation — can affect fire behavior inside those buildings. In addition, firefighters must be aware of the effects on fire behavior of various building materials. Some new materials change the fire environment by keeping the heat and other products of combustion confined within the building, rather than allowing them to be vented to the outside by breaking windows or by burning through the roof. Other materials may add massive volumes of fuel and/or toxic products as they pyrolize due to the heat of the fire.

There are many ways in which the construction of a building that is on fire can affect truck company operations, and firefighters must include these factors in their overall size-up of a fire situation. Among the factors that can impact these operations are the age of the building, the type of construction, its collapse potential, the nature and extent of any modifications, and how the fire is likely to behave in this particular building.

Age of Building

The age of a burning building can be a very critical factor for firefighters to assess in their size-up of the structure. Buildings in a given neighborhood tend to be of generally the same age and have similar construction features and characteristics, but this is not always the case. Depending upon the geographic region in which the building was constructed, very old wood frame buildings may be of **balloon-frame construction** that allows fire to travel unseen inside the walls from the basement to the attic **(Figure 6.13)**. Older wood frame buildings are more likely to have substandard wiring, and the combustible structural components are likely to be tinder dry. These are characteristics that lend themselves to fires starting easily and spreading rapidly. Older brick (unreinforced

> **Balloon-Frame Construction** — Type of structural framing used in some single-story and multistory wood frame buildings wherein the studs are continuous from the foundation to the roof. There may be no fire stops between the studs.

Figure 6.13 Old wood-frame buildings are likely to incorporate balloon-frame construction.

Figure 6.14 Domed hangars and other structures often have arched roofs and large unsupported spans.

masonry [URM]) buildings often trap heat and smoke inside and are sometimes prone to wall collapse. Some buildings may have unsupported arched roofs, such as the **bowstring** or Lamella types, and be covered with many layers of composition roofing or other materials **(Figure 6.14)**. Older residential structures may have extraordinarily high ceilings unless they have had false ceilings installed at some point — a common practice.

Bowstring Truss — Lightweight truss design noted by the bow shape, or curve, of the top chord.

On the other hand, newer wood-frame buildings are more likely to have some type of lightweight construction that may fail early in a fire. Newer buildings of all types may contain building materials that liberate toxic products when subjected to the heat of a fire. However, in many jurisdictions, newer buildings are much more likely to be fully sprinklered so the likelihood of full fire involvement is reduced. The more that firefighters know about the requirements of the local building code, the more likely they are to be able identify exceptionally dangerous buildings within their response districts during size-up.

Type of Construction

In sizing up a burning building, firefighters need to consider the type of construction. Obviously, wood-frame buildings of any age may contain large quantities of highly combustible wooden structural components **(Figure 6.15)**. Masonry buildings may resist the effects of fire but add to the risk of wall collapse. Buildings with arched roofs, lightweight roofs, or similar assemblies

Figure 6.15 Many structures contain large quantities of combustible structural materials.

may be prone to sudden and unexpected roof collapse when subjected to a major fire within. Metal buildings, especially if well insulated, may contain a fire long enough that it can develop into major proportions before it is discovered. In addition, unprotected steel components are more likely to distort and fail earlier in a fire than would wooden beams. For more information on the types of construction, refer to the IFSTA **Building Construction Related to the Fire Service** manual.

Building Modifications

Unless preincident planning information on a particular building has been kept current, assessing how and to what extent it has been modified (renovated or remodeled) can be a challenge when firefighters arrive at the scene of a structure fire (**Figure 6.16**). Renovations in older buildings using lightweight construction materials and methods may be disguised in the finishing process, and this can sometimes result in an inaccurate size-up. Therefore, it is critically important to identify how and to what extent buildings have been renovated by conducting preincident planning surveys as often as necessary to keep the plans up to date. Frequent surveys are the best way for firefighters to become familiar with the characteristics of the buildings in their response districts and to keep that knowledge current.

Figure 6.16 Structural modifications during remodeling can leave holes in floors and stairwells without adequate railings or support. *Courtesy of the McKinney (TX) Fire Department.*

Both residential and commercial buildings constructed before the middle of the twentieth century commonly had high ceilings, some 10 feet (3 m) or more, but many of them have since had dropped (false) ceilings installed during renovation. A fire burning between a false ceiling and the original ceiling may be unaffected by a vertical ventilation opening cut in the roof or by a fire in the attic burning through the roof.

> If a firefighter crawling on the floor of a smoke-filled Victorian-style residence can touch the ceiling with a 6-foot (2 m) pike pole, there is probably a false ceiling in that room.

Rain Roof — A second roof constructed over an existing roof.

Another modification that can greatly hinder firefighters' efforts to vertically ventilate some roofs is the so-called **rain roof**. A rain roof is a second roof assembly constructed over an older existing roof (**Figure 6.17**). When the original roof has deteriorated beyond repair, property owners will sometimes choose to have a second roof installed over the first instead of removing it. This creates a void space between the two roof assemblies. If firefighters are unaware of the rain roof and cut a ventilation opening in it, they may assume that they have vented the building when they have not.

Other structural modifications, perhaps in violation of local building codes, may result in unsprinklered rooms being created in what were previously fully sprinklered buildings. This happens when someone divides an existing room with one or more interior walls but does not modify the sprinkler sys-

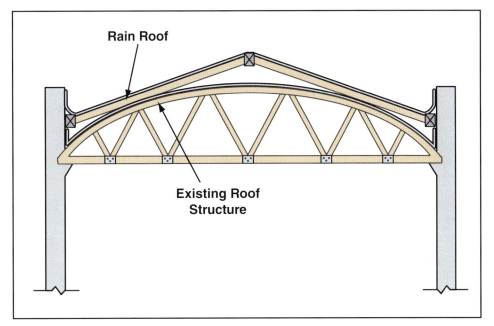

Figure 6.17 Rain roofs may be encountered and often pose an additional challenge during vertical ventilation.

Figure 6.18 Reinforcing stars are an indication from the outside of the structure that structural stabilization has been performed and additional structural issues may be present.

tem to cover each of the separate spaces created by the modification. When firefighters observe heavy fire involvement in one area of a fully sprinklered building, it may be because of storage blocking the sprinklers, some accelerant causing the fire to overwhelm the sprinkler system, or the system is faulty or has been disabled.

Other unauthorized modifications involve rooms being added to the exterior walls of a building. Access into such a room from inside the building may be through what was formerly a required exit door. Obviously, anyone trying to exit the building through that door would find themselves in another room — which may or may not have an exit door to the outside. These add-ons can sometimes be identified from the outside because they do not match the construction of the original building.

If reinforcing stars or plates are seen on the walls of older buildings, firefighters should know that the building either underwent modifications requiring the additional support, or the building has weakened over time and needed reinforcement **(Figure 6.18)**. Either way, firefighters need to survey these buildings to become familiar with them in order to forecast how a fire inside these structures might behave.

Another common modification is for building occupants to add deadbolts, padlocks, metal security doors or windows, or other security devices **(Figure 6.19)**. In zero visibility conditions, these devices may make it much more difficult for people (including firefighters) to escape through these exit openings. If firefighters are aware of these modifications when they arrive at the scene, they can take the necessary tools and equipment with them into these buildings. Some of these procedures are discussed in Chapter 3, Firefighter Safety and Survival.

Figure 6.19 While window bars are good at keeping intruders out, they also prevent victims and firefighters from escaping if necessary.

Fire Characteristics

If firefighters are to accurately size-up interior structure fires, they must not only know basic fire behavior and basic building construction, but also understand how these two major components of interior structure fires interact with each other. While the physics and chemistry of fire behavior remain the same, understanding how fire may behave when confined in various types of structures or parts thereof is critical to accurately sizing up these fires. Therefore, how fires may behave in attics, basements, townhouses, Victorians, large dwellings, warehouses, and office buildings is discussed in the following section.

Attics

These confined spaces are constructed in various sizes and configurations, and from a wide variety of materials. However, regardless of whether it is the typical small crawl space between the ceiling and roof of a suburban dwelling, the common attic in a strip mall, or the cavernous **cockloft** or interstitial space above a large commercial or manufacturing occupancy, most attics have certain characteristics in common. In most cases, there are no openings between the attic and the occupied space below except the covered access hatch **(Figure 6.20)**. Most, but not all, attics are vented to the outside in some way. During a fire, attic vents allow air in — fanning the fire — but also provide a means for the products of combustion to escape. Therefore, attic fires can grow to significant proportions before creating enough internal pressure to force smoke down into the occupied space below. Because the occupied space may be completely clear of smoke or unusual odors, the occupants may be unaware that a fire is burning above their heads.

Cockloft — Concealed space between the top floor and the roof of a structure.

Figure 6.20 The attic hatch or scuttle may be the only means of accessing the attic.

In general, attic fires in single-story residences are relatively easy to size-up. If smoke and/or fire are seen issuing from attic vents under the eaves or from under roof shingles, but there is little or no indication of fire or smoke in the living space below, a fire in the attic is a reasonable conclusion. On the other hand, multistory residential structures, especially very old ones, may be of balloon-frame construction that will allow smoke and fire to travel upward through the walls into the attic. This can give the outward appearance of a typical attic fire when the seat of the fire is actually in the basement or in void spaces throughout the shell of the building. Fires in the attics of large commercial buildings can be very difficult to locate because the smoke may travel a considerable distance within the attic before escaping through a vent or scuttle. In these situations, the seat of the fire may be some distance from the point where the smoke is showing.

Basements

Some basement fires may be difficult to size up; others not. However, basement fires are almost always difficult to control and extinguish. Basement fires in buildings with balloon-frame construction can and often do quickly spread throughout the structure. The key to accurately sizing up fires in these buildings is knowing beforehand (because of preincident planning) which buildings or types of buildings in the jurisdiction have or are likely to have balloon-frame construction. Because of its fire spread characteristics, balloon-frame construction has been prohibited by building codes in many jurisdictions for so many years that few if any of these old buildings are still standing. Other jurisdictions still have many older buildings with this type of construction.

In buildings of more modern design, basement fires may be somewhat easier to size up. With the exception of buildings with one or more subbasements, basement fires have only one way to spread — up. Basement fires may reveal themselves by smoke and/or fire issuing from ground level windows, dead lights, cellar doors, vents, cracks in the exterior walls, or from the interior wall/floor junction **(Figure 6.21)**. Smoke on the first floor may be relatively cool from floor to ceiling without obvious layering. The floor may be noticeably hot, but with no sign of fire in that room or adjacent rooms. In some cases, vent pipes run from the basement up to and through the roof. Therefore, if smoke is issuing from a roof vent but there is no other indication of fire in the attic or the occupied spaces, the basement should be checked.

Figure 6.21 Cellar doors provide access to the basement.

Certain building features may also make sizing up a basement fire difficult. For example, smoke from a basement fire may spread throughout the building through the ventilation system. It may also spread from floor to floor in a trash or laundry chute. In some older buildings, lightweight concrete floors have been poured over existing wooden floors above the basements. As has been seen in historical fires, these floors can hide a basement fire until the floor supports burn away and the floor collapses into the basement.

Townhouses

Because they make efficient use of space, a growing number of townhouse apartments and condominiums can be found in many cities and towns in North America **(Figure 6.22, p. 166)**. Most are two- or three-story, wood-frame, multiple-residential buildings that may or may not have **fire walls** separating the units. Some not only do not have fire walls, but also have common attics or

Fire Wall — Fire-rated wall with a specified degree of fire resistance, built of fire-resistive materials and usually extending from the foundation up to and through the roof of a building, that is designed to limit the spread of a fire within a structure or between adjacent structures.

attics in which the smoke barrier may have been compromised. These characteristics can allow fires to spread through the attic beyond the unit of origin to involve the entire building. However, the most common fire spread problem related to the typical townhouse design is an open stairway that allows fire to spread from the ground floor to the upper floor or floors.

Typically, the living room and kitchen are on the ground floor and the bedrooms are on an upper floor. A fire that develops on the ground floor, especially during the late night or early morning hours, may trap those sleeping in rooms on an upper floor. This is because their primary exit (the stairway) acts as a chimney that channels fire and smoke upward into the upper floor hallway. Because the multi-story design can make vertical ventilation of a ground-floor fire extremely difficult, horizontal ventilation is often used. However, this can allow fire on the ground floor to lap up the outside of the building and spread to an upper floor and/or the attic. Because townhouse units often have skylights that incorporate a plastic bubble, the bubble will often melt and fall out, creating a vertical opening through which smoke and heat from a fire on the ground floor can escape from the roof.

From a size-up standpoint, smoke from a ground-floor fire can sometimes be seen exiting from openings on an upper floor because that is where the highest internal pressure is. Sizing up a fire on an upper floor, or in the attic, is no different than sizing up a similar fire in a single-story residence. From a life safety standpoint, laddering the upper floor windows, front and rear, is usually a very high priority.

Figure 6.22 Townhouses are common in densely populated areas.

Victorians

Older neighborhoods in many cities and towns have Victorian-style residences in them **(Figure 6.23)**. While many of these ornate buildings are still single-family dwellings or have been converted to office or retail space, many of the larger ones have been converted to apartment houses such as the one in the case history cited at the beginning of this chapter.

From the standpoint of size-up, Victorians contain one or more of each of the undesirable characteristics already discussed. In general, they have many features that make them vulnerable to fires starting and, once started, spreading rapidly. These features may include old substandard wiring inside walls made of wood that is extremely dehydrated. Victorians are typically of balloon-frame construction which lends itself to rapid fire spread. Many have been remodeled to a greater or lesser extent creating hidden void spaces in which fire can burn for a considerable time before being discovered.

Large Dwellings

A recent trend in residential construction in North America has been the emergence of extremely large dwellings compared to those built in the middle to late twentieth century **(Figure 6.24)**. These single-family residences are commonly between 5,000 and 10,000 square feet (550 m² to 1 100 m²), and some even larger. Because of the variations in design and style, sometimes combined in the same house, and the use of a variety of building materials, sizing up fires in these mansions can be challenging. The key to making realistic forecasts of fire behavior, and accurate size-ups when fires are burning, is to conduct frequent preincident familiarization and planning surveys while these buildings are under construction.

Warehouses

Depending upon when, where, and how warehouse buildings were constructed, they have the potential to produce some of the largest and most dangerous structure fires that many firefighters will ever face. Given that they may be packed full of highly flammable, toxic, or explosive materials, warehouses can produce some of the most spectacular and deadly blazes **(Figure 6.25)**.

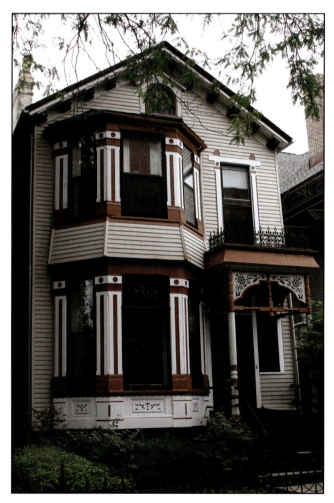

Figure 6.24 Large single-family residences pose a challenge for firefighters.

Figure 6.23 Victorian style homes are often located in older neighborhoods and utilize balloon-frame construction.

Figure 6.25 Warehouses often contain materials that are hazardous when burned.

Since warehouses typically have large open spaces within them, any fire that starts inside has an abundant supply of oxygen. In order to create these large open interior spaces, the roof assemblies often span considerable distances — sometimes unsupported by columns or posts — greatly increasing the collapse potential. Even though many warehouses are fully sprinklered, if the contents are stacked too close to the sprinklers, they can reduce the system's effectiveness. Likewise, if the sprinkler system has been disabled — intentionally or through lack of maintenance — the fire may grow to such proportions that the IC will decide that the fire must be fought from the outside only — even if it means that the building may burn down completely.

From a size-up standpoint, one of the first determinations that must be made is if it is merely a small fire in a big building — such as a fire in a waste basket or trash bin that could be handled with a portable extinguisher — or if it is a big fire that is likely to get bigger. If it is the latter, the IC may order a defensive attack from outside the building.

Office Buildings

Whether single-story or high-rise, fires in office buildings can often be difficult to accurately size up **(Figure 6.26)**. Many of the fires that occur during office hours are relatively small because they are discovered early and perhaps even extinguished before firefighters arrive. However, after office hours, fires can go undetected until they have reached major proportions. Just as in warehouses, an office building full of smoke may or may not indicate the existence of a big fire within. It may only be a small, well-contained fire that has smoldered for many hours – which may also pose a potential backdraft situation. Carefully checking the doors and windows as described earlier in this chapter can help to confirm or rule out backdraft conditions. If conditions allow entry, finding the seat of the fire in a maze of cubicles and offices in a smoke-filled building can be tedious and time-consuming. Otherwise, fires in offices generally behave as they do in any other structure of similar size and construction.

Figure 6.26 Fires in office buildings can be challenging to size up.

Structural Collapse

Historically, the sudden and unexpected collapse of burning buildings has been the cause of numerous firefighter deaths. The following case histories are two more examples of what can and does occur.

> According NIOSH Report F2007-08, a Pennsylvania firefighter was killed when a heavy wooden canopy collapsed on him and another firefighter in February of 2007. While fighting a fire in an attached residential garage with a hoseline, the firefighters were forced to back out due to deteriorating conditions inside. The two firefighters stopped at the open garage door and continued to fight the fire from that location. The wooden canopy, which was attached to the garage roof with steel bars, suddenly collapsed without warning onto the firefighters. One of the firefighters, although badly injured, was able to crawl to the edge of the canopy where a rapid intervention team extricated him. When the second firefighter was located and extricated, he was unresponsive. Both firefighters were transported to a local hospital where one was pronounced dead of crushing injuries and the other received treatment for his injuries.

It is not only the roof and walls of a building that can collapse and endanger firefighters. The collapse of a fire-weakened floor can drop firefighters into an inferno below. Even if a basement fire has been extinguished, firefighters can die from injuries suffered in the fall, be asphyxiated by dense toxic smoke, or even drown in water collected in that area.

In a second incident, firefighters were barely inside the front door when a floor collapse proved fatal for one of them. While it is vitally important for firefighters to know the limitations and inherent dangers of construction methods and materials used in their districts, the need for them to maintain situational awareness cannot be overemphasized.

> According to NIOSH Report F2007-07, a Tennessee firefighter was killed in January of 2007 when he fell through a floor supported by unprotected wooden I-beams into a fire in the basement below. In zero visibility conditions on the main floor of the residence, the initial attack team had backed out because they couldn't find the seat of the fire and the floor was becoming spongy. Two other firefighters took the nozzle and reentered the main floor hallway. A few feet inside the door, the floor suddenly gave way under the nozzle operator and he fell into the fire below. Crews attempted to rescue the firefighter from the heavily involved basement, but were forced to suspend rescue efforts when the entire main floor collapsed into the basement. All firefighters were ordered out of the structure before the remainder of the building collapsed. After the firefighter's body was recovered it was determined that he had died of smoke inhalation.

Collapse Potential

As described in the case histories cited earlier, one of the things that firefighters must assess in their initial and ongoing size-up of a burning building is its collapse potential. Making such an assessment involves both of the foregoing factors – age of the building and type of construction – as well as the effects of the fire itself. The age of the building may indicate the amount and type of reinforcing material used in its construction. The mortar in older brick buildings may have deteriorated to the point where the potential for wall collapse during a fire or earthquake is greatly in-

Figure 6.27 Deteriorated mortar joints are an indicator that the structure may not be sound.

Figure 6.28 Structural components are often added to older buildings to reduce the potential for structural collapse.

creased **(Figure 6.27)**. On the other hand, reinforced concrete buildings are designed to be both fire and collapse resistant. Many newer buildings, or older buildings that have been retrofitted to meet current standards, are likely to have structural components and assemblies designed to reduce collapse potential **(Figure 6.28)**. However, regardless of the age of a building or its construction, as the tragic events of September 11, 2001 clearly showed, virtually any building may collapse if it is exposed to a sufficient volume of fire for an extended period of time.

Occupancy Type

In many interior structure fires, the most serious concerns for firefighters are related more to the contents of the building than its construction. Some of these concerns are related to the occupant loads while others are related to the nature of the materials that are stored and used in the buildings. When sizing up a fire in any building, the life safety of both occupants and firefighters is the highest priority.

Life Safety

During their normal hours of operation, certain types of occupancies can be expected to house vast numbers of people. Some of the most heavily occupied are as follows:

- Office buildings
- Condominiums
- Apartment buildings
- Schools
- Movie theater complexes
- Sports arenas

Firefighters must also be concerned with smaller groups of people who may not be able to escape a burning building without assistance. Some of the most common of these occupancies are as follows:

- Assisted living facilities
- Convalescent hospitals
- Full-service hospitals
- Correctional facilities

Hazardous Materials

When sizing up fires in certain occupancies, firefighters need to be concerned for their own safety and survival, perhaps more so than for the occupants of the buildings. Because some businesses store and use potentially dangerous and very toxic raw materials, they have trained their personnel to deal with fires and other emergencies in their facilities. Firefighters need similar training to protect themselves when fires occur in these facilities. To obtain this level of awareness and knowledge, firefighters must conduct thorough and repeated preincident planning surveys in these occupancies. If any such facilities are not round-the-clock operations, obtaining and maintaining emergency call lists is a high priority for firefighters.

From a size-up standpoint, some of these occupancies are readily identified because of exterior signage **(Figure 6.29)**. Other occupancies housing hazardous materials or processes may not provide these clues. Again, to protect themselves and do their jobs more effectively, firefighters need to be familiar with the buildings and occupancies in their response districts, and that means preincident planning.

Figure 6.29 Buildings that contain hazardous materials are often – but not always – labeled as such.

Size-up scenario:

At dusk on a snowy winter evening, you and your engine company are the first to arrive at a large, single-story, brick warehouse next to an interstate highway. There are large "For Sale or Lease" signs on the exterior of the building. Dark gray smoke is issuing from a few broken windows and from roof ventilators. A civilian approaches you and says that he thinks some homeless people have been living in the building.

- What would be your first concern?
- How would you characterize the fire situation?
- Are additional resources needed to handle this situation?
- What factors might affect the availability of additional resources?

Summary

Size-up is defined as the initial and ongoing assessment of a fire emergency from the first alarm to incident termination. Depending upon the nature and scope of the incident, size-up can be a relatively straightforward process, or it can be very difficult. Accurately sizing up a working structure fire is one of the most critical functions during the incident. How the initial size-up is performed sets the tone for the entire incident and directly affects the safety and effectiveness of the entire operation.

Performing an accurate size-up of a working structure fire requires knowledge of fire behavior, building construction, and resource availability and capability. However, it also requires the experience and judgment to determine how these individual factors combine to affect the plan of attack on the incident at hand.

Review Questions

1. What is size-up? What is its relationship to firefighter safety?
2. What information is gathered during a preincident size-up of a structure?
3. What size-up information is gathered during a fireground operation — dispatch through ongoing operations?
4. What is the NIOSH model of size-up?
5. What important size-up information is provided by the characteristics of the smoke coming from the structure?
6. What is the relationship between a building's construction features and fire behavior in that building?
7. What are the characteristics of fires in attics and basements?

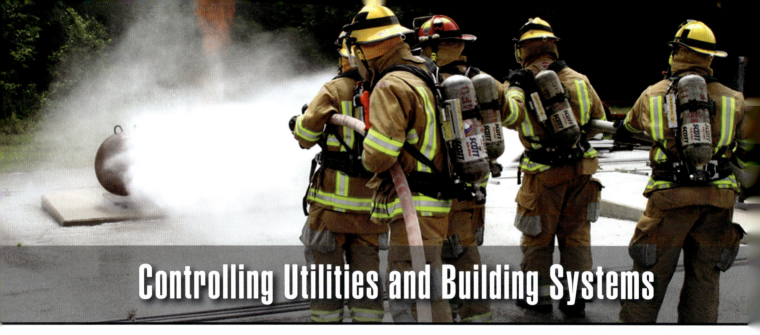

Controlling Utilities and Building Systems

Chapter Contents

CASE HISTORY 177	**Electricity Control** 188
Fuel Control 178	Controlling Electricity in Structure Fires 188
Situational Differences 179	Downed Electrical Wires 191
Gas Leaks without Fire 185	**Water Control** 195
Approach 185	Water Control in Structure Fires 196
Perimeter Control 185	Water Leaks without Fire 198
Hazard Assessment 186	**Summary** 199
Hazard Mitigation 187	**Review Questions** 199

chapter 7

Key Terms

Boiling Liquid Expanding Vapor Explosion (BLEVE) 181
Carcinogen 191
Combustible Gas Indicator (CGI) 185
Control Zone 185
Liquefied Petroleum Gas (LPG) 178
Lower Explosive Limit (LEL) 186
Short Circuit 195

Controlling Utilities and Building Systems

Learning Objectives

After reading this chapter, students will be able to:

1. Explain the purpose of controlling utilities and building systems during fireground operations.
2. Describe the procedures for controlling the natural gas fuel supply to a building.
3. Describe the procedures for controlling the LPG supply to a building.
4. Describe the procedures for controlling fuel oil supply to a building.
5. Describe the procedures for controlling a natural gas or LPG leak in a building with no fire present.
6. Describe the procedures for controlling the electrical supply in residential occupancies during a structure fire.
7. Describe the procedures for controlling the electrical supply in commercial and industrial occupancies during a structure fire.
8. Describe the factors to consider when shutting off the water supply to a sprinklered building during a fire.

Safety Points

When reading this chapter, keep the following safety points in mind:

- Control of the building's utilities must be coordinated by the Incident Commander.
- Building utilities should be controlled with a specific purpose in mind and must not be shut down arbitrarily.
- All gas or fuel leaks should be approached from a direction that is upwind of the reported location.
- Pulling an electrical meter is potentially hazardous and may not even completely stop the flow of electricity to the building.

Chapter 7
Controlling Utilities and Building Systems

Case History

In January of 1998, a construction crew severed an underground gas main in the downtown commercial district of Phoenix, Arizona. The construction crew called 9-1-1. Because there was a confirmed natural gas leak, the PFD notified the utility company and dispatched two engines, a ladder truck, a rescue unit, and a chief officer to the scene. On arrival, PFD personnel established a perimeter, set up a protective hoseline, and stood by while waiting for utility company personnel and equipment to arrive.

Shortly after the utility crew arrived with a large truck and a backhoe, a huge fireball blew out of the front windows of the nearest building. Since the open window area was not large enough to completely relieve the overpressure created by the explosion, the walls and roof of the building also disintegrated. This sent debris flying in every direction. The utility crew and several firefighters were knocked down by the blast, but no one was seriously hurt.

Had fire personnel not secured the scene and controlled entry, the results might have been much worse. This incident is typical of countless others in which firefighters and civilians have been injured or killed by explosions and fires.

Historically, firefighters and others have been injured or killed by fires and explosions that were either caused or fueled by flammable substances used in residential and industrial occupancies. Others have been injured by flash burns from electrical arcs or killed by electrocution. Victims have also been scalded by fire-heated water, or have drowned while trapped in basements or cellars because the water supply to the structure was not shut off. Unfortunately, such incidents continue to occur and these incidents highlight the importance of utility and building system control.

At working structure fires, securing a burning building's utilities is one of the best ways in which to protect firefighters and occupants who may be trapped inside. However, arbitrarily securing all of a burning building's utilities may not always be the best course of action. For example, arbitrarily shutting down all electrical power to a burning high-rise building can preclude the use of the building's elevators, HVAC systems, fire pumps, and lighting. In some industrial occupancies, shutting down the power can interrupt critical processes and

Figure 7.1 It may be necessary to shut down the electrical service to industrial machines to prevent accidents.

Liquefied Petroleum Gas (LPG) — Any of several petroleum products, such as propane or butane, stored under pressure as a liquid.

may disrupt essential cooling systems, which could lead to overheating and fires or explosions. As with every other aspect of truck company operations, control of a burning building's utilities must be coordinated with search and rescue and fire suppression efforts.

Securing the utilities to a burning building is not always related to preventing explosions and electrocutions. For example, it may be necessary to secure the gas service because it is also supplying fuel to a malfunctioning industrial oven or other gas-fired device. Likewise, it may be necessary to shut down the electrical service to prevent machines or other appliances from accidentally being reenergized at a critical moment (**Figure 7.1**).

Not all gas and electrical emergencies are related to structure fires because some occur outside of buildings and other structures. For example, as in the case history cited earlier, construction crews sometimes sever gas mains, water mains, or underground electrical cables while excavating or trenching. Vehicles sometimes crash into gas meters, electrical transformer boxes, and other utilities and create serious problems for the occupants and for firefighters. These contingencies can create incidents that are limited to the location where the service was damaged, or their effects may spread over a large area and impact a large population.

As mentioned earlier, uncontrolled utilities at structure fires and other emergency incidents can result in increased property damage, injuries, and even fatalities. To prevent or reduce these excessive property losses and traumatic injuries, utility services must be controlled in a safe and timely manner. This chapter begins with a discussion of fuel control, which includes natural gas (methane), **liquefied petroleum gas (LPG)**, and fuel oil. The chapter continues with discussions of controlling electrical utilities (including solar panels) and water supplies.

Fuel Control

Many of the utility-related calamities in which firefighters have been injured or killed were caused by or fueled by natural gas, LPG, or heating oil. Some of these incidents involved gas leaks that went undetected until the buildings exploded. Other incidents involved gas explosions that occurred as firefighters investigated a report of *an odor in the area*. Still others involved gas explosions inside burning buildings as firefighters operated on scene.

> According to an NFPA® report, firefighters in New York State were called to a reported propane leak in December of 1983. While a large propane tank was being moved, it had fallen from a forklift in the basement of a three-story warehouse. When the tank struck the concrete floor, the valve broke off and liquid propane began escaping. The forklift driver immediately called the fire department, but just as the first-due units arrived, the propane vapors reached an ignition source and a tremendous explosion followed. The explosion blew a ladder truck and two engines across the street. Five firefighters and two civilians were killed; 26 other firefighters and dozens of civilians were injured.

Situational Differences

While the universal priorities of life safety, incident stabilization, and property conservation remain the same, situational differences may necessitate different approaches to addressing these priorities. For example, the most common fuel control problem that truck company personnel face is making sure that the gas supply to a burning building is secured. Securing this utility reduces the chances of an explosion from escaping fuel gas within the building and keeps the escaping gas from adding fuel to the fire. Therefore, following the universal priorities in this situation is best done by securing the building's fuel supply as quickly as possible. In most cases, the tools and techniques described in **Essentials** can be used to accomplish this task.

On the other hand, if the call is to a reported gas leak without fire, the universal priorities dictate that the responding units approach the scene from upwind and stage a safe distance away. Of course, there are other considerations involved that include establishing isolation zones, eliminating sources of ignition, and evacuating those downwind from the scene. How the universal fireground priorities are followed in these instances will vary with the situation.

The two most common gas control situations that firefighters face are those in structure fires and those in which there is a gas leak without fire. As mentioned earlier, uncontrolled utilities can complicate a fire situation and perhaps result in increased property damage, injuries, or fatalities. Therefore, it is critically important that a burning building's utilities be secured as dictated by the situation at hand.

Controlling Natural Gas in Structure Fires

Stopping the flow of natural gas into a burning building is one of the most common gas control operations that firefighters perform. In many cases, the tools and techniques for securing a building's gas supply are as described in **Essentials**. This is not always the case, however. For example, many industrial sites and some larger commercial buildings have gas meters that are much larger than those shown in **Essentials.** These meters may have a different type of control valve than firefighters are accustomed to.

The main control valve on heavy-duty gas meters may simply be a larger version of the quarter-turn crossbar valve common to residential and light commercial buildings **(Figure 7.2)**. However, some heavy-duty control valves are installed in either a horizontal or vertical section of the main line close to the meter housing. In addition, the operating nut is usually square instead of the crossbar design found on most residential meters. Turning the square-operating nut one-quarter turn in either direction closes the valve. Turning this nut requires a properly sized open-end or box wrench or a large adjustable wrench. The type of shutoff valve should be identified during preincident planning surveys so that firefighters can take the correct tool to the meter initially.

Another item to verify during preincident planning is the location of the gas meter on the property. Gas meter location varies greatly from region to region. In some areas, gas meters are located at or near the curb, making them easy to locate during an

Figure 7.2 Commercial gas meters are often similar in nature to those of residential occupancies. These gas meters are simply of a larger scale.

emergency **(Figure 7.3)**. In other areas, meters are typically located at one of the front corners of the building, making them accessible from the street. Just because a meter is accessible from the street does not mean it will be readily visible **(Figure 7.4)**. This is especially true if the property owner plants shrubbery in front of the meter for aesthetic reasons. Gas meters in other areas may be located along the rear property line, in the basement, or under exterior stairways, making them more difficult to find during an emergency. In many industrial properties, gas meters are located in underground vaults or in utility rooms inside the buildings. Once again, familiarity with the property gained through preincident planning surveys is critically important to the process of cutting off the gas supply to a structure **(Figure 7.5)**.

In buildings with multiple occupancies, there is usually a gas meter for each occupancy or unit within the building **(Figure 7.6)**. If the meters are not clearly labeled to identify which occupancy each meter serves, it may be necessary to shut off the gas service to the entire building. This can cause a disruption of service to those occupancies not affected by the fire and may result in critical industrial processes being interrupted needlessly. Therefore,

Figure 7.3 Gas meters located near a curb are typically easy to locate, but run the risk of being struck by a wayward vehicle.

Figure 7.4 Gas meters are often obscured by landscaping and other items.

Figure 7.5 Obscure gas meters and the location of other utility connections are important to identify during preincident planning.

Figure 7.6 Gas meters that serve multiple occupancies should be properly labeled to prevent shutting off the wrong meter.

firefighters should work with property owners during preincident planning to get each gas meter correctly labeled.

It is SOP in many fire departments that firefighters are not allowed to restore natural gas service to any occupancy once the flow of gas has been turned off. Others make a distinction based on where the shutoff is located; firefighters are allowed to open valves located above ground, but are not allowed to open those in underground vaults or rooms.

If a natural gas leak has caused gas to infiltrate a building – even one in which there is no unfriendly fire burning – a high priority for firefighters is to prevent a natural gas explosion. Because natural gas is lighter than air, it will tend to rise. Therefore, firefighters need to be most concerned about evacuating everyone and eliminating ignition sources located above the point of release.

Controlling LPG in Structure Fires

In areas not served by a natural gas distribution system, buildings of all types — residential, mercantile, agricultural, institutional, and industrial — often use liquefied petroleum gas (LPG) for heating and industrial processes. In some areas, LPG tanks are housed in underground vaults which reduce the chances of the tanks or piping being struck by vehicles. While homes and small businesses may have relatively small LPG tanks on site, the quantities needed at some sites require very large storage tanks on the premises **(Figure 7.7)**.

If a large horizontal tank is involved in fire, and especially if LPG is venting from the tank, firefighters should not attempt to control the leak. They may be able to set up master streams to cool the tank and any adjacent exposures and withdraw a safe distance away. Fire streams should be directed at the upper portion of the tank in order to cool the vapor area.

When any LPG tank — regardless of size — is involved in fire, the possibility of a **boiling liquid expanding vapor explosion (BLEVE)** is ever-present. Therefore, if the fire has the potential of reaching a portable LPG tank, it may be prudent to disconnect the tank and move it away from the building. A forklift or similar vehicle may be needed to move larger tanks. Otherwise, these situations must be handled as described in **Essentials** and according to local SOPs.

The DOT *Emergency Response Guidebook* (*ERG 2008*) recommends pulling back ½ mile (800 m) in these instances **(Figure 7.8, p. 182)**. However, any decision to approach a propane tank with direct flame impingement must be

Boiling Liquid Expanding Vapor Explosion (BLEVE) — Rapid vaporization of a liquid stored under pressure upon release to the atmosphere following major failure of its containing vessel; failure is the result of over-pressurization caused by an external heat source, which causes the vessel to explode into two or more pieces when the temperature of the liquid is well above its boiling point at normal atmospheric pressure.

Figure 7.7 Industrial occupancies may use large LPG storage tanks.

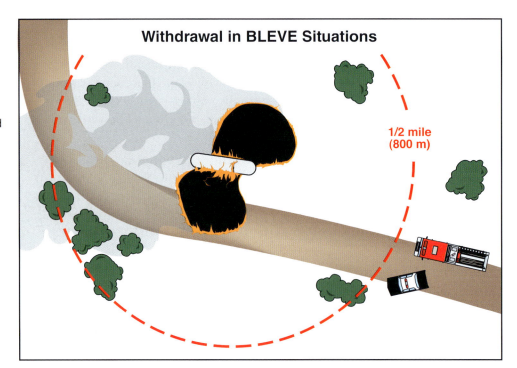

Figure 7.8 Evacuations should be made at least ½ mile away from a LPG tank that has the potential for BLEVE. This illustration is not to scale.

Figure 7.9 LPG tanks involved by fire can be difficult to control.

> **WARNING!**
> Regardless of its size, if an LPG tank is exposed to the heat of direct flame impingement it can undergo a boiling liquid expanding vapor explosion (BLEVE), with devastating force.

made on a case-by-case basis after weighing the risks against the benefits and assessing whether available water supply and pumping capacity are adequate.

At structure fires, there are two different scenarios firefighters may have to face involving LPG tanks. The first is when the LPG tank is threatened by or involved in fire **(Figure 7.9)**. The other very common scenario is when the LPG is or may be fueling a fire inside a building but the LPG tank itself is not involved.

If the LPG tank is not threatened by or involved in the fire, the flow of gas can be stopped by turning off the valve located where the piping connects to the tank. On portable LPG tanks, the control valve is located on the top of the tank, sometimes protected by a hinged weatherproof cover **(Figure 7.10)**. On fixed installations with large horizontal tanks, the control valve may be located on the side of the tank or in a manifold box at the end of the tank **(Figure 7.11)**. Where multiple tanks are installed side by side, the flow from any or all of the tanks may be controlled from a central manifold location.

Figure 7.10 The white bubbles on top of these LPG tanks lift up to reveal the control valve for the tank.

Figure 7.11 Large fixed LPG tanks have a control panel on the side or adjacent to the tank. *Courtesy of Keith Flood.*

Figure 7.12 LPG is heavier than air and will collect in low areas.

Because LPG is heavier than air, leaking gas will tend to stay close to the ground and collect in depressions, basements, underground vaults, and other low areas **(Figure 7.12)**. Therefore, if there is an LPG leak without fire, firefighters should eliminate sources of ignition located below and downwind from the leak source. If evacuations are necessary, those located downhill and downwind of the leak are the most at risk and should be evacuated first.

Controlling Fuel Oil in Structure Fires

Many buildings in North America are heated with oil rather than natural gas or LPG. Some industrial boilers are fired with pulverized coal and a variety of other similar fuels. These other fuels are far less common than fuel oil, so this discussion is confined to heaters and boilers using ordinary heating oil. Heating oil is sometimes stored in underground tanks that are connected to the heating appliance by copper or aluminum tubing. In multifamily residential buildings, there can be hundreds of gallons (liters) of fuel oil located in the basement. Firefighters should be aware of this potential hazard when responding to a report of a heating oil leak or fire in the basement.

In other situations, heating oil tanks are mounted on stanchions aboveground to increase gravity pressure. These stanchions may or may not be fire resistive. In locations where the stanchions are made of wood or unprotected steel, jurisdictions usually require that the tanks be surrounded by an earthen dike or other means of containment.

Even though a BLEVE of a fuel oil tank is theoretically possible, it is highly unlikely because fuel oil tanks are not pressure vessels. Fuel oil tanks usually rupture in a fire before the conditions required for a BLEVE develop. However, this does *not* mean that fuel oil tanks are not dangerous when exposed to direct flame impingement. The fire-related rupture of a fuel oil tank can result in the spread of flaming oil over a large area around the tank.

As a combustible liquid, heating oil must be preheated before it will burn. The preheating process may increase the risk to firefighters because this is usually done with either electricity or steam. In most appliances, the oil is also atomized into a fine spray as it is introduced into the firebox. Some industrial heaters or boilers use steam or air atomizers, but most residential units use mechanical atomizers. Considering that the oil pressure required for maximum efficiency ranges from 600 to 1,000 psi (4 100 kPa to 6 900 kPa), any of these systems may be dangerous to firefighters who are unfamiliar with them. For their own safety, firefighters must familiarize themselves with the types of heating systems in use in their respective response districts. In large residential buildings, firefighters should work closely with building engineers or maintenance supervisors.

If a fuel oil tank is not threatened by or involved in fire, the flow of oil can be stopped at the tank by closing the gate valve where the tubing connects to the tank. If the valve is inoperable for any reason, crimping the tubing can stop the flow of oil. The tubing can sometimes be crimped with heavy-duty pliers or with a hydraulic cutter equipped with crimping blades **(Figure 7.13)**.

Perhaps the most dangerous phenomenon associated with oil-fired appliances is commonly called a *white ghost*. The name comes from the white cloud of fuel oil vapor that forms in and around an oil-fired appliance when the pilot light fails to ignite a fine spray of fuel oil introduced into an already heated firebox.

In these instances, all occupants of the building should be evacuated, and the fuel oil should be shut off at the remote control switch (usually located near the utility room door), or at the tank. The utility room should be thoroughly ventilated and firefighters should avoid entering the vapor cloud unless absolutely necessary.

> **WARNING!**
> A white ghost has a strong odor of fuel oil and is within its explosive range. If the cloud cannot be dispersed before it reaches an ignition source, it can explode with devastating force.

Figure 7.13 The tubing for fuel oil tanks can sometimes be crimped with pliers to shut off the flow. *Courtesy of Mark Pare.*

Gas Leaks Without Fire

The case history cited earlier in this chapter involving an LPG tank falling off a forklift is only one type of call involving an uncontrolled release of a flammable gas. A more common call that fire departments receive is a report of an odor of gas from an unknown source in a building or neighborhood. When investigating an odor of gas where the source of the leak is not immediately apparent, adjacent buildings should also be checked because gas can migrate through the ground and emerge some distance from the leak. In addition, soil may filter out the additives that give natural gas and LPG their distinctive odors. This means that it is possible that buildings may be filling with flammable gas that has no odor. The occupants of these buildings may be unaware of the danger until an explosion takes place. Therefore, firefighters must not become complacent when dealing with these incidents. Crews should establish a perimeter or isolation zone, charge one or more protective hoselines, and wear full PPE while investigating the source of the leak with properly calibrated **combustible gas indicators (CGI)** or multigas meters.

Combustible Gas Indicator (CGI) — Device that indicates the explosive levels of combustible gases.

In other instances, such as the case history from Phoenix cited earlier, the source of the gas leak is definitely known. Even though there may be no fire when the leak is initially reported, this situation can change in an instant. Uncontrolled flammable gas leaks are never *routine*. They are always potentially lethal, and firefighters should treat them that way. Safely handling these incidents involves using the correct approach, establishing and controlling the perimeter, and assessing and mitigating the hazard.

WARNING! Sparks from static electricity can ignite flammable gases, especially when relative humidity is low.

Approach

Because the responding fire apparatus could provide a source of ignition, the approach to the area of a reported odor should be from upwind. Apparatus responding from the downwind direction should stage well beyond the affected area or, if necessary, detour around the area of the odor and approach from the upwind side. Depending upon the size and location of the leak, wind speed and direction, topography, and local SOPs, apparatus should be staged as much as a block away and upwind from the leak. The *DOT ERG 2008* recommends staging anywhere from 160 to 330 feet (50 m to 100 m) from the source of both LPG and natural gas leaks. Those assigned to assess the hazard can approach the leak source on foot.

Perimeter Control

One of the first-arriving units should be assigned to establish a perimeter or **control zone** around the hazard area and maintain control of that perimeter. As the incident progresses, it may be necessary or desirable to set up hot, warm, and cold zones as described in **Essentials**. Initially, the goal is to establish a perimeter a safe distance from the leak. What constitutes a *safe* distance is a judgment made by the IC based on information supplied by firefighters and others at the scene. One critical piece of information relating to the establishment of the perimeter is an accurate assessment of the hazard, which is discussed in the next section. The perimeter should be marked with either CAUTION or FIRELINE tape, and only utility company personnel or those in full PPE should be allowed to enter the hazard area. Control of the perimeter should be passed to law enforcement as soon as possible if firefighters were used to establish the initial perimeter **(Figure 7.14, p. 186)**.

Control Zone — System of barriers surrounding designated areas at emergency scenes intended to limit the number of persons exposed to the hazard, and to facilitate its mitigation. At a major incident there will be three zones — restricted (hot), limited access (warm), and support (cold).

Chapter 7 • Controlling Utilities and Building Systems 185

> **CAUTION**
>
> If there are civilians inside the perimeter, they should be advised to leave the area immediately. Civilians must be warned against using cell phones or turning on or off any lights, televisions, computers, or other electrical devices until they are outside the control zone. Vehicle engines should not be started and evacuations should be done on foot.

Figure 7.14 Law enforcement personnel should be left to control the perimeter, freeing firefighters to perform more critical functions.

Lower Explosive Limit (LEL) — Lowest percentage of fuel/oxygen mixture required to support combustion. Any mixture with a lower percentage would be considered *too lean* to burn.

> **CAUTION**
>
> To function as designed, CGI units must be maintained according to the manufacturer's instructions and properly calibrated. Firefighters must also be trained on the proper use of these instruments.

These instructions are necessary to prevent people from inadvertently creating a spark (source of ignition) when an electrical switch is used or an internal combustion engine is started. The instructions may be announced over a public address system or by handheld electronic bullhorns. Firefighters should also work closely with the local electrical utility to ensure that proper instructions are given and actions are coordinated.

Hazard Assessment

One way to assess a flammable gas leak is by using combustible gas indicators (CGI). These handheld devices not only detect the presence of a combustible gas, they also indicate its concentration. Some of these units express the gas detected in parts per million (ppm) and others as a percentage of the **lower explosive limit (LEL)**.

One way of establishing a control zone is for the CGI operator to move from a point that registers no detectible concentration toward the suspected leak source, taking samples at frequent intervals until a reading is noted. Because natural gas is slightly lighter than air, the readings should not be taken near the ground. Instead, they should be taken at waist height or higher **(Figure 7.15)**. Departmental SOPs must be followed, but in general, the point at which the first detectible reading appears is one point at which the perimeter may be established. Since the LEL for natural gas is 5 percent (50,000 ppm), many fire departments establish the perimeter at 10 percent of that figure — 0.5 percent (5,000 ppm). However, because the lower explosive limit for propane is 1.5 percent (15,000 ppm), any reading above 0.15 percent (1500 ppm) may be too dangerous, and it may be advisable to locate control points where readings indicate a lower concentration. This process is repeated at various points around the leak until the entire hazard area has been defined and cordoned off.

When monitoring for LPG, readings should be taken close to the ground. One characteristic that makes establishing the perimeter of an LPG leak somewhat easier than with natural gas is that the cloud may be visible. When sufficient humidity is present, an LPG leak may form a white cloud in air. Because LPG is heavier than air, the cloud hugs the ground and collects in depressions and other low areas. The fact that LPG is heavier than air also makes it more likely that the gas will enter storm drains, utility vaults, culverts, and open basement windows. Areas such as basements are of particular concern because they

Figure 7.15 Readings with the CGI should be taken at waist height.

often contain sources of ignition such as heating appliances with pilot lights. Firefighters should also be aware that the white cloud formed by an LPG leak is not the only dangerous area.

Hazard Mitigation

The main tasks that firefighters can perform to follow the universal priorities in a gas leak without fire are to establish a safe perimeter or control zone, deny unauthorized entry, and prevent the gas leak from becoming a gas explosion. The process of preventing a leaking gas from reaching a source of ignition before the leak can be controlled can vary.

Control of Natural Gas and LPG Leaks

Some fuel gas leaks may be controlled by firefighters; others should be left to utility company or gas supply company personnel. Many fire departments allow their personnel (wearing full PPE) to shut off the flow of gas at aboveground gas meters, but insist that utility company crews handle shutoffs below grade. Utility company emergency response personnel are trained and equipped to handle these contingencies. Even when utility company or gas supply company personnel control the flow of gas, the IC may order firefighters to conduct or assist with the evacuation of those downwind of the leak. The IC may choose to shelter those people in place rather than evacuating them. This can be done

WARNING! The visible cloud of LPG is surrounded by an invisible envelope of gas that is within its explosive range.

using a public address system to instruct the occupants of buildings downwind of the leak to close all exterior windows and doors, remain indoors, and not to turn any electrical or electronic device on or off until notified otherwise.

The other way that firefighters may help reduce the hazard of a fuel gas leak is by systematically eliminating sources of ignition downwind of the leak. This is usually done in areas from which the occupants have been evacuated. Starting from a point within the perimeter that is farthest from the leak source and working slowly toward it, firefighters turn off the gas supply to every building within the perimeter. This should extinguish any pilot lights within these buildings. Firefighters should be aware that exceptionally long gas distribution lines in large buildings or complexes may take some time to bleed down.

Many fire departments do not allow their firefighters to restore gas service to buildings following a fire or other emergency. That task is left to the utility company or gas supplier because it involves making sure that there are no leaks and relighting all pilot lights.

Electricity Control

The electrical power to a burning building may come from the conventional power grid, photovoltaic (PV) solar panels installed on the roof of the building, or an on-site wind turbine generator **(Figure 7.16)**. Regardless of its source, controlling the electrical power can be one of the most critical functions of truck company personnel. While control of the electrical service to a structure is important, arbitrarily shutting off the service is not always advisable. Just as in controlling gas service, there are situational differences that affect how and when the flow of electrical power should be interrupted. For truck company personnel, the two most common emergency situations involving electricity are structure fires and downed electrical wires.

Figure 7.16 Solar panels are becoming more common in new buildings. *Courtesy of the McKinney (TX) Fire Department.*

Controlling Electricity in Structure Fires

In many structure fires, one of the most important safety considerations is shutting down electrical service to the burning building. Eliminating the flow of electrical power to the building helps protect firefighters and others from electrical shocks – even electrocution – and prevents additional fires from being started by electrical arcs and overheated wiring or components.

When the IC orders the electrical supply shut off, firefighters must know where and how to do so safely. The location and means of shutting off a building's electrical service varies depending upon whether power to the building is supplied exclusively by the power grid or is supplemented by rooftop PV panels or a wind turbine, and whether the building was designed for residential, commercial, or industrial occupancy.

Residential Occupancies

Most single-family residences take power from the grid so they have only one main electrical panel, located with the electrical meter and main switch. If PV panels or a wind turbine also supply power, the shutoff switch for these sys-

> **CAUTION**
> Because shutting off power may preclude the use of elevators and fire pumps, and because loss of power can damage some industrial equipment or disrupt critical processes, shutting off electrical power should only be done when ordered.

tems is most likely to be located near the main electrical switch, but may be elsewhere. Where power is distributed to the neighborhood through overhead wires from the power grid, the building's main electrical panel is usually located directly below the weather head where power from a pole-mounted transformer enters the building **(Figure 7.17)**. In many areas, newer housing developments or subdivisions have underground power lines. In these areas, firefighters must locate the electrical panel on or in the building to access the main electric switch. However, some very large residences and many apartment buildings and condominiums have a number of subpanels serving various parts of the building. Having one or more subpanels permits electricity to be shut off to some sections of a building while leaving electrical power on in other parts of the building. This may be desirable or necessary so that emergency lighting, HVAC systems, or fire pumps can continue to operate.

Historically, some fire departments trained their personnel to secure the electrical service to a residential building by pulling the electrical meter. This can be extremely dangerous for the firefighter pulling it. Furthermore, this action does not necessarily guarantee that all electrical power to the building is eliminated. Many departments also trained their firefighters to cut the drip loop at the weather head.

Today, electrical utility companies recommend neither of these practices. If an electrical meter must be pulled or the drip loop needs to be cut, it should be done only by utility company personnel.

Many fire departments prohibit their firefighters from cutting electrical wires that *might* be energized. This is because their nonconductive tools and equipment may not have been properly maintained and tested, and their firefighters may not have been trained in the proper use of the tools and equipment. As described in **Essentials**, firefighters should assume that all electrical wires are energized.

To secure electrical service to a burning residential building, firefighters in most departments are trained to locate the main electrical panel and to open the main switch or circuit breaker. Most agencies do not advocate removing the circuit breaker. In some departments, but not all, it is SOP that once the switch or breaker has been opened, it should be locked in the open position and tagged (lockout/tagout) **(Figure 7.18, p. 190)**. However, opening any electrical switch can create an arc or spark sufficient to ignite any flammable gases or vapors present.

As mentioned earlier, in high-rise and other large residential buildings, it may be desirable to maintain the electrical service to some portions of the building so that elevators, HVAC systems, fire pumps, and other vital components can remain operational. Whenever possible, building maintenance personnel should operate system controls, including those that control electrical power.

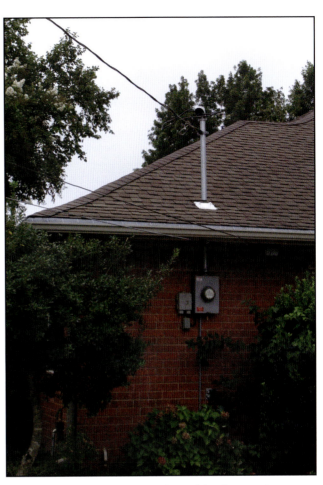

Figure 7.17 The main electrical panel for the structure can usually be found directly below the weather head.

WARNING!
Pulling an electrical meter or cutting a drip loop or any other electrical wire can be hazardous to the firefighter performing the operation.

WARNING!
Electrical switches should not be opened or closed if flammable gases or vapors are present.

Figure 7.18 Facility personnel can be utilized to assist in lockout/tagout procedures if it is safe for them to do so.

Firefighters should rely on the building engineer or maintenance staff to open switches or circuit breakers that will interrupt power to selected portions of the building while maintaining electrical power to the remainder.

Commercial Occupancies

The same reasons for securing electrical utilities in residential buildings apply to commercial buildings. However, because there may be several subpanels, simply finding the right electrical switch in a commercial building can sometimes be difficult. In some commercial occupancies, shutting off the main electrical switch activates a generator or other source of emergency power. In addition, on-site battery banks or solar panels may continue to provide power to areas that need to be shut down. The presence of generators, PV panels, storage batteries (a source of flammable hydrogen gas), and other emergency power sources should be identified during preincident planning. Otherwise, the tools and techniques required for securing electrical power to commercial buildings are, in most cases, little different from securing power to large residential buildings.

In other cases, shutting off electrical power to commercial buildings can be much more hazardous than securing the power supply to residential occupancies. The hazards involved are related to the size of the electrical components (including pad-mounted transformers) installed in many commercial buildings, especially older buildings. The main electrical switches in many older commercial buildings are much larger than those in the typical residential building **(Figure 7.19)**. Opening these large switches often results in an electrical arc. In addition to being a source of ignition if flammable vapors or gases are present, this arc can damage the eyes of anyone looking at the switch. Therefore, when opening large main electrical switches, firefighters should take appropriate precautions to protect themselves and others as they operate the lever arm on these switches. If possible, utility personnel should be used to operate these controls.

Industrial Occupancies

Unlike those in either residential or commercial buildings, the electrical utilities in industrial buildings or facilities can be extraordinarily large and complex. Because of the power demands of some industrial processes, the on-site electrical utilities may be as large as those for some small communities. Some

Figure 7.19 A typical commercial electrical panel and main switch.

Figure 7.20 This electrical substation serves an adjacent industrial plant.

industrial facilities have fenced enclosures containing banks of high-voltage transformers **(Figure 7.20)**. Even though banned by the U.S. Environmental Protection Agency (EPA) for many years, the oil in some older transformers may contain polychlorinated biphenyls (PCBs), which are known **carcinogens**.

Other facilities may have their high-voltage electrical equipment housed in concrete utility vaults. Through preincident planning surveys conducted as often as necessary, firefighters should become as familiar as possible with the industrial electrical utilities in their response districts. However, during a major fire, firefighters may have to rely upon plant personnel who know how to safely manipulate the system as needed. Indiscriminately shutting down industrial power sources can deactivate safety devices, overpressure pumps, and cause numerous other hazardous situations. Because of these dangers, plant personnel are responsible for working closely with the fire department to help carry out the incident action plan.

Carcinogen — Cancer-producing substance.

> **CAUTION**
> Even transformers marked *No PCB* can still contain trace amounts, so firefighters should assume that all transformers contain PCBs.

Downed Electrical Wires

The other major category of electrical emergencies to which truck company personnel are often called involves electrical wires that have fallen to the ground for some reason. Wires are sometimes blown down in windstorms, or they break under the weight of snow or ice. At other times they fall because the pole or tower supporting them is knocked down, often as a result of being

Chapter 7 • Controlling Utilities and Building Systems

hit by a vehicle. Regardless of why and how the wires fell, the priorities for the responding firefighters are still the same — life safety, incident stabilization, and property conservation.

> One of the most important actions firefighters can take in dealing with downed electrical wires is to contact the responsible utility provider, describe the situation, and request its emergency response team.

> According to an NFPA® report, in 1994 a vehicle struck a power pole beside a rural road and the driver was thrown out. A paramedic and five firefighters strapped the victim to a backboard and attempted to slide the backboard under the uninsulated high-voltage power lines hanging close to the ground. When one of the firefighters holding the backboard brushed against one of the power lines, the paramedic, the victim on the backboard, and two firefighters were electrocuted. The other three firefighters holding the board were injured but somehow survived.

Unfortunately, this type of incident is not uncommon. Similar incidents occur even in newer residential neighborhoods with underground electrical service.

> In San Jose, California, a speeding automobile jumped a curb and came to rest on top of the metal housing of a pad-mounted distribution transformer. When the police officer investigating the incident touched the vehicle, he was electrocuted.

Handling these potentially lethal incidents is sometimes very similar to the procedures for handling the gas leak incidents discussed earlier in this chapter. In most cases involving downed electrical wires, firefighters should do nothing more than establish a perimeter and deny entry to all except utility company personnel. However, there are incidents in which firefighters must to do some basic hazard assessment in order to decide where the perimeter should be established.

Perimeter Control

Controlling the scene and denying unauthorized entry while waiting for utility company personnel to arrive is a very important and potentially lifesaving action (**Figure 7.21**). However, utility personnel may be overtaxed with numerous downed wires as the result of a major storm. In areas with widespread storm damage, the response of local utility crews to any particular scene can be delayed — sometimes for hours or days. When there are numerous wires down in a fire department's response area, fire crews are unlikely to have enough resources to stand by at every downed wire. In these cases, it may be necessary for individual companies to simply cordon off each hazard zone with either CAUTION or FIRELINE tape or mark it with traffic cones and move on to the next incident (**Figure 7.22**).

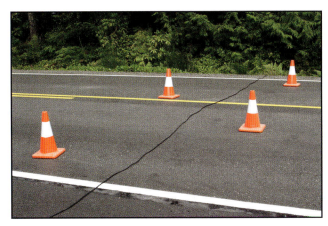

Figure 7.22 Traffic cones are often used to mark areas of downed power lines.

Figure 7.21 In some instances, it may be necessary to delay emergency operations until the utility company has rendered the electrical service safe.

In some incidents involving downed electrical wires, establishing and controlling the perimeter is relatively easy; in others it can be quite difficult. For example, if a single strand of power line has parted, it may be relatively easy to see where the break is and where the perimeter should be established to isolate the break. On the other hand, if an energized electrical wire falls across a metal fence (chain link, barbed wire, etc.), the entire length of the fence can become energized. If the fence is enclosing a large institutional, industrial, or agricultural property, the fence may be miles (kilometers) in length. Anyone touching the fence may then complete the circuit to ground and suffer a severe electrical shock – even electrocution. Similarly, innocuous-looking telephone wires or cable TV lines that are down may be energized with electrical power if they are in contact with live power lines at any point.

Establishing a perimeter around a downed electrical wire may be as simple as placing traffic cones around the hazard zone to direct motor vehicles around the scene. In other cases, it may be necessary to close a street at both ends of the block in which a wire has fallen.

A common error is to establish a perimeter that is too small. As described in **Essentials**, the recommended isolation distance is that equal to one full span between the adjacent poles or towers in all directions from a break in a wire or the point of contact with the ground. If curious pedestrians are converging on the scene, it may be necessary to cordon it off with CAUTION tape,

> **CAUTION**
> All downed wires should be treated as energized high-voltage lines until proven otherwise.

Chapter 7 • Controlling Utilities and Building Systems **193**

WARNING!
Do *not* attempt to remove a power line that is in direct contact with a vehicle unless you are properly trained and equipped to handle energized electrical wires. Avoid touching the vehicle — even if there are injured passengers still inside. Call the responsible utility company and keep everyone away from the vehicle and the downed wire until utility company personnel have shut off the power.

FIRELINE tape, or rope. In most cases, the method and degree of perimeter control established depends upon the nature and scope of the situation, the available resources, and on local SOPs.

If the wire is down because a vehicle struck the pole or tower supporting it, and the driver and passengers are still inside, it is necessary to establish hot, warm, and cold zones as described in **Essentials (Figure 7.23)**. The occupants of the vehicle should be advised not to attempt to exit the vehicle.

Hazard Identification

While the general rule for perimeter placement can be used in most downed wire incidents, it may not always be adequate. In some situations, such as following an explosion or structural collapse, it may be necessary to more clearly define the hazard area. For example, if a downed wire is obscured by building debris, smoke, or darkness, firefighters may need to use various forms of technology to identify the hazard area. Two of the most useful devices available to fire departments are *alternating current detectors* and *thermal imaging cameras*.

Alternating current detectors. Alternating current detectors can detect unshielded AC current through snow, ice, and many solid objects. These battery-operated devices are handheld wands similar in size and shape to a police officer's baton **(Figure 7.24)**. In the presence of an alternating current, they emit an intermittent beep. The closer the device is to the source, the more rapid the beep. The detection range (distance from the source at which the device detects the current) varies with the situation. In general, the higher the line voltage, the greater the range of detection will be. Under ideal conditions, these devices may be able to detect AC current in a single 120-volt line from as far as 15 feet (3 m). However, if the conductor is lying on wet soil, the range may be reduced to as little as 1 foot (300 mm). With higher potentials, such as those in distribution and transmission lines, the detection range can increase to more than 500 feet (150 m).

Because power outages often result from very temporary causes, such as a tree limb being blown against a wire by high wind, most electrical distribution systems are programmed to automatically reenergize a few seconds after the circuit breaker in the substation trips. If

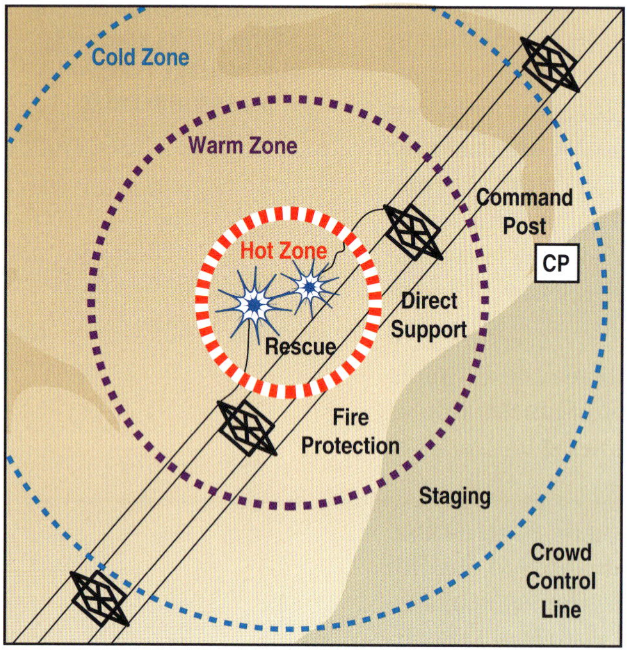

Figure 7.23 Typical control zones around a downed electrical wire.

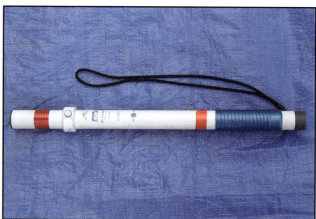

Figure 7.24 A typical AC detector.

the breaker trips again, many of these programs reenergize the system one more time before remaining off-line. Therefore, even if a handheld detector fails to activate near a downed wire, it only means that the line is dead at that given moment, not that the line itself is necessarily dead.

When power from the normal utility source fails, some emergency generators may start automatically. If these units are not disconnected from the system, the power lines can be reenergized with 240 volts from the generators. Also, many overhead power lines are supplied from both directions. This means that a line broken at a single point can still be energized on both sides of the break.

Thermal imaging cameras. Thermal imagers can also be used to detect hidden wires. Electrical current creates heat whenever it encounters resistance in a circuit, and the heat is created at the point of resistance, not throughout the circuit. This phenomenon can be seen in the operation of an electric range or space heater. Resistance occurs when an uninsulated conductor (wire) is in contact with the ground or there is a kink in or damage to a conductor, insulated or not. This resistance creates heat and thermal imagers can detect that heat.

> Even though the technology just discussed allows firefighters to locate energized electrical conductors more safely and more reliably than in the past, most fire departments still do not allow their personnel to move or cut electrical wires under any circumstances. The majority of electric utility companies also support this practice. Therefore, unless directed otherwise by the IC or by local SOPs, firefighters should locate and isolate downed electrical wires, establish and control a perimeter, and wait for utility company personnel to shut off the power to those wires.

Water Control

The case history discussed in Chapter 4 involving the collapse of a hotel undergoing renovation is another reminder of the dangers associated with water accumulation during fire attack. While there were a number of factors that contributed to the collapse of that hotel, the weight of the water used to extinguish the fire was almost certainly one of them, perhaps the primary one. This is easy to understand when the following hypothetical example is considered:

If extinguishing a fire on an upper floor of a 50- × 100-foot (15 m by 30 m) building results in 6 inches (150 mm) of water accumulating on the floor, the total weight of that water exceeds 75 tons (68 *t*). This amount of water can be discharged from automatic sprinklers or hoselines (or both) in a few minutes. In addition, the water may not have to be that deep if any of its volume has been absorbed into the contents of the building.

Controlling the water supply in a structure fire incident can be a lifesaving action. Uncontrolled water flow can contribute to structural instability and collapse, fill basements or cellars, and sometimes result in scalding injuries or steam burns to firefighters **(Figure 7.25, p. 196)**. When water fills a basement, it can **short circuit** the main electrical service and extinguish pilot lights in gas-fired appliances. In some cases, this can add a flammable gas leak to an already hazardous situation. However, just as there are variations in when

Short Circuit — An abnormal, low-resistance path between conductors that allows a high current flow that normally leads to an overcurrent condition.

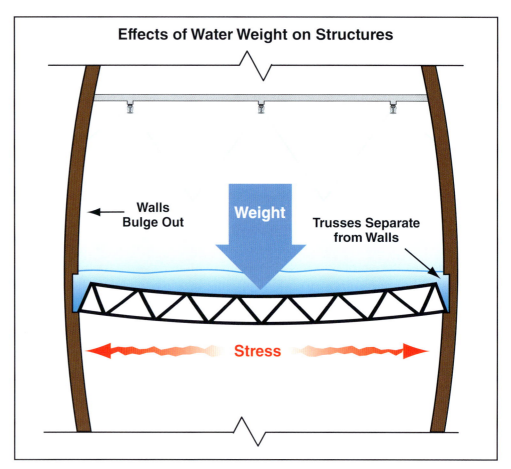

Figure 7.25 Water from sprinklers or hoselines can add substantial weight to upper floors of a structure, greatly adding to the collapse potential.

and how other utilities are controlled, there are also situational differences with regard to controlling water supplies. The two most common situations relating to water control by truck company personnel are in structure fires and in buildings with major water leaks without fire.

Water Control in Structure Fires

There are several differences in water control during structure fires, depending on the structure. The most prominent examples of these differences are between fires in sprinklered and unsprinklered buildings.

Sprinklered Buildings

Controlling the water supply to a sprinklered building that is on fire requires careful coordination between all operational aspects on the fireground. The primary need is to maintain and sometimes increase the water supply to activated sprinklers. Water may also be needed to supply hoselines operating from standpipes within the building. Shutting off the building's water supply too soon could rob operating sprinklers and standpipes of the water needed to control the fire — and could increase the danger for firefighters.

As in the case history cited in Chapter 6, operating sprinklers can reduce the effectiveness of vertical ventilation efforts. In addition, the runoff water can be heated to scalding temperatures by the fire. When this extremely hot water cascades down from above, it can deny firefighters and others on that floor access to a means of egress — perhaps the only means. Shutting off the water supply to a building at the proper time can help reduce these effects, but timing is critically important. If water is shut off too soon, the fire may be allowed to overwhelm the on-scene fire fighting resources. Water that is shut off too late can contribute to structural instability because of the weight of the water accumulating inside the building. Allowing sprinklers to continue discharging water after the fire has been controlled also adds to the live load of the building and may unnecessarily increase property damage.

In some cases, it may be prudent to shut down the sprinkler system water supply after the fire has been controlled so that open sprinklers can be plugged or replaced. The water supply must then be restored if the standpipe system is to be used during overhaul.

A growing number of single-family residences have full or partial sprinkler systems installed. As in the larger commercial systems, a separate valve from the one that controls the domestic water supply controls the water supply to the sprinklers. But unlike the commercial systems, the valve controlling the water supply to residential sprinklers may be either a small OS&Y valve or the same type of gate valve as is used to control the domestic water supply.

Figure 7.26 A typical water valve cover.

Unsprinklered Buildings

In most cases, the decision regarding when to shut off the water supply to an unsprinklered building that is on fire is relatively simple. Unless the water supply is contributing to the fire suppression effort, it should be shut off as soon as possible. The only reason to delay shutting off the water supply would be because of resource limitations and other, higher fireground priorities. But as soon as someone is available, the water supply should be turned off.

On most small residential buildings, a single gate valve in the main line between the water meter and the building controls the water supply. When the water supply comes from a domestic well, there is usually a gate valve somewhere between the well and the building. On larger, multiple residential and other buildings, the water supply is controlled by a subsurface valve — often found in the sidewalk — between the water main and the building **(Figure 7.26)**. In even larger buildings and complexes, the water supply is controlled by a large subsurface valve in the street adjacent to the front of the property. A large T-handle water key may be needed to operate this valve **(Figure 7.27)**. Because municipal water systems can be damaged by street valves being closed too quickly, many agencies allow only water utility personnel to operate these valves. If local SOPs permit firefighters to operate these valves, they must be trained in the proper valve-closing procedures.

Figure 7.27 T-handle water keys are used to shut off water service to a structure.

Water Leaks without Fire

Major water leaks can develop in buildings for a variety of reasons. Seismic activity can break pipes or loosen fittings. Water hammer caused by large valves being closed too quickly can also damage plumbing or cause numerous pressure relief valves to open simultaneously. In addition, the effects of age, intermittent fluctuations in pressure, and the expansion and contraction due to changing temperatures (alternately freezing and thawing) can loosen pipe fittings over time or cause pipes to burst. All these causes, and any number of others, can produce water leaks that can have disastrous effects within buildings — especially if the leaks go undiscovered for an extended period of time.

Buildings with Basements or Cellars

The fact that a major water leak is not in the basement or cellar of a building does not necessarily mean that these spaces will not fill with water. Water is directly affected by gravity and will take the path of least resistance. Therefore, a water leak anywhere above may cause the basement or cellar to eventually fill with water. Because of insulation within the walls and high ambient noise levels inside and outside many buildings — especially those in densely populated urban areas — water leaks can go undetected for long periods of time.

The first indication of a leak is often when the lights suddenly fail or the furnace does not respond to commands from the thermostat. Water collecting in a seldom-used basement or cellar can short out the building's electrical system and/or extinguish the pilot lights in gas-fired furnaces and water heaters. If these gas-fired units are old enough, they may not have the thermocouple-controlled gas shutoff valves found on newer units. If they are not so equipped, the gas can continue to bubble up through the water and escape upward into the rest of the building. Should the gas reach another ignition source, an explosion and fire could result. Anyone falling into the basement or cellar as the building collapses may drown in the water collected there, or they may be electrocuted if the main electrical panel is compromised.

> **Utility control scenario:**
>
> A major fire is working on the upper floors of an older 10-story manufacturing building that has been converted to condominiums. A pumper is connected to the FDC supplying the sprinklers and interior standpipes. You and your company are assigned to control the utilities.
>
> - Would you shut off the natural gas? If not, why not?
> - Would you shut off the electricity? If not, why not?
> - Would you shut off the water supply? If not, why not?
> - Where would you look for the utility controls?
> - How would you maintain control of the building's utilities?

Summary

Some emergency incidents to which firefighters are called are initiated by uncontrolled utilities. Accumulations of inert gases may asphyxiate people by excluding the oxygen from the room in which they are sleeping, or flammable gases may reach an ignition source and explode. A malfunctioning electrical system may start a fire in an occupied building, or power lines may fall to the ground and electrocute anyone coming into contact with a downed wire. Leaking water can short out electrical systems in buildings, cause scald injuries and steam burns to firefighters and others in fires, and even drown anyone trapped in low areas following structural collapse.

Other incidents may not be caused by uncontrolled utilities but are made worse by them. Uncontrolled flammable gases can feed a structure fire and make it much more difficult to extinguish. Electrical wires that fall across a vehicle or other metal object can energize those objects and make rescues from them more difficult and much more dangerous for firefighters. Making rescues from collapsed buildings can be much more difficult if leaking water is rising in the areas where victims are trapped under the debris.

In all these situations and many other possible scenarios, firefighters must be aware of the dangers to themselves and others when utilities are uncontrolled. So they know how to safely and quickly control the utilities in an incident when ordered to do so, firefighters must become familiar with the utilities in their response districts through an ongoing program of preincident planning.

Review Questions

1. Why is it important to control a building's utilities and other systems during a fireground operation?
2. What are the procedures for controlling the natural gas fuel supply to a building during a structure fire?
3. What are the procedures for controlling the LPG fuel supply to a building during a structure fire?
4. What are the procedures for controlling the fuel oil supply to a building during a structure fire?
5. What is the procedure for controlling a natural gas or LPG leak in a building with no fire present?
6. What are the differences in procedures for controlling the electrical supply to a residential occupancy, a commercial occupancy, and an industrial occupancy during a structure fire?
7. What factors should be considered before shutting off the water supply to a building in which sprinklers have activated?

Access to Structures

Chapter Contents

CASE HISTORY 203	Vinyl Fences 211
Topography and Landscaping **203**	Decorative Metal Fences 211
Overcoming Site Obstacles 206	Masonry Walls 211
Gates **206**	**Security Measures** **212**
Manually Operated Gates 207	Barbed Wire 212
Automated Gates 207	Razor Ribbon 212
Lockboxes 208	Fence Spikes 213
Fences **209**	Wall Tops 213
Wire Fences 209	Guard Dogs 214
Chain-Link Fences 209	Booby Traps 214
Wooden Fences 211	**Summary** **215**
	Review Questions **215**

chapter 8

Key Terms

Hasp 207
Razor Ribbon 210
Topography 203

Access to Structures

Learning Objectives

After reading this chapter, students will be able to:

1. Describe the impact of topography and landscaping on accessing a structure.
2. Describe the procedures used to gain access through manual and automated gates.
3. Summarize the types of fences encountered during structural operations.
4. Describe procedures used to gain access through fences.
5. Summarize common security measures which may pose a threat to the safety of firefighters attempting to access a structure.
6. Describe procedures used to gain access through structural security measures.

Safety Points

While reading this chapter, keep the following safety points in mind:

- Some bridges will not support the weight of fire apparatus.
- If the wheels on one side of an emergency vehicle suddenly sink in soft or wet soil, the vehicle can become unstable and roll over.
- An electric fence can deliver a shock if touched while it is energized.
- Some masonry walls have broken glass embedded along the top.
- Some chain-link fences have razor ribbon at their bases or along their top rails.
- Some wrought iron fences have sharp spikes along their top rails.
- Ground ladders positioned on soft soil can fall over.

Chapter 8
Access to Structures

Case History

According to NIOSH Report F2006-25, firefighters were called to a structure fire in rural Alabama in July of 2006. While responding to the fire, a water tanker crashed through the guardrail of a narrow one-lane bridge and landed upside down in the creek bed twenty feet below. A 17-year-old volunteer firefighter riding in the vehicle was killed in the crash and two others were injured but survived.

Before firefighters can force doors or take other steps to gain access into a burning building, they must first be able to reach the building. This is not always an easy task because a variety of barriers or obstacles can impede firefighters from reaching the structure **(Figure 8.1, p. 204)**. As in the case history just cited, some of these impediments are related to the design of access roads, bridges, and driveways. Other impediments are related to the topography of the building site or result from steps that building owners have taken to protect their privacy and their property.

This chapter discusses a variety of exterior access challenges and how to overcome them. It begins with a discussion of natural exterior barriers such as roads and driveways, **topography**, and landscaping. Manmade exterior obstacles such as fences, walls, and gates are also discussed. Finally, security measures that can delay access to a building, and how to deal with them, are discussed.

Topography — Physical configuration of the land or terrain.

Topography and Landscaping

As illustrated by the case history cited earlier, the first impediment to reaching a burning building may be the streets, roads, and driveways that must be used to access it. Some access roads are narrow, winding, and obstructed by overhanging tree branches. Others are so steep that using them may be unsafe when they are wet or icy. Many rural bridges are narrow and some have height and weight limits that can restrict access by emergency vehicles **(Figure 8.2, p. 204)**.

Figure 8.1 Gates and other barriers often pose a challenge to firefighters.

Figure 8.2 Many older bridges and those in rural areas have weight limits that will not accommodate fire apparatus.

Figure 8.3 Homes are often built on the edge of hills to allow for scenic views.

The manner in which some buildings are situated on the property can present a challenge for fire department access. For example, many older mill buildings were built on the banks of rivers or streams because the water flow provided energy to operate machinery and to carry away industrial wastes. Because many of these buildings were built on the very edge of the bank, approaching the rear of the building is often difficult if not impossible.

Likewise, some other buildings are situated on mesas and other natural promontories to take advantage of scenic vistas **(Figure 8.3)**. Very large and expensive homes sometimes occupy the only flat area on promontories or ridges and may even be cantilevered over the edge. Once again, access may be readily available to only the fronts of these buildings.

To take advantage of lower land values and natural scenic beauty, office buildings and even manufacturing facilities are sometimes situated in relatively pristine outskirts of cities and even in rural areas. The sites chosen are often on ridge tops or other locations that provide a commanding view of the area. The sometimes steep slopes of these sites and the natural vegetation that covers them can severely limit access to all but the front of such buildings **(Figure 8.4)**. The access roads to some of these facilities may be restricted by their narrow width and overhanging tree limbs.

Even buildings that are located on relatively flat sites can be difficult to reach. In some areas where property costs are very high, structures are built extremely close together to maximize land use. These zero-lot structures often have a fire-resistive exterior, but prove to be extremely challenging to ladder, ventilate, or force entry. Buildings located in office or industrial parks are sometimes surrounded by man-made lakes or ponds or stone or brick walls that are part of the park's landscaping **(Figure 8.5)**. Some have large flower beds that will not safely support a ground ladder and certainly not the weight of an aerial device. Many buildings also are set back a considerable distance from the street and can only be reached by narrow, meandering walkways that may be difficult to negotiate in an emergency vehicle. Even the lawn areas may be so well irrigated that they will not support the weight of fire apparatus **(Figure 8.6)**. Access to these buildings also may be restricted by trees and other decorative vegetation.

Figure 8.4 Structures in heavily wooded areas often make access difficult.

Figure 8.5 Buildings that are located adjacent to bodies of water may not allow access from all sides.

Figure 8.6 Lawn areas in front of buildings often force the fire apparatus to be positioned away from the structure.

Figure 8.7 Barriers in front of government buildings pose another challenge for fire department access.

An additional problem on some sites is abandoned septic systems left over from a time when they were occupied by farmhouses. These underground tanks may not support the weight of fire apparatus and could cave in if driven over.

After the 1995 bombing of the federal building in Oklahoma City and terrorist attacks on U.S. military facilities in Saudi Arabia in 1996, many government agencies and private businesses in the U.S. installed barricades to protect their facilities **(Figure 8.7)**. These barricades may be massive metal or concrete bollards, or they may be similar to the types of barricades (Jersey barriers) used on streets and highways. Regardless of the type of barricade used, they are intended to keep vehicles from approaching too close to the buildings. Unfortunately, these barriers can also impede access by emergency vehicles.

Overcoming Site Obstacles

As just discussed, merely getting to the exterior of a burning building may be difficult. However, firefighters must size up the situation and take advantage of whatever the situation allows. The majority of site obstacles can and should be identified during preincident planning. Once the obstacles have been identified, plans can be devised and resources identified that will allow them to be overcome.

Figure 8.8 If used, the aerial apparatus may need to be positioned at an adjacent location to provide best access. *Courtesy of District Chief Chris Mickal, NOFD Photo Unit.*

Some fire departments require all-weather access to all sides of a planned structure as a condition of approving the building permit during the plans review process. Some departments also require the building owner to provide whatever means are necessary to allow access to all sides of the building. Allowing access may involve clearing and maintaining a specified area that is free of vegetation or the construction of all-weather access roads that will support the weight of fire apparatus.

However, when a building is on fire and firefighters need to access the outside of the building, they may have to be very innovative in their approach. For example, if a building is inaccessible because it is situated atop a steeply sloped promontory, it may be necessary to position an aerial device on an adjacent driveway, street, or access road close enough to allow the building's exterior to be reached **(Figure 8.8)**

Gates

Obviously, the quickest way through a fence is by using a gate made for that purpose. However, for security reasons or simply for convenience, a growing number of gates are fully automated. Having the means to operate an automated gate or the knowledge of how to override the mechanism and allow it to be opened manually can be extremely important during emergencies when time is critical. The time spent trying to get through an automated gate may mean the difference between having to fight a small fire or a larger and more hazardous one, or between a rescue and a body recovery. However, not all gates are automated. Many are simply manually operated gates that are locked with a padlock. Again, it is critically important that firefighters familiarize themselves with the gates in their response districts and how to open them.

Manually Operated Gates

The majority of manually operated gates are either wooden, aluminum, steel farm gates, or steel gates in chain-link fences. Most manually operated gates have a simple latching mechanism, and its operation is usually obvious. Many are locked with a padlock or a padlock and chain. If a gate is locked with only a padlock, it may be possible to cut the shackle of the lock with bolt cutters **(Figure 8.9)**. However, some locks have case hardened shackles that are virtually impossible to cut with bolt cutters — and may even damage the tool. In these instances, it may be possible to cut the staple on the **hasp**. If the gate is locked with a padlock and chain, the chain link closest to the lock should be cut so that the chain is long enough for the property owner to use again after the incident. When forcing a padlock open, the tools and techniques described in **Essentials** can be used. If a padlock cannot be forced open or cut, removing the hinges or hinge pins may allow access. If this is also unsuccessful, breaching the fence as described in the section on fences is another option. To avoid having to cut a chain or padlock, some departments add their own locks to the chains securing gates through which access is likely to be needed.

In some cases, a padlock used to secure a gate will be protected by a sturdy metal shell which is often a short length of steel pipe with the ends welded shut. There is usually only a small hole cut in the bottom of the shell through which someone can insert the padlock key. The shell often precludes cutting the padlock because bolt cutters will not fit through the opening. In that case, the shell may have to be cut away using a rotary saw or a cutting torch. These situations also lend themselves to the addition of a lockbox containing a key to the padlock or other instructions for opening the gate.

Automated Gates

Automated gates can be found in many different settings and configurations; however, they all have certain things in common. For instance, most are electrically operated and electronically controlled. However, some newer gates may be hydraulically operated or electrically operated with a hydraulic override. Some of the gate controls are actuated by a small radio transmitter that is similar to a garage door opener or toll pass **(Figure 8.10, p. 208)**. Others require a card key to be inserted into a scanner or a series of numbers entered into a keypad. Some automated gates are designed to be opened

Hasp — Fastening device consisting of a loop, eye, or staple and a slotted hinge or bar; commonly used with a padlock.

Figure 8.9 It is sometimes possible to cut a padlock with bolt cutters.

with the emergency vehicle's traffic signal controller, radio, or electronic siren. While automated gates have similarities, they also have unique features. Some are swinging gates hinged at one or both sides. Other automated gates are designed to move horizontally on small wheels attached to the top or bottom rail (or both) of the movable section.

Some gates have backup batteries that allow the gates to operate during a power failure. Others are designed to open automatically when there is a power failure. As always, it is important for firefighters to know the specific emergency operating procedures of the gates in their response districts.

All automated gates can be opened without the required transmitter or card key, but it may take more time. Some of those that have a sensor wire imbedded in the pavement of the exit lane can be opened by placing a metallic object such as a pry bar, halligan bar, or other metal tool onto the area where the wire is located. If this method is to be used, it must be tested during preincident planning. Some of these gates are equipped with a hand crank to allow them to be operated during a power failure. The crank is inserted into the proper opening in the motor housing and it can be used to open or close the gate manually. Others have a drive chain release that allows the gate to be pushed open or closed by hand. If not, the chain can be cut and the gate pushed open. In other cases, it may be necessary to disconnect or even cut the swing arm that normally opens and closes the gate. Ideally, the

Figure 8.10 Some gate controls have sensors that pick up transmitter signals from authorized vehicles.

swing arm can be disconnected by removing a pin or bolt from the point of connection to the gate or the drive motor. If this is not possible, it may be necessary to use a rotary saw equipped with a metal-cutting blade to simply cut the arm.

To limit access to residents and other authorized entrants, some gated communities have security guards in gate houses. These guard-controlled gates may be so restrictive that they create traffic congestion and limit access by emergency vehicles.

Lockboxes

The owners of many properties that implement automated gates have installed lockboxes or keypads nearby. They have done so because they do not want to risk their rather expensive gates being damaged if firefighters need to enter quickly. Many fire departments refuse to accept keys or gate controllers, making lockboxes a necessity. Some of the lockboxes contain a gate controller; others may contain a key that operates the gate without the controller, a card key, or numeric keypad combination that opens the gate. Some keypad gate controllers are designed with a lockbox key receptacle so that the gate can be opened or closed with the fire department's lockbox key

Figure 8.11 Gate controls often have a lock box that is provided for fire department use.

(Figure 8.11). However, for security reasons it is extremely important that emergency vehicles leave the protected property by the same entrance they used to gain access and that they close the gate behind them. They should also lock the gate if possible.

Fences

If for any reason a gate cannot be used or if access is needed where no gate exists, firefighters may have to breach a fence or scale a wall to reach a burning building. Just as with topography, landscaping, gates, and other on-site obstacles, the importance of identifying fences within the response district during preincident planning cannot be overemphasized. Identifying fences that could delay access to a building, developing the necessary plans for getting over or through them, and acquiring the needed resources before a fire starts is by far the best way to approach the problem.

Wire Fences

Most fences are constructed to either keep something or someone in or to keep something or someone out. Many rural and agricultural fences are designed to keep livestock in — that is, in a pasture or feedlot — or to keep them out of a crop field. Farm fences often consist either of three strands of barbed wire or wire fabric (sometimes called *hog wire* or *field fence*) attached to wooden or metal posts. Others are a combination of barbed wire and wire fabric. The gauge of the wire is small enough that that it is easily cut with bolt cutters or even electrical wire cutters. However, some agricultural fences are electrified to keep cattle from damaging the fence and breaking out. These fences are easily recognized by the insulators that hold an uninsulated conductor wire **(Figure 8.12)**. If the power to the fence cannot be shut off, only insulated wire cutters should be used to cut the charged conductor wire.

Figure 8.12 Electric fences pose a shock hazard for firefighters.

Chain-Link Fences

Almost as common as barbed wire fences are the chain-link fences that surround schools, playgrounds, parks, correctional facilities, military installations, commercial

Figure 8.13 Barbed wire is often found atop chain link fences.

Figure 8.14 Chain link fences are easily cut with a rotary saw.

Razor Ribbon — Coil of lightweight, flexible metallic ribbon with extremely sharp edges; often installed on parapet walls and on fence tops to discourage trespassers.

and industrial properties, and a growing number of single-family residences. Chain-link fences consist of heavy-gauge steel fence fabric attached to steel posts. Many of these fences have a steel top rail to add strength to the fence. Some chain-link fences have brackets atop the posts that hold strands of barbed wire in place, depending upon where they are installed and their intended purpose **(Figure 8.13)**. Others, especially those around correctional facilities, have coils of **razor ribbon** attached to the top of the fence to discourage potential escapees. Such security measures also make it more difficult for firefighters to get through these fences without injury.

If a chain-link fence must be breached to allow access to a burning building, firefighters have a number of options. The chain-link fence fabric is attached to the posts and top rail (if any) with wire bands. These bands are usually of a smaller gauge than the strands of fence fabric. Therefore, they are more readily cut than the fabric itself. The wire bands can be cut with wire cutters, bolt cutters, or a rotary saw. Simply cutting the wire bands between two or more adjacent posts will allow enough slack in the fence fabric to lay it down on the ground. Firefighters can then walk under the top rail, if there is one. If necessary, the fence fabric can be quickly cut using a rotary saw equipped with a metal-cutting blade **(Figure 8.14)**. Or, if necessary and time allows, the fence fabric can be cut one strand at a time using bolt cutters. The fence fabric should be cut as close to a post as possible to facilitate repair after the emergency.

Wooden Fences

Many homes, office buildings, and other commercial structures are surrounded partially or completely by wooden fences. If a wooden fence prevents access to a burning building, the fence will have to be breached. While wooden fences are found in many heights and styles, the majority consist of individual vertical boards nailed to horizontal wooden stringers between posts spaced about 8 feet (2.5 m) apart **(Figure 8.15)**. In most cases, the fence can be quickly dismantled simply by cutting the framework with a chain saw or by pulling the individual boards off the fence frame.

Figure 8.15 Wooden privacy fences are found in many subdivisions.

Vinyl Fences

A growing number of properties are enclosed with rail fencing made of vinyl plastic or similar materials **(Figure 8.16)**. In some, the rails may be filled with plastic foam for added rigidity, and posts may be filled with plastic foam or concrete for added strength. Regardless of the constituent materials, these fences are easily cut with a rotary or chain saw if they cannot be quickly dismantled.

Figure 8.16 Vinyl plastic fences are a common alternative to wooden privacy fences.

Decorative Metal Fences

Some single-family homes and multiple-residential developments are surrounded by wrought iron or steel fences **(Figure 8.17)**. If time allows when emergency access is needed, the individual vertical members or the framework to which they are attached can be cut using a rotary saw equipped with a metal-cutting blade. If this type of fence must be cut, the fastest way is to cut the ends of the horizontal frame members and remove an entire section at once **(Figure 8.18)**. A less destructive way to cross these fences is by using two ground ladders, one placed on each side of the fence. Or, a combination ladder can be set up in an A-frame configuration over the fence. For more information on these techniques, refer to Chapter 5, Ground Ladders.

Figure 8.17 Wrought iron fences are popular due to their style and strength.

Masonry Walls

Because of personal security concerns, a growing number of upscale homes and even entire housing developments, called gated communities, are enclosed within masonry walls **(Figure 8.19, p. 212)**. Most of the walls are about 6 feet (2 m) high and roughly 1 foot (300 mm) thick. The same equipment and techniques described in the foregoing section can be used to cross these walls.

Figure 8.18 The removal of sections of wrought iron fence may be necessary to gain access.

Figure 8.19 Masonry walls often totally encompass residences and neighborhoods.

Security Measures

Some security measures, such as automated gates, may slow firefighters attempting to gain access. However, other security devices can be a threat to their safety and survival if firefighters cannot exit the same way they entered. Security measures such as barbed wire, razor ribbon, spiked iron fences, and trained guard dogs also have the potential to seriously injure firefighters — and prevent them from completing their assignments.

Barbed Wire

Whether barbed wire is strung between wooden or metal posts as part of a farm fence or on brackets atop a chain-link fence, this common fencing material can be a serious impediment for firefighters. Barbed wire can snag protective clothing and equipment straps to slow firefighters down **(Figure 8.20)**. And, if they are not careful, firefighters can be injured by the steel barbs. Whenever barbed wire must be cut, it should be securely held with pliers or similar tools on both sides of the point to be cut. This prevents the wire ends from recoiling and perhaps hitting someone standing nearby. To cross a wire fence rather without cutting it, a partially unfolded salvage cover draped over the wire will protect firefighters enough to allow them to place ladders as described in the section on wire fences.

Figure 8.20 Barbed wire can easily snag and tear firefighters' turnout gear.

Razor Ribbon

Also called *concertina wire*, razor ribbon represents an even greater threat to firefighters than does barbed wire **(Figure 8.21)**. Razor ribbon is usually installed in flexible coils atop chain-link fences and sometimes on the ground adjacent to them. It may also be found along the tops of parapet walls on commercial or institutional buildings. However, razor ribbon may be found anywhere that property owners have serious concerns about trespassing. Firefighters must handle this material very carefully if they are to avoid injury. The same tools and techniques described for barbed wire also apply to cutting and crossing razor ribbon.

Fence Spikes

Iron and steel fences often have vertical members (sometimes referred to as *spikes*) that are sharply pointed at the top end to make them look menacing and thereby discourage trespassers **(Figure 8.22)**. While these spikes are rarely sharp enough to injure a firefighter (except in a fall onto them), they can snag protective clothing or equipment straps and thereby slow the firefighter down. The best way to avoid these obstacles is to remove them as previously described. If that is not possible, draping a partially unfolded salvage cover across the top of the fence will allow firefighters to place ladders as previously described, or to crawl over without interference from the spikes.

Wall Tops

Some masonry walls are constructed with security measures built in, and others have them added. It is not uncommon for the columns or posts to extend above the top of the wall with sections of iron or steel fencing installed between the columns. These can be handled as described in the foregoing section on iron or steel fences. Other masonry walls have broken glass embedded in the top surface of the wall **(Figure 8.23)**. These, too, can be handled in the same way as the iron or steel fences.

Figure 8.21 Razor ribbon is much more dangerous than barbed wire and must be handled with great care. *Courtesy of Razor Wire International, L.L.C.*

Figure 8.22 Spikes atop fences can cause serious injury to firefighters.

Figure 8.23 Broken glass is sometimes embedded at the top of masonry walls to deter intruders.

Guard Dogs

Some of the fences and walls previously described are not intended to keep trespassers out. They are merely intended to slow them down and cause them to make enough noise to alert a guard dog within. Guard dogs may be found in almost any type of occupancy — single-family residences, salvage yards, warehouses, and even on the roofs of commercial buildings. These highly trained, extremely agile, and totally focused animals can easily overpower firefighters and inflict serious injuries on them **(Figure 8.24)**. They are a force to be reckoned with.

Figure 8.24 Guard dogs can quickly overpower unsuspecting firefighters.

If firefighters are being prevented from approaching a burning building by a guard dog, they should immediately inform their supervisor or Command and be guided by the instructions they receive. Depending upon the circumstances, they may be told to wait outside the fence until the animal can be restrained by the property owner or an animal control officer. Or, they may be told to lure or coax the dog into a confined area where a gate can be closed behind it and thereby remove the threat. However, if a guard dog attacks or threatens to attack firefighters already within the fenced or walled area, they may be able to fend the animal off with a stream from a hoseline or with a pike pole or other tool. If all else fails, a police officer may be called to destroy the animal.

Booby Traps

Some property owners or occupants, especially those engaged in illegal activity on the property, may set up elaborate booby traps to discourage anyone from approaching. These traps may include camouflaged holes or pits in the ground into which an unwary firefighter might fall. Booby traps may even include loaded firearms set up inside a building with trip wires across door and window openings.

The best way for firefighters to protect themselves from booby traps and dangerous animals is to know of their existence prior to the incident and have appropriate procedures in place beforehand **(Figure 8.25)**. Such procedures may include firefighters staging nearby until law enforcement personnel have secured the scene.

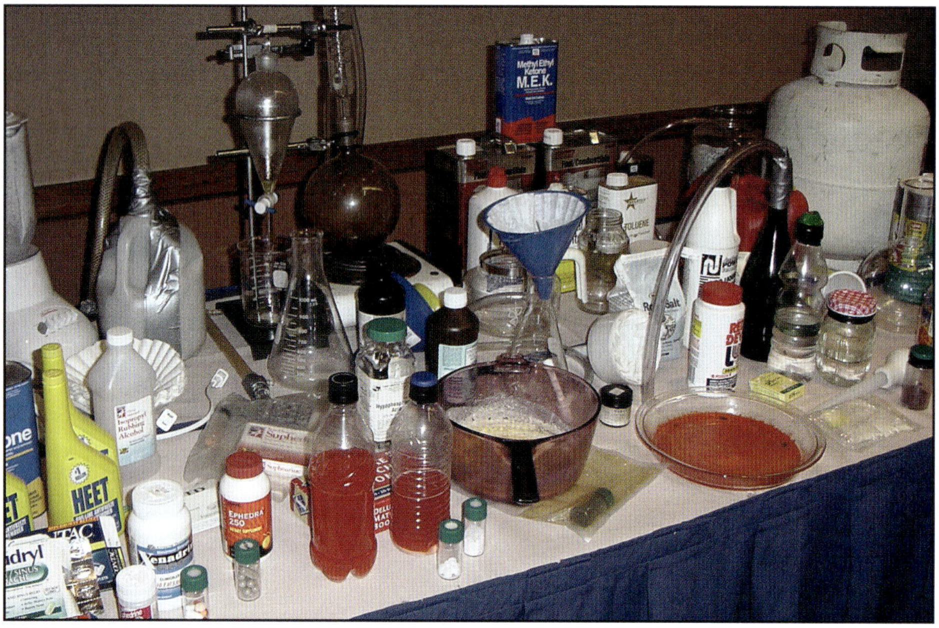

Figure 8.25 Firefighters should be familiar with items commonly found in clandestine methamphetamine labs.

Building Access Scenario:

A fire is burning inside a large, two-story office building located on a narrow peninsula of land jutting out into a man-made lake. There is an automatic swinging metal gate blocking the lone access driveway. The first-arriving engine does not have a controller for the gate.

- What is the best way to gain access to this building?
- How would you open the gate without a controller?
- How would you access the rear of this building?
- How would you access the roof of this building?
- What additional resources might be needed at this location?

Summary

Before firefighters can force any doors or take any other steps to gain access into a burning building, they must be able to reach the building. Because of substandard access roads, height- or weight-restricted bridges, topography, landscaping, fences, walls, and a variety of other security measures, this may not be easy to do. Firefighters may have to employ some innovative techniques to overcome these obstacles. However, if they are to perform search and rescue instead of a body recovery, firefighters must be able to deal with these obstacles quickly. By far, the easiest way to deal with these impediments is to know of their existence before an incident occurs and have the proper tools and techniques ready to use when needed. This can only be done through preincident familiarization and planning.

Review Questions

1. What is the impact of topography and landscaping on access to a structure during a fireground operation?
2. What procedures can be used to gain access through manual and automated gates?
3. What types of fences are commonly used to enclose structures?
4. What procedures can be used to gain access through fences during a fireground operation?
5. When trying to access a structure during a fireground operation, what is the threat to firefighters from barbed wire, razor ribbon, fence spikes, wall tops, guard dogs, and booby traps?
6. What procedures can be used to gain access through structural security measures including barbed wire, razor ribbon, fence spikes, wall tops, guard dogs, and booby traps?

Access into Structures

Chapter Contents

CASE HISTORY 219	Breaking Windows 237
Forcible Entry Tools 220	Window Security Systems 238
Doors 222	**Walls** 242
Door Size-Up 222	Types of Exterior Walls 243
Residential/Commercial Doors 224	**Summary** 248
Industrial/Institutional Doors 228	**Review Questions** 249
Door Security Systems 234	
Windows 235	
Window Size-Up 237	
Types of Windows 237	

chapter 9

Key Terms

Course 246	Panic Hardware 224
Deadbolt 234	Rabbet 224
Forcible Entry 220	Rebar 247
Gypsum Wallboard 244	Solid-Core Door 224
Header Course 246	Tempered Glass 224
Laminated Glass 241	Triangular Cut 231
Lexan® 239	Veneer 244
Oriented Strand Board (OSB) 243	Wired Glass 241

Access into Structures

Learning Objectives

After reading this chapter, students will be able to:

1. Summarize the characteristics of a door considered during door size-up.
2. Describe the procedures used to force residential and commercial doors.
3. Describe the procedures used to force industrial doors.
4. Describe methods for overcoming door security systems.
5. Describe the procedures for breaking residential, commercial, and industrial windows.
6. Describe methods for overcoming window security systems.
7. Describe the procedures for breaching wood frame, masonry, concrete, and metal walls.

Safety Points

While reading this chapter, keep the following safety points in mind:

- Evaluate the potential effect on fire behavior before opening any doors or windows.
- Make sure that any ground ladders placed in use are positioned on a stable surface.
- Use proper tools and techniques when breaking windows.
- Always use proper PPE and correct techniques when using saws or other power tools.

Chapter 9
Access into Structures

Case History

According to NIOSH Report 98-F07, California firefighters responded to a reported fire in a one-story commercial building in March of 1998. The first-arriving firefighters saw light smoke coming from the building, and a ventilation crew proceeded to the roof and began opening up. Another crew began forcible entry into the front of the building through two metal security doors. According to the report, it took between 7½ and 9 minutes for them to get the doors open. While fire attack crews waited for the doors to be opened, conditions inside the building changed dramatically, and fire erupted from the ventilation hole that had been cut in the roof.

Once the front doors were open, the crews advanced hoselines inside to look for the seat of the fire. Approximately 15 feet (5 m) inside the front door, they encountered heavy smoke and near-zero visibility. The crews advanced their lines approximately 30 to 40 feet (10 to 12 m) inside the building, but they could not locate the fire. Because conditions inside were rapidly deteriorating, the company officers ordered their crews to withdraw from the building. However, one of the officers became separated from his crew and remained inside. Approximately one minute later, a partial roof collapse blocked the front door, trapping the officer inside. After a rapid intervention crew located the victim, CPR was started immediately and continued on the way to the hospital. At the hospital, the victim was pronounced dead of smoke inhalation and burns.

Among other things, this case history illustrates the importance of being able to force entry into a burning building quickly. Scientifically controlled fire tests conducted by the NFPA® indicate that the *time available for escape* (TAE) from a burning building can be as little as 11 minutes after ignition due to heat buildup in a confined space such as a bedroom. In the same tests, the TAE was even less when lethal smoke concentrations were considered. Even if a fire is detected quickly and reported promptly, it still takes time for the nearest fire department units to receive the call, respond to the scene, size up the situation, devise an incident action plan (IAP) and begin to carry it out. Therefore, any significant delay in gaining access into a building increases the likelihood that a small fire will develop into one that is larger, more difficult to control, and more dangerous for the firefighters assigned to extinguish it. And, it may mean the difference between a rescue and a body recovery.

When a fire is burning inside a building, the IC has two basic choices: (1) allow the building to burn and use the on-scene resources to protect any exposures, or as is most often the case, (2) order a search of the building and an aggressive interior attack on the fire. Allowing the building to burn is certainly justified if the risk to firefighters is clearly greater than the possible benefit from ordering them inside. For instance, if the building is so heavily involved by fire that the chances of anyone inside surviving are virtually nil or if the building is unoccupied and abandoned, the risks to firefighters in an aggressive interior attack are far greater than any possible benefit. However, such incidents are a small fraction of the structure fires to which firefighters respond in North America each year. In the vast majority of cases, firefighters are justifiably put at some risk by being ordered to enter the burning building to conduct a search for trapped occupants and to control and extinguish the fire.

Given the case histories discussed in the preceding chapters, it should be clear that accurately sizing up a structure fire is critically important to the success of the operation and to firefighter safety and survival. Accurate size-up is also critically important when deciding where and how to gain access into a burning building. If the building is showing signs of potential backdraft, entry should be delayed until the backdraft factors are mitigated. In addition, the doorways and other openings that firefighters need for access into the structure may be congested by the occupants fleeing the building.

Gaining access into a burning building may be as simple as walking into the open doorway through which the occupants fled the building. Or, it may be as involved as having to overcome a security system, force a door or window, or even breach a wall. The best way to force entry into any burning building is to know in advance what tools and techniques will be needed and to bring those tools to the building initially.

There are several reasons why firefighters might need to gain access into a burning building. Of course, the most important reason is for search and rescue. Unless informed by a credible person that all occupants are out of the building, firefighters must enter to conduct a primary and secondary search of the building. They may also need to create openings through which other firefighters trapped inside the structure can escape. Firefighters may also need to enter the building to perform ventilation. And, unless it is a very small fire that can be handled with a portable extinguisher, firefighters will need to take one or more hoselines inside to extinguish the fire.

This chapter discusses the tools and techniques that firefighters may need when forcing locked doors in order to enter a burning building. Various types of windows and how to force them are also discussed. Finally, the tools and techniques needed for breaching exterior walls and overcoming various types of security systems are discussed.

Forcible Entry — Techniques used by fire personnel to gain entry into buildings, vehicles, aircraft, or other areas of confinement when normal means of entry are locked or blocked.

Forcible Entry Tools

Any of the **forcible entry** tools described in **Essentials** might be capable of performing the tasks discussed in this chapter. However, the use of those tools may be different because of unique situations and applications. To function safely and effectively in the situations described in this chapter, firefighters must be fully proficient in the use of these tools.

While all of the standard forcible entry tools are important, one of the most important and most versatile forcible entry tools is the rotary saw, sometimes referred to as a *rescue saw*. **Table 9.1, p. 222,** shows the various blades that are available for rotary saws and their applications.

When using the rotary saw for forcible entry, firefighters must be aware of its capabilities and limitations. For example, when equipped with the correct blade for the material being cut, these saws are extremely fast and efficient cutting tools. However, attempting to cut wooden doors with a metal-cutting blade — or vice versa — will significantly reduce the cutting speed and efficiency, and the saw could be damaged in the process. Also, when cutting metal, these saws produce a tremendous amount of sparks that can ignite adjacent combustibles **(Figure 9.1)**. Therefore, rotary saws should not be used to cut metal where there are flammable fuels in close proximity. In some cases, the blade of a rotary saw can bind in the material being cut. To avoid damage to the saw and possible injury to the operator, the saw should be shut off until the blade can be freed from the bind.

As with all other fire service tools, the rotary saw must be maintained properly if it is to perform safely and effectively. One of the most important ways of ensuring the saw's safety and effectiveness is by making sure that the saw blades are serviceable. While the manufacturer's recommendations and departmental SOPs must be followed, the FDNY SOP on rotary saw blades provides an example of reasonable guidelines. Its SOP reads as follows:

- Replace 12-tooth woodcutting blades when two or more teeth are damaged or worn down more than the other teeth or when the tips are worn down to the circumference of the blade.
- Replace 24-tooth woodcutting blades when eight or more teeth are damaged or worn excessively, or the tips are worn down to the circumference of the blade.
- Replace composite concrete- or metal-cutting blades when they have been worn down sufficiently for the blade to fit inside an 8-inch (200 mm) circle.

Figure 9.1 Rotary saws can produce a significant amount of sparks when used to cut metal objects. *Courtesy of the Los Angeles Fire Department – ISTS.*

Table 9.1 Rotary Saw Blades	
Blade	**Uses**
Carbide Tipped	• Heavy tar roof covering • Light-gauge metal roof coverings • Composition roof coverings • Wooden shingle roof coverings • Wooden structural members • Metal clad wood
Composite Carbide	• Heavy roof coverings • Wooden roof coverings • Wooden structural members • Light-gauge metal roof coverings • Metal clad wooden components • Forcible entry
Composite Metal	• Metal roof coverings • Steel structural components • Heavy forcible entry
Composite Masonry (Dry Cut)	• Brick • Concrete block • Concrete • Tile • Stucco

All other forcible entry tools should be maintained according to the manufacturer's recommendations, departmental SOPs, or as described in **Essentials**.

Doors

The process of sizing up a building for truck company operations, including its doors, begins with preincident familiarization and planning. Preincident planning surveys allow firefighters to identify unusual or highly secure doors that will require tools and techniques other than those needed to force entry through standard exterior doors. With this information, firefighters can save critical time by bringing the needed tools directly to the door instead of having to retrieve them later. However, because of the pace of new building construction and renovation in some areas, it may be difficult for firefighters to know which tools and techniques will be required to force entry through every door in a particular response district.

Door Size-Up

In some fire departments, preincident planning information on exterior doors is supplemented during incidents with a door size-up process. This process includes a quick 5-point size-up that will indicate the tools and techniques needed to force entry through any particular door. This size-up process includes the following:

- Type of door (Style/material)
- Type of frame around the door (Wood/metal)
- Type of wall into which it is set (Wood/metal/masonry)
- Type of hinges/locks (Exposed/recessed/protected)
- Door movement (Swinging [inward/outward]/roll-up/sliding)

During this quick size-up, firefighters identify the weakest part of the door assembly and exploit the weakness. For example, if firefighters are faced with a metal-clad door with a protected lock, it may be faster and easier for them to drive out the hinge pins and remove the door. Or, if the hinges are not exposed, it may be faster and easier to simply cut around the lock mechanism with a rotary saw or chainsaw.

> ⚠ Before forcing any exterior door in a burning building, firefighters must read the fire behavior indicators so they can anticipate how opening the door may change the fire behavior.

As stated in **Essentials**, before trying to force any door, firefighters should attempt to open it in the normal way. In other words — *try before you pry*. Having to explain to an irate property owner why an unlocked door was damaged or destroyed by overeager firefighters is not something that chief officers enjoy.

While firefighters may occasionally find doors that are unlocked, the large majority of exterior doors into burning buildings will be locked and will have to be forced open. To force entry quickly and safely, firefighters must be familiar with a wide variety of doors and locks and how to force them open. But before spending time and effort forcing door locks, firefighters should take the time to quickly evaluate other alternatives that may provide faster access. For example, the building may have a lockbox with door keys inside, the door may have a glass pane, or there may be a window (called a *sidelight*) next to the door **(Figure 9.2)**. In these cases, it will usually be faster to unlock the doors with the keys from the lockbox, or to break the glass in the sidelight and reach inside to unlock the door. Replacing a pane of glass is usually cheaper than repairing or replacing a damaged door, doorframe, or lock set. Of course, firefighters reaching through a sidelight opening to unlock a door must be careful to avoid being cut by broken glass.

As mentioned earlier, to be most efficient at opening doors as quickly as possible, firefighters must bring the most effective tools to the door initially. Firefighters assigned to perform these activities must always work as a team with each member taking a different type of forcible

Figure 9.2 Sidelight panes can often be broken to gain access to the door lock. This is much cheaper for the property owner to repair than purchasing a new door or lockset.

entry tool as they leave the apparatus. Obviously, it is counterproductive for every member of a crew to carry the same type of tool because different tools may be needed to force different types of doors. Preincident planning surveys can help crews determine what will be needed to force open any particular door.

The following sections discuss both typical and atypical types of doors and locks and how to open them quickly. For more detailed information about door construction, refer to the IFSTA **Building Construction Related to the Fire Service** manual.

Residential/Commercial Doors

Many residential and commercial buildings have similar exterior doors. Some are conventional hollow-core or solid-core wooden doors as described in **Essentials**. Others are **tempered glass** or **solid-core** metal doors. In smaller buildings and occupancies that have relatively low occupant loads, the exterior doors open inward so the hinges are on the inside. In occupancies with higher occupant loads, the exterior doors must swing outward in the direction of exit travel. In most cases, the hinges on outward-swinging doors are on the outside **(Figure 9.3)**. However, the exterior doors in some commercial buildings are double-acting doors; that is, they swing both inward and outward on pivot pins top and bottom.

Some commercial buildings house public assembly occupancies such as theaters and auditoriums with fixed seating or large open banquet halls or ballrooms. These buildings are designed to accommodate very large occupant loads, and they commonly have exterior exit doors with **panic hardware** on the inside and no exterior hardware other than hinges.

Forcing Residential/Commercial Doors

Many residential and office doors can be forced open quickly using standard forcible entry tools with little or no damage to the door or doorframe. However, some exterior doors in these occupancies are solid-core metal doors set in steel frames. These doors resist being forced open with the tools and techniques described in **Essentials**. Therefore, other tools and techniques must be used if entry is to be gained quickly.

A rotary saw equipped with a metal-cutting blade is one of the best tools to use for forcing an inward-swinging metal door set in a metal frame. The blade can be plunged through the **rabbet** or doorstop to cut the deadbolt **(Figure 9.4)**. Or, the saw can be used to make two intersecting 45-degree cuts around the locking mechanism so that the door is free to open **(Figure 9.5)**. On some of these doors, it may be necessary to make three perpendicular cuts around the locking mechanism **(Figure 9.6)**. Again, to open a door quickly with a rotary saw, firefighters must know in advance that the saw will be needed and bring it to the door initially.

Once a cut has been made around a door lock, the door will usually open with little pressure from the outside. However, for a variety of reasons, some doors resist being opened even after cuts have been made around the locking mechanism. In these cases, considerable force may have to be applied to open the door. If pushing on the door with a gloved hand does not open it, additional force will have to be used. Striking the door with a shoulder is *not* recommended because it may injure the shoulder and, if the door opens sud-

---

Tempered Glass — Type of glass specially treated to become harder and more break-resistant than plate glass or a single sheet of laminated glass. Tempered glass is most commonly used in side windows and some rear windows.

Solid-Core Door — Door whose entire core is filled with solid material.

Panic Hardware — Hardware mounted on exit doors in public buildings that unlocks from the inside and enables doors to be opened when pressure is applied to the release mechanism.

Rabbet — Groove cut in the surface or on the edge of a board to receive another member.

Figure 9.3 The hinges for outward swinging doors are usually placed on the outside of the building.

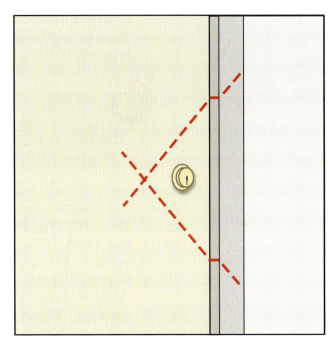

Figure 9.5 Two intersecting 45 degree cuts can be made around the locking mechanism.

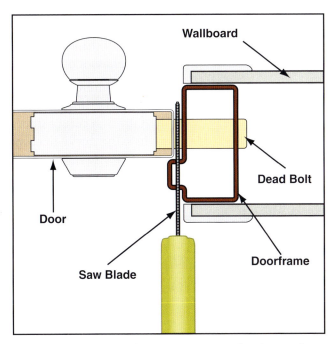

Figure 9.4 The blade of a rotary saw can often be used to cut the deadbolt.

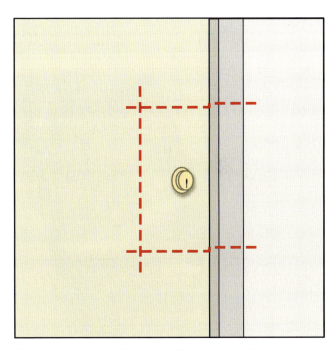

Figure 9.6 In some instances, three perpendicular cuts are necessary to cut around the locking mechanism.

Chapter 9 • Access into Structures **225**

denly, the firefighter could fall into a room that might be engulfed in flames. Likewise, standing in front of a door and kicking it also leaves the firefighter exposed.

> ⚠️ Some fire departments prohibit their firefighters from using anything but their hands to force a door open; other departments allow them to use whatever is necessary.

If allowed by departmental SOP, one effective technique is what some call a *mule kick* (**Figure 9.7**). The advantages of this backward kick technique are that it uses the firefighter's strongest muscles to strike the door, the foot is protected by the boot, and the firefighter is protected by the wall if fire erupts from the doorway when the door opens. Departments that do not allow their firefighters to use their bodies to force doors open must use a different tool or technique (**Figure 9.8**).

On double doors, the rotary saw blade can be plunged through the weather strip and into the crevice between the door panels to cut the lock bolt (**Figure 9.9**). Once the locking panel is open, the upper and lower latch pins of the other panel can be opened in the usual manner.

If the door is an outward-swinging type and the hinges are exposed on the outside, it may be possible to drive the hinge pins out from the bottom so that the door can be removed (**Figure 9.10**). If the pins cannot be driven out, it may be possible to pull the hinges with the fork of a Halligan or a claw tool or be cut off flush with the doorframe using a rotary saw (**Figure 9.11**). If readily available, a cutting torch or similar device can also be used. Regardless of which tool is used, once the hinges have been cut off, the door can be pried out of the frame. As always, before opening a door into a burning building, firefighters must consider the effects that opening the door may have on the behavior of the fire.

Finally, many residential and some commercial buildings have large single-piece slab doors that tilt up to open. These doors are most often used as garage doors in residential buildings and on loading docks of com-

Figure 9.8 Battering rams can be used to force open a door.

Figure 9.7 A mule kick can be an effective way of forcing open a door if approved by department SOP.

mercial buildings. Slab doors pivot on spring-assisted hardware attached to the doorframe on each side. Some of these doors have a simple latch handle at one side that can be locked with a padlock. Others have a lock in the handle located on the centerline of the door, near the bottom. This type of latch is similar to that shown in **Essentials** and can be opened as described there.

Figure 9.9 A rotary saw can be plunged between the panels of a double door to cut the locking mechanism.

Figure 9.10 It is sometimes possible to drive the hinge pins up from the bottom to remove the door.

Figure 9.11 It may be possible to pull the hinges off of a door with the fork from a Halligan tool.

Figure 9.12 Softening the building involves forcing all doors open in the structure for both firefighter access and emergency egress.

Forcing doors into burning structures is not always for the purpose of *entering* the building. Firefighters and others may be trapped inside and need an emergency escape route. It is SOP in some departments to force open *all* doors into a structure (sometimes called *softening the building*) when there is significant fire inside **(Figure 9.12)**. However, softening a building is done only if it is consistent with the IAP and if it will not change the ventilation profile. When properly done, the softening of a building will not affect fire behavior because the doors are not necessarily left open, but if firefighters or others inside need to escape through one of these doors, their progress will not be impeded.

In addition to the challenges of gaining access just discussed, many exterior doors also have some form of security device or system. These can be found in a variety of forms. Means of overcoming these impediments to forcible entry are discussed later in this chapter.

Industrial/Institutional Doors

In addition to the standard pedestrian doors at the office entrances to industrial and institutional occupancies, these buildings may also have large tilt-slab, roll-up, bi-fold, or telescoping service doors. Service doors are found wherever large unobstructed wall openings are needed, such as at loading docks. Some roll-up doors are also used as fire doors in required separation walls. Many roll-up doors do not have an exterior latching mechanism.

One of the most common types of industrial/institutional service doors that firefighters may have to force open is the steel roll-up door **(Figure 9.13)**. These doors are constructed of dozens of interlocking horizontal steel slats that move up and down in tracks at both sides of the door opening. Unlike sectional doors (discussed next), the ends of the slats in roll-up doors do not have wheels or rollers attached to them, but the ends of every other slat have small metal guides that slide up and down in the track. These doors are usually raised and lowered from inside the building using a manually operated or electrically driven chain hoist at one side of the door **(Figure 9.14)**.

Other common industrial/institutional roll-up service doors consist of a number of horizontal panels connected by hinges. Sometimes called *sectional* doors, they are merely larger versions of some residential garage doors. These doors usually have small steel wheels attached to the ends of each panel or section that move in steel tracks at each side of the doorway opening. This type of roll-up door is commonly opened and closed by an electrically driven chain mechanism attached at the center of the topmost panel of the door.

Another type of industrial/institutional service door is called a *sheet-curtain* door. These metal roll-up doors look exactly like conventional steel roll-up doors so their existence in a particular occupancy must be identified during preincident planning. Even though sheet-curtain doors look like conventional roll-up doors, they are quite different. Instead of dozens of individual interlocking slats, sheet-curtain doors are made up of a few interlocking flexible panels of relatively light-gauge metal **(Figure 9.15)**. Each panel is embossed to give it the appearance of a conventional roll-up door. These doors function in the same way as conventional roll-up doors.

Many roll-up doors have a conventional pedestrian doorway next to the service door **(Figure 9.16)**. These doorways typically utilize metal-clad solid-core doors or solid metal doors set in metal frames.

Figure 9.13 Steel roll-up doors are commonly found on industrial and institutional structures.

Figure 9.14 Roll-up doors can typically be opened by pulling the chain driven mechanism.

Figure 9.15 Sheet curtain doors often appear similar to traditional roll-up doors.

Figure 9.16 Many roll-up doors have a pedestrian door in close proximity.

Chapter 9 • Access into Structures **229**

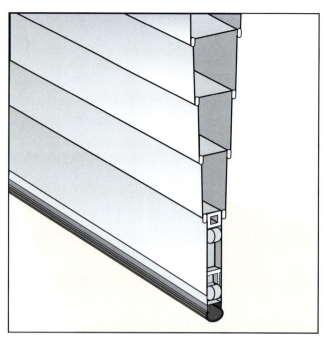

Figure 9.17 A cross section of a horizontal telescoping door.

Figure 9.18 Aircraft hangars often incorporate heavy-duty bifold doors.

Another type of industrial/institutional service door is called a telescoping door. These doors consist of a number of interlocking, inverted U-shaped metal sections. When the door is open, the sections are nested together at the top of the doorway opening. As the name implies, the door sections telescope into position as the door is closed. When a telescoping door is closed, it forms a barrier of hollow interlocking sections, each with a rectangular cross-section **(Figure 9.17)**. Like roll-up doors, telescoping doors are operated by chain-hoist mechanisms at one side of the doorway opening. These mechanisms can be operated manually or electrically, but unlike roll-up and sheet-curtain doors, telescoping doors are raised and lowered with internal cables and there are no springs or counterweights in the lifting mechanisms.

Some older warehouses and similar buildings have single- or double-panel horizontal sliding doors. These doors may be all metal, all wood, or a combination of the two. The door panels are suspended from steel rollers at the top that move on a horizontal rail above the doorway opening. Depending upon the size of the doors and other factors, these doors may be manually or power-operated. Some horizontal sliding doors are secured with a hasp and padlock on the outside; others are locked from the inside.

Some large industrial buildings, such as aircraft hangars, have heavy-duty bifold doors. Some of these doors are installed to open horizontally and others to open vertically **(Figure 9.18)**.

Forcing Industrial/Institutional Doors
In many cases, the quickest and most efficient way to gain access through any type of industrial or institutional service door is by forcing the pedestrian door beside it and then using the mechanism inside to open the service door. Pre-incident planning surveys will confirm whether the pedestrian door provides access to the inside of the service door. The pedestrian door can be forced using the tools and techniques described in **Essentials** and in the preceding

section on forcing residential/commercial doors. If there is no pedestrian door or if opening it does not provide access to the door-opening mechanism for the service door, another method will have to be used.

One of the most common methods of cutting through a roll-up or sheet-curtain door is to make a large **triangular cut** (sometimes called a tepee cut), in the center of the door **(Figure 9.19)**. While this type of cut is popular, it does have some disadvantages. The triangular cut typically does not create an opening large enough for access by fire attack crews. The openings are usually only large enough to provide an escape route for firefighters trapped inside or to enable firefighters to use the door-opening mechanism to open the door fully for interior access. In addition, making these cuts sometimes bends or distorts the door components enough that they do not roll up when firefighters attempt to use the door-opening mechanism. For these reasons, some fire departments are beginning to use other methods than the triangular cut.

If a triangular cut is used, firefighters must be careful to protect the door from damage so that it will not jam when the door-opening mechanism is used. The triangular cut is most often made with a rotary saw equipped with a metal-cutting blade. In this type of cut, the base of the triangle is the bottom of the door, and the sides are formed by two 45-degree cuts. The apex of the triangle should be at least 6 feet (2 m) high in the middle of the door, but the higher the better. The cuts should not quite intersect at the apex. Once the triangular cut has been completed, the cut section of door can be flapped down in front of the door, or removed **(Figure 9.20, p. 232)**. Then, if fire conditions inside allow, firefighters can enter to raise the service door using the operating mechanism inside.

If the door cannot be raised for any reason, the ends of the cut slats can be pulled from each side to enlarge the unobstructed opening. The slats can sometimes be pulled by hand (wearing gloves), but pulling them with heavy-duty pliers is safer and more effective. The first slats or panels to be pulled should be those at chest height where most firefighters are strongest, and they should be pulled as close to parallel with the wall as possible.

If the door operating mechanism is not locked, the top of the service door will usually roll up after the first few slats are pulled because of the spring tension in the mechanism. If it is locked, the lock should be cut off using the tools and techniques described in **Essentials**.

While the triangular cut is a commonly used technique, it typically takes a long time to create a relatively small opening. And, if the bottom of the service door is not at ground level, such as on some loading docks, the triangular cut is particularly ineffective. Triangular cuts are not recommended for telescoping doors.

Triangular Cut — Triangular opening cut in a roll-up or tilt-slab door to provide access into the building or a means of egress for those inside.

WARNING!
Firefighters should not stand below older roll-up doors that are automatically retracting by the spring-operated mechanism because these doors may break loose from the wall and come crashing down.

Figure 9.19 The triangular or tepee cut is often made in the center of the roll-up door.

Many fire departments use an alternative to the triangular cut for opening roll-up or sheet-curtain doors. They simply make a single vertical cut down the middle of the door and pull the cut slats from both sides of the door **(Figure 9.21)**. This creates an opening the full width of the doorway. The opening is large enough for access by fire attack crews and eliminates the problem of the door not opening fully because of damage. As with the triangular cut, the higher that the vertical cut can be started, the better, as this creates the largest possible opening. If flames or excessive heat do not erupt from the vertical cut, a firefighter can lean against one half of the cut section and begin removing slats or panels from the opposite half of the door **(Figure 9.22)**. If fire does show through the first cut, a firefighter can push on one half of the door with a long-handled tool while another firefighter pulls slats from the other half with pliers. Once the slats or panels are removed from both

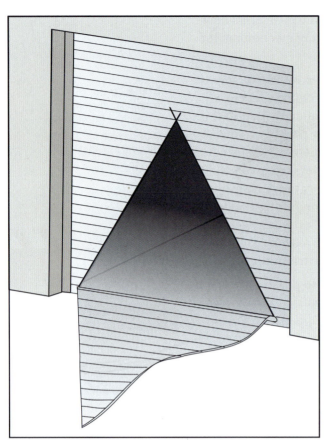

Figure 9.20 Once the triangular cut is made, the entire section can be flapped down.

Figure 9.21 Instead of the triangular cut, a vertical cut can be made down the center of the door and the slats removed. *Courtesy of the Cedar Rapids (IA) Fire Department.*

Figure 9.22 To remove the slats, a firefighter can lean on one side of the door and pull slats from the other side. *Courtesy of the Cedar Rapids (IA) Fire Department.*

sides, the upper part of the door will roll up if the operating mechanism is not locked. If the mechanism is locked, the opening created by the cut is still more than adequate for access through the doorway.

In some situations, roll-up or sheet-curtain doors are inset far enough that the slats or panels cannot be pulled out parallel to the wall in which the door is installed. In these cases, the cut slats can be pulled laterally as far as possible and then cut again in the middle to shorten their length **(Figure 9.23)**. This may allow the slats or panels below to fall and the upper part of the door to roll up.

If fire conditions inside an exterior roll-up or sheet-curtain door make a single cut in the center unsafe to use, an alternative is to make a horizontal cut across nearly the full width of the door, stopping about 1 foot (30 cm) from the doorframe on each side **(Figure 9.24)**. This horizontal cut should be made about 6 feet (2 m) above the bottom of the door. A vertical cut (which does not quite intersect with the horizontal cut) is then made from each end of the horizontal cut down almost to the bottom of the door. Finally, when the vertical cuts are connected with the ends of the horizontal cut, the full section of door components between the cuts will fall away creating a large access/egress opening **(Figure 9.25, p. 234)**.

When cutting a large opening in a telescoping door, the procedure just described should be used to cut the outer skin of the door sections. However, since these doors consist of hollow, box-like sections, once the outer skin is removed a second (slightly smaller) opening must be cut in the inner skin to finish the job **(Figure 9.26, p. 234)**.

Some institutional buildings are designed to restrict the movement of those inside. Jails, prisons, and other correctional and detention facilities have a variety of highly secure doors, gates, and other barriers. The quickest and most efficient means of gaining access into one of these facilities is to enlist the aid of a member of the institutional staff who can accompany the firefighters and unlock these items. If the fire inside such a facility is

Figure 9.23 It may be necessary to make another vertical cut to shorten the slats. *Courtesy of the Cedar Rapids (IA) Fire Department.*

Figure 9.24 A firefighter makes a single horizontal cut across a roll-up door. *Courtesy of the Cedar Rapids (IA) Fire Department.*

Figure 9.25 Vertical cuts are made at each end of the horizontal cut to create the opening. *Courtesy of the Cedar Rapids (IA) Fire Department.*

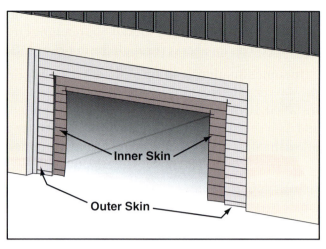

Figure 9.26 Both the outer and inner surfaces of telescoping door sections must be cut.

beyond the incipient stage, access inside will involve entering an Immediately Dangerous to Life and Health (IDLH) atmosphere, so wearing SCBA will be required. Therefore, it may be necessary to enlist the aid of the institution's fire department or fire brigade. If the building is on fire and threatening the lives of those inside but the institution does not have fire-trained and equipped personnel — or if these personnel are unavailable — firefighters will have to use whatever means are at their disposal to gain access. Because the locks and latching mechanisms in these facilities are designed to resist being forced open, it may be quickest to simply cut around them as previously described in the section on forcing residential/commercial doors. However, because these interior doors and gates may be made of hardened steel, it may be necessary to use some form of exothermic cutting device to force them open. These considerations should be addressed during preincident planning at the facilities.

Door Security Systems

Many exterior and some interior doors in a variety of different occupancies, including those just discussed, have security devices or systems designed to deny access except to those authorized to enter. Some of these devices are as simple as several **deadbolts**, a horizontally movable scissor gate, an overhead roll-up door, a horizontal security bar in stirrups, or panic hardware on the inside of an exterior door. Others are electronic systems that require a series of numbers to be entered into a keypad or a card key to open them. Some even have sophisticated electronic fingerprint or iris recognition systems. Regardless of what type of device or system is installed, firefighters must be able to gain access into the building, or egress from it, quickly and efficiently when the building is on fire.

Exterior doors in some federal facilities are equipped with security systems that will not allow firefighters to forcibly enter or exit under any circumstances. Firefighters must identify these doors during preincident familiarization surveys and work with facility security staff to devise plans that will allow for emergency entry and exit.

> **Deadbolt** — Movable part of a deadbolt lock that extends from the lock mechanism into the door frame to secure the door in a locked position.

Overcoming Door Security Systems

The best way to overcome door security devices or systems is to identify them during preincident planning surveys and develop contingency plans. Except in jails and correctional institutions, one plan for overcoming door security devices or systems might be (if allowed by department policy) to encourage a property owner or occupant to install a lockbox **(Figure 9.27)**. If a lockbox is installed, whatever is needed to open the door — conventional key, card key, numeric code, etc. — can be placed inside for firefighters to use in an emergency. Using the means contained in the lockbox may be faster than forcing the door and is almost certainly less destructive.

Figure 9.27 Lockboxes provide quick access to fire crews without having to create costly damage during forcible entry.

In the absence of a lockbox, firefighters may have to cut the lock or force the door. The fact that there is no lockbox on the building should be identified during preincident planning surveys. These surveys will allow firefighters to also determine the most efficient means of cutting the lock or forcing the door so that there is no delay in getting the necessary tools and equipment to the door when the building is on fire. Whatever method is chosen, it should be one that allows access into the building as quickly as possible. This may involve cutting off exposed locks or hinges, or it may involve cutting around the locking mechanism as described earlier.

If a scissor gate or roll-up door is locked with a padlock, the lock can be cut off using the tools and techniques described in **Essentials**, or the staple through which the lock shackle passes can be cut with bolt cutters or a rotary saw. Scissor gates or roll-up doors with built-in locks may be forced open with a manual or powered hydraulic spreader but using a rotary saw to cut around the lock might be faster **(Figure 9.28)**. If double doors have a horizontal security bar in saddles on the inside, the blade of a rotary saw can be inserted into the crevice between the door panels to cut the bar. Or, the heads of the bolts holding the saddles can be cut off by plunging the blade of a rotary saw behind the bolt heads at a 45-degree angle to cut through the bolts **(Figure 9.29, p. 236)**. If firefighters know that a door has several deadbolts installed, they will also know to cut the door from top to bottom about one foot (300 mm) from the edge on the door handle side **(Figure 9.30, p. 236)**. If the doors are equipped with panic hardware, a chain saw equipped with a carbide-tipped chain can be plunged through the door a few inches (cm) above the panic bar. The bar of the saw can then be tilted down to operate the panic bar and open the door **(Figure 9.31, p. 236)**.

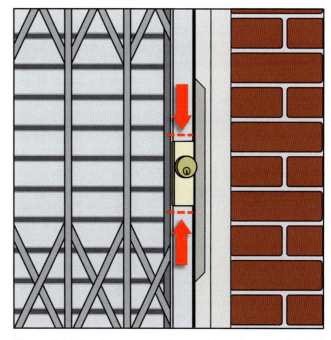

Figure 9.28 A rotary saw can be used to cut around the lock of a scissor gate.

Windows

There are perhaps as many different types of windows and window latches as there are doors and locks. Staying current on all the various types can be a daunting task for firefighters. However, just as with doors, the amount of time

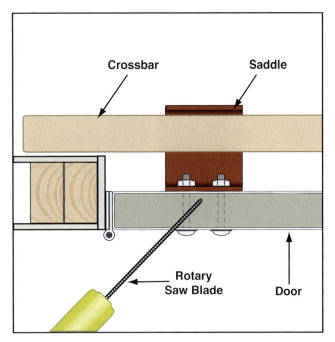

Figure 9.29 Rotary saws can be used to cut the blind bolts holding the security bar saddles.

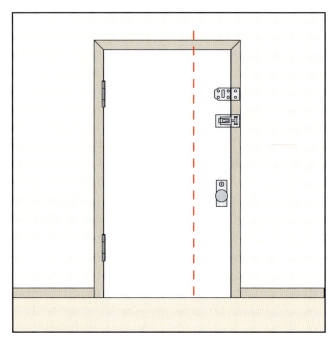

Figure 9.30 If it is known that a door has numerous locks, firefighters can make a single vertical cut down the length of the entire door.

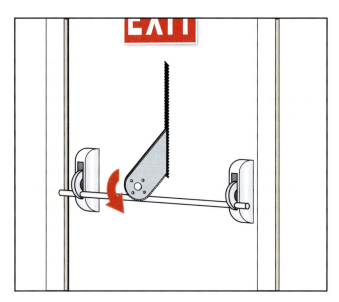

Figure 9.31 A chainsaw can be plunged through a door with panic hardware above the lever and the blade used to open the door.

and effort firefighters invest in learning about the different types of windows installed in their districts, and how to force them open quickly and safely, can translate into lives and property saved. The following sections describe a variety of windows and how to open them.

For gaining access into buildings, opening windows may sometimes be the quickest means of forcing entry. Even when the windows cannot be opened, the panes may be broken out relatively easily and quickly. If the frame is undamaged, the cost of replacing the broken glass is usually, but not always, less than the cost of repairing damaged doors or walls. On the other hand, leaded glass windows, especially large, stained-glass windows in churches, temples, and fraternal buildings are sometimes priceless works of art that should be protected if at all possible **(Figure 9.32)**. However, when any window glass is removed to allow access into a building, the open window can unintentionally change the ventilation profile and may have other adverse effects on the behavior of the fire. If the entire window or even just the glass has been removed, it can be difficult to reverse the effects during an incident. Therefore, when circumstances permit, opening a window is preferable to breaking the glass.

Window Size-Up

The size-up for windows is similar to that of doors. Key factors in the size-up of windows for forcible entry include the following:

- Type of window
- Type of glass
- Type of frame or casement
- Type of locking or latching mechanism
- Type of security devices in use

Types of Windows

A wide variety of windows exist in both new and old buildings in most communities. Some of the more common types described in **Essentials** are as follows:

- Double-hung (Checkrail) windows
- Hinged (Casement) windows
- Projected (Factory) windows
- Awning and Jalousie windows
- Hurricane windows
- High-security windows

Breaking Windows

As with doors, *try to open a window instead of breaking it.* If it is necessary to break a window, the entire pane should be broken out and the frame cleared of broken shards by scraping the frame with the breaking tool. The firefighter breaking the glass should be upwind of the window and in full protective clothing – including hand and eye protection. If using an axe to break the window, the firefighter should strike the window with the flat side of the blade. Regardless of which tool is used, the handle should be held higher than the blade to prevent glass from sliding down the handle toward the firefighter (**Figure 9.33, p. 238**) When working aboveground, windows should be broken inward whenever possible to avoid the *flying guillotine* hazard that may cut hoselines and injure anyone working below.

Figure 9.32 Ornate stained glass windows should be protected if at all possible.

CAUTION
Using the tip of a ground ladder to break a second-story window is dangerous and not recommended.

Figure 9.33 Proper technique should be used whenever breaking glass.

There are other specialized windows designed for very specific applications. Regardless of the design or application, windows that resist being opened from the outside usually can and should be broken out when access is needed. However, many newer windows are glazed with or constructed entirely of extremely resilient plastics that are very difficult to break. In these situations, removing the entire frame with the window intact may be quicker and more efficient for entry purposes.

Residential/Commercial Windows

Most windows in residential/commercial occupancies can be forced open using the tools and techniques described in **Essentials**. However, there are some windows that require special knowledge and/or special tools and techniques to open them quickly. For example, those that have security bars, heavy screens, or sheet curtains over them can be a challenge if they have not been identified during preincident planning. If they have been identified (and they should have been), the necessary tools and techniques can be planned in advance and the personnel trained in their use so that there is little or no delay when needed during an emergency.

Industrial/Institutional Windows

As described in **Essentials**, the more common types of industrial/institutional windows can often be opened by simply breaking a pane of glass and reaching inside to release the latch. However, other types of windows in these occupancies present a more formidable challenge. Many have some form of security glass such as wired glass, laminated glass, or break-resistant plastic. Other windows have hurricane shutters that can add another layer of protection that must be overcome if they are closed. The tools and techniques needed to force entry through these windows are discussed in the following section on window security systems.

Window Security Systems

Some of the most common types of window security systems are rigid metal grilles attached to the outside of the building. These grilles may consist of heavy-gauge steel wire screen or bars made of wrought iron or steel **(Figure 9.34)**. The grilles are normally blind-bolted to the wall of the building or the window frame. Other windows may be protected by metal sheet-curtains or

> **CAUTION**
> If fire crews are operating inside a burning building, all window bars should be removed to facilitate the emergency escape of the interior crews if necessary.

Figure 9.35 Hurricane shutters are commonly found in areas that are affected by hurricanes. *Courtesy of the Florida State Fire College.*

Figure 9.34 Heavy security bars can pose a challenge for fire department access. *Courtesy of the Los Angeles Fire Department – ISTS.*

hurricane shutters **(Figure 9.35)**. Still other windows are designed to increase security by having a windowpane that resists breakage.

Historically, laminated windows or those with wire mesh embedded in the glass have been used. Modern security windows are more likely to have panes made of **Lexan®**, a polycarbonate plastic that is many times stronger than safety glass or Plexiglas® of the same thickness. Because Lexan® cannot be broken with standard forcible entry tools, it is critical that windows utilizing this material be identified during preincident planning surveys.

Overcoming Window Security Systems

To remove security screens or bars from windows, the fastest way is to cut the points of attachment rather than cutting each individual bar. If the security system is attached with bolts, and the heads are exposed, they can be cut off with a rotary saw. If the bolt heads cannot be reached with the saw blade, they can sometimes be removed by driving the fork of a Halligan or a rambar under them and snapping them off. Otherwise, a cutting torch or other exothermic cutting device can be used to cut the points of attachment **(Figure 9.36, p. 240)**. If the points of attachment cannot be cut, both ends of the upper horizontal bar may be cut and this will often allow the vertical bars to hinge on the lower horizontal bar and swing downward out of the way. If that does not create the necessary access, both ends of the lower horizontal bar will have to

Lexan® — Polycarbonate plastic used for windows. It has one-half the weight of an equivalent-sized piece of glass, yet is 30 times stronger than safety glass and 250 times stronger than ordinary glass. It cannot be broken using standard forcible entry techniques.

Figure 9.36 Exothermic cutting devices are often used to cut metal items.

be cut also and the entire unit removed from the window. Windows protected by metal sheet curtains or hurricane shutters can be forced using the tools and techniques described earlier for opening roll-up doors.

In addition to exterior security bars or screens, many building in high-crime areas have windows that are also designed to resist breakage. The tools and techniques needed to break these security windows are as follows:

Thermoplastic windows. Plexiglas® acrylic, Lexan® polycarbonate, and other thermoplastic windows may have to be opened to gain access into a burning building. A rotary saw with a medium (40 tooth) carbide-tipped blade is most effective when entry must be made through all types of plastic windows **(Figure 9.37)**. As always, eye and ear protection are critically important whenever a rotary saw is used. However, a rotary saw is the *only* fire service tool that will cut Lexan® polycarbonate. The following technique described for cutting Plexiglas® will *not* work with Lexan® windows.

Figure 9.37 It is usually necessary to cut thermoplastic windows in order to gain access.

Figure 9.38 In order to shatter a Plexiglas® window, it is often necessary to score a large X with a pick head axe.

Figure 9.39 The Plexiglas® pane can often be broken with a sledgehammer.

In the absence of a rotary saw, Plexiglas® windows can be broken out. Shattering a Plexiglas® window is done by scoring a large *X* on the pane and then striking the intersection of the *X* with the point of a pick-head axe **(Figure 9.38)**. The pane will usually break along the *X*, and if so, the pieces can be pulled or bent out. Another method is to strike the pane in the center with a sledgehammer **(Figure 9.39)**. If this does not break the pane, it may bend it enough to cause it to slip out of its frame.

Laminated windows. Some security windows are glazed with **laminated glass** similar to that in automobile windshields. A sheet of plastic is sandwiched between two layers of plate glass. When broken, the glass shards cling to the plastic laminate **(Figure 9.40)**. Firefighters can take advantage of this characteristic and simply cut out the panes of glass with an axe, hatchet, or a glass saw such as those used during vehicle extrication.

Figure 9.40 Shattered laminated glass often stays in place after it is broken.

Laminated Glass — A type of glass consisting of two layers of glass with a transparent layer of vinyl bonded into the center.

Wired-glass windows. Another common form of security window uses wire mesh imbedded in the glass **(Figure 9.41, p. 242)**. Like laminated glass, the pieces of broken glass cling to the wire mesh and therefore can be cut out in one piece. The same tools used to cut laminated glass can be used to cut **wired glass**.

Wired Glass — Flat sheet glass containing a wire mesh that is embedded in it during manufacture, which increases resistance to breakage and penetration.

Chapter 9 • Access into Structures **241**

Film-coated glass. The windows of many buildings, especially those in the south and west walls, have a reflective film applied to the inside of the glass to reduce glare from the sun (**Figure 9.42**). When broken, film-coated windows will sometimes behave in a manner similar to laminated windows. That is, the glass shards may cling to the film, and the window can fall out in one large piece. When breaking these windows, firefighters must be careful that a large pane of glass does not fall on them.

Shuttered windows. Windows in some areas are covered by metal roll-up sheet curtains, and those in areas subject to hurricanes and similar extreme weather may be equipped with shutters. These security systems can be breached using the same tools and techniques described in the section on forcing entry through roll-up metal doors.

Walls

The types of walls that firefighters may have to breach to gain access into burning buildings are many and varied. As with all other truck company operations, the key is to be able to breach any type of wall as safely and as quickly as possible. One of the most important aspects of wall breaching operations is a thorough knowledge of the building gained through preincident planning. These surveys allow firefighters to identify in advance which tools and techniques would be needed to breach the exterior walls of a particular structure. The tools most commonly used to breach exterior walls are the rotary saw, chain saw, circular saw, battering ram, sledgehammer, concrete breaker (jackhammer), and the air chisel.

Whenever an exterior wall must be breached, eye protection is a critical part of the firefighters' protective ensemble. In such situations, *both* helmet faceshields *and* goggles or safety glasses are needed. In situations where a concrete or masonry wall must be breached, considerable dust can be produced so respiratory protection is also needed. In some cases, filter masks may be sufficient. However, because the firefighters should be wearing their SCBA, the facepieces may provide both respiratory and eye protection (**Figure 9.43**).

Figure 9.41 Wired-glass is a common security measure found in doors and windows.

Figure 9.42 Film coated glass often breaks in the same manner as laminated glass.

Another important aspect of breaching an exterior wall for access into a structure is deciding where to cut. Just as in cutting ventilation openings, when cutting through an exterior wall it is usually better to cut one large opening instead of several smaller ones. Both time and effort will be saved if the job is done right the first time. Knowledge of the structural design of the particular building, gained during preincident planning surveys, will often help firefighters decide where openings should be made — and where they should not. For example, choosing a section of wall at random (without knowing the structural

Figure 9.43 Due to inhalation hazards and flying debris, it is necessary for firefighters to wear full PPE and SCBA when cutting masonry walls.

design) may result in opening the exterior wall where an interior wall intersects. A good deal of time and effort could therefore be wasted because the interior wall would also have to be removed before the opening would be usable, or an entirely new opening might have to be made.

In the absence of detailed knowledge of a particular building, and sometimes with it, one of the fastest ways to make a usable opening in an exterior wall is to make two vertical cuts down from the bottom corners of a window opening to the floor. The window and the section of wall below it can then be removed and a relatively large opening is created with less time and effort being expended than by cutting the same size opening in a blank wall **(Figure 9.44, p. 244)**. Obviously, if there are no window openings in a wall that must be breached, knowledge of the building is critical to deciding where to cut.

> **CAUTION**
> Hollow exterior walls often contain electrical wiring and/or piping for natural gas or LPG. Therefore, the utilities to the building should be shut off before any cuts into exterior walls are made.

Types of Exterior Walls

There are many types of exterior walls that firefighters may have to breach to gain entry into a building. The most common types of exterior walls are as follows:

- Wood-frame
- Masonry
- Concrete
- Metal

Breaching Wood-Frame Walls

Gaining access into ordinary wood-frame buildings sometimes involves breaching an exterior wall. Wood-frame walls are often covered by some form of wooden siding such as plywood or **oriented strand board (OSB)** panels, vertical or horizontal wooden planks, or wooden shingles **(Figure 9.45, p. 244)**. Some wood-frame walls are covered with siding made of vinyl plastic,

> **Oriented Strand Board (OSB)** — Construction material made of many small wooden pieces (strands) bonded together to form sheets, similar to plywood.

Chapter 9 • Access into Structures **243**

Figure 9.44 Cutting the section of a wall below a window creates a large access opening with much less effort.

Figure 9.45 Typical wooden siding.

Gypsum Wallboard — Widely used interior finish material. Consists of a core of calcined gypsum, starch, water, and other additives that are sandwiched between two paper faces. Also known as gypsum wallboard, plasterboard, and drywall.

Veneer — Surface layer of attractive material laid over a base of common material.

aluminum, or a cement-based composite **(Figure 9.46)**. Other wood-frame walls are covered by stucco over wire mesh, which is often backed by **gypsum wallboard** attached to the studs **(Figure 9.47)**. However, some older stucco walls consist of the finish layer of plaster over wire and tar paper covering diagonal wooden planking. Some wood-frame walls are covered by a **veneer** of brick or stone **(Figure 9.48)**. The exterior walls of some older residences, warehouses, and former military buildings are covered with large asbestos shingles over plywood or planking.

In many cases, breaching exterior walls of wood-frame structures can be done relatively quickly **(Figure 9.49)**. However, firefighters cutting through these materials must wear respiratory and eye protection as part of their protective ensemble. Because of the possibility of plumbing or electrical wiring inside the walls, the building's utilities should be secured before cutting begins.

Breaching Masonry Walls

As mentioned in the previous section, masonry walls are often just a veneer over wooden or metal structural members. In those cases, the tools and techniques discussed earlier can be used. However, in some buildings the exterior masonry walls are full-thickness assemblies that are made entirely of mineral material. For example, they may be cement-filled concrete blocks or a double-course brick wall. Double-course brick walls (also called unreinforced masonry [URM]) can usually be identified

Figure 9.46 Vinyl siding being installed.

Figure 9.47 A typical stucco wall.

Figure 9.48 Wood frame walls are often covered with a brick veneer. *Courtesy of the McKinney (TX) Fire Department.*

Figure 9.49 Breaching an exterior wood wall can often be done quickly.

Chapter 9 • Access into Structures **245**

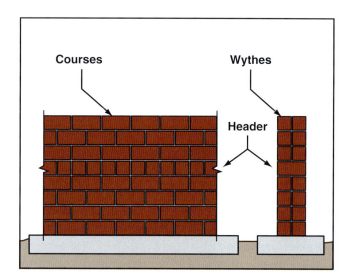

Figure 9.50 In a header course, the ends of the brick are visible.

Course — Horizontal layer of individual masonry units.

Header Course — Course of bricks with the ends of the bricks facing outward.

by certain bricks or **courses** being laid perpendicular to the other courses. In this **header course**, which may be every fifth, sixth, or seventh course, the ends of the bricks are visible **(Figure 9.50)**. Walls may simply be brick or stone veneer over concrete blocks or a metal framework.

In some cases, URM walls can be breached with a rotary saw equipped with a masonry blade. It may also be possible to break out a section of wall using a battering ram or a sledgehammer. However, all these tools and techniques tend to be slower than using electric or pneumatic concrete breakers (jack hammers). Obviously, eye protection is extremely important when using these tools to breach a masonry wall. In addition, the decibels produced by these tools make hearing protection critical also.

Breaching Concrete Walls

Some exterior walls may be reinforced or unreinforced poured concrete. Some are poured in place; others are tilt-up. Depending upon the age, quality, and thickness of the concrete, these walls can be some of the most difficult and time consuming to breach. Therefore, breaching poured concrete walls is usually considered too difficult and time consuming to be a reasonable option except in some structural collapse situations. Poured concrete walls are much more difficult to breach than other types of walls, but if deemed necessary, it can be done.

Manual breaching tools, such as battering rams and sledgehammers, are ineffective on poured concrete walls. A variety of power tools can be used to breach walls that have knockout panels built into them. Sometimes called blowout panels, knockout panels are large sections of concrete walls that are designed to be removable so that large vehicles or machinery can be brought into or removed from the building **(Figure 9.51)**. With these panels, a rotary saw equipped with a masonry blade can be used to cut around the perimeter of the panel. A chain saw equipped with a carbide-tipped chain will also work. But, as mentioned earlier, an electric or pneumatic concrete breaker may be most efficient.

In many older concrete and masonry buildings, window and doorway openings that are no longer used have been bricked-up **(Figure 9.52)**. These bricked-up areas are often easier to breach than the surrounding wall ar-

Figure 9.51 An exterior wall with a blowout panel.

Figure 9.52 In older buildings, window and door openings that are no longer used are often bricked up.

eas. The brickwork can sometimes be knocked out with a sledgehammer or battering ram.

Breaching reinforced concrete walls is so time consuming that it is rarely done until after a fire is extinguished. However, if these walls must be breached, it is likely that the reinforcing steel (rebar) will have to be cut to create a large enough opening for access by firefighters. The **rebar** can be cut with hydraulic cutters, such as those used to cut brake pedals during vehicle extrication, or with a rotary saw equipped with a metal-cutting blade. Rebar can also be removed with a cutting torch or other exothermic device if it is available on scene.

Rebar — Steel bars that are placed inside concrete structural elements to reinforce and strengthen the element.

Chapter 9 • Access into Structures **247**

Breaching Metal Walls

Lightweight metal walls are common on a wide variety of building types. The metal siding panels are usually attached to horizontal wooden or sheet metal framing members with screws. An access opening can be created by removing the screws, but this may be too slow to be practical. In many cases, the metal panels are thin enough that they can be cut with an axe. Metal walls can also be cut with an air chisel such as is used in vehicle extrication. But the tool of choice is often the rotary saw because it is almost always readily available and it is very effective **(Figure 9.53)**. However, because of the amount of sparks produced by these saws when cutting metal, they should only be used where flammable materials are a safe distance away or a charged hoseline is close at hand.

Figure 9.53 A charged hoseline should be close by when cutting a metal wall near combustible materials.

Forcible Entry Scenario:

You and your engine crew answer an automatic fire alarm call at a large single-story all-metal building. On arrival, a bright orange glow can be seen through the windows near the front of the building and smoke and flames are billowing from existing roof vents. You and your crew are ordered to open the building for access by the first fire attack crew.

- What are the most likely fire conditions inside the building?
- Where should the first opening be made?
- What tools and techniques would you use to create the opening?
- Which door or window would you open first?

Summary

Once firefighters have reached the outside of a burning building, they must use information gathered during preincident planning surveys and information gathered during size-up to decide which are the best access locations and what are the fastest ways of gaining access into the building. Forcing doors and windows is usually the safest and fastest way to get inside. However, the doors and windows may be protected with security systems that must be overcome before these openings can be used. In some situations, firefighters may have to breach an exterior wall to gain access into a building. One of the keys to making entry quickly and safely is preincident planning. Such planning allows firefighters to know what tools and techniques will be needed to force entry into any particular building. Armed with this knowledge, they can approach a burning building with the correct tools to do the job right the first time.

Review Questions

1. What characteristics of common doors are considered during size-up for gaining access into a building?
2. What procedures are commonly used to force residential and commercial doors?
3. What procedures are commonly used to force industrial doors?
4. What methods can be used to overcome door security systems?
5. What procedures are commonly used for breaking residential, commercial, and industrial windows?
6. What methods can be used to overcome window security systems?
7. What procedures are commonly used for breaching wood frame, masonry, concrete, and metal walls?

Fireground Search and Rescue

Chapter Contents

CASE HISTORY 253
Search and Rescue 253
    Search Size-Up 254
Conducting a Search 258
    Building Search Safety 258
    Primary Search 259
    Vent, Enter, Search (VES) 266
    Marking Systems 266
    Large-Area Search 268
    Rescue 270
    Secondary Search 272

Searching Multistory Buildings 273
    Multistory Search Methods 273
Rapid Intervention 274
    RIC Formation 275
    Tools and Equipment 275
    Operational Modes 279
Summary 281
Review Questions 281

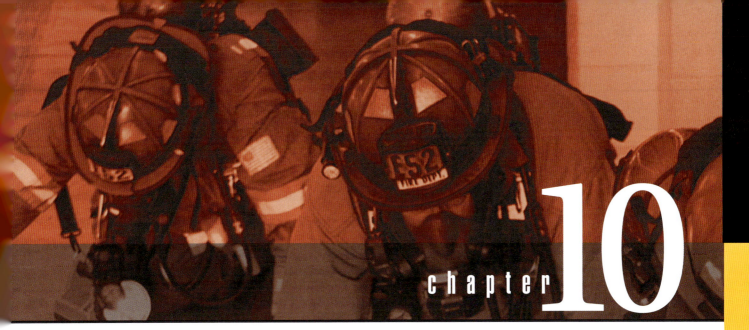

chapter 10

Key Terms

All Clear 254	Index Gas 272
Buddy System 260	Litter 278
Carabiner 268	Mayday 276
Dead Load 255	Shelter in Place 271

Learning Objectives

After reading this chapter, students will be able to:

1. Describe the difference between a primary and secondary search.
2. Describe three variables which impact the type and number of resources needed to conduct search operations during structural fires.
3. Describe the two objectives of a building search.
4. Describe the priorities of a primary search.
5. List the tools commonly used during primary searches.
6. Describe the methods used to conduct a primary search.
7. Describe the vent, enter, search (VES) technique.
8. Describe the procedures used for searching a large area.
9. Describe the process of sheltering in place during a fire emergency.
10. Describe the methods used to conduct a secondary search.
11. Describe the methods for conducting a multistory search.
12. Explain the OSHA rule known as 'two in-two out'.
13. Describe the role of a rapid intervention crew (RIC).
14. Summarize the tools that are commonly used by a RIC.
15. Describe the rapid intervention operational modes.

Fireground Search and Rescue

Safety Points

While reading this chapter, keep the following safety points in mind:

- Perform a risk/benefit analysis before beginning an interior search. Determine that there are savable lives.
- Attempt entry only after potential backdraft conditions have been mitigated.
- Work according to the incident action plan (IAP) – no freelancing.
- Wear full personal protective equipment, including SCBA and PASS device (and be sure the PASS device is turned ON).
- Use the established personnel accountability system without exception.
- Work in teams of two or more and stay in physical, voice, or visual contact with each other. Rescuers are responsible for themselves and each other. Maintain radio contact with your supervisor (Command, Division or Group Supervisor, etc.), and monitor radio traffic for important information.
- Stay alert – maintain your situational awareness. Continuously monitor fire conditions that might affect the safety of your search team and other firefighters.
- Maintain awareness of the secondary means of egress (line of retreat) established for the search team.
- Monitor the structure's integrity and communicate any significant change.
- Open windows to relieve heat and smoke during search only if consistent with the IAP.
- Close the door, report the condition, and follow your supervisor's orders if fire is encountered during a search.

Chapter 10
Fireground Search and Rescue

Case History

According to a newspaper report, Illinois firefighters were called to a fire in a one and one-half story, wood-frame residence in October of 2006. On arrival, firefighters saw heavy smoke coming from the dwelling. A neighbor told them that an 8-year-old boy was still inside so a search and rescue team, equipped with a thermal imaging camera, entered the house. When a search with the TIC failed to locate the child, the team switched to a conventional search. They soon discovered the boy unconscious and unresponsive behind a mattress where he had taken refuge from the fire. They began CPR and moved the boy outside to a waiting ambulance which transported him to a local hospital. Because of a quick but thorough search by the firefighters, and CPR begun immediately, the boy survived.

Most of the search and rescue operations conducted by firefighters are on the fireground. The foregoing case history is but one example. While too many people die in fires each year in North America, many others are successfully rescued by firefighters. This chapter begins with an overview of fireground search and rescue and the most common variables in fireground search and rescue incidents. Also discussed are conducting a primary search, search safety, search priorities, search tools (including thermal imagers), search methods, and marking systems. Additional items are large-area searches, rescuing trapped occupants, sheltering in place, evacuation, and secondary searches. Finally, the search and rescue of downed firefighters in the form of rapid intervention is addressed.

Search and Rescue

In structure fires, one of the primary ways in which fire departments meet their responsibility to save lives is by conducting a thorough search of the building and rescuing anyone who is in peril and needs assistance. In virtually every structure fire, firefighters search the building if it is reasonable and safe to do so. Even in relatively minor fires, there may be occupants in the building who are incapable of leaving on their own. Failing to locate a victim until after a relatively minor fire is extinguished or, worse yet, missing a victim entirely is both unprofessional and unacceptable. However, the decision to conduct a primary search is always based on a risk assessment and a determination that there may be savable victims.

Search Size-Up

While the initial size-up is the responsibility of the first-arriving officer, all firefighters should observe the exterior of the building and its surroundings as they approach. Careful observations may give them some indication as to the size and location of the fire, whether the building is likely to be occupied, the possible structural integrity of the building, and some idea of the amount of time it will take to effectively search the structure. Firefighters can greatly maintain their orientation within the building if they use the size-up to identify their possible alternate escape routes (windows, doors, fire escapes) *before* they enter. Once inside, a firefighter's specific location can sometimes be confirmed by looking out of the windows. The assessment of fire and building conditions must continue throughout the incident.

If occupants who have escaped the fire are available to be questioned, firefighters may be able to obtain information about anyone who might still be inside. Because neighbors may be familiar with the building occupants' habits and room locations, they may be able to suggest where occupants are likely to be found. They may also have seen an occupant near a window prior to the fire department's arrival. In addition, firefighters can obtain information about the location and extent of the fire (**Figure 10.1**). To the extent possible, all information should be verified. In any case, firefighters should not assume that all occupants are out until the building has been searched and an **all clear** declared. Information on the number and location of trapped occupants should be relayed to the incident commander (IC) and all incoming units.

If possible, the fire attack should be started before or simultaneously with any interior search operations. The safety of both the trapped occupants and the firefighters conducting the search can be increased by attacking and controlling the fire. In some cases, fire control may need to precede search.

All Clear — Signal given to the incident commander that a specific area has been checked for victims and none have been found or all found victims have been extricated from an entrapment.

Figure 10.1 Residents of the structure should be asked if there are other occupants inside if possible.

However, despite the sense of urgency that is part of every emergency scene and the pressure from bystanders for firefighters to take action, the IC and all firefighters on scene should carefully assess the situation and be guided by the IFSTA Risk Management Model described in Chapter 3. Firefighters are trained to function in high-risk environments, but the risks in any situation must be weighed against the potential for saving lives. Firefighters should never be put in mortal danger to recover a body.

As described in **Essentials**, almost all structure fires require both a primary and a secondary search. However, the number and types of resources needed to conduct these search and rescue operations safely and effectively can vary from one fire to another, depending upon a number of variables in each situation. While there may be other variables, the most common ones are the type of building that is burning, the time period in which the incident is taking place, and the fire situation.

Building Type

In this context, building *type* includes the construction type, occupancy type, and the age of the building. As discussed in earlier chapters, some types of construction tend to contain a fire while others contribute to its spread. For example, fire can spread more rapidly in an open warehouse than in a highly compartmentalized office building. Some building types are more vulnerable than others to losing their structural integrity during a fire, making them more prone to early collapse. For example, buildings that have lightweight roof assemblies supporting heavy **dead loads** may collapse sooner than those with other types of roof construction.

Dead Load — Weight of the structure, structural members, building components, and any other feature permanently attached to the building that is constant and immobile. Load on a structure due to its own weight and other fixed weights.

In addition, some buildings make forcible entry relatively easy while others make it much more difficult. Gaining entry into buildings with window bars, metal-clad exterior doors, and other security measures is more difficult than in buildings without such devices. All these variables can and should be identified during preincident planning so that any potential problems can be analyzed and plans developed to overcome them.

NOTE: For more information on preincident planning, see NFPA® 1620, *Recommended Practice for Pre-Incident Planning*.

Some types of buildings pose a greater life safety hazard than others **(Figure 10.2)**. For example, fully occupied places of public assembly and high-rise office buildings have a greater life safety hazard than most other building types. However, residential type buildings such as single-family dwellings, apartments, dormitories, and hotels may also have a greater life safety hazard than some other types of buildings. The occupant loads to be expected in these and other occupancies may vary significantly with the time period involved.

Figure 10.2 Buildings, such as hospitals, have larger than normal life safety hazards.

Time Period

In this context, time period refers to both the time of day and the day of the week when a fire is burning. In most residential occupancies, the highest occupant loads are to be expected during the late night and early morning hours when people are likely to be at home and asleep. Elementary and secondary schools are likely to be most heavily occupied during the daytime on weekdays. Post-secondary schools may also be occupied in the evening hours and on weekends. Retail, commercial, and industrial occupancies are likely to have their highest occupant loads during the day and early evening. Bars, nightclubs, movie theaters, and other public assembly occupancies are most likely to have their heaviest occupancy between noon and about 2:00 a.m., depending upon local laws **(Figure 10.3)**.

The occupant loads in other buildings, such as hospitals, nursing homes, and residential care facilities are not affected by the time of day or the day of the week. These facilities have a relatively constant occupant load at all hours of the day and night. When search and rescue operations are necessary in heavily occupied residential or public assembly occupancies, it can be expected that significant numbers of firefighters will be needed. While the time period involved can be a factor in the occupant loads of these occupancies, the other major variable affecting search and rescue operations is the fire situation.

Figure 10.3 Restaurants and bars are typically most heavily populated in the evening.

Fire Situation

The volume of fire, its intensity, its rate and direction of spread, and what is being threatened by it are all variables related to the fire itself. Variables related to the need for search and rescue include the following considerations:

- Type of construction
- Fire load **(Figure 10.4)**
- Occupancy type
- Occupant load
- Size of the fire
- How the fire is behaving.

Some of these variables will increase the need for search and rescue; others will reduce it. For example, if a residential building is *heavily* involved when the first fire department unit arrives, the firefighters must quickly try to determine whether anyone is still inside the building. If the answer is yes — based on direct observation or information from a credible person — firefighters may be put at considerable risk to conduct an immediate search for the occupants. Of course, the fire conditions must be such that firefighters have a reasonable chance of finding someone alive inside the building. It is *not* appropriate to put firefighters in mortal danger to recover a body. Given that immediate action by the first-arriving crew may save a life, a rapid intervention crew (RIC) is not required for them to enter the hazard zone for search and rescue, but a RIC should be established as soon as possible.

Figure 10.4 Heavy fire loads can greatly increase the size and intensity of the fire.

> The immediate action exception to the OSHA two-in/two-out rule does not include a search to determine whether lives are in jeopardy. The exception applies only to situations where lives are known to be at risk.

Firefighters conducting a search of the floor above a fire are in a very dangerous location because of the potential for the fire to cut off their means of egress or to extend upward onto that floor. Therefore, it is extremely important that charged hoselines be in place to protect their exit stairway and that a secondary means of egress be provided. This secondary means of egress can sometimes be provided by ground ladders placed at the windows on that floor. However, these ladders are vulnerable to fire issuing from a window below them. If firefighters are performing a search on a floor that is above the reach of the available ground ladders, an aerial device may be needed.

On the other hand, if the building is *fully* involved — regardless of the other variables — interior search and rescue could be precluded by the fire situation In this case, protecting any exposures and mounting an exterior fire attack are probably all that can be done until the fire is controlled **(Figure 10.5)**. After

Figure 10.5 Protecting exposures and mounting an exterior attack is appropriate if the structure is fully involved and no occupants are inside. *Courtesy of the Los Angeles Fire Department – ISTS.*

the fire has been controlled, fire crews can conduct a slow and methodical search for bodies. Because victim recovery is not an emergency operation, firefighters should not be put in serious danger during what is the equivalent of a secondary search.

Firefighters are often faced with a situation where there are reported victims and marginal fire conditions. In these instances, the incident commander must make the difficult decision of whether or not to allow a search. The sense of urgency and moral pressure to search for reported occupants should not overwhelm sound situational assessment, decision making, and tactical action to control the fire environment so that a search may be completed when conditions are more favorable.

Conducting a Search

The two objectives of a building search are: (1) locating victims, and (2) obtaining information about the location and extent of the fire. As previously mentioned, locating trapped occupants involves both primary and secondary searches.

In some cases, however, a third type of search – rapid intervention – is needed to locate and rescue firefighters in distress. Rapid intervention is discussed later in this chapter. If the decision is made to conduct an interior search of any burning building, firefighters must do so in a calculated and careful way.

Building Search Safety

While searching for victims in a fire, firefighters must always consider their own safety. In addition, incident commanders must consider the hazards to which firefighters may be exposed while conducting search and rescue operations. Safety is the primary concern of rescuers because hurried, unsafe search and rescue operations may have serious consequences for rescuers as well as victims. Firefighters can enhance their own safety if they and their officers make a good initial size-up, continue the size-up throughout the operation, and perform a risk/benefit analysis before each major step in the operation.

If the building is filled with smoke (zero visibility), firefighters are more likely to become disoriented and lose track of where they are in the building. Such conditions can slow the search process to the point that firefighters may run out of breathing air before completing their assignments. If they run out of air and are disoriented, they cannot tell other firefighters where they are located.

> ⚠ In zero-visibility conditions, firefighters must use a tag line or take a charged hoseline with them into the building.

When conducting a primary search, firefighters must work quickly but safely if they are to complete their assignments and avoid becoming victims themselves. As they search a burning building, especially when visibility is limited because of smoke and/or darkness, firefighters must always be alert for weakened or hazardous structural conditions, especially the floors. Firefighters should continually feel the floor in front of them with their hands or a tool to be sure that the floor is still intact **(Figure 10.6)**. Otherwise, they may blindly crawl into an open elevator shaft, a stairway, an arsonist's trap, or a hole that may have burned through the floor.

Firefighters on or directly below the fire floor should also be alert for signs such as sagging floors or ceilings or the sound of structural members creaking or groaning that may indicate that the floor/ceiling assembly above them has weakened. Any of these signs should be immediately reported to command.

Primary Search

As discussed in **Essentials**, a primary search is a rapid but thorough search that is performed either before or simultaneously with fire suppression operations. Therefore, a primary search is often carried out in extremely hostile conditions. However, in situations where there is a high probability of the building being occupied, a primary search must be conducted as soon as possible. Because time is of the essence in these situations, some departments allow search teams to enter a burning building without taking a charged hoseline with them; others do not. There are advantages and disadvantages to both procedures. Having a charged line allows a search team to protect themselves from any fire they encounter during their search; on the other hand, they could become focused on fighting the fire and lose sight of their original assignment. A conscious decision must be made in each situation if taking a charged hoseline is not required by departmental SOP.

Figure 10.6 A tool can be used to feel the floor for stability.

During primary search, firefighters must be sure to check the known or likely locations of victims as quickly as conditions allow. They should then move quickly to search all other affected areas of the structure as soon as possible. During the primary search, the search team or teams can also confirm that the fire conditions are as they appeared from the outside or report any differences they may encounter.

Primary Search Priorities

During a primary search, many fire departments follow a standard set of priorities that have been developed through experience with countless fires. These standard priorities dictate that search teams focus their efforts as follows:

- *Most severely threatened* — In most cases, the victims most severely threatened by fire are those closest to it. Therefore, whenever possible, firefighters should begin their primary search as close to the seat of the fire as conditions allow. If the search team is operating independently from a hose crew, they should have a charged hoseline with them when close to the seat of the fire. The next most seriously threatened are those on the floors above the fire because of the potential for fire and smoke to spread upward. Once the fire floor has been searched, the floor directly above should be checked.

- *Largest numbers* — In an ideal situation there would always be sufficient resources available to search all areas of a burning building at once. However, if on-scene resources do not allow all areas to be searched simultaneously, the IC may decide that searching areas that are likely to be occupied by the most people is the best choice.

- ***Remainder of hazard zone*** — Once the foregoing search priorities have been satisfied, either by conducting a search or by a conscious decision not to search, the balance of the hazard zone should be checked. If the hazard zone is closest to the seat of the fire, the remainder would be the immediately adjacent area.
- ***Exposures*** — After an all clear has been declared in the foregoing areas, the exposures should be searched. In a structure fire, the exposures may be internal or external. Both should be checked.

During primary search, firefighters must always use the **buddy system** — working in teams of two or more. By working together, two rescuers can conduct a search quickly while maintaining their own safety. When searching an IDLH atmosphere such as the smoke-filled areas in a burning building, firefighters must remain in physical, voice, or visual contact with other team members **(Figure 10.7)**.

> **Buddy System** — Safety procedure used in rescue work. When rescuers work in a hazardous area at least two rescuers must remain in contact with each other at all times.

Primary Search Tools

In addition to any specialized tools or pieces of equipment identified during preincident planning of a building or occupancy, every search team should carry at least the following:

- Portable radio
- Handlight
- Forcible entry tools
- Thermal imaging camera (if available)
- Marking devices

Valuable time will be lost if firefighters have to return to their apparatus for basic search tools and equipment. Tools used to force entry may be needed to force a way out of the building if search team members become trapped by a sudden increase in fire intensity or a structural collapse.

Many fire departments also require their search teams to take a search rope (tag line) with them when they enter the hazard zone. Some of these departments supply their teams with lighted search ropes that consist of a series of tiny white lights encased in a clear plastic sheath **(Figure 10.8)**. Available in lengths of up to 300 feet (100 m), the rope operates on 120-volt AC power and is carried in a canvas bag. These lighted ropes provide at least some illumination to help rescuers see their surroundings and identify potential hazards. However, the lighted rope's greatest value may be that it makes the search rope easier for firefighters to find when visibility is limited.

A growing number of fire departments are equipping their search teams with thermal imagers or *thermal imaging cameras* (TIC). Several different types of thermal imagers are available to fire/rescue agencies. Most imagers use one of two technologies — microbolometer technology, or BST (barium, strontium, titanium) technology.

A thermal imager functions by detecting the heat signature (minute amounts of thermal radiation) produced by fires and some living organisms **(Figure 10.9)**. They will also detect the residual heat signature, such as footprints, left after the removal of an object or organism that is warmer than its surroundings.

Figure 10.7 Firefighters should be in physical, voice, or visual contact with one another when operating in the hazardous area.

Figure 10.8 Some departments use lighted search ropes to improve visibility. *Courtesy of Rock-N-Rescue and Middlesex VFC.*

Figure 10.9 The difference between night vision equipment (top) and thermal imaging equipment (bottom) can be clearly seen. *Courtesy of Bullard.*

Handheld thermal imagers are available — some with pistol grip handles and some without **(Figure 10.10, p. 262)**. Others are designed to be mounted on a helmet **(Figure 10.11, p. 262)**. Some units are capable of remote transmission so that the image can be seen on a monitor at the incident command post (ICP) or some other location. Some imagers are designed primarily for locating the seat of a fire by being calibrated to respond to temperatures in excess of 900°F (465°C). Others are capable of differentiating between body temperature and that of surrounding materials.

Because the heat of a fire or other exothermic reaction may be detected through smoke and some walls, the seat of a fire may sometimes be detected from the exterior of a building. Thermal imagers can also be used on the roof of a burning building to help identify the best location for a ventilation exit opening, and to locate roof supports **(Figure 10.12, p. 262)**. For more information on this application, see Chapter 13, Vertical Ventilation.

All thermal imagers have certain limitations. For example, even though they are designed for use on the fireground, some are relatively fragile. Dropping one may put it out of service until it can be recalibrated. Imagers can also be

Chapter 10 • Fireground Search and Rescue **261**

Figure 10.10 Many thermal imaging cameras have pistol grip handles.

Figure 10.12 Thermal imaging cameras can be used to locate good areas for vertical ventilation.

Figure 10.11 Some thermal imagers are designed to be helmet-mounted. *Courtesy of the Allen (TX) Fire Department.*

put out of service, at least temporarily, by becoming overheated or by a condition known as a *whiteout*. A whiteout occurs when the imager is overwhelmed by the heat signature produced by a very intense fire and the screen suddenly goes white.

While thermal imagers will detect the heat signature produced by a fire or a live person, in some cases — as in the case history cited at the beginning of this chapter — the signature can be blocked by walls and other solid objects. In addition, window glass, mirrors, or other reflective surfaces may prevent thermal imagers from detecting a heat source.

Another possible disadvantage to using thermal imagers is that only the team member operating the camera sees what the device is detecting. The other team members must depend upon the TIC operator to keep them informed of any possible dangers or changes in fire behavior. If the operator fails to do so, the other team members could be in jeopardy if they do not maintain their situational awareness.

The two major advantages of using a thermal imager during primary search are speed and effectiveness. If an entire room can be scanned from the doorway, the time-consuming and sometimes difficult task of physically searching the room may not be necessary **(Figure 10.13)**. This can save a considerable amount of time; however, scanning too fast can result in victims being missed. Victims overcome by oxygen deprivation sometimes collapse in areas that cause them to be missed during a physical search. The sensitivity of a thermal imager can greatly reduce the likelihood of this happening and thereby increase the effectiveness of the search.

Another major benefit of using thermal imagers is a reduced likelihood of firefighters becoming lost or trapped. This is especially true if every team operating inside a burning building is equipped with a TIC. However, search teams should still employ standard search techniques such as using a tag line because TICs can and do malfunction. In these relatively rare instances, firefighters need to be able to find their way out.

Preincident planning is critically important in identifying occupancies that have a greater-than-normal life hazard and/or are configured in a way that would make a physical search both labor-intensive and time-consuming. Considering the resource demands involved in conducting an effective primary search in these occupancies, the expense of purchasing one or more thermal imaging cameras and training department personnel in their use may be justified.

Figure 10.13 An entire room can often be scanned from the doorway using a TIC.

Primary Search Methods

Depending on conditions within the building, firefighters may be able to search while walking upright or they may have to crawl on their hands and knees. If there is only light smoke and little or no heat, walking is the fastest way of moving about. Searching on hands and knees (beneath the smoke and heat) can increase visibility for firefighters and reduce their chances of tripping or falling into open stairways or holes in floors. While crawling is much slower than walking, and firefighters may consume their breathing air faster, it is usually noticeably cooler near the floor. When visibility is limited, firefighters should move up and down stairs on their hands and knees, ascending head first and descending feet first.

> ⚠ If firefighters can't see their feet because of the smoke, they shouldn't be walking upright.

Some departments train their firefighters to control the search environment to the greatest extent possible. They do so by applying *safe zoning* techniques and *guarding the line of retreat*.

Safe zoning. This technique is used in support of a fire attack or independently of it. Firefighters create safe zones by closing interior doors to isolate the fire and then remove heat and smoke from uninvolved areas with positive-pressure ventilation (PPV) or hydraulic ventilation **(Figure 10.14, p. 264)**.

Guarding the line of retreat. When search teams must progress deep into large and complex buildings, their line of retreat must be maintained. This can be done by positioning hose teams at intervals along the line of retreat to cool the hot gas layer and maintain control of the exit corridor.

When searching within a burning building, firefighters must be very cautious when opening doors. They should first feel the top of the door and the doorknob to determine the heat level. If the door is hot to the touch, it should not be opened until a charged hoseline is in position. Doors should be opened just enough to allow conditions in the room to be assessed.

Firefighters should not remain in front of any door while it is being opened, especially outward-opening doors. They should stay to one side, keep low, and open the door slowly. If there is fire behind the door, staying low may allow the heat and flames to pass overhead. With outward-opening doors, firefighters should stay on the hinge side (not the latch side) of the doorway so that the door can provide some protection if flames and heat erupt from the doorway opening. Some departments train their firefighters to apply a short burst of water fog above the door to cool the gases at the ceiling, and then to open the door and apply another short burst into the hot gas layer inside the room before attempting to enter. However, the risk to search teams can be reduced by simply keeping the door closed.

If an inward-opening door is difficult to open, firefighters should not kick the door to force it open because a victim may have collapsed behind it. Kicking the door could injure the victim further as well as the firefighter. Kicking the door will also leave firefighters unable to control the door. Instead, they should place a strap around the door knob to maintain control of the door and slowly push it open to check the area behind it for possible victims **(Figure 10.15)**.

When searching within a structure, firefighters should use the search patterns described in **Essentials**. They should move systematically from room to room, searching each room completely, while constantly listening for sounds from victims. On the fire floor, firefighters

Figure 10.14 Hydraulic ventilation is an effective way to remove smoke from the structure.

Figure 10.15 Straps can be used to maintain control of the door.

should tie a tag line to a standpipe or other stationary object before they enter the fire area if a hoseline is not being used. Once inside the room, firefighters should start their search as close to the fire as possible and then work back toward the entry door. This allows the team to reach those in the most danger first — those who would be overtaken by any fire spread that might occur while the rest of the search was in progress.

Because those who are a greater distance from the fire may be in less immediate danger, there is enough time for them to be located as a search team works its way back toward the starting point. Search teams should proceed as directly as possible from the entry point toward the fire pulling their hose or paying out their taglines as they go. This will provide a way for the team to remain oriented so they can find their way out quickly if fire conditions change rapidly during the search.

As in the case history cited at the beginning of this chapter, people instinctively seek any available shelter from a threatening fire. Therefore, it is very important for search teams to check all areas such as bathrooms, bathtubs, shower stalls, closets, basements, and attic rooms, as well as under beds, behind furniture, and any other areas where occupants might seek shelter from the fire **(Figure 10.16)**.

Teams should search the perimeter of each room, and because occupants may be overcome while trying to escape, firefighters should always check behind doors and on the floor below any windows. As they move around the perimeter, firefighters should extend their arms or legs or use the handle of a tool to reach completely under beds and other furniture. After the perimeter has been searched, they should then search the middle of the room.

Visibility may be extremely limited during the primary search, so firefighters should use a TIC if they have one. If one is not available, searching by touch may provide the only clue to what type of room the team is in. Poor visibility due to smoke should be reported to the IC because it may indicate a need for additional ventilation.

As they search, teams should maintain radio contact with their supervisor and should report only essential information (initial fire conditions found, significant changes in fire behavior or spread, etc.) to their supervisor or Command. They should also periodically report their progress in accordance with departmental SOPs. During a primary search, it is just as important to report negative information as positive information. For example, if the fire has spread farther than it appeared from the outside, if a large number of trapped occupants are found, or if the search has to be aborted for any reason, Command should be notified immediately. Informing the IC of any areas that have not been completely searched is especially important so that additional search teams can be assigned to these areas if necessary.

Figure 10.16 Victims can often be found in shower stalls and other concealed locations.

In some departments, small rooms are searched by using a TIC to scan the room. If a TIC is not available, the procedure is for one firefighter to stay at the door while another searches the room. The firefighter performing the search remains oriented by maintaining a steady dialogue with the firefighter at the door. The searcher keeps the firefighter at the door informed of the progress of the search. When the room search is completed, the two rejoin at the doorway, close and mark the door (see later section), and proceed to the next room. Firefighters may exchange their roles of searching the room and standing by at the door in order to preserve energy.

This last method reduces the likelihood of rescuers becoming lost within the room and makes the situation less stressful. When searching relatively small rooms, this technique is often quicker than when both members search together because the searcher can move along more quickly without the fear of becoming disoriented.

Another form of the oriented search involves the team using a charged hoseline. In this technique, the firefighter on the nozzle stays at the doorway while the other firefighter searches each room.

Vent, Enter, Search (VES)

In certain situations, some departments use a technique called Vent, Enter, Search (VES) in addition to the required primary search. VES is used where the fire has cut off the normal means of entry into or egress from some parts of a burning building and credible reports indicate that one or more occupants are trapped in a room that is accessible from the outside. Because people trapped in areas filled with smoke and heat cannot survive for very long, the decision to use an unconventional technique such as VES may be justified.

VES involves forcing entry from the exterior into rooms, such as bedrooms, where trapped occupants are most likely to be found. This most often involves opening or breaking an exterior window (venting) and entering through that window to search the room **(Figure 10.17)**. To increase both firefighter safety and access into the room, the entire window should be removed. To avoid drawing fire and smoke to the room because of the open window, firefighters should locate and close the interior door as quickly as possible. As with any other tactical operation, implementing VES should be coordinated with the fire attack and primary search operations.

Firefighters performing VES must be aware of the possibility of initiating a backdraft in the room when they break the glass or open the window. This requires firefighters to assess the fire behavior and backdraft indicators before creating any opening. If conditions within the room are too hostile for firefighters to enter, they can still search for victims by probing through the open window with the handle of a pike pole or similar tool **(Figure 10.18)**. Victims who were overcome while attempting to escape a fire are often found on the floor just below the window, so firefighters may be able to reach in and pull a victim out.

Marking Systems

As described in **Essentials**, the means most often used for marking searched rooms inside a burning building include: construction chalk or crayon, masking or duct tape, specially designed door markers, and latch straps over doorknobs

> **CAUTION**
> When VES is used, positive-pressure ventilation (PPV) must be delayed until the fire is controlled or all occupants have been removed from the building.

Figure 10.17 In VES, the window is opened from the outside to allow for ventilation and firefighter access.

Figure 10.18 If conditions do not allow firefighters to enter the area, the handle of a pike pole or other tool can be used to search for victims.

(Figure 10.19). Latch straps also serve the secondary function of preventing RIC members from having to force entry into a locked room when a search team is inside and needs help. Marking methods that might contribute to fire spread, such as blocking doors open with furniture, or methods that require subsequent searchers to enter the room to find the marker are *not* recommended.

Departmental SOPs usually dictate one accepted method of marking; however, all department personnel must be trained to understand and use whatever method is selected. Regardless of the marking method used, the marks should be placed on the lower third of the wall or door so they are more likely to be visible below the smoke layer.

Some departments train their search teams to use a two-part marking system. This involves marking the door with a slash when entering the room **(Figure 10.20)**. When the room search is finished, they add a second slash to form an X **(Figure 10.21)**. This avoids duplication of effort by alerting other search teams that the room is being or has been searched. If a search team fails to report and does not respond to calls for a personnel accountability report (PAR), this mark can serve as a starting point for others to begin searching for the missing team.

Figure 10.19 Latch straps are one means of marking a room during a search.

Figure 10.20 One slash is placed on the door when entering the room.

Figure 10.21 A second slash is placed on the door when exiting the room.

Chapter 10 • Fireground Search and Rescue

Large-Area Search

When searching large or complex spaces that are filled with smoke, some fire departments employ a primary search system that uses a dedicated search line. The search line consists of 200 feet (60 m) of ⅜-inch (10 mm) rope with a Kevlar™ sheath for maximum abrasion protection and heat resistance. Every 20 feet (6 m) along its length, a 2-inch (50 mm) steel ring is tied into the search line **(Figure 10.22)**. Immediately after each ring, one or more knots are tied in the search line to indicate distance. After the first ring, one knot indicates 20 feet (6 m) from the beginning of the line **(Figure 10.23)**. After the second ring, there are two knots indicating 40 feet (12 m) from the beginning of the line. After the third ring, three knots, and so on.

The knots indicate the distance from the beginning of the line and they are always *after* the ring, so they provide a directional indication – knots toward the fire; rings toward the exit. The rings also provide an anchor point for lateral tethers. The lateral tethers are 20 foot (6 m) lengths of ¼-inch (6 mm) rope with a Kevlar™ sheath. Each tether has a ¾-inch (18 mm) steel ring tied to one end, a knot at the midpoint, and either a nonlocking **carabiner** or a snap hook on the other end **(Figure 10.24)**. Each firefighter on the search team carries a tether, usually wrapped around one wrist.

Implementing a primary search using a search line system requires a team with a minimum of three firefighters, although more is better. All team members must be in full protective ensemble including SCBA. About 10 feet (3 m) outside of the entry point (or as close as possible) to the area being searched, the end of the search line is tied to a fixed object about 3 feet (1 m) above the floor **(Figure 10.25)**. A company identifier is left at that point. Some departments using this system choose to station an attendant at the entry point to maintain communication with the search team and act as their air management timekeeper; others do not.

One team member, sometimes called the *Lead*, carries the rope bag into the search area. The Lead is accompanied closely (shoulder to shoulder) by another member often called the *Navigator*. The Navigator is equipped with a radio, handlight, and TIC if available **(Figure 10.26)**. The Navigator uses the light and/or the TIC to direct the Lead while crawling forward in the search

> **Carabiner** — A steel or aluminum D-shaped snap link device for attaching components of rope rescue systems together.

Figure 10.22 A steel ring is tied into the search line every 20 feet (6 m). *Courtesy of Jeff Seaton.*

Figure 10.23 Knots are tied in the rope at predetermined intervals. Note: The knots in this photo are for effect and are not to scale. *Courtesy of Jeff Seaton.*

area. One or more radio-equipped searchers follow them in. Each searcher carries a tether wrapped around one wrist and a forcible entry tool in the other hand **(Figure 10.27)**. As they progress into the building, the search line pays out behind them and all team members maintain contact with the search line.

If it becomes necessary to search areas perpendicular to the search line, team members can either snap their tether onto one of the 2-inch (50 mm) rings and begin searching laterally, or tie the tether to the search line at any point between rings **(Figure 10.28, p, 270)**. Maintaining radio contact with the Navigator, the searchers pay out the tether as they progress. Reaching the knot in the middle of the tether allows each searcher to make a 10 foot (3 m) diameter arc from the attachment point. If a searcher does not find a victim, he or she can progress an additional 10 feet (3 m) to the end of the tether. There, the searcher can sweep a 20 foot (6 m) arc.

If there is still more area to be searched beyond the first 20-foot (6 m) tether, a second searcher can attach a tether to the ring on the end of the first searcher's tether **(Figure 10.29, p. 270)**. This effectively doubles the area that can be searched from one point of attachment to the search line. As they return to the

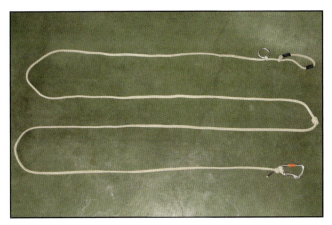

Figure 10.24 Lateral tethers are 20 foot (6 m) sections of rope that have a steel ring at one end and a carabiner at the other. *Courtesy of Jeff Seaton.*

Figure 10.25 The end of the search line is tied to a secure object outside the search area. *Courtesy of Jeff Seaton.*

Figure 10.26 The navigator should be equipped with a portable radio, handlight, and TIC if available. *Courtesy of Jeff Seaton.*

Figure 10.27 Searchers should have their lateral tethers wrapped around their wrist. *Courtesy of Jeff Seaton.*

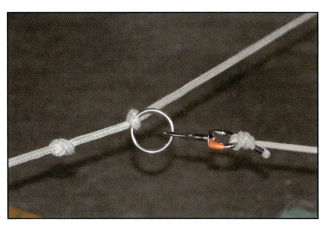

Figure 10.28 The lateral tethers allow for areas to be searched away from the main search line. *Courtesy of Jeff Seaton.*

Figure 10.29 A second searcher can tie on to the first searcher's tether, effectively doubling the amount of area that can be searched. *Courtesy of Jeff Seaton.*

search line, the searchers wind their tethers around their wrists again. As the team progresses into the building, the Navigator keeps Command informed of their progress by reporting how many knots they are into the building, what the conditions are, and what they have found.

For this or any other search technique to be most effective, firefighters must be thoroughly trained in its application, and that training tested periodically with realistic exercises. In addition, fire departments should consider the advantages and disadvantages of any search system – especially one that does not include the use of a charged hoseline – before adopting it or using it during a major incident. The inherent risks involved in using any search technique must be weighed against the value of simply staying out of the burning building.

Rescue

When occupants are found during a primary search, their condition and their overall situation must be assessed. This assessment is necessary to determine whether they merely need assistance in leaving the building or whether they are incapable of escaping because of impairments, injuries, or entrapment. It is critical that Command be informed of the situation and of any additional resource needs.

Some building occupants, especially the very young and the very old, or those impaired by drugs or alcohol, may be frightened, confused, or disoriented by the sounds of a smoke alarm, fire alarm bell, and/or the sirens and air horns of arriving emergency vehicles. Some who are physically capable of escaping without assistance are mentally incapable of doing so. Individuals who are not fluent in English may have difficulty following instructions. These individuals may instinctively remain in or return to their rooms where they feel safe. If the atmosphere outside the victims' rooms is clear enough for them to breathe without SCBA and they would not otherwise be in danger from the fire, they can be escorted out of the building. If conditions outside their rooms will not allow them to be escorted out, they may have to be rescued through an exterior window. The equipment and techniques described in **Essentials** can be used to rescue these victims.

If occupants are injured or they are trapped because the fire has cut off their normal means of escape, their medical condition and situation will have to be assessed and appropriate action taken. These actions include keeping Command informed of the situation and may include stabilizing the victims before any rescue attempt is made. However, if the victim's location is immediately threatened by the fire or imminent structural collapse, it may be necessary to rescue the victims before medically stabilizing them. It is a choice between risking further injury during the rescue and risking death from the fire. In some situations, it may be possible to protect trapped and/or injured victims without immediately rescuing them. This technique is known as **sheltering in place**.

> **Shelter in Place** — Having occupants remain in a structure or vehicle in order to provide protection from a rapidly approaching hazard (fire, hazardous gas cloud, etc.).

Sheltering in Place

It may be impractical and unnecessary to evacuate the entire population of a heavily occupied burning building — not to mention rescuing them. For example, in fully occupied high-rise office or residential buildings it is often neither practical nor necessary to evacuate or rescue every building occupant. Instead, those not in immediate danger from the fire — primarily those located below the fire floor — may be better protected by being allowed to remain in the building and perhaps in their own rooms. Even occupants above the fire floor may be out of danger if the fire is well contained and the occupants are several floors above it. The fire situation must be continually monitored and any change that might put occupants at risk would trigger an immediate change in the plan. Obviously, these alternate plans must be thought out and ready to be implemented if needed.

Some residential and commercial buildings are designed with sheltering in place as part of their life safety plan. The design of these buildings includes what are called *areas of refuge*. An area of refuge is a protected location in a structure where occupants can gather and wait for assistance. While the Americans with Disabilities Act (ADA) uses the term *area of rescue and assistance*, the practical meaning is the same as for an *area of refuge*, provided that the area meets all other requirements for wheelchair access, etc. **(Figure 10.30)**. Both areas of refuge and areas of rescue and assistance must be equipped with emergency communications systems. For more information on areas of refuge, refer to NFPA® 101, *Life Safety Code®*.

Figure 10.30 Areas of refuge are often labeled as such in buildings.

If the burning building is equipped with a common communications system that allows all occupants to hear an announcement at the same time and is still operational, it can be used to notify occupants about which floors or areas of the building need to be evacuated and which are safe for them to continue to occupy. If there is no such system available, electronic bullhorns or other public address systems may be used for this purpose **(Figure 10.31)**.

Figure 10.31 Bullhorns may be needed to communicate with occupants during an evacuation.

Figure 10.32 School gymnasiums and other large facilities are commonly used as relocation centers during long-term incidents. *Courtesy of Patsy Lynch/FEMA.*

Evacuation

Even though the occupants of some burning buildings can be moved to an area of safe refuge within the structure, other fires may require the evacuation of the building, a city block, or even an entire neighborhood. In some cases, large-scale evacuations can go quickly and without incident. In others, evacuations can be extremely complex. For example, those involving convalescent hospitals, nursing homes, or correctional facilities can require the cooperation of numerous agencies.

Before people are asked to leave, an adequate temporary relocation site must be identified and security for their unoccupied homes and businesses must be provided. Churches, school gymnasiums, and similar facilities can be used as relocation centers **(Figure 10.32)**. The responsible law enforcement agency may control the perimeter of or increase patrols in the evacuated area. Individuals who cannot evacuate themselves should be assisted in doing so.

While firefighters may be initially involved in the evacuation, many jurisdictions assign this responsibility to law enforcement and emergency management organizations. In some jurisdictions, law enforcement has the sole legal authority to order people from their homes. Obviously, law enforcement personnel must conduct any evacuations from correctional facilities.

As with other emergency operations, preincident planning is critical to safe and efficient evacuations. Protocols, procedures, and contingency plans should be worked out in advance with all agencies that might be affected. Like other emergency procedures, evacuation plans need to be tested periodically in order to be effective.

Secondary Search

A secondary search is conducted *after* the fire is under control and the most serious hazards have been mitigated. Ideally, firefighters other than those who conducted the primary search should be assigned to conduct a secondary search of the building. During the secondary search, speed is not as important as thoroughness. The secondary search is conducted just as systematically as the primary search to ensure that no rooms or spaces are missed, but the secondary search is conducted more slowly and carefully than the primary search. As in the primary search, any negative information, such as the fire beginning to rekindle, should be reported immediately. In addition, firefighters assigned to conduct a secondary search must maintain their situational awareness because the structural integrity of the structure may be compromised from the fire and water used for extinguishment.

SOP for some departments calls for firefighters to continue to use their SCBA until the atmosphere of the hazardous area is deemed to be within safe limits. As a way of defining what *safe limits* means in these situations, departments have historically used carbon monoxide (CO) as an **index gas**. These departments assumed that when CO readings fell below a designated concentration, any other toxic gases present would also be at similarly low levels. Any reading above the designated level for CO meant that firefighters inside the fire

> **CAUTION**
> Even though the interior of a building may appear to be free of smoke, firefighters conducting the secondary search must not remove their SCBA until the atmosphere has been sampled and found to be within safe limits.

Index Gas — Any commonly encountered gas, such as carbon monoxide in fires, whose concentration can be measured. In the absence of devices capable of measuring the concentrations of other gases present, the CO measurement may be assumed to indicate their concentrations as well.

damaged area had to continue to breathe air only from their SCBA. However, CO as an index gas has proven to be unreliable. Scientifically controlled tests have shown that even when CO levels are quite low, other toxic gases can be present in dangerous concentrations. Therefore, firefighters inside a building after fire control has been achieved should continue to breathe supplied air only.

Searching Multistory Buildings

When searching multistory buildings, the order in which the floors are searched can influence the success of the search and rescue operation. As discussed earlier in this chapter, areas most threatened by the fire should be searched first. In order of priority, the most critical areas in a multistory building are as follows:

- The fire floor
- The floor directly above the fire
- The topmost floor

These floors should be searched first because this is where any remaining occupants will be in the greatest jeopardy due to rising smoke, heat, and fire. The majority of victims are likely to be found in these areas. Once these floors have been searched, the intervening floors should also be checked.

During the primary search, doors to rooms not involved in fire should be closed to prevent the spread of fire or smoke into these areas unless they are part of the ventilation process. Opening doors can change the ventilation profile and can even spread the fire by drawing it toward the openings. Exits, hallways, and stairs should be kept as clear as possible of hoselines and other equipment to facilitate the egress of occupants and to reduce tripping hazards **(Figure 10.33)**. In buildings with multiple stairways, one should be designated for occupant egress and another for fire fighting operations.

Figure 10.33 Stairwells can easily become congested during firefighting efforts.

Multistory Search Methods

When rooms, offices, or apartments are situated along both sides of a center hallway, the large-area search system described earlier can be used effectively. Otherwise, teams should be assigned to search both sides of the hallway. If two teams are available, each can take one side of the hallway. If there is only one search team, they should search all the rooms on one side of the hallway before reversing direction to search those on the other side. During this or any search operation, it is critically important to control the line of retreat to ensure that search teams can escape if fire conditions suddenly deteriorate.

As described in **Essentials**, when a search team enters the first room, they turn right or left and follow the walls around the room until they return to the starting point. As they leave the room, they turn in the same direction they turned to enter the room and continue to the next room to be searched. For example, if they turned left when they entered the room, they turn left when they leave the room.

When removing a victim to safety or to exit the building, firefighters must turn in the opposite direction from that which they used to enter the room. It is important that firefighters exit each room through the same doorway they entered to ensure a complete search and to avoid getting lost or disoriented. This technique may be used to search most buildings, from a one-story, single-family residence to a large high-rise building.

Rapid Intervention

Whenever firefighters are ordered into the hostile environment inside a burning building, the possibility exists for one or more of those firefighters be injured, lost, disoriented, or trapped. This text refers to firefighters in any of these dire situations as being *downed* or *in distress*. To most effectively assist downed or distressed firefighters in burning buildings, other firefighters must first be aware of the situation, be able to locate the firefighter or firefighters, and be able to rescue them as quickly as possible.

Occupational Safety and Health Administration (OSHA) respiratory protection regulations in 29 CFR 1910.134 state that whenever firefighters are in an IDLH atmosphere, including the interior of burning buildings when the fire is beyond the incipient or early growth stage, the firefighters must work in teams of two or more. These regulations also require that at least two fully equipped firefighters be standing by outside of the hazard zone ready to immediately enter if needed to search for and rescue firefighters in distress. This requirement has become known as the *two-in/two-out rule*.

Although stated in slightly different terms, similar requirements are also included in NFPA® 1500, *Standard on Fire Department Occupational Safety and Health Program*. In fire departments across North America, the firefighters assigned to stand by outside the hazard zone are identified by a variety of names and acronyms such as RIC, RIT, FAST, and others. However, NFPA® uses the term *rapid intervention crew/company* (RIC), and this terminology is used in this and all other IFSTA manuals.

Because regulations require two firefighters to stand by outside the hazard zone whenever a team is inside, a total of four firefighters must usually be on scene before firefighters are allowed to enter a burning building for primary search and rescue. However, the regulations allow an exception to the two-in/two-out rule if, by taking immediate action, the first-arriving company can save a life or lives. While this exception allows for entry without adequate personnel on scene, OSHA stipulates that this is *only* to be done in cases where lives are *known* to be at risk.

NOTE: The exception to the two-in/two-out rule does not allow firefighters to conduct a primary search to determine if there are trapped occupants. The firefighters must have seen or heard the occupants from outside the burning building, or have been informed by a credible person that someone is still inside.

To limit possible abuses of this exception, NFPA® 1500 requires an investigation into every case where the two-in/two-out rule was not followed. The results of this investigation must be submitted in writing to the fire chief.

RIC Formation

It should be understood that compliance with the two-in/two-out rule and establishing a formal rapid intervention crew (RIC) are *not* the same thing. Having two firefighters, a firefighter and a driver/operator, or a driver/operator and a chief officer on scene when two other firefighters are inside meets the OSHA requirement, but may or may not provide a sufficient number of personnel to locate and rescue the interior crew if necessary. On the other hand, a RIC may be composed of two or more firefighters – perhaps many more – equipped and ready to make entry if needed **(Figure 10.34)**. Firefighters assigned to the RIC are not distracted by having to operate a pumping apparatus or needing to organize and manage the fire suppression operation. While RIC members may be assigned to perform certain functions on the fireground, they must be able to drop those assignments at a moment's notice if they are needed for rapid intervention. In addition, RIC members are charged with setting up a dedicated RIC equipment cache so that the necessary tools and equipment will be immediately available if needed.

Figure 10.34 RIC personnel ready to make entry.

One possible limitation on the effectiveness of rapid intervention crews may be the number of personnel assigned compared to the number actually needed to complete the task in a safe and timely manner. Tests conducted by the Phoenix (AZ) Fire Department under controlled but very realistic conditions revealed serious limitations on the work that can be accomplished by a two-member RIC. These tests showed that while a two-member RIC may be capable of locating a downed firefighter, it may take a dozen or more firefighters to provide a reliable air supply, stabilize any injuries, and package and remove even a single firefighter from the contaminated atmosphere to a place of safety **(Figure 10.35)**.

Figure 10.35 Numerous firefighters are often needed to remove a downed firefighter from the hazardous area.

When fire departments are developing or reviewing their SOPs on rapid intervention, they should consider the results of these tests or conduct their own. At the same time, they should consider the tools and equipment that may be needed to safely and effectively conduct rapid intervention operations.

Tools and Equipment

Most of the gear needed for any type of rapid intervention is standard, and many fire departments have a list of tools and equipment to be gathered when needed. Other departments have developed dedicated RIC kits which are equipment caches kept separate from those staged for the fire attack **(Figure 10.36, p. 276)**. Whether in kit form or not, rapid intervention crews need the following tools and equipment at structure fires:

- Full PPE and SCBA
- Appropriate communications equipment

Figure 10.36 A typical RIC equipment cache.

- Thermal imaging cameras
- Personal illumination equipment
- Forcible entry tools
- Rescue air supply
- Rescue ropes
- Rescue litters

Full PPE and SCBA

A **Mayday** or other distress call from a fellow firefighter can increase the level of anxiety and stress for firefighters assigned to a RIC. Although these firefighters naturally want to locate and rescue their coworker as quickly as possible, they must not enter a burning building wearing anything less than full PPE and SCBA. Any time saved by cutting corners on their PPE can be more than offset by reduced safety and effectiveness. Being able to survive and function effectively in such a hostile environment depends upon the RIC members being able to protect themselves.

Appropriate Communications Equipment

The regulations governing rapid intervention operations require that RIC members remain in visual, voice, or physical contact with each other. Physical contact can be maintained using a rope. However, RIC members may not use a radio to maintain the required contact with other members of their crew. The designated leader of a RIC should use a radio to maintain communications with the supervisor and Command **(Figure 10.37)**.

Thermal Imaging Cameras

If available, a thermal imaging camera (TIC) can be an extremely useful search tool. A TIC's ability to detect the heat signature (thermal radiation) produced by fires, warm-blooded organisms, and even the minute levels of residual heat left by recent footprints can help firefighters locate unconscious victims.

Mayday — International distress signal broadcast by voice.

Personal Illumination Equipment

Each member of the RIC should be equipped with at least one effective lighting device. Flashlights and other handheld lights can be used if they are the only lights available, but they can be cumbersome if they have to be held. Lights that attach to the helmet, waist strap, or a neck strap allow both hands to be free to perform work **(Figure 10.38)**. However, lights attached to neck straps are potentially dangerous because the straps can be an entanglement hazard.

Some departments include chemical light sticks in their RIC kits. These intrinsically safe devices glow for several hours when activated. While their primary purpose is as a locator beacon, they do produce a limited level of illumination that may be useful at very close range.

Some departments include illuminated ropes in their RIC caches. These devices are discussed in the preceding ropes section.

Forcible Entry Tools

The forcible entry tools that may be needed by a RIC vary with the scope and complexity of the incident. At a minimum, each RIC should take the basic tools needed to force open locked interior doors. This could be as simple as a standard set of *irons* consisting of a Halligan bar nested with a flat-head axe **(Figure 10.39, p. 278)**. Some RICs also take a short pike pole inside with them. The RIC cache of some departments includes a power saw, hydraulic spreaders, and a variety of prying tools; although these may be needed more by those assigned to rescue a downed firefighter than by those who merely locate him or her.

NOTE: Tools driven by gasoline engines may not function in a smoky atmosphere and electric tools may be unsafe where flammable vapors are present. Hydraulic spreaders, saws, and other tools are generally safe and functional in these situations.

Rescue Air Supply

In addition to their personal SCBA, RICs should take a spare air cylinder or a complete SCBA unit with them into the hazard zone for each firefighter reported to be in distress. Spare air cylinders should be equipped with the appropriate regulators and/or trans-fill fittings to allow RIC members to provide rescue air to a downed firefighter without needing share their personal air supply **(Figure 10.40, p. 278)**. Firefighters should *never* compromise their SCBA in any way to share their personal air supply with anyone — not even another firefighter.

Figure 10.37 The RIC leader should stay in contact with the IC.

Figure 10.38 There are numerous different styles of lights that firefighters can use.

Chapter 10 • Fireground Search and Rescue **277**

Figure 10.40 Spare air cylinders can be attached to the down firefighter's SCBA unit to provide additional breathing air.

Figure 10.39 A set of irons is an important part of the RIC equipment cache.

> ⚠ According to both NFPA® and NIOSH, so-called buddy breathing techniques are unreliable and more likely to produce two victims instead of one. Therefore, these techniques are not recommended. NIOSH recommends providing respiratory assistance and quickly moving the victim to a clear atmosphere.

The rescuers must be able to provide the downed firefighter (and themselves) with breathing air for as long as needed. If the firefighter is seriously injured or trapped under rubble and debris, several air cylinder changes may be needed before the rescue operation is completed.

Rescue Ropes

As in other search and rescue operations, ropes are an integral part of the equipment needed for rapid intervention and serve multiple purposes. Ropes are needed as tag lines to help the RIC and other firefighters find their way out of a burning building if necessary. In addition, ropes may be needed to rescue the downed firefighter.

Rescue Litters

Litter — Portable device that allows two or more persons to carry the sick or injured while keeping the patient immobile.

Like rescue ropes, **litters** can have a number of uses in rapid intervention operations, and can take a variety of forms. Some litters used for rescue are rigid plastic or metal/wire baskets; others are simple frames with canvas stretched over them, or even full backboards can be used. Basket-type litters can be used as originally intended – to carry injured victims out of a burning building to a waiting ambulance **(Figure 10.41)**. They can also be used as a basket in which to place tools and equipment that need to be carried into a burning building or hoisted to an upper floor **(Figure 10.42)**.

Operational Modes

Rapid intervention operations on scene can be classified into two modes: stand-by and deployment. The stand-by mode includes all RIC activities outside of the building or hazard zone. The deployment mode includes all activities by the RIC once it has been determined that a firefighter is in distress and cannot escape without assistance.

Stand-by Mode

In stand-by mode, those assigned to a RIC perform a quick reconnaissance to familiarize themselves with the building and size up the fire situation. They also gather the tools and equipment that will be needed if they are deployed into the hazard zone. In some fire departments, tarps slightly smaller than standard salvage covers, and of a different color, are marked as dedicated RIC equipment caches. RIC kits or the tools and equipment on the RIC equipment list are placed on the designated tarp. Once the RIC equipment has been gathered and inspected for readiness, the crew is ready for deployment.

NOTE: Depending on the size and complexity of the burning building, how many firefighters are inside, and how many entry points were used, there may be more than one RIC, each assigned to a different location.

Under certain conditions, NFPA® 1500 allows members of a RIC to perform other duties outside of the hazard zone as long as one member remains at the entry point. RIC members must be able to:

- Maintain communication with the interior crew
- Perform outside duties that do not limit their ability to perform search and rescue
- Abruptly abandon the outside duties without putting other firefighters in danger

Strenuous activities, such as repeated heavy lifting, might reduce a firefighter's readiness for rapid intervention if needed. Therefore, some departments limit the types of outside duties to which RIC members can be assigned.

Typical tasks for RIC members in stand-by mode include placing ladders for access and egress, forcing doors, removing security features, and making additional

Figure 10.41 Litters are a good means of carrying downed firefighters out of the hazardous area.

Figure 10.42 Litters also allow for tools and other equipment to be carried efficiently.

openings to the building. This is commonly referred to as *softening* the building. As mentioned earlier, these tasks can be performed by RIC members *only* if the task can be immediately abandoned without putting other firefighters in danger.

Entry or Deployment Mode

Once a Mayday or other distress call has been received or it has been determined that a firefighter is missing inside a burning building, the RIC will be deployed. Unless the downed firefighters are equipped with electronic locator devices that pinpoint their locations within the building, the RIC leader must obtain the following information:

- How many firefighters are in distress
- The last known location of the missing firefighters
- If radio contact been established or a distress signal has been received
- The radio channel on which the missing firefighters may transmit or receive
- If a tag line or hoseline can be used to help locate the missing firefighters

Because the firefighters in distress are probably breathing air from an SCBA that is depleted, time is critical. Therefore, the search should be delayed only long enough to gather this information. If possible, the information should be obtained face-to-face instead of over the radio to avoid tying up a channel over which the distressed firefighters may attempt to communicate. While the RIC leader is obtaining the information, the other member or members can pick up the needed tools and equipment from the RIC cache.

Once entry is made, the RIC proceeds as directly as possible to the downed firefighters or to their last known location. As they make their way toward the firefighters in distress, the RIC should stop at intervals to listen for signals or other sounds from the downed firefighters. At each stop, an attempt should be made to establish radio contact with the missing firefighters. If radio or physical contact is made, Command should be informed of the situation immediately. The air supply and medical condition of the downed firefighters should be assessed, and their most immediate survival needs addressed first. If additional equipment or other resources are needed from outside the hazard zone, they should be requested immediately.

If the firefighters are seriously injured, they should be medically stabilized before being moved if conditions allow. However, if fire conditions or imminent structural collapse make the location untenable, they should be moved immediately regardless of their injuries.

Fireground Search Scenario:

Arriving at the scene of a working fire in an older multistory apartment building, you and your engine company are ordered to conduct a primary search of the building.

- What variables might affect the search and rescue resources needed in this building?
- How would you assess the likelihood of there being occupants trapped inside?

- If it is not obvious from the outside, how could you determine where the fire is located?
- How would the location of the fire affect the search priorities in this building?
- What tools and equipment would you take with you into the building?

Summary

In structure fires, one of the primary ways in which fire departments meet their responsibility to save lives is by conducting a thorough search of the building and rescuing anyone who is in jeopardy but cannot escape without assistance. Regardless of how small a structure fire may look upon arrival, firefighters almost always search the building if it is reasonable and safe to do so. Even in relatively minor fires, there may be occupants in the building who are incapable of leaving on their own.

Firefighters have a variety of means available to determine the need for search and rescue in any given situation and to conduct search and rescue operations safely and effectively. However, to use these means to their greatest advantage, firefighters need to have identified potential rescue scenarios through preincident planning, developed contingency plans to address those scenarios, and trained on the use of the available tools and equipment.

Review Questions

1. What is the difference between a primary and a secondary search?
2. What are the variables that impact the resources required to conduct search operations at a structure fire?
3. What are the two objectives of a building search?
4. What are the priorities of a primary search?
5. What tools are commonly used by firefighters when conducting a primary search?
6. What methods are used to conduct a primary search?
7. What is the vent, enter, search (VES) technique? In what situations is it used?
8. What procedures are used to search a large area in a building?
9. What is sheltering in place? In what situations can it be used?
10. What methods are used to conduct a secondary search?
11. What methods are used to search a multi-story building during a fire operation?
12. What is the purpose of the OSHA rule known as "two in-two out"?
13. During a fireground operation, what is the role of the RIC? Who can make up the RIC?
14. What tools are commonly used by a RIC and for what tasks are they used?
15. What are the rapid intervention modes?

Ventilation Size-Up

Chapter Contents

CASE HISTORY 285	**Coordination with Rescue and Fire Attack** 299
Ventilation Overview 285	Timing of Ventilation 300
Natural Ventilation 286	Location of Ventilation Opening 300
Tactical Ventilation 286	Method of Ventilation 302
Ventilation Size-Up 287	**Other Ventilation Size-Up Considerations** 303
Review of Fire Behavior 289	Exposures 303
The Burning Regime and Extreme Fire Behavior 289	Weather 304
Reading the Fire 290	**Summary** 306
Smoke Behavior 290	**Review Questions** 306
Building Construction 292	
Age and Type of Building 293	
Positive Construction Features 295	
Negative Construction Features 298	

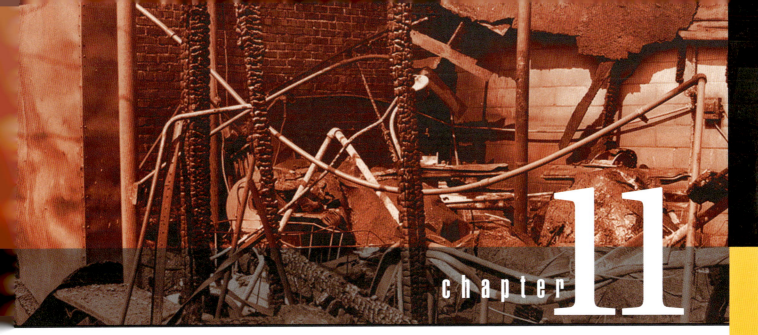

chapter 11

Key Terms

Compartmentalization 296
Hydrocarbon Fuel 291
Mechanical Ventilation 287
Natural Ventilation 286
Tactical Ventilation 286
Ventilation 285

Ventilation Size-Up

Learning Objectives

After reading this chapter, students will be able to:

1. Define ventilation.
2. Explain the concept of a ventilation profile.
3. Describe tactical ventilation.
4. Describe the building construction factors that must be considered during ventilation size-up.
5. Describe the procedures for coordinating ventilation with rescue and fire attack.

Safety Points

While reading this chapter, keep the following safety points in mind:

- Ventilation should be performed strategically and with a purpose. Arbitrarily breaking windows and creating roof openings can contribute to fire spread and places victims and firefighters in great danger.
- The IC should carefully coordinate ventilation activities with attack and rescue crews.
- Wind speed and direction should be reassessed regularly while on scene.

Chapter 11
Ventilation Size-Up

Case History

According to NIOSH Report F2004-10, firefighters in Missouri were called to a fire in a single-story wood-frame restaurant in February of 2004. Firefighters took a charged hoseline inside to try to locate the seat of the fire, but once inside they found dense black smoke and zero visibility. When one of the firefighters experienced an SCBA malfunction, he abandoned the nozzle and another member of the hose crew followed him out. A short time later, the IC ordered an emergency evacuation of the structure and a personnel accountability report (PAR) because of the danger of roof collapse. The PAR revealed that one firefighter was missing. Following a partial roof collapse, several unsuccessful search attempts were made. The victim was eventually located inside the building with his SCBA mask dislodged. He was pronounced dead at the scene.

Among the conclusions drawn from the foregoing case history, the importance of early and aggressive tactical ventilation operations on interior structure fires — especially attic fires — cannot be overstressed. Had this building been ventilated before attack crews were sent inside, the results might have been different. Before ventilation or any other fireground action is ordered, the fire should first be accurately sized up. Then, using the information gained in the size-up process, the IC can weigh the risks and benefits of tactical ventilation and other possible actions.

This chapter begins with an overview of tactical ventilation. As it affects ventilation size up, fire behavior is reviewed. Also discussed is how building construction may affect ventilation size-up. Finally, the coordination of tactical ventilation with rescue and fire suppression related operations is discussed along with other ventilation size-up considerations.

Ventilation — Systematic removal of heated air, smoke, gases or other airborne contaminants from a structure and replacement with cooler and/or fresher air to reduce damage and to facilitate fire fighting operations.

Ventilation Overview

As discussed in **Essentials**, one of the most effective tactics available to firefighters is **ventilation**. Unfortunately, ventilation is often a much-discussed but little-understood concept in the fire service. Virtually every fire has some type of naturally occurring ventilation. Factors that contribute to the ventilation of a fire are known as a *ventilation profile*. Ventilation profiles are unique for each incident because no two fires and structures are the same.

Natural Ventilation

Natural ventilation profiles are composed of factors that occur without outside intervention. Open or closed windows and doors, progress of the fire through the roof, and wind are all aspects that contribute to a structure's natural ventilation profile. A fire is often termed *self vented* if it progresses through the roof or compromises windows on its own. This term may be a bit misleading. While a structure has a natural ventilation profile and may be venting outside the structure, it may not be doing so in a desirable manner for fire fighting operations.

> **Natural Ventilation** — Techniques that use the wind, convection currents, and other natural phenomena to ventilate a structure without the use of fans, blowers, or other mechanical devices.

Tactical Ventilation

Tactical ventilation is a methodical, thought-out approach to changing the ventilation profile of a structure. This is done to improve conditions for fire fighting operations inside the structure, limit or prevent the spread of fire, and create a more tenable environment for firefighters and victims. Any actions on the part of firefighters to ventilate a structure – from opening doors and breaking windows to setting up ventilation fans – are tactical ventilation efforts because they are done with intent and purpose.

> **Tactical Ventilation** – A methodical, thought-out approach to changing the ventilation profile of a structure.

Decisions on how to implement tactical ventilation efforts should be made by the incident commander. As the foregoing case history indicates, some incident commanders tend to ventilate too little rather than too much — and often too late. It is also clear that firefighters sometimes allow a legitimate concern for property conservation — doing the absolute minimum of property damage in the ventilation process — to dictate the type and amount of ventilation that is done. For example:

- Time is lost trying to force open a window rather than breaking the glass.
- A ventilation opening is not cut in a roof, allowing the attic fire below to spread.
- A ventilation opening is made, but it is too small so the fire spreads as if there were no ventilation opening.

Even when a ventilation opening of adequate size is made, ventilation is too often done as an afterthought. An example of this is clearing residual smoke after the fire inside the building has been extinguished. However, experience has shown that if tactical ventilation is not implemented properly and with appropriate aggressiveness or coordination, the fire often continues to grow and spreads to unintended areas of the structure (**Figure 11.1**). Properly done, tactical ventilation can contribute significantly to the achievement of all three of the universal goals on every incident: life safety, incident stabilization, and property conservation.

Life Safety

Effective tactical ventilation of a structure fire can draw heat, smoke, and toxic fire gases away from both trapped occupants and firefighters. Tactical ventilation also decreases the chances of a rollover, flashover, or backdraft

Figure 11.1 Fires can quickly spread to unintended areas of the structure if improper ventilation is performed. *Courtesy of the Oklahoma State Fire Marshal's Office.*

and reduces the likelihood of firefighters being injured. In addition, ventilation reduces the amount of physical stress firefighters have to endure inside a building during search and rescue and fire suppression operations. When firefighters are not fatigued by extreme temperatures within the building and are not in danger of heat-related conditions such as heat exhaustion or even heat stroke, they can attack the fire more aggressively.

Incident Stabilization

Properly executed tactical ventilation improves visibility inside a burning building and releases heat, which makes it easier for attack crews to locate the fire and control it. Faster control of a fire translates into earlier stabilization of the incident.

Property Conservation

A properly sized and placed ventilation opening will provide the shortest possible path by which the fire and its products can leave the building. Ventilation openings also channel heat and smoke away from uninvolved portions of the building. Both of these effects contribute to a reduction in property loss.

Whenever possible, tactical ventilation should be implemented in concert with existing atmospheric conditions, taking advantage of natural ventilation. However, in some situations – such as with an adverse wind – natural ventilation may be inadequate and may have to be supplemented or increased with **mechanical ventilation**. Also called *forced ventilation*, mechanical ventilation involves the use of fans, blowers, nozzles, and other mechanical devices to create or redirect the flow of air within an involved compartment or building (**Figure 11.2, p. 288**).

Ventilation Size-Up

One of the most important elements in the size-up of a structure fire is that of ventilation. Before orders are given to ventilate a burning structure, the IC must consider the effects that ventilation will have on the behavior of the fire.

> **Mechanical Ventilation** — Any means other than natural ventilation. This type of ventilation may involve the use of fans, blowers, smoke ejectors, and fire streams.

Figure 11.2 Firefighters may have to be creative when ventilating large buildings. *Courtesy of the Florida State Fire College.*

Figure 11.3 Ventilation of the structure must be considered prior to making entry.

Before actually opening the building, consideration must be given to the readiness of attack crews to advance hoselines to facilitate fire attack, search and rescue operations, and exposure protection **(Figure 11.3)**. To be both safe and effective, ventilation operations must be coordinated with fire attack.

The IC must first determine whether ventilation is necessary and, if so, when, where, and in what form it should be initiated. Conditions present upon arrival will heavily influence ventilation decisions. Some situations may simply require locating and extinguishing the fire and then ventilating afterward to clear residual smoke from the building. Other situations will require early and aggressive ventilation to enable firefighters to enter the building to conduct search and rescue and fire suppression operations.

For ventilation to be most effective, it must be done sooner rather than later — sometimes even before the fire attack has begun — provided that it is performed as part of a coordinated strategic effort. The type of ventilation used (vertical vs. horizontal or natural vs. mechanical) must also be the most appropriate for the situation. Ventilation must be adequate, meaning it must be capable of handling the volume of heat, smoke, and toxic gases being produced by the fire. In addition, ventilation efforts must be aggressive enough to be efficient.

In their zeal to do the best possible job, firefighters assigned to ventilate a burning building sometimes develop tunnel vision and fail to recognize elements in the situation that could threaten their safety or that of others. Therefore, firefighters must be trained to quickly but thoroughly size up the situation, weigh the risks and benefits of the tactical options available, and base their actions on what is safe and of the greatest benefit to the overall operation. Some agencies use the simple approach:

- What do we have?
- What are we going to do?
- What do we need?

The answers to these questions provide a general outline of ventilation size-up. However, to more accurately size up a ventilation situation, firefighters must have at least a basic understanding of how fire, smoke, and gases behave under various conditions. In addition, firefighters must understand what effect ventilation will have on the fire.

Review of Fire Behavior

In addition to other factors discussed later in this chapter, tactical ventilation size-up and decision-making are based on an understanding of fire behavior and the influence of changes in ventilation profile. Earlier chapters have addressed fire development and extreme fire behavior in depth. The following section reviews the critical aspects of fire behavior as they relate to ventilation size-up.

The Burning Regime and Extreme Fire Behavior

Unless interrupted by some outside intervention such as fire attack or automatic fire suppression system activation, fires in compartments start with ignition and progress through four stages:

- Incipient
- Growth
- Fully developed
- Decay

In the incipient and early growth stages, a fire will be fuel-controlled. Development of fuel-controlled fires is limited by the characteristics and availability of the fuel involved. Increasing ventilation (air supply) to a fuel-controlled compartment fire will initially slow its progress toward flashover by removing hot gases and cooling the interior of the compartment with fresher air. However, if the fire is not quickly controlled, it may grow larger before reaching flashover.

As the fire develops through the growth stage and approaches the fully developed stage, it is likely to become ventilation-controlled. When a compartment fire is ventilation-controlled, fire development is limited by the available air supply. Increasing the air supplied to a ventilation-controlled compartment fire will cause the heat release rate to rapidly increase. If the accelerated heat release rate is not mitigated through effective fire control and ventilation tactics, ventilation-induced flashover may result.

In a closed compartment, a ventilation-controlled fire may progress into the decay stage as the available fuel and oxygen are consumed. Of these two variables, the major concern is when the fire decays due to a limited air supply. This condition presents a severe threat as combustion becomes less efficient, smoke production increases and becomes more fuel-rich, and the temperature in the compartment remains high. Providing an increased air supply to a ventilation-controlled fire in the decay stage can result in a ventilation-induced flashover or backdraft.

The hazards presented by ventilation-controlled fires may extend beyond the involved compartment. Smoke may push into and accumulate in uninvolved compartments and void spaces. Smoke is unburned fuel and it may form a flammable mixture with the air in these spaces, increasing the risk of a smoke explosion. All that is needed for this to occur is an ignition source.

Analyzing the Fire

Ventilation size-up requires an assessment of the burning regime and the potential for extreme fire behavior. For a review of fire behavior indicators, refer to **Table 2.1** in Chapter 2. Different stages of fire development may require different ventilation tactics. For ventilation size-up to be performed safely and effectively, it is critically important that firefighters be able to recognize the stage of fire development inside the building. In addition, firefighters must also consider the burning regime and potential for extreme fire behavior — rollover, flashover, and backdraft. Review fire behavior information in Chapter 2, Enhanced Fire Behavior, for more information on these concepts.

Smoke Behavior

From a ventilation size-up perspective, one of the most important indicators of the fire conditions within a burning building is the behavior of the visible smoke. For their own safety, firefighters must remember that smoke contains a variety of toxic substances. Therefore, firefighters should follow the safety behaviors listed in Chapter 3, Firefighter Safety and Survival, especially the one that says — *never* breathe smoke. Also for their own safety, firefighters must remember that smoke is unburned fuel that may be ready to ignite. In addition, firefighters must be able to accurately assess smoke behavior. As discussed in Chapter 6, the variables in smoke behavior that firefighters should look for when sizing up a working structure fire are:

- Smoke volume
- Smoke color and density
- Air flow (pressure)

Smoke Volume

There are differences in the volume of smoke produced by various materials when they burn and by the conditions in which they burn, but the volume of smoke is still a good general indicator of fire conditions. In general, the greater the volume of smoke, the bigger and more intense the fire is. While it is possible for a large fire to produce little smoke, these conditions rarely exist outside of the laboratory or in certain industrial processes. It is far more likely that a small fire will produce a large volume of smoke. However, in most structure fires, firefighters should assume — until proven otherwise — that a lot of smoke equals a lot of fire **(Figure 11.4)**.

Smoke Color and Density

As was discussed in Chapter 6, the color of the smoke being produced by a fire is a more reliable indicator of fire conditions than the volume of smoke being produced. For example, whitish-gray smoke generally indicates that cellulose-based materials (wood, paper, etc.) are burning in an atmosphere with abundant oxygen. On the other hand, dense black smoke is generally produced by **hydrocarbons** such as petroleum and petroleum-based materials. But, as discussed earlier, this dense black smoke may also be the result of virtually any material burning in an atmosphere where the oxygen supply is limited — such as in a developing backdraft condition. To make these distinctions, firefighters must consider the overall situation and not just the color of the smoke **(Figure 11.5)**.

> **Hydrocarbon Fuels** — Petroleum-based organic compounds that contain only hydrogen and carbon.

In addition to the color of the smoke being produced by a structure fire, firefighters should observe its density. From a size-up perspective, there are two categories of smoke density — optical density and opacity, and physical density.

Optical density and opacity. These terms describe how difficult it is to see through the smoke. Smoke containing high concentrations of particulates is both very dense (thick) and opaque (not transparent). Therefore, it is virtually impossible to see through.

Physical density. This describes how buoyant the smoke is. Smoke that is buoyant will rise quickly and smoke that is not will hang close to the floor. In general, buoyancy is related to the temperature of the smoke — the higher the temperature, the more buoyant the smoke (**Figure 11.6, p. 292**).

Figure 11.4 Large volumes of smoke typically indicate the presence of a large fire. *Courtesy of the Los Angeles Fire Department – ISTS*.

Figure 11.5 All indicators must be taken into account when analyzing fire conditions. *Courtesy of the Los Angeles Fire Department – ISTS*.

Figure 11.6 Cool smoke will tend to linger in the air.

Air Flow (Pressure)

As a fire burns within a structure, convection causes the hot smoke and gases to expand and rise. If the smoke and gases are confined, pressure is created. As a confined fire grows larger and more intense, more pressure is created. When the entire space within a compartment has been filled with smoke, the smoke will be forced out under pressure through every available opening. The higher the pressure, the greater the movement.

When firefighters see a large volume of very dense smoke billowing out of a structure under great pressure, there can be little doubt that a large and intense fire is burning inside the building. However, if firefighters see only a light haze of smoke moving lazily on the top floor of a building, it could be from a fire burning very intensely in the attic space above them. Once again, firefighters must not base their entire ventilation size-up on a single observation. Each observation must be considered in relation to the overall situation.

Building Construction

In addition to sizing up the location and extent of the fire, firefighters must also consider the building age, type, design, and occupancy when making tactical ventilation decisions. Type and design features that have a bearing on these decisions include the types of materials of which the building is constructed, the number of stories, the number and size of roof vents and wall openings, and the availability of roof access **(Figure 11.7)**. Also to be considered are security devices on windows and doors, as well as the direction in which these openings face in relation to exposures and the prevailing wind. Building construction features are discussed in greater detail in Chapter 13, Vertical Ventilation, and Chapter 14, Special Ventilation Operations.

For purposes of ventilation size-up, the following four critical building construction factors should be considered:

- Age and type of building
- Positive construction features
- Negative construction features
- Occupancy-specific construction features

Age and Type of Building

Knowing approximately when a particular building was constructed can provide firefighters with information that may be critical to safe and effective ventilation of the structure. Older buildings, newer buildings, and all those in between have certain advantages and disadvantages with regard to their fire resistance, fire spread characteristics, and susceptibility to structural collapse.

Figure 11.7 Unique architectural features must be taken into account during the ventilation size-up.

The type of building involved can also affect the ventilation size-up process. Single- or multi-family residences, commercial buildings, industrial buildings, and high-rises all have characteristics in common as well as those that are unique to their types and specific occupancies.

Older Buildings

Even though many older buildings — those built before building codes were adopted — are unique, others share common characteristics. Many older buildings were constructed with walls of unreinforced masonry (URM), primarily brick, giving them the capacity to contain the heat of a fire longer than wood-frame buildings. While this can reduce fire spread to other structures, it can also increase the chances of backdraft conditions developing. URM structures are also prone to structural collapse **(Figure 11.8)**.

Older wood-frame buildings were most often built from full-dimension lumber. When damaged by fire, full-dimension lumber retains its strength longer than the nominal-dimension lumber used in newer buildings. However, because the lumber is so old, it is more likely to be dehydrated and therefore more susceptible to ignition than newer lumber. In addition, older buildings are more likely to have balloon-frame construction that allows fire to spread inside the walls from the basement to the attic or even from top to bottom **(Figure 11.9, p. 294)**.

Figure 11.8 Unreinforced masonry (URM) buildings are especially prone to structural collapse. *Courtesy of Ed Prendergast.*

Unless they have been remodeled, and many of them have, older buildings may have knob-and-tube wiring with substandard insulation on the wires. In older buildings, the number of circuits and outlets may also be inadequate to handle the many electrical devices commonly used today. This makes these buildings more susceptible to electrical fires. Many older buildings used lamella arch roof systems or bowstring arch roof assemblies. These roof assemblies have a history of sudden collapse in fire situations.

During renovations of many older buildings, heavy HVAC units were added to roof systems that were not designed to support that sort of dead load. These additions can increase the collapse potential of a roof assembly significantly. Some older buildings have had a second roof assembly added above the first one. Discussed more in Chapter 13, Vertical Ventilation, these so-called *rain roofs* can make cutting ventilation openings more difficult and dangerous **(Figure 11.10)**. Many older buildings had false ceilings installed, which created concealed spaces where fire could burn undetected. The original wooden window frames in many older buildings were replaced with aluminum or vinyl plastic frames. A number of older buildings had siding composed of asbestos shingles; others had aluminum or vinyl siding. Still other older buildings had massive metal grilles added to their exteriors to improve their appearance. These grilles add another layer of material that must be breached when gaining access to exterior windows for rescue or horizontal ventilation.

The exteriors of many older buildings have been extensively changed with the addition of decorative fascia, awnings, marquees, and cornices **(Figure 11.11)**. These modifications often added heavy overhead frameworks that increase the danger to firefighters from structural collapse. The exteriors of other older buildings have been refurbished using polystyrene foam cov-

Figure 11.9 Balloon-frame construction does not utilize firestopping between studs and allows products of combustion to travel between floors. *Courtesy of Wil Dane.*

Figure 11.10 A rain roof under construction. Note the gap that will exist between the new roof and the existing roof.

Figure 11.11 Decorative fascia is often added to existing structures for visual appeal.

ered with a weatherproof coating of a granular plastic material such as Dryvit®, USG®, and others. Although the polystyrene foam is flammable, these materials are extremely lightweight and represent little collapse threat to firefighters.

The net result of these modifications is that many older buildings are not as they appear from the outside. They may appear to be modern but are really old, pre-code buildings with a new front that may have significant fire spread and/or collapse potential. Numerous modifications may have replaced original features with newer ones made of synthetic materials, increasing the potential for highly toxic smoke being produced when these buildings burn (**Figure 11.12**).

Figure 11.12 These composite glulam beams give the appearance of heavy timber construction.

To increase the accuracy of their ventilation size-ups, firefighters need to be aware of the modifications that have been made to older buildings in their response districts. This awareness is usually gained through a conscientiously applied program of ongoing preincident planning surveys.

Newer Buildings

Even though many buildings constructed since the middle of the 20th century were erected in compliance with a building code, they may not necessarily meet current code requirements. For example, when copper was in short supply during the Korean and Vietnam wars, some newer buildings had aluminum wiring installed, which has been identified as the probable cause of numerous structure fires.

Newer buildings also contain a greater percentage of synthetic materials than older buildings. These materials are found in carpeting, furniture, interior doors, window frames, and interior finishes. As mentioned earlier, these materials add to the fuel load and significantly increase the toxicity of the gases produced during an interior structure fire.

Many newer buildings are also more likely than older ones to incorporate lightweight construction materials, methods, and systems. These buildings often use parallel chord trusses or engineered wooden I-beams to support floor and roof assemblies **(Figure 11.13, p. 296)**. Other newer buildings incorporate panelized roof systems. Many newer residential and office buildings incorporate factory-assembled lightweight wooden roof trusses **(Figure 11.14, p. 296)**. These construction methods and materials generally reduce the cost of construction, but the long spans and enclosed voids increase the likelihood of early structural collapse under fire conditions.

Positive Construction Features

A number of building construction features are of some help to firefighters on the fireground. Generally, these features tend to resist the effects of the fire, reduce fire spread of fire, and reduce the likelihood of structural collapse. During the size-up of a structure fire, firefighters should look for these features and factor them into their assessment of the building.

> **WARNING!**
> Because lightweight construction can fail suddenly and unexpectedly during a fire, the IC should be notified whenever these materials are found during ventilation operations.

Figure 11.13 Engineered wooden I-beams are often used to support floor and roof assemblies. *Courtesy of Dave Coombs.*

Figure 11.14 Lightweight roof trusses are often assembled in factories and shipped to the jobsite. *Courtesy of McKinney (TX) Fire Department.*

Steel Framing Members

Buildings that incorporate steel framing members are far less likely to contribute to fire spread than those with traditional wooden framing **(Figure 11.15)**. Steel framing that is protected by gypsum drywall is virtually impervious to fire, and this contributes to the maintenance of structural integrity.

Self-Closing Fire Doors

Among the most positive building construction features are self-closing fire doors **(Figure 11.16)**. Whether activated by fusible links or by fire/smoke detection systems, these doors limit the spread of fire on any particular floor by employing the principle of **compartmentalization**. As long as these doors are not blocked open or otherwise prevented from operating as designed, they can be of tremendous benefit to firefighters.

> **Compartmentalization** — The systematic venting of a structure by controlling which windows and doors are opened at any given time.

Automatic Sprinkler Systems

Another positive building feature is an automatic sprinkler system. When functioning properly, these systems generally keep fires in check long enough that firefighters need only do final extinguishment, salvage, and overhaul **(Figure 11.17)**. However, automatic sprinklers can be overwhelmed by rapidly accelerating fires in certain fuels. These systems can also be rendered ineffective by anything that prevents the water from the sprinklers reaching the fire. If firefighters face a major fire in a fully sprinklered building, they must assume that either the system is not operational or that an extremely intense fire has overwhelmed the system.

Built-In Fire Suppression Systems

Other built-in fire suppression systems are also of help to firefighters. Flooding systems that discharge CO_2, halogenated agents, or dry-chemical agents have generally the same capabilities as automatic sprinkler systems — but on a more limited scale **(Figure 11.18)**. These systems are usually designed to protect a single compartment within a building and not the entire building as are most automatic sprinkler systems. However, the same ventilation size-up conclusions apply to compartments with built-in systems as those that have automatic sprinkler systems.

Figure 11.15 Metal studs are commonly found in commercial and institutional applications.

Figure 11.17 Fire Department Connections (FDCs) are an important component of automatic sprinkler systems.

Figure 11.16 Magnetic fire door holders like this one are connected to a smoke detection system. When the system is activated, the electromagnetic charge in the door holder is deactivated closing the door automatically.

Figure 11.18 Built-in fire suppression systems are often found in restaurant kitchens and industrial occupancies.

Chapter 11 • Ventilation Size-Up **297**

Elevator Shafts

One construction feature that is common to most multistory buildings is one or more elevator shafts **(Figure 11.19)**. Elevator shafts can be both a hindrance and a help during interior fires. They can be a hindrance when they provide an avenue for fire and smoke spread from one floor to the next. On the other hand, they can also allow vertical ventilation of a fire below the top floor by providing an avenue by which smoke and hot gases can be vented through the roof without having to pass through intervening floors.

Automatic Smoke Vents

From a ventilation standpoint, one of the most helpful features a building can have is automatic smoke vents. Some automatic vents open when a fusible link within the vent hood separates. Others are opened automatically by smoke detectors inside the building. Still others are designed with plastic panels that soften from the heat of a fire and fall out. Ideally, buildings with panelized roof systems, or any other system that is prone to early collapse during a fire, will have automatic smoke vents. Having these vents prevents firefighters from having to walk on these sometimes unstable roof structures to cut ventilation exit openings.

Figure 11.19 Elevator shafts often allow smoke and other products of combustion to spread to other floors.

Negative Construction Features

To most effectively size up construction features that can hinder tactical ventilation operations, firefighters must be familiar with the buildings within their districts before a fire call is received. Frequently touring the district and observing building construction and renovations in progress is time well spent for firefighters. As new construction or major modifications to existing structures are being done, firefighters should visit the sites as often as possible to identify the materials and methods being used in these buildings. The knowledge gained could save their lives and the lives of others.

As mentioned in the preceding section, some of the construction features that help firefighters can also hinder tactical ventilation operations. Negative construction features include those that do not resist effects of fire, those that promote fire spread, increase the likelihood of structural collapse, and make entry by firefighters more difficult. Recognizing these features during ventilation size-up is critically important to the success of fireground operations.

Elevator Shafts

As mentioned earlier, elevator shafts can be used to vertically ventilate a building. However, they can also make fire spread from floor to floor more likely. In buildings not protected by automatic sprinklers, elevator shafts act as chimneys to channel convected heat, smoke, and fire upward to the roof. If there is no opening at the top, the products of combustion will spread laterally and be forced downward. Smoke and heat will spread into compartments on the top floor and below through cracks around and between the doors at each elevator landing.

Synthetic Materials

As previously mentioned, many newer buildings, and older buildings that have been extensively remodeled, contain large quantities of synthetic materials. These materials may be found in structural components, trim pieces, finishes, or furnishings — or all of these **(Figure 12.20)**. Regardless of how these materials are incorporated into the building, they tend to increase the rate of fire spread and significantly increase the volume of smoke and the toxicity of the combustion products when these materials burn. For the firefighters ventilating these occupancies, wearing SCBA is not an option; it is an absolute necessity.

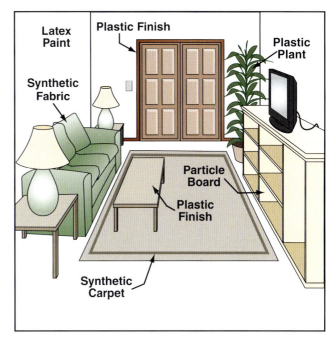

Figure 11.20 Synthetic interior furnishings under combustion can release toxic products into the atmosphere.

Planters and other Landscape Features

Whether installed for aesthetic reasons or as barriers, masonry planters and similar features can keep fire apparatus some distance from a burning building. This can force firefighters to carry all their equipment farther from the apparatus to the building, and makes it much more difficult for them to place ground ladders at strategic positions around the exterior of the building.

Security Measures

These features are intended to deny access to vandals and burglars, who often start fires to destroy evidence of their crimes. However, security doors and window bars or screens also make entry by firefighters more difficult and time consuming.

Occupancy-Related Features

In many cases, construction features that can either help or hinder tactical ventilation operations are directly related to the occupancy or use of the building. For example, the cocklofts and exterior walls of industrial buildings often contain high-voltage electrical wiring. Highly toxic gases may be piped through the walls to various locations within the building. If firefighters are unaware of these potential hazards or are unfamiliar with how to recognize them, they can inadvertently cut into the wiring or piping with catastrophic results.

Coordination with Rescue and Fire Attack

A critically important part of the ventilation size-up of a structure fire is coordinating the ventilation with other fireground operations — particularly with rescue and fire attack. This coordination is necessary because the fire often increases in intensity when ventilation is initiated. This happens because of the inrush of oxygen-rich air replacing smoke and other fire gases that exit through doors, windows, and other openings.

Establishing and maintaining the required level of coordination demands that everyone on the fireground know and understand the incident action plan (IAP) and how the plan affects each part of the operation. In other words, the required coordination demands a high level of communication and co-operation. When the IC has decided that ventilation is needed, coordinating the ventilation operation with rescue and fire attack generally involves three components: timing, location, and method.

Timing of Ventilation

The timing of tactical ventilation can be one of the most critical aspects of the operation, in both effectiveness and safety. Regardless of the location or type of ventilation opening, if the operation is started too soon or too late, it can seriously affect both rescue and fire attack operations. For example, if a large ventilation opening is made before rescue and attack crews are ready to enter the building, the fire can grow and spread faster than it otherwise would because of the increased oxygen that is made available. On the other hand, if a ventilation opening is not created until after rescue and attack crews have entered the building, they may have to endure unnecessary discomfort from the heat and smoke until the opening is made. Therefore, the ventilation crew must get into position and be ready to make the ventilation opening as soon as forcible entry is completed and rescue and attack crews are ready to enter.

Location of Ventilation Opening

Deciding where to create the ventilation opening is often dictated by where the fire is located in the building and the stage of fire development. In general, the ventilation opening should be made as close to the seat of the fire as safely possible. This provides the greatest effect for the amount of resources invested. However, one of the most important considerations is that the ventilation opening be located where it will draw the fire, heat, and smoke away from any trapped occupants. Because suppression crews should be attacking the fire from the unburned side, channeling the heat and smoke away from any occupants should also draw it away from the firefighters inside. Some of the factors that have a bearing on where to ventilate include the following:

- Location of the fire
- Location of occupants
- Interior and exterior exposures
- Type of construction
- Purpose or use of the occupancy
- Extent to which the fire has progressed
- Condition of the building and its contents
- Existing openings (skylights, ventilators, monitors, etc.)
- Direction and velocity of the wind
- Resource availability and capability

Even locating the seat of the fire may not always be easy to do. When the smoke is not readily visible, such as at night, other indicators must be used. One additional indicator that can be used is heat. As a structure fire develops, progressively higher temperatures are produced. Unless the fire breaks a window or burns through to the outside, these high temperatures continue to build well into the fully developed stage. Firefighters can sometimes locate the main body of the fire from the outside by using a thermal imaging camera (TIC) **(Figure 11.21)**. If a TIC is not available, they can get some indication of the location and intensity of the fire by feeling walls, doors, or windows for heat or by looking for discolored or blistered paint. These visible indicators may reveal the location of the seat of the fire. For example, a basement fire may sometimes be located by a hot spot on the floor above it, or an attic fire may be revealed by an area of melted snow on the roof.

When the involved building is but one of a connected series in a commercial block or strip mall, checking the interior walls or exterior windows of adjoining occupancies may disclose the fire's location. If interior crews find an exceptionally hot area, this information should be communicated to the ventilation crew to help them decide where to ventilate. Knowing the exact location and severity of the fire is critical to making sound ventilation decisions.

If a fire is found to be in the attic, the ventilation opening should be made over the area of heaviest fire involvement **(Figure 11.22)**. If this area is deemed to be unsafe, the ventilation opening should be made between the fire and the uninvolved portion of the building in a location where fire-

Figure 11.21 The main body of the fire can sometimes be located from the outside of the structure by using a thermal imaging camera (TIC).

Figure 11.22 The ventilation opening should be made directly above the area of greatest fire involvement if it is safe to do so.

fighters will not be in jeopardy. If neither option is available, a defensive tactic (such as trench/strip ventilation discussed in Chapter 13) may have to be considered.

If the fire is one or more floors below the top floor of a multistory building, vertical ventilation may not be the best option unless an elevator shaft or other vertical channel is available. Without an adequate vertical channel, horizontal ventilation may be indicated.

Method of Ventilation

The decision regarding the most appropriate method of ventilation must include consideration of where to ventilate (based on the variables just discussed) and the results to be expected from the various ventilation options. The major considerations are whether to ventilate horizontally or vertically and whether to use natural or forced ventilation. While some aspects of vertical ventilation may also apply to horizontal ventilation, ventilating a room, a floor, a cockloft, an attic, or a basement will each require somewhat different techniques. A more complete discussion of horizontal ventilation is presented in Chapter 12, and vertical ventilation is discussed in Chapter 13.

Horizontal vs. Vertical Ventilation

As described in **Essentials**, *horizontal ventilation* is accomplished by opening doors or windows to allow smoke to escape and fresh air to enter. Structures in which horizontal ventilation may be appropriate include those:

- In which the fire is not large enough to necessitate opening the roof
- With windows or doors close to the seat of the fire
- In which the seat of the fire is below the top floor
- In which fire has not entered structural voids or concealed spaces

Vertical ventilation is accomplished by opening a structure at the highest point by cutting a hole in the roof or by opening doors, scuttles, or skylights to allow the heat and smoke to travel upward and out of the structure. Structures in which vertical ventilation may be appropriate include those:

- With fire in the attic, cockloft, or the top floor
- With no windows and few exterior doors
- With large vertical channels (light wells, elevator shafts, hoistways, etc.)
- In which fire has entered structural voids or concealed spaces

Natural vs. Mechanical Ventilation

Whenever possible, tactical ventilation should be in concert with existing atmospheric conditions, taking advantage of natural air flow. If conditions allow, natural ventilation is the best option because it requires no additional personnel or equipment to set up and maintain. However, in some situations natural ventilation may be inadequate and may have to be supplemented or replaced by mechanical ventilation to provide a tenable atmosphere for rescue and suppression operations. Mechanical or forced ventilation involves the use of fans, blowers, nozzles, or other mechanical devices to create or redirect the flow of air inside a burning building.

Within limits, using mechanical ventilation can eliminate or reduce the effect of wind on tactical ventilation efforts. Having a reliable and controllable airflow allows for greater control of the movement of heat and smoke. Mechanical ventilation can channel the airborne products of combustion out of a building by the most efficient and least destructive path and allow fresh air to be reintroduced into the space. When the fire situation permits, using forced ventilation in conjunction with natural ventilation allows a tenable atmosphere to be restored faster and more efficiently than with natural ventilation alone.

Situations Requiring Mechanical Ventilation

Whenever natural ventilation is inadequate or causes air to flow in the wrong direction, or if other elements in the situation limit or preclude natural ventilation, mechanical ventilation is needed **(Figure 11.23)**. Otherwise, there are no definite rules governing when mechanical ventilation should or should not be employed. In general, mechanical or forced ventilation is indicated when:

- The location and size of the fire have been determined
- The layout of the building is not conducive to natural ventilation
- Natural ventilation slows, becomes ineffective, and needs support
- Fire is burning below grade in structures
- The involved area within a compartment is so large that natural ventilation is inefficient
- It is dictated by the type of building or the fire situation

Figure 11.23 Mechanical ventilation is often needed on the fireground for a number of reasons.

Other Ventilation Size-Up Considerations

Other items that need to be considered when sizing up a ventilation situation are exposures, both internal and external, and the weather. Ventilation operations can be seriously affected by both wind and temperature.

Exposures

Because horizontal ventilation does not normally release heat and smoke directly above the fire, some routing of the smoke and fire gases to an exterior opening is often necessary. Firefighters must consider the threat to internal exposures that channeling heat and smoke through a building can create. The routes that the smoke and heated gases must travel to reach the exterior openings may be the same corridors and passageways that occupants need for egress. In horizontal ventilation, fire and heated gases are released through window openings or doorways. Consequently, there is sometimes a danger that they will ignite the structure above the point where they escape or that they may be drawn into windows above the ventilation opening by lapping, also known as autoexposure **(Figure 11.24, p. 304)**.

Firefighters must also consider the possible threat to external exposures from tactical ventilation efforts. Horizontal ventilation can threaten exposed buildings through radiation and/or direct flame contact. Smoke may also be

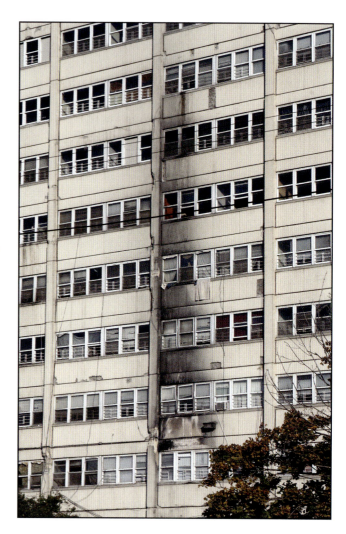

Figure 11.24 Lapping is a common result of fires in multistory buildings.

drawn into adjacent buildings by window-mounted AC units. Vertical ventilation may also threaten nearby structures if hot brands or embers that are carried aloft by convection fall onto combustible roofs or into dry vegetation. If adjacent structures are taller than the burning building, fire may be drawn into exterior windows.

Weather

All buildings are designed to resist the effects of weather. However, any opening in a building, whether man-made or caused by the fire, allows the surrounding atmosphere to affect what is happening inside the building. The most important weather-related influences on tactical ventilation are *wind* and *temperature*.

Wind

Wind conditions must always be considered when determining the proper ventilation method. Wind blowing fire toward an external exposure, supplying oxygen to the fire, or blowing the fire into uninvolved areas of the building can reduce the benefits of horizontal ventilation (**Figure 11.25**). Firefighters must remember that ventilation methods used should be in concert with the prevailing wind, not against it.

> **CAUTION**
> A strong enough wind can overpower the natural convective effect of a fire and drive the smoke and hot gases back into the building.

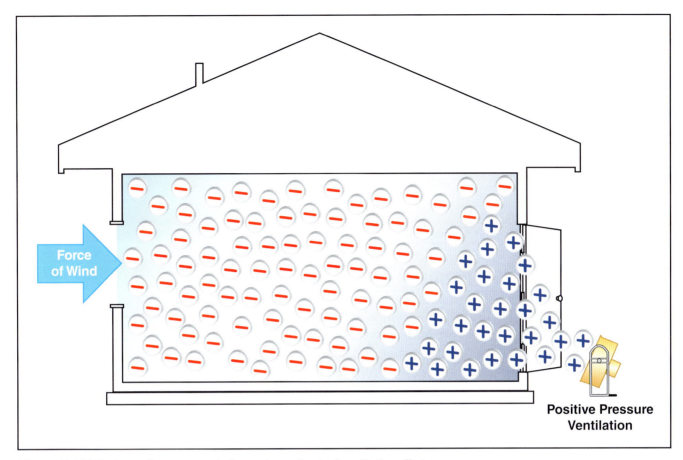

Figure 11.25 Wind can often pose a challenge to mechanical ventilation efforts.

Temperature

While the effect of atmospheric temperature on fire behavior inside a structure may be limited, temperature can have a profound effect on some tactical ventilation operations. As discussed in Chapter 14, Special Ventilation Operations, atmospheric temperature can affect the neutral pressure plane in high-rise buildings. The temperature on the flat roof of a commercial building — often black or dark gray and surrounded by parapet walls — can be significantly higher than the temperature at street level. The effects of elevated roof temperature on ventilation crews doing very strenuous work in full PPE must be considered. The crews are at risk of heat exhaustion or even heatstroke, and their productivity may be reduced because of fatigue and dehydration. These conditions can cause vent crews to take longer than normal to complete their assignments, and will require earlier and more frequent rest breaks and/or crew rotations.

Cold atmospheric temperatures can also affect ventilation operations. In winter, snow and ice accumulations on the roofs of buildings can increase live loads, conceal potential hazards, and delay the completion of vertical ventilation operations. Firefighters may also be at increased risk because of wet or icy roofs being very slippery.

> **Ventilation Size-Up Scenario:**
>
> **On a hot and windy summer afternoon, you and your engine company are ordered to ventilate a two-story brick office building in which a fire is burning on the ground floor.**
>
> - **What fire behavior indicators would you look for?**
> - **How might the weather affect the ventilation operation?**
> - **What effect might wind have on ventilation location?**
> - **What method of ventilation would you choose?**
> - **How would you determine where to ventilate?**
> - **How would your decisions change if the fire were on the top floor?**

Summary

For firefighters to effectively size up a ventilation situation in a burning building, they must have at least a basic understanding of tactical ventilation and how fire and smoke behave under a variety of fire and environmental conditions. They must understand how the construction of the burning building may affect the ventilation process. Finally, they must understand the effects that ventilation may have on fire behavior and know how to coordinate tactical ventilation operations with rescue and fire attack.

Review Questions

1. What is ventilation?
2. What is a ventilation profile for a building involved by fire?
3. What is tactical ventilation?
4. What are the building construction factors that are considered during ventilation size-up?
5. What are the procedures for coordinating ventilation with rescue and fire attack?

Horizontal Ventilation

Chapter Contents

CASE HISTORY 311	
Use of Horizontal Ventilation Tools and Equipment 312	
Ventilation Tools 312	
Ventilation Equipment................................... 312	
Building Construction Related to Horizontal Ventilation 316	
Windows 316	
Doors 320	
Walls 324	
Establishing and Supporting Horizontal Ventilation 329	
Location of Fire.. 329	
Wind Direction and Speed 329	
Location of Ventilation Openings 329	
Natural Horizontal Ventilation 330	
Doors 331	
Windows 332	

Mechanical Horizontal Ventilation 333

Using Smoke Ejectors 333

Using Blowers 333

Using Nozzles (Hydraulic Ventilation) 334

Precautions against Upsetting Established Horizontal Ventilation 337

Improper Implementation............................ 337

Inadequate Control of Exit Openings 337

Improperly Located Exit Opening 338

Improperly Directed Fire Streams 338

Improper Placement of Salvaged Contents 338

Building Construction 338

Wind 339

Summary 340

Review Questions 340

chapter 12

Key Terms

Churning 333	Negative Pressure Ventilation (NPV) 313
Fire Door 321	Positive Pressure Ventilation (PPV) 313
Fog Stream 334	Target Hazard 324
Intrinsically Safe Equipment 316	Unprotected Openings 325
Leeward 329	Windward 329
Mullion 318	

Horizontal Ventilation

Learning Objectives

After reading this chapter, students will be able to:

1. Describe how tools and equipment are commonly used for horizontal ventilation.
2. Describe building construction features which impact horizontal ventilation.
3. Describe the factors that are considered when planning for horizontal ventilation.
4. Describe the methods used for natural horizontal ventilation.
5. Describe the methods used for mechanical horizontal ventilation.
6. Summarize actions that can negatively impact established horizontal ventilation.

Safety Points

While reading this chapter, keep the following safety points in mind:

- **Check for indicators of backdraft or ventilation-induced flashover potential before making any horizontal openings.**
- **Coordinate horizontal ventilation actions with interior operations.**
- **Use horizontal ventilation tools within their design limitations.**
- **Wear proper PPE and use proper tools and techniques to avoid injury when performing horizontal ventilation.**

Chapter 12
Horizontal Ventilation

Case History

According to NIOSH Report F2001-23, firefighters in New York were called to a fire in a two-story hardware store with full basement in June of 2001. Upon arrival, it was determined that the fire was burning in the basement which contained a large inventory of flammable materials such as propane, acetone, alcohol, and paints of various kinds. While fire attack crews were attempting to gain entry into the basement through a reinforced steel security door, other firefighters were starting to ventilate the basement through ground-level windows. As a hose crew was about to begin an attack, an explosion occurred in the basement. The blast blew firefighters in and around the building off their feet. It also destroyed much of the main floor and caused a partial collapse of the structure. Firefighters on the main floor fell into the basement, and one died of asphyxiation. Two of the firefighters attempting horizontal ventilation died of blunt-force trauma when they were buried under a collapsing brick wall.

As this case history shows, even firefighters attempting horizontal ventilation from the outside of a burning building can be at great risk. As discussed in earlier chapters, structure fires are uncontrolled environments where it can be extremely difficult to anticipate every potential contingency.

Despite the potential for tragedies such as in the foregoing case history, horizontal ventilation remains the most frequently used form of tactical ventilation. This is true because the majority of fires in buildings are extinguished while they are relatively small, so they do little damage and produce more smoke than fire. In these situations, once the fire is out, it may only be necessary to open the windows and doors of the affected occupancy to allow the residual smoke to escape through natural ventilation. In other situations, natural ventilation may have to be supplemented with smoke ejectors or blowers. In every interior structure fire, firefighters actually start a form of horizontal ventilation when they open doors or windows to make entry for search and rescue or fire attack. Also, in fires located on intermediate floors of multistory buildings, horizontal ventilation may be the most practical form of tactical ventilation.

Just as properly implemented horizontal ventilation can help reduce fire loss, it can also increase loss by spreading the fire when done improperly. Windows that are opened to allow heat and smoke out of a burning building can also let fire spread to adjacent areas by permitting flames to lap upward into uninvolved floors in the structure. Fire issuing from open windows can also spread into the attic through vents under the eaves of the building.

This chapter reviews the tools and equipment needed to initiate horizontal ventilation, as well as the construction of the closures over horizontal openings such as doors and windows. The importance of establishing and supporting horizontal ventilation and the techniques involved in natural and mechanical horizontal ventilation are also discussed.

Use of Horizontal Ventilation Tools and Equipment

Under the right conditions, virtually every forcible entry tool described in **Essentials** can be applied to horizontal ventilation. In the removal or opening of doors, windows, or other barriers, axes and more specialized prying and cutting tools may be required.

Ventilation Tools

Bolt cutters or rotary saws may be needed for removing locks and security bars from doors and windows. Pike poles, ceiling hooks, and similar tools may be needed for breaking windows. As described in Chapter 9, Access into Structures, axes, rotary saws, or air chisels can be used to create openings in metal walls. Openings in wooden or metal roll-up doors are most often made with rotary saws.

It is important that firefighters know the capabilities and limitations of the available ventilation tools as well as how to use and maintain them for maximum safety and efficiency. Regular preventive maintenance of ventilation tools improves their performance and maximizes their safety.

CAUTION
Using a tool for something other than its intended purpose can damage the tool and endanger the operator.

Ventilation Equipment

The mechanical devices necessary to supplement or alter the natural airflow in a structure or other confined space can take a variety of forms. Some of this equipment, such as smoke ejectors and blowers, are very familiar to most firefighters. Other devices, such as HVAC systems, may be less familiar and will require further investigation and study. Many new devices and systems have led to greater efficiency and versatility, enabling firefighters to accomplish ventilation operations more rapidly than ever before. In addition, accessories, such as flexible ducts, stacking and hanging devices, and other support systems allow for flexibility in the placement of smoke ejectors.

NOTE: For purposes of clarity, in this manual the term *ejector* refers to any device positioned within the space or in the exit opening to *expel* or *exhaust* contaminated air from the space. The term *blower* refers to any device positioned outside of a space to blow fresh air in to create a slight positive pressure within. The term *fan* will be used interchangeably with blower and ejector.

Fans

Fans can be driven by electric motors, gasoline-powered engines, or water (hydraulic) pressure. Each type has advantages and disadvantages. For example, those driven by electric motors are quieter than those driven by gasoline engines and they do not contaminate the air with exhaust smoke **(Figure 12.1)**. Therefore, electric fans are preferred for ventilating burned areas during overhaul. However, those driven by gasoline engines may move a greater volume of air than do electric fans **(Figure 12.2)**. Fans driven by hydraulic pressure can add water damage to the loss if they leak **(Figure 12.3)**.

Figure 12.1 A typical smoke ejector. *Courtesy of Super Vac.*

Figure 12.2 A typical smoke blower. *Courtesy of Tempest Technologies.*

Figure 12.3 A typical hydraulic smoke blower. *Courtesy of Ramfan Corp.*

Flexible Ducts

The flexible ducting that some departments use for ventilation is similar to but larger than that used by utility workers when they are required to work in confined spaces, especially in spaces below grade. The ducting consists of a treated fabric tube (usually yellow in color) over a continuous steel coil that provides support and keeps the duct open throughout its length **(Figure 12.4, p. 314)**. Because it is supported by the steel coil, flexible ducting can be used in either **positive pressure ventilation (PPV)** or **negative pressure ventilation (NPV)** operations **(Figure 12.5, p. 314)**. This type of ducting is available in a variety of sizes.

Fire departments also use flexible ducting that is up to 24 inches (10 cm) in diameter, and is made of smooth, translucent plastic **(Figure 12.6, p. 314)**. This ducting has no steel reinforcement and is kept open by the pressure of the air being forced through it. To expel smoke from a compartment, an electrically driven blower must be positioned inside the compartment **(Figure 12.7, p. 314)**. If an electric blower is not available, the blower must be positioned outside the building or compartment and the duct deployed in the innermost portion of the compartment **(Figure 12.8, p. 315)**. Because this ducting is larger and has a smooth inner surface, there is less friction

> **Positive Pressure Ventilation (PPV)** — Method of ventilating a confined space by mechanically blowing fresh air into the space in sufficient volume to create a slight positive pressure within and thereby forcing the contaminated atmosphere out the exit opening.

> **Negative Pressure Ventilation (NPV)** — Technique using smoke ejectors to develop artificial circulation and to pull smoke out of a structure. Smoke ejectors are placed in windows, doors, or roof vent holes to pull the smoke, heat, and gases from inside the building and eject them to the exterior.

Figure 12.4 Flexible ducting can be used in numerous ventilation applications.

Figure 12.5 Flexible ducting can be used in both negative and positive pressure ventilation operations.

Figure 12.6 Clear plastic ducting does not have reinforcement and utilizes air pressure to keep open.

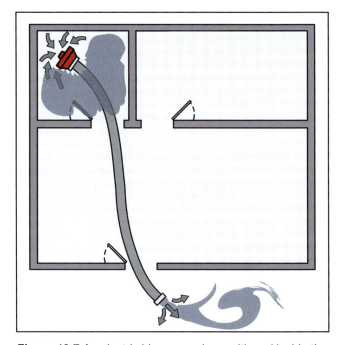

Figure 12.7 An electric blower can be positioned inside the compartment to expel smoke outside the structure.

Figure 12.8 If an electric blower is not available, a gas powered blower must be positioned outside the structure and the ducting extended into the compartment.

Figure 12.9 Flexible ducting allows for smoke to be expelled from affected compartments without spreading smoke throughout the rest of the structure.

loss than with conventional ducting. With less friction loss to overcome, a considerably larger volume of air or smoke can be blown through this ducting with the same size blower.

This technique is usually not appropriate as part of the initial fire attack due to the time involved in setting up flexible duct ventilation systems. However, using these devices to move cold smoke and/or other airborne contaminants to the outside can be very effective once the fire is controlled. Using flexible ducts in this way allows smoke and gases to be channeled through a building without contaminating undamaged areas. For example, with a fan and flexible duct combination, an exhaust line can channel smoke down a hallway, through a room, or through an entire building without causing smoke damage or contamination **(Figure 12.9)**. Being able to channel smoke or gases through a flexible duct to the outside without contaminating other areas is particularly useful in shopping malls where there are many unrelated occupancies, and in hospitals, schools, or office buildings.

By using flexible ducting, two or more smoke ejectors can be coupled to ventilate smoke from basements, attics, suspended ceilings, and other confined spaces. Also, ducting can provide fresh air for rescue crews involved in long-term confined space operations such as in utility vaults, sanitary sewers, silos, and other hostile environments.

When using smoke ejectors for ventilation, it is important to remember that replacement air must be brought into the area from which contaminants are being expelled. This can be difficult when ventilating areas that have only one relatively small opening for exhaust and replacement air. However, by providing the replacement air (positively) via a flexible duct to the most distant part of the compartment, it is possible to exhaust the contaminants and bring replacement air through the same doorway or access opening **(Figure 12.10, p. 316)**.

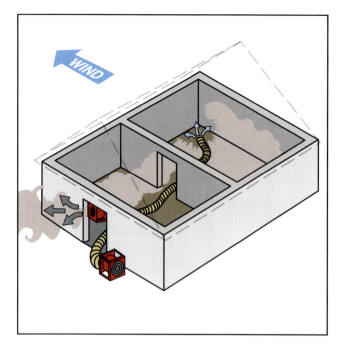

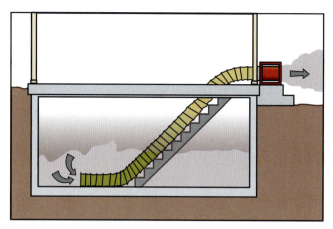

Figure 12.11 Flexible ducting is extremely useful when ventilating areas below grade.

Figure 12.10 Replacement air can be provided by PPV to support negative pressure ventilation.

Using the ejector/flexible duct combination is also an excellent method of ventilating areas below grade **(Figure 12.11)**. This combination works well for removing heavier-than-air gases that settle near the floor and in low areas. A smoke ejector can be positioned at ground level or above, with the flexible duct running through a window or down a stairway or elevator shaft into the basement. Replacement air can be channeled through the same opening in which the fan is located or through other available openings. Because of the hazards associated with heavier-than-air gases and/or oxygen deficiency, it is important to remember that even with replacement air being supplied, personnel working below grade and the atmosphere itself should be constantly monitored.

> **WARNING!**
> Whenever firefighters work below grade, they must wear SCBA. If there is any chance that the atmosphere below grade may be flammable, only fans that are **intrinsically safe** can be used.

Intrinsically Safe Equipment — Equipment designed and approved for use in flammable atmospheres that is incapable of releasing sufficient electrical energy to cause the ignition of a flammable atmospheric mixture.

Building Construction Related to Horizontal Ventilation

As discussed in earlier chapters, having a working knowledge of common construction methods and materials will help firefighters create ventilation openings for horizontal ventilation safely and efficiently. The construction practices described in this section are those in general use across North America but may not be typical of those used in some local areas. Firefighters should conduct preincident planning surveys as often as necessary to become familiar with the construction practices used in their particular areas.

The following sections discuss the most common construction features that firefighters may have to breach during horizontal ventilation. These construction features are windows, doors, and walls.

Windows

For horizontal ventilation purposes, windows are some of the best means of creating the necessary exterior openings. Even when the windows cannot be opened, the panes may be broken out quickly and with relative ease. If the frame is undamaged, the cost of replacing the broken glass is usually, but not always, less than the cost of repairing damaged doors or walls. However, leaded glass windows, large stained-glass church windows, and windows with unusual shapes should be protected if at all possible.

A wide variety of windows exist in both new and old buildings in most communities. As described in Chapter 9, Access into Structures, the most common types are fixed windows, single- and double-hung windows, casement windows, horizontal-sliding windows, awning windows, jalousie windows, projected windows, hopper windows, and energy-efficient windows.

Fixed Windows

As the name implies, a fixed window does not open but has a permanently glazed pane or panes set in a wooden, vinyl, or metal frame. They range from small, sometimes irregularly shaped windows to large picture windows **(Figure 12.12)**. Fixed windows are often flanked by double-hung or casement windows or are stacked with awning or hopper windows that can be opened.

Single- and Double-Hung Windows

Single-hung windows have one movable section; in double-hung windows, both halves are movable **(Figure 12.13)**. In both cases, only half of the window area is available for ventilation unless the panes are broken out.

Figure 12.12 The windows of this building are fixed and are not manufactured to be opened. *Courtesy of McKinney (TX) Fire Department.*

Figure 12.13 Typical single-hung windows.

Casement Windows

Casement windows are usually opened and closed using a small hand crank built into the frame **(Figure 12.14)**. They have one or two side-hinged, outward-swinging sashes, and the screens are on the inside. Double-casement windows may be separated by a fixed pane or simply by a vertical post called a **mullion**. The entire window area is available for ventilation when open **(Figure 12.15)**.

> **Mullion** — Vertical division between multiple windows or a double door opening.

Horizontal-Sliding Windows

These windows have two or more sashes, one of which is fixed and the other or others are movable. From the inside, the movable sash can often be lifted out of the frame without damaging the window. In most designs, half of the window area is available for ventilation without breaking the glass.

Awning Windows

These windows have one or more top-hinged, outward-swinging sashes **(Figure 12.16)**. Single-awning windows are often combined with a fixed sash in a larger unit. All the openable area is available for ventilation.

Figure 12.14 Casement windows are usually opened with a hand crank.

Figure 12.15 Casement windows allow for the entire window area to be opened.

Figure 12.16 A typical awning window.

Jalousie Windows

These windows consist of narrow horizontal panes of glass set in pivoting brackets at each end **(Figure 12.17)**. The panes overlap in a louver-like fashion. They are very difficult to open from the outside without breaking the panes. When open, they offer the entire area for ventilation.

Projected Windows

These windows, also known as *factory windows*, may be hinged at the top or bottom and may swing inward or outward **(Figure 12.18)**. All the openable area is available for ventilation.

Hopper Windows

Hopper windows have bottom-hinged, inward-swinging sashes. These windows look like awning windows that have been installed upside down **(Figure 12.19)**. Like awning windows, hopper windows offer all the openable area for ventilation.

Energy-Efficient Windows

Some energy-efficient windows are double- or triple-glazed. Regardless of how many panes are in each window, there is always a space between the panes **(Figure 12.20)**. This space may be filled with air, argon, or some other inert gas.

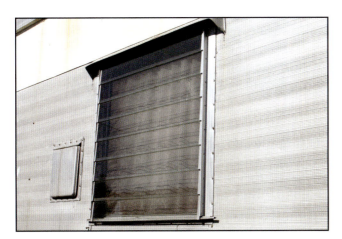

Figure 12.17 A typical jalousie window.

Figure 12.18 Typical projected windows.

Figure 12.19 These hopper windows open inward.

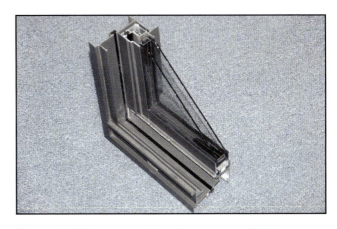

Figure 12.20 A cross section of an energy-efficient window.

Figure 12.21 It is often quicker to cut the entire window frame than try to break a thermoplastic window.

Although there are several brands of energy-efficient windows, they are all commonly referred to as *thermal* windows. While these windows offer some additional protection from an exposure fire, they can also present some disadvantages for firefighters. Because of their superior insulating properties, thermal windows hold in more heat than conventional windows. This can delay the fire being seen by passersby, accelerate the development of flashover conditions, and increase the likelihood of backdraft conditions developing.

There are other specialized windows designed for very specific applications. Regardless of the design or application, windows that resist opening from the outside usually can and should be broken out when a horizontal ventilation opening is needed. However, many newer windows are glazed with or constructed entirely of Lexan® or other extremely dense plastics. As also discussed in Chapter 9, these windows are very difficult to break. In these situations, removing the entire frame with the window intact may be quicker and more efficient for ventilation purposes **(Figure 12.21)**.

One additional aspect of window construction must also be considered — security measures. Because a tool can often be inserted between the bars of security devices and still break the glass, security devices are more of a problem for forcible entry than for ventilation. However, windows covered with heavy-gauge screen may not even allow a tool to pass through, and the screen will have to be removed if that window is to be opened for horizontal ventilation.

WARNING!
Doors opened to provide access for fire attack change the ventilation profile.

Doors

Doors present the same sorts of challenges for ventilation as for forcible entry, but they also provide opportunities to make horizontal ventilation very effective. Doorway openings are larger than many window openings. So, for the same investment of time and effort, opening a door often results in a bigger and therefore more effective ventilation opening.

Regardless of its design or location, a door opened for tactical ventilation purposes should be blocked open, but not removed **(Figure 12.22)**. Removing a door makes it more difficult to close the opening if the ventilation profile needs to be changed later. Blocking a door open prevents it from being closed inadvertently during the ventilation operation, which could seriously affect fire behavior.

There are numerous different types of doors that can be encountered on the fireground. The most common types of exterior doors used for tactical ventilation purposes are:

- Swinging doors
- Sliding doors
- Overhead-type doors
- Roll-up doors

Also of importance to horizontal ventilation are various types of interior doors. Described in the following sections are the construction features of the types of doors that are the most useful for horizontal ventilation. For a more complete discussion of doors and any other aspect of building construction, refer to the IFSTA **Building Construction Related to the Fire Service** manual.

Swinging Doors

In addition to the most common types of swinging doors described in **Essentials**, some residential occupancies, care facilities, and hospitals have self-closing, rated **fire doors** in the interior hallways **(Figure 12.23)**. These doors may be held open by fusible links as described earlier for sliding fire doors, or they may be held open by electromagnets connected to the fire detection system. When the system is activated by either heat or smoke, the power to the electromagnets is interrupted, which releases the doors and allows them to close. Such systems are designed to compartmentalize a building and thereby confine a fire to its area of origin.

> **Fire Door** — A specially constructed, tested, and approved fire-rated door assembly designed and installed to prevent fire spread by automatically closing and covering a doorway in a fire wall during a fire to block the spread of fire through the door opening.

Sliding Doors

From the standpoint of horizontal ventilation, the two most important types of sliding doors are exterior sliding doors and interior sliding fire doors. Exterior sliding doors are most common on storage, commercial, industrial, or agricultural buildings. They are generally suspended from a horizontal track on the exterior wall of the building **(Figure 12.24)**. Most doors of this type

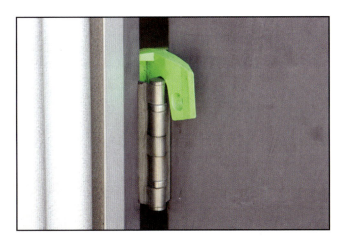

Figure 12.22 Doors opened for tactical ventilation should be blocked in the open position.

Figure 12.23 A typical swinging door closer.

Figure 12.24 This hangar uses sliding metal doors to create a large opening.

move laterally when they are manually pushed open or closed. Because the track is level, these doors will remain in the position in which they were left, so blocking them open is usually not necessary. These doors are usually metal or metal clad. They have a variety of locking mechanisms but often feature just a hasp and padlock. Because these doors usually cover relatively large openings, they can be very advantageous for horizontal ventilation. The other common type of exterior sliding door is the wooden or metal framed-glass sliding door most often found in residential occupancies and some offices **(Figure 12.25)**.

Many sliding-type interior fire doors are metal-clad assemblies suspended from slanting tracks mounted on the surface of a rated firewall **(Figure 12.26)**. In high-traffic areas where it would be impractical to continually open and close a fire door, the door is held in the open position by a cable connected to a fusible link located at the top of the doorway opening. When the heat of a fire passes through the doorway, the link fuses and separates to release the cable. Gravity then rolls the door into position, closing off the opening. Because the track is slanted, once the fusible link separates and the door rolls into the closed position it will remain closed unless manually opened. Before fire doors are reopened, firefighters must make sure that there is no longer any danger of fire spread through that doorway.

Figure 12.25 A typical residential sliding door.

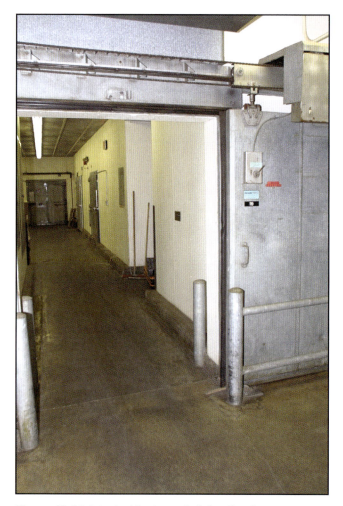

Figure 12.26 A typical horizontal sliding fire door.

Sliding doors on a slanted track may also represent a hazard to firefighters working within a building. The heat of a fire may cause the fusible link to separate and the door to close behind them, thereby cutting off one (and perhaps their only) escape route. The door may also close on a hoseline and crimp it enough to restrict or stop its flow. Therefore, when these doors are being used by firefighters, they should be blocked open with a pike pole or other suitable tool. Because they are intended to remain closed once activated, these doors tend to be quite heavy and may be very difficult to push back up the track, especially if obstructed by fallen debris.

Overhead-Type Doors

These doors also come in a variety of types and styles. They vary from wooden slab doors or lightweight wooden or metal sectional doors (typical of residential garage doors) to heavy-duty service doors used in commercial and industrial occupancies **(Figure 12.27)**. Some of the heavy-duty doors are also rated fire doors, held in the open position by fusible links as described previously. The same safety precautions apply.

Roll-Up Doors

There is also a variety of commercial roll-up doors. Most are heavy-duty metal doors **(Figure 12.28)**. From a horizontal ventilation standpoint, roll-up doors are sometimes a problem because they can be difficult to force open. In addition to the time required to force these doors, the door components may be bent in the process, and the door may not open fully because of the distorted components. As described in Chapter 9, if a triangular or other type of cut is made in the door, which may be faster than forcing the door, the size of the opening will be smaller than the door being fully open. This smaller opening will obviously reduce the volume of airflow compared to that available with the fully open door, so this opening should be used to gain access to the interior where the regular door-opening mechanism can be used to open the door fully. As also mentioned in Chapter 9, roll-up doors often have a conventional pedestrian door adjacent to them. If so, it may be easier and faster to enter through this door and open the roll-up door from the inside.

Figure 12.27 Some residential garages use tilt-slab doors.

Figure 12.28 Steel roll-up doors are often found in commercial occupancies.

Telescoping Doors

As discussed in Chapter 9, telescoping doors have characteristics in common with other large service doors, but they also have certain unique features. The most significant difference between telescoping doors and other types of service doors is that telescoping doors consist of two layers (skins) separated by at least 2 inches (50 mm) of air space. From the bottom of the door, the space between the inner and outer skins becomes progressively larger toward the top of the door. Depending upon the size of the door, the space between the inner and outer skin can be more than 13 inches (325 mm). The techniques described in Chapter 9 can be used to open telescoping doors for horizontal ventilation.

Walls

If the available windows and doors do not provide enough ventilation to be effective, firefighters may have to create openings in the walls of a burning building **(Figure 12.29)**. To create horizontal ventilation openings in walls safely and efficiently, firefighters must be able to recognize the various types of walls when they see them. To do this, they need to be familiar with the types of walls present in their response districts, and with the types of walls in specific **target hazards (Figure 12.30)**. This familiarity can only be obtained through an ongoing program of preincident planning surveys. The following section discusses some of the most common types of walls that firefighters may have to breach for horizontal ventilation — stem walls, interior firewalls, and exterior walls.

> **Target Hazard** — Facility in which there is a great potential likelihood of life or property loss in the event of an attack or natural disaster.

Figure 12.29 It is sometimes necessary to breach an exterior wall in order to create a ventilation opening.

Figure 12.30 Daycare centers are typical target hazard occupancies.

Stem Walls

Many modern buildings have continuous concrete foundations, although older structures may have foundations of brick or stone. The stem wall, located between the foundation footing and the first floor, may extend well above the ground if the building occupies a sloping site **(Figure 12.31)**. A high stem wall may make it necessary for firefighters to work from ladders when creating openings in walls for horizontal ventilation.

Interior Firewalls

Firewalls are rated assemblies designed to reduce the likelihood of horizontal fire spread by compartmentalizing a building with fire-resistive separations. Fire walls are constructed of masonry or a specified thickness of gypsum drywall over a wood or metal frame. Firewalls must extend the entire width of the building and, in most cases, extend up to and above combustible roofs **(Figure 12.32)**. If these walls have been penetrated with **unprotected openings**, fire may pass through the openings and spread beyond the occupancy of origin. This may require ventilation to be performed on both sides of the wall.

There is the potential for flammable fire gases to accumulate on the uninvolved side of a firewall in an attic or cockloft, thereby increasing the chances of fire spread or smoke explosion. This emphasizes the need for early and effective ventilation of these areas. Otherwise, unburned fire gases may accumulate, unknown to the firefighter, until they reach a source of ignition. Depending on the availability of oxygen within the space, the ignition of these gases may result in an intense fire, a smoke explosion, or both.

Generally, firewalls should not be breached for ventilation purposes. Holes in firewalls can provide additional oxygen to the fire and/or provide a path of travel for heat, smoke, and fire gases. Drafts created by the holes may also draw the fire toward the openings because of the availability of oxygen at the openings and on the other side of the wall.

Unprotected Openings — Openings in floors, walls, or partitions that are not protected against the passage of smoke, flame, and heat; generally used to refer to such openings in fire walls.

Exterior Walls

As described in earlier chapters, to protect a building and its contents from the elements and to support its roof structure, most buildings have substantial exterior walls. Exterior walls may be solid masonry, masonry or other veneer over frame, or metal.

Figure 12.31 A typical stem wall.

Figure 12.32 Interior fire walls are often labeled as such above the finished ceiling. *Courtesy of the McKinney (TX) Fire Department.*

Masonry and concrete walls. Exterior masonry walls usually range from 8 to 12 inches (200 mm to 300 mm) or more in thickness, depending upon the material used. The walls may be of reinforced concrete (poured in place, tilt-up, or precast panel), concrete block, or unreinforced masonry of brick, or stone **(Figure 12.33)**. Windowless masonry/concrete walls, regardless of the specific material, are formidable barriers that are so difficult and time-consuming to penetrate they are rarely breached for ventilation purposes. If they must be breached, heavy-duty power equipment such as electric or pneumatic jackhammers (concrete breakers) should be used.

Veneer-over-frame walls. These walls are essentially frame walls in which 2×4-inch or 2×6-inch (50 mm by 100 mm or 50 mm by 150 mm) wood or metal studs are covered with a layer of plywood or oriented strand board (OSB) for shear strength. One layer of brick or stone (real or imitation) is added to the exterior and/or interior surface to give the appearance of a solid brick or stone wall **(Figure 12.34)**. In other cases, a veneer of stucco is applied over a gypsum wallboard base or over chicken wire and tar paper directly over the studs. In some areas, exterior plywood siding is nailed directly to the studs because this provides the required shear strength and the exterior finish in one layer **(Figure 12.35)**. As described in Chapter 11, some buildings have a foam veneer called an exterior insulation and finishing system (EIFS) that is applied to the outside for aesthetic purposes. The EIFS veneer may be as much as one foot (300 mm) thick. After the base foam is applied to the wall, it is sealed against the weather with a granular finish, giving the appearance of a solid masonry wall **(Figure 12.36)**. These walls can be recognized by the hollow sound they make when tapped with a tool.

> **CAUTION**
> Gas lines or electrical wiring may be inside walls that are covered with brick or stone veneer. Care must be taken when breaching these walls.

Unlike solid masonry walls, veneer-over-frame walls are much easier to breach with conventional forcible entry tools. For example, if a windowless building with a stucco or plywood veneer must be breached for hori-

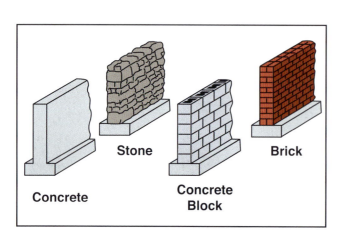

Figure 12.33 Common types of exterior concrete and masonry walls.

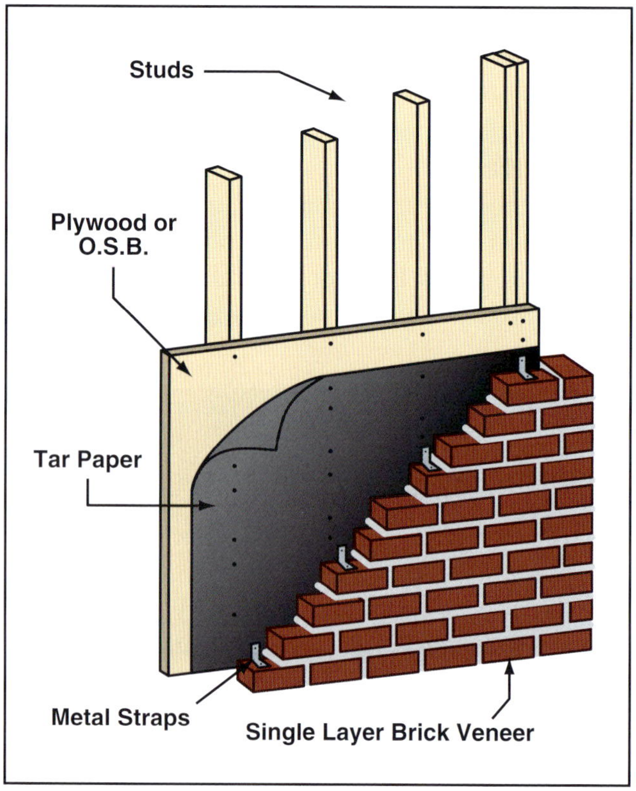

Figure 12.34 A single layer of brick is often added to the exterior of wood frame walls.

Figure 12.35 In some applications, plywood or OSB sheathing is all that is used for exterior walls.

Figure 12.36 This structure has an EIFS finish.

zontal ventilation, the wall can be sounded with a tool to locate the studs, the perimeter of the opening cut with an axe or power saw, and the veneer stripped away with axes or rubbish hooks **(Figure 12.37)**. Likewise, a rotary saw equipped with a masonry blade can quickly cut through a single layer of brick or imitation stone to allow the veneer to be stripped away. Masonry veneer can also be breached with sledgehammers or battering rams, although this is a relatively slow process.

Tall masonry veneer walls can present a substantial collapse potential because of the way some of them are attached to the studs. Some veneers, such as brick or stone (real or imitation), are attached to the studs with thin, corrugated pieces of sheet-metal called wall ties **(Figure 12.38, p. 328)**. On a concrete block wall, one end of the tie is embedded in the mortar joint between the blocks and the other end in the mortar joints between the bricks or stones. On a wood frame wall, one end of each tie is nailed or screwed to a stud, and the other end is embedded in the mortar joint between the bricks or stones. Under fire conditions, these ties can fail because they pull out or because they snap when weakened by the heat of the fire. Firefighters should keep this potential collapse hazard in mind during breaching operations.

Metal walls. The exterior walls of metal buildings are usually of light-gauge sheet metal formed into rectangular panels that are applied vertically over a wooden or metal frame **(Figure 12.39, p. 328)**. The panels are attached to horizontal wooden or light-gauge metal stringers with screws. In most metal walls there are no vertical studs, but some are supported by a rigid structural steel frame with heavy steel pillars **(Figure 12.40, p. 328)**. Metal wall panels are easily cut with conventional hand or power tools, and they lend themselves to being opened using the same tools and techniques used to open metal roll-up doors. Or, if time allows, the individual panels can be removed using an electric screwdriver.

Figure 12.37 Wood exterior walls can often be breached with an axe, although the use of a power saw may be more efficient.

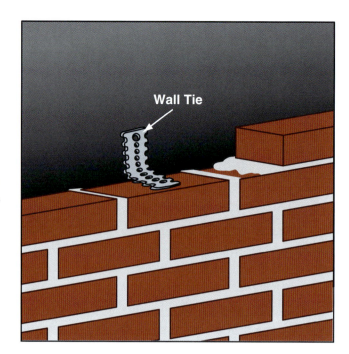

Figure 12.38 Brick veneers are often attached to the structural frame with metal wall ties.

Figure 12.39 Metal siding will be applied to this wood frame structure.

Figure 12.40 A metal building using heavy steel structural members.

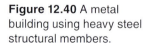

Establishing and Supporting Horizontal Ventilation

Horizontal ventilation is intended to support fire control and extinguishment. Generally, this involves creating an exhaust opening close to the seat of the fire and using the entry point to the structure as the inlet opening. However, it is critical to consider the potential influence of wind direction and speed when selecting inlet and exhaust opening locations. Whether intentional or not, horizontal ventilation is started when firefighters make entry into a building for search and rescue or fire attack. However, under ideal circumstances, implementing horizontal tactical ventilation will be intentional and will result from a conscious decision and deliberate actions. Important factors that must be considered in a plan for horizontal ventilation include:

- Location of the fire
- Wind direction and speed
- Location of ventilation openings

Location of Fire

One of the most important factors in deciding how to horizontally ventilate a burning building is where the seat of the fire is located within the structure. Whether the fire is in a basement, on the top floor, an intermediate floor, or in the attic of a building has a major impact on the other ventilation decisions that must be made.

Wind Direction and Speed

The direction from which any prevailing wind is blowing and wind strength are also critical factors in the decision-making process regarding horizontal ventilation. A favorable wind can facilitate horizontal ventilation; an adverse wind can complicate it.

Location of Ventilation Openings

Both wind direction and speed must be considered when deciding where to locate the inlet and exit openings for horizontal ventilation. While generally on opposite sides of the fire, these openings must be located where the inflow of air will move smoke and heat out of the structure without causing the fire to intensify and grow.

In addition to wind intensity and direction, where the seat of the fire is located determines where the inlet and exit openings should be made. The exit opening is usully made as close to the seat of the fire as possible and opposite the point from which the fire attack will be made **(Figure 12.41, p. 330)**. However, if the seat of the fire is on the **windward** side of the building, creating an opening on the windward side (closest to the seat of the fire) could spread the fire throughout the building **(Figure 12.42, p. 330)**. Under these conditions, it may be possible to counteract the effects of an adverse prevailing wind by pressurizing the building from the **leeward** side with PPV blowers before creating an exit opening on another side **(Figure 12.43, p. 330)**.

Windward — Unprotected side; the direction from which the wind is blowing.

Leeward — Protected side; the direction opposite from which the wind is blowing.

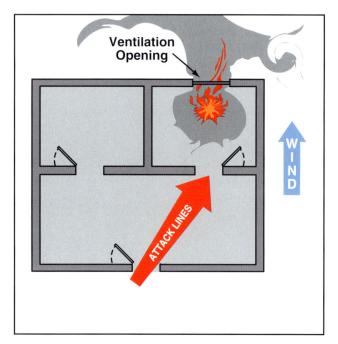

Figure 12.41 The ventilation opening should usually be made as close to the seat of the fire as possible.

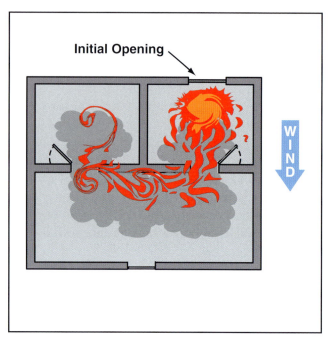

Figure 12.42 An exit opening made on the windward side of the structure may increase fire growth and spread.

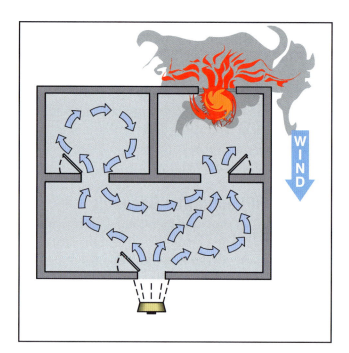

Figure 12.43 It may be possible to overcome adverse wind conditions with the use of PPV.

Natural Horizontal Ventilation

Of all the various methods of ventilating burning buildings, natural horizontal ventilation is by far the most often used. Unaided by any mechanical means, this method depends entirely on the buoyancy of the smoke, the prevailing wind, and the layout and design of the building. Natural horizontal ventilation is most often done through existing openings such as doors and windows.

Doors

Both exterior and interior doors can play an important role in horizontal ventilation. Because exterior doors are the most likely points of entry for search and rescue or fire attack, they will become part of the ventilation operation whether intentional or not. Doors have to be forced before they can be opened for ventilation or entry, which can be a frustrating and time-consuming task. The doors may be metal clad, have heavy security bars, or be otherwise reinforced for security purposes. If metal roll-up doors resist being forced open, cutting a large hole in them may be the only choice. However, before any door is forced, the old rule of *try before you pry* should always be followed.

If a door that has been opened for ventilation should suddenly close for any reason, fire behavior could change dramatically, perhaps endangering occupants and firefighters. Therefore, whenever any swinging door is opened for ventilation purposes, whether for natural or mechanical ventilation, the opening should be maintained by blocking the door open with wooden or rubber doorstops, pieces of furniture, or special hinge hooks **(Figure 12.44)**.

Interior doors should be opened or closed in order to facilitate horizontal ventilation and accomplish the objectives specified in the incident action plan (IAP). Doors will have to be opened to facilitate searching each room, but if there are open windows in the room, opening the door may change the ventilation profile. The doors to interior rooms that have been searched should be closed and marked. For ventilation purposes, interior doors may be opened and closed one by one in a systematic process of ventilating an entire floor **(Figure 12.45)**.

Figure 12.44 Hinge hooks are specially made to hold doors open.

Figure 12.45 Windows and doors should be opened and closed systematically to remove smoke.

Windows

When windows are opened for tactical ventilation, screens, curtains, drapes, or blinds should be removed because they will hinder airflow. In most cases, the exit opening should be about twice as large as the inlet opening. In other words, open the windows on the leeward side fully, and those on the windward side about half way.

If the seat of the fire is on the leeward side of the building, the procedure for ventilating horizontally (cross ventilation) is to first open the top windows on the leeward side, allowing the superheated gases to begin to escape. The next step is to open the lower windows on the windward side to introduce replacement air into the compartment **(Figure 12.46)**.

If the seat of the fire is on the windward side, natural horizontal ventilation may not work. In that case, before an exit opening is created on the windward side, the building should be pressurized as described later in the section on mechanical horizontal ventilation. If the building cannot be pressurized, opening windows on the windward side should be delayed until after the fire is controlled.

Breaking Windows

As always, before breaking any window, try to open it first. If it is necessary to break the window, break out the entire pane and clear the sash of broken shards by scraping the sash with the breaking tool. As described in **Essentials**, the firefighter breaking the glass should be in full protective clothing, including hand and eye protection, and should be upwind of and higher than the window. To review the tools and techniques for breaking windows, refer to Chapter 9, Access into Structures.

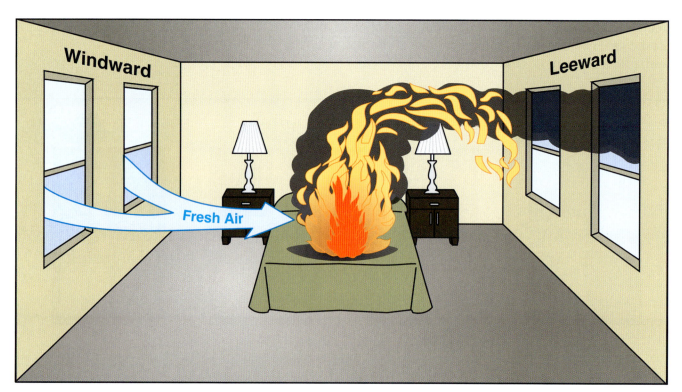

Figure 12.46 Natural cross-ventilation of a room.

Mechanical Horizontal Ventilation

Whether in horizontal or vertical ventilation operations, mechanical (forced) ventilation is primarily a means of supplementing or augmenting natural ventilation. Horizontal ventilation has traditionally been the area where smoke ejectors and/or nozzles have been used. Both of these methods are applied at the point of exit for the heat and smoke and are almost always applied from inside the structure. Another option is to force contaminated air out by using blowers to force replacement air into a structure from the outside at the point of entry.

Using Smoke Ejectors

Smoke ejectors are capable of being set up to blow air into a structure, but this is not the purpose for which they were designed. These units were designed to withstand the heat and contamination of drawing smoke through the fan in the process of exhausting it to the outside.

While smoke and heated air may pass harmlessly through the unit, actual flame passing through it can seriously damage or destroy it. Unless they are equipped with intrinsically safe motors, smoke ejectors are capable of igniting certain combustible gases encountered in fires. For these reasons, smoke ejectors are most often employed after initial control of the fire and not as part of the fire attack.

Smoke ejectors are usually set up in openings on the leeward side of the building. They may be suspended in window or doorway openings, positioned on the floor, or elevated on a door, ladder, or some other object. Using a special platform with telescoping legs, smoke ejectors can be made freestanding, and their height can be adjusted to the most effective level.

When smoke ejectors are placed in doorways, windows, or other exterior openings, they should be positioned near the top of the opening because convection causes the majority of the heat and smoke to rise to the top of the compartment **(Figure 12.47, p. 334)**. In addition, the open area around the units should be sealed with salvage covers or some similar means if churning is to be prevented **(Figure 12.48, p. 335)**. **Churning** (sometimes called *recirculation*) is the phenomenon of smoke being blown out the top of the opening, only to be drawn back into the compartment at the bottom of the opening by the slight vacuum created by the action of the ejector. Churning is obviously counterproductive to clearing the building of smoke.

Churning —Movement of smoke being blown out of a ventilation opening only to be drawn back inside by the negative pressure created by the ejector because the open area around the ejector has not been sealed. Also called recirculation.

Using Blowers

Blowers can be extremely effective adjuncts to natural horizontal ventilation. Slightly larger in diameter than smoke ejectors, blowers are most often powered by gasoline-driven engines but may be powered by electric motors or by water pressure from a hoseline. Because gasoline engines require fresh air to operate, these units are not well suited to being set up in a contaminated atmosphere. For PPV, blowers are set up about 6 feet (2 m) outside the point of entry into the building so the cone of air they create completely covers the inlet opening **(Figure 12.49, p. 335)**. When properly applied, blowers can effectively support the efforts of the search and rescue and fire attack crews by enhancing visibility and reducing interior temperatures. For these reasons, they are often used as part of the initial attack.

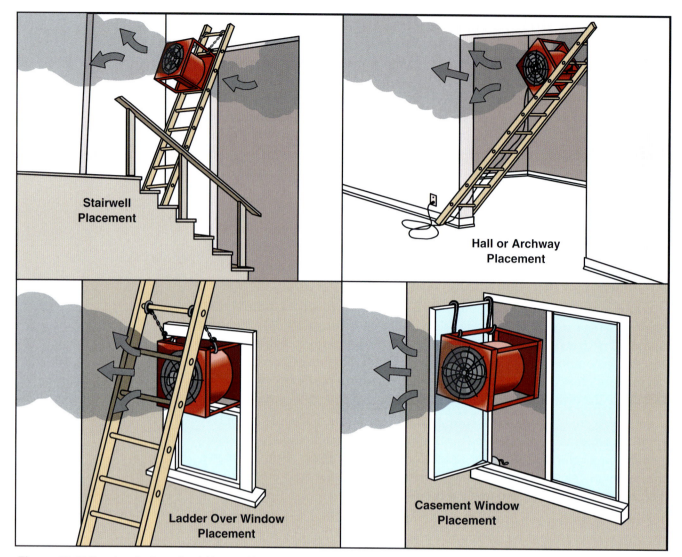

Figure 12.47 Smoke ejectors should be positioned at the top of the opening.

CAUTION
PPV can be used to help determine the location and extent of the fire, but it is SOP in many departments that these facts be known before PPV is started.

Blowers function by creating a slight positive pressure within the structure, thus forcing the heat and smoke out the exit opening. A single blower is often sufficient to pressurize a building, but two blowers working in tandem can be used if needed **(Figure 12.50)**. The keys to effective use of blowers are to apply positive-pressure ventilation (PPV) as soon as the first attack crew is ready to enter and to maintain the size of the exit opening in proportion to the size of the entry opening

Departmental SOPs for using PPV should be based on experimentation with the technique conducted in a safe, controlled training environment. Once the capabilities and limitations of PPV are understood and SOPs have been developed, firefighters must be thoroughly trained in the use of PPV before it is implemented on the fireground.

Using Nozzles (Hydraulic Ventilation)

Fog Stream — Water stream of finely divided particles used for fire control.

The terms **fog stream** and *spray stream* are used interchangeably in this section. As described in **Essentials**, a fog or spray stream directed through a window or door opening will entrain heat and smoke into the stream and transport it out

334 Chapter 12 • Horizontal Ventilation

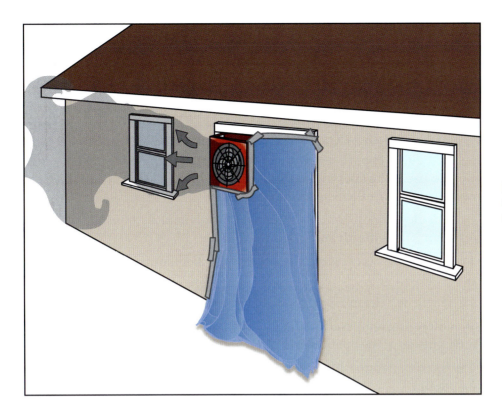

Figure 12.48 The open area around smoke ejectors should be covered to prevent churning.

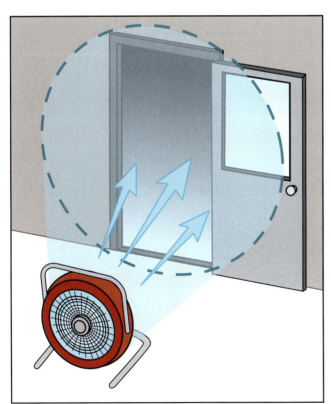

Figure 12.49 The cone of air from PPV blowers should completely cover the inlet opening.

Figure 12.50 Two blowers placed in tandem may be needed to ventilate larger structures.

of the compartment. Compared with mechanical smoke ejectors, fog streams are capable of removing two to four times more smoke, depending on the type and size of the nozzle, the angle of the spray pattern, and the location of the nozzle in relation to the ventilation opening.

A fog or spray stream directed through a window or doorway with a 60-degree pattern covering 85 to 90 percent of the opening provides the best results for ventilation **(Figure 12.51)**. The ideal nozzle position will vary, but in most cases it should be about 2 feet (.6 m) inside the room being ventilated. Regardless of the size of the opening, the spray pattern should not exceed 60 degrees because it will lose efficiency at greater angles.

As with any other technique, there are disadvantages to using hydraulic ventilation. These disadvantages are as follows:

- There may be an increase in the amount of water damage within the structure.
- There will be a drain on the available water supply.
- In subfreezing temperatures, additional ice may form in the area immediately outside of the opening being used.
- The nozzle operator must remain in the hostile environment during the operation.
- The operation may have to be interrupted each time the operator runs out of breathing air.

Figure 12.51 Hydraulic ventilation in use.

Precautions against Upsetting Established Horizontal Ventilation

Firefighters should be careful not to block or close openings that channel fresh air into the area being ventilated. Established ventilation may also be upset if additional openings are made that redirect the air currents intended for ventilating the area. Some things that can upset established horizontal ventilation are addressed in the following sections.

Improper Implementation

Because ventilation will almost always increase heat release rate, the fire may be intensified if operations are begun before attack lines are ready to be taken into the building. This can spread the fire to uninvolved areas of the building and may threaten occupants and firefighters inside **(Figure 12.52)**.

Inadequate Control of Exit Openings

Effective horizontal ventilation can be rendered ineffective by crews arbitrarily opening windows without being ordered to do so. To be effective, a proper balance between the volume of air being introduced and the size of the exit opening must be maintained **(Figure 12.53)**.

Figure 12.52 Improperly implemented PPV can spread the fire throughout the structure and poses a significant threat to firefighters inside.

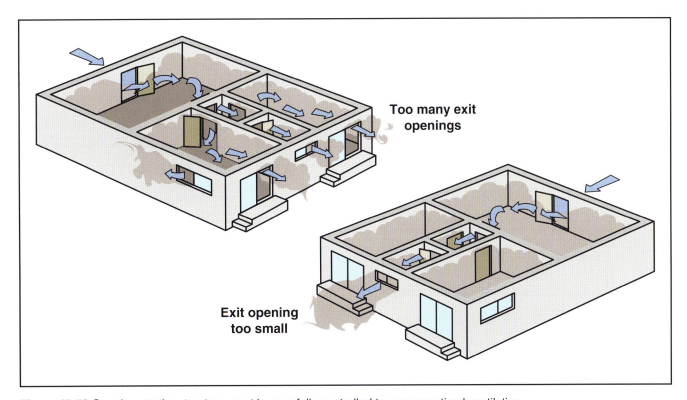

Figure 12.53 Openings to the structure must be carefully controlled to ensure optimal ventilation.

Chapter 12 • Horizontal Ventilation **337**

Improperly Located Exit Opening

If the exit opening is improperly located so that heat and smoke are drawn into uninvolved portions of the building, escape routes may be denied to occupants, attack crews may be subjected to unnecessary harm, and fire damage may be increased **(Figure 12.54)**.

Improperly Directed Fire Streams

If fire streams are directed into ventilation exit openings, whether horizontal or vertical, the results can be disastrous. Natural convection currents can be reversed, causing turbulence within the structure. Also, the additional steam generated can injure firefighters inside, or drive them from the building.

Improper Placement of Salvaged Contents

If furniture or other building contents are stacked in the wrong location during loss control operations, they can have a detrimental effect on horizontal ventilation efforts. Contents stacked in hallways or too near doorways or windows can impede the flow of air into and out of the structure. This can reduce the effectiveness of natural or mechanical ventilation **(Figure 12.55)**.

Building Construction

Even though smoke from a fire in a single compartment may have completely filled a building by seeping through cracks and other tiny openings, removing all that smoke with horizontal ventilation can be very difficult. Air flow can be obstructed by walls, partitions, closed doors, and stacks of stored material **(Figure 12.56)**. If buildings contain a large number of rooms or are heavily loaded with contents, these conditions may make it very difficult to ventilate horizontally.

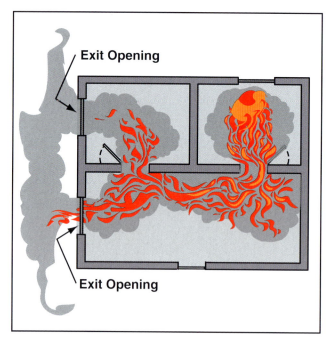

Figure 12.54 Improperly located exit openings can cause unintended fire spread.

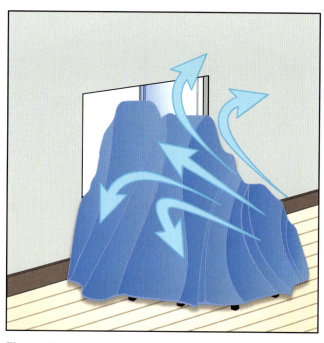

Figure 12.55 Salvaged contents that are improperly placed can block ventilation openings.

Figure 12.56 A heavily compartmentalized building can be a challenge for horizontal ventilation.

Wind

Under ideal circumstances, wind can provide all the air circulation necessary for effective horizontal ventilation. Opening the structure on the windward side and ventilating on the leeward side often works very well. However, as discussed earlier, if the seat of the fire is on the windward side of the building, air flow created by the wind could spread the fire into uninvolved areas.

Depending on the size and efficiency of the blower or blowers used and the rate at which the wind is blowing, it is sometimes possible to counteract an adverse wind with positive pressure ventilation. If higher wind speeds are present, and if vertical ventilation is impractical or impossible, delaying ventilation until after the fire is controlled may be the only available option. If ventilation is to be delayed, firefighters must be alert for sudden changes in fire behavior if windows break or the fire burns through to the outside.

Horizontal Ventilation Scenario:

When you and your company arrive at a three-story brick office building that is completely filled with smoke, you are ordered to ventilate the building.

- **What information would you gather first, and how would you obtain it?**
- **What tools and equipment would you gather for this assignment?**
- **Where would you begin the ventilation process?**
- **How would you avoid making the situation worse?**

Summary

Because horizontal ventilation is the most frequently used means of channeling smoke and other products of combustion out of buildings, firefighters should be well trained in its capabilities, applications, and limitations. They must know how to use the available horizontal ventilation tools and equipment to their best advantage. Firefighters should also know which occupancies within their response districts are most likely to require horizontal ventilation. Finally, firefighters need to be familiar with the requirements and application of their department's SOPs regarding horizontal ventilation.

Review Questions

1. What tools and equipment are commonly used for horizontal ventilation? How are they used during the ventilation operation?
2. What building construction features impact horizontal ventilation?
3. What factors should be considered when planning horizontal ventilation?
4. What methods are used for natural horizontal ventilation?
5. What methods are used for mechanical horizontal ventilation?
6. What actions taken by firefighters can negatively impact established horizontal ventilation?

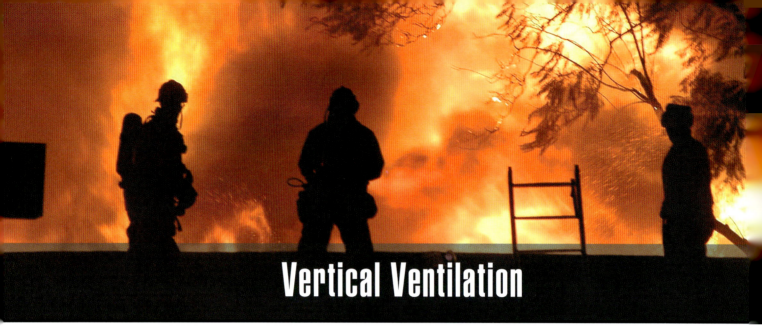

Vertical Ventilation

Chapter Contents

CASE HISTORY 345	Urethane/Isocyanate Foam........................ 392
Establishing and Supporting Vertical Ventilation 346	Single-Ply/Synthetic Membrane............................ 393
Vertical Ventilation Safety 347	Tile and Slate 393
Opening a Roof 352	Light-Gauge Metal or Fiberglass 394
Vertical Ventilation Tools................... 355	Steel Clad................................ 394
Cutting Tools 355	**Existing Roof Openings** 396
Stripping Tools 359	Scuttle Hatches 396
Roof Construction 361	Penthouses (Bulkheads)............................ 396
Pitched Roofs 361	Skylights................................ 396
Flat Roofs........................ 368	Monitors 397
Arched Roofs........................ 379	Turbine (Rotary Vane) Vents 397
Lightweight Roof Construction 383	Light and Ventilation Shafts 398
Panelized Roofs........................ 383	Ridge Vents 398
Trussed Roofs........................ 385	Clerestory Windows 399
Wooden I-Beams........................ 388	**Cutting the Ventilation Exit Opening**.......399
Roof Coverings 389	Louver Vents................................ 401
Wooden Shakes and Shingles 390	Rolling Back Panelized Roofs................................ 402
Composition Roofing and Shingles........................ 391	Trench (Strip) Ventilation 403
Tar and Gravel................................ 392	**Summary**....................................... 405
	Review Questions 405

Divider page photo courtesy of The Los Angeles Fire Department-ISTS.

chapter 13

Key Terms

Bar Joist 386	Purlin..378
Furring Strips 393	Sheathing 390
Gang Nail 385	Substrate 389
I-Beam 388	Thermoplastic 392
Louver Cut 379	Trench Ventilation 403
Pilaster 383	

Vertical Ventilation

Learning Objectives

After reading this chapter, students will be able to:

1. Describe vertical ventilation safety considerations.
2. Describe the tools and equipment commonly used for vertical ventilation.
3. Describe the various types of common roof construction and the hazards associated with each.
4. Describe types of lightweight roof construction.
5. Describe the hazards associated with lightweight roof construction.
6. Describe the common types of roof coverings.
7. Describe the types of existing roof openings that can be used for vertical ventilation.

Safety Points

While reading this chapter, keep the following safety points in mind:

- Read the fire and assess structural integrity before and during vertical ventilation operations.
- Evaluate the impact of changes to the ventilation profile before making vertical openings.
- Ensure that a charged attack line is in place before making ventilation openings.
- Wear proper PPE and use proper tools and techniques when conducting vertical ventilation.
- Coordinate vertical ventilation with interior operations.
- Have at least two means of egress from a roof when firefighters are on it.
- Determine if a charged hoseline is needed on a roof.
- Beware of drop-offs behind high parapet walls.
- Read and sound any roof before stepping onto it – and continually while on it.
- Walk perpendicular to outside walls and only over roof supports.
- Avoid contact with solar panels, especially with metal tools.
- Make roof cuts with the wind at your back.
- Work from involved areas back toward uninvolved areas.
- Exit the roof as soon as the assignment is finished.

Chapter 13
Vertical Ventilation

Case History

According to NIOSH Report F2002-40, firefighters in Iowa responded to a dwelling fire in September of 2002. On arrival, they saw smoke issuing from the eaves of a 96-year-old, 2½-story wood-frame residence. Because heat and smoke prevented interior attack crews from reaching the top floor of the residence, roof ventilation was ordered. The dwelling had a steeply pitched roof covered by several layers of asphalt shingles. One firefighter wearing full PPE and SCBA, and the aerial apparatus driver/operator who was wearing full turnouts but no SCBA, used an aerial platform to take a chain saw to the roof. Because of heavy smoke on the roof, the firefighter with the saw went on air, but the driver/operator could only cover his face with his hands. After the last saw cut was made, the driver/operator indicated to the other firefighter that they needed to leave the roof immediately. Leaving the cut section of roof unopened, the firefighter abandoned the saw to try to help the driver/operator. The two retreated toward the aerial platform, but before reaching it the driver/operator fell to his knees. Seconds later, the roof under the driver/operator collapsed and he fell into the fire below. Flames erupted from the collapse opening as the fire vented through it. With help from a rapid intervention crew, an interior attack crew located and removed the driver/operator within five minutes. He was transported to a local hospital where he was pronounced dead.

While the foregoing case history shows how dangerous vertical ventilation operations can be, experience by many fire departments on countless structure fires shows that properly implemented and coordinated vertical ventilation can be a part of a safe and successful fire suppression operation. Properly implemented vertical ventilation can positively influence fire behavior, prevent or reduce the loss of life, and prevent or reduce property damage. After the IC has sized up a structure fire, decided that tactical ventilation is needed, determined that vertical ventilation would be most effective, and made sure that fire attack and protection lines are ready, the next step is to open the building at its highest point or as close to the seat of the fire as safely possible.

Just because a building is filled with smoke does not necessarily mean that a backdraft or flashover is imminent. However, releasing heat and smoke vertically may reduce the chances of these contingencies occurring and will facilitate search and rescue and interior fire attack.

While many structure fires contain elements that might lend themselves to either vertical or horizontal ventilation, only those conditions that relate to vertical ventilation are discussed in this chapter. This chapter discusses establishing and supporting vertical ventilation, safety considerations, and the most commonly used vertical ventilation tools. Building construction related to vertical ventilation is also discussed, including roof construction, lightweight roofs, roof coverings, and existing roof openings. Finally, the various ways of opening a roof are discussed.

Establishing and Supporting Vertical Ventilation

Before and during the actual opening of the roof, the following items must be considered:

- Verifying that attack lines are charged and ready
- Evaluating roof construction type and condition
- Providing a second means of egress from the roof
- Observing weather (temperature, humidity, visibility, wind direction/speed)
- Noting any obstructions or dead loads on the roof
- Reading (observing) the roof continually
- Locating the seat of the fire
- Using existing roof openings when appropriate
- Cutting one large opening instead of several small ones
- Enlarging the original opening instead of cutting an additional hole if more ventilation is needed
- Tracking elapsed time into the incident

Figure 13.1 The vertical ventilation opening should be made as close to the seat of the fire as possible. *Courtesy of Dr. George McClary.*

Vertical ventilation is intended to allow heat, smoke, and other fire gases to escape into the atmosphere and replace them with fresh air. In performing vertical ventilation, firefighters should attempt to give the heat and smoke the most direct path out of the structure that is safely possible without spreading the fire or interfering with occupants exiting the building. Ideally, the ventilation exit opening should be made directly over the seat of the fire. This is the preferred location, *but only if it is judged to be a safe one* **(Figure 13.1)**.

Roof features can either help or hinder vertical ventilation operations. Some features, such as solar panels, may be obstructions. Others, such as air-handling units, process vents, machinery vents, and dust-collection units may assist in ventilation efforts under certain conditions. All such roof features should be assessed during preincident planning surveys of buildings within the response area. If it is determined that a particular roof feature will hinder tactical ventilation, alternative methods of ventilation can and should be devised and written into preincident plans.

Vertical Ventilation Safety

Because there are numerous ways in which firefighters can be at risk, vertical ventilation operations are potentially some of the most hazardous operations at structure fires. Vision on rooftops is often obscured by weather, smoke, or darkness. The tools that firefighters use to cut ventilation holes in roofs can be dangerous for the operator and for other firefighters nearby. Fire-weakened roofs may collapse — sometimes without warning **(Figure 13.2)**. Creating an opening through which heat and smoke can escape may expose firefighters to flames and high levels of radiant heat, as well as to extremely toxic gases. These and other conditions encountered during vertical ventilation operations make the following discussion of firefighter safety especially important.

Figure 13.2 Structural members can give way quickly, causing total failure of the roof system. *Courtesy of Ed Prendergast.*

Identifying Vertical Ventilation Hazards

One of the most important safety considerations for firefighters assigned to perform vertical ventilation is a roof that is potentially being weakened by fire below them. Therefore, firefighters must become familiar with the various types of roof construction and the effects that fire exposure is likely to have on each. Before stepping onto any roof, firefighters should *read* (observe the condition of) and *sound* (test the condition of) the roof and they should continue to do so as long as they are on the roof. Techniques for reading a roof and sounding a roof are discussed later in this section.

Reading and sounding reduce the chances of firefighters getting on or remaining on a roof that is structurally unstable. However, smoke or darkness may reduce visibility and make reading a roof difficult. Using a thermal imaging camera may be useful under these conditions. Firefighters should sound every roof with a hand tool as they advance, except for roofs covered with tile or slate. Rain, snow, and ice may also interfere with accurately reading a roof and will increase the live load on the roof and make the surface slippery. As soon as a ventilation operation is completed, or when conditions indicate that the roof is or may soon become unstable, firefighters should immediately leave the roof **(Figure 13.3, p. 348)**.

While there are numerous potential hazards in vertical ventilation operations, the primary ones are that firefighters must work aboveground (often far above) on sometimes steeply sloped surfaces that can lead to slips and falls. They also face the possibility of roof collapse. Firefighters must beware of the possibility of falling onto roofs from high parapet walls, of falling off roofs because of tripping over low parapets, and of poor footing on steep roofs. They must also be aware of the potentially dangerous levels of electrical power (up to 600 volts DC, at up to 8 amps) inherent in rooftop solar panels. Finally, firefighters must be aware of the toxic products of combustion released through their ventilation efforts and of the dangers of fire spread beneath them.

> **CAUTION**
> Firefighters should *never* get on a roof wearing anything less than full protective clothing, SCBA, and a PASS device. As a minimum, the vent group leader should also be equipped with a portable radio.

Figure 13.3 Firefighters should leave the roof immediately if conditions begin to deteriorate. *Courtesy of the Los Angeles Fire Department – ISTS.*

> **CAUTION**
> Whenever firefighters ascend to a roof, a secondary means of egress from the roof *must* be provided. This can be accomplished by placing ladders on two or more sides of the building.

Getting Firefighters to the Roof

Because truck company personnel – or those assigned to perform truck functions in the absence of an on-scene truck company – are responsible for performing vertical ventilation when the IC deems it necessary, they should be trained to automatically determine the best means of access to the roof of a burning building. As discussed in Chapter 3, whenever firefighters are on a roof, the building should be laddered on at least two sides. In fact, it should be laddered on all sides if on-scene resources permit **(Figure 13.4)**. Some of these ladders may be used for roof access.

Aerial devices may also be used for roof access if they are not already committed to rescue or fire suppression operations. It is SOP in many fire departments to automatically position an aerial device for best access to the roof at every structure fire to save valuable time in ventilation and fire suppression operations **(Figure 13.5)**. In those cases where firefighters cannot reach the roof by using fire department ladders, they may have to use the interior stairway, exterior fire escapes, or those on adjoining buildings if they can be used safely.

Reading a Roof

To *read a roof* means to observe the roof, construction features, and other indicators that can warn firefighters of potentially unsafe conditions. If firefighters are familiar with common local roof and building construction design practices, they can read a roof from a position of stability such as a parapet wall or an aerial device. Features that can be read before stepping onto a roof include the following:

- Age of the building
- Type of roof structure
- Location and orientation of supporting members
- Type and condition of the roof coverings

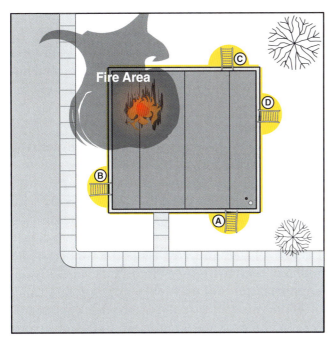

Figure 13.4 It is preferable to ladder all sides of the structure if possible.

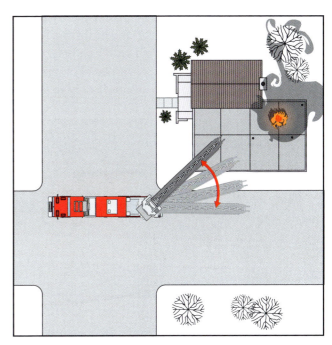

Figure 13.5 An aerial device is often the safest and most efficient means of gaining access to a roof and should be positioned to gain the greatest advantage possible.

- Heavy tanks, machinery, solar panels, or other loads
- Visible smoke
- Visible fire

Because vents, skylights, and other features penetrate a roof *between* the rafters or joists, they can offer other clues to the location and orientation of roof supports **(Figure 13.6)**. Also, the weathering of roof coverings over time will often reveal where rafters are located and the direction in which they are oriented. If a thermal imager is available, it can be used to locate hot spots and to identify the location and orientation of roof supports **(Figure 13.7)**. Other factors that firefighters should look for before stepping onto a roof include the following:

- Sagging roof surface
- Roof vents that appear to be unusually tall (indication that the roof is sagging)
- Large puddles of water
- Smoke or fire coming from roof vents
- Heavy dead loads
- Drop-offs due to light wells or varying roof elevations
- Solar panels

All of these signs and conditions will help firefighters decide whether a roof is stable enough to support their weight or whether ventilation work must be done from

Figure 13.6 The positioning of skylights can indicate the location of roof supports.

Figure 13.7 Roof supports and hot spots can often be identified with the use of a TIC.

Chapter 13 • Vertical Ventilation **349**

an aerial device or other position of safety such as from the roof of an adjoining building. If the roof appears stable, the factors observed while reading the roof can help identify the strongest and weakest areas and the safest routes of travel on the roof. If the roof appears unstable, the IC must be notified immediately so that consideration can be given to withdrawing interior crews.

Sounding a Roof

Firefighters should sound the roof (if possible) with the blunt end of a pike pole, rubbish hook, or axe any time they attempt access. In poor visibility, probing with a tool handle will also reveal if the roof is covered with solar panels or vegetation **(Figure 13.8)**. If there are no such obstructions, when a roof surface is struck by a tool, some will feel solid over structural supports, and the tool will tend to bounce off the surface. Between the supports, the roof may feel softer and less rigid. The roof may also *sound* solid when struck over a rafter or joist and produce a hollow sound when struck between the supports. By practicing on a variety of intact roofs, firefighters can learn to recognize the difference in the feel and the sound of supported and unsupported areas.

Figure 13.8 Solar panels on a roof are a significant electrocution hazard and may not be visible under heavy smoke conditions. *Courtesy of McKinney (TX) Fire Department.*

However, roofs that have several layers of composition shingles or other roof coverings may not provide clear indicators when sounded. They may sound quite solid when struck with a tool even though the roof supports may have been severely damaged by the fire. Also, roofs covered with tile or slate cannot be sounded and the individual pieces must be removed to reveal the underlying structure.

> When vertically ventilating a burning building, firefighters should do the following:
>
> - Continuously read the fire and evaluate the effect of the fire on structural stability.
> - Place ladders away from windows.
> - Place ladders away from electrical wires.
> - Sound the roof with a tool in one hand while holding onto the ladder with the other hand.
> - Walk only over structural members.
> - Progress from the uninvolved area toward the involved area.
> - Work between the involved area and the egress route.
> - Get off the roof as soon as the assignment is finished.

CAUTION
The roof surface may sound stable even when the underlying structure has been weakened by the fire. This is especially true with trusses. Sounding alone is not a guarantee of roof stability.

As mentioned earlier, as long as firefighters remain on the roof of a burning building, they should continue to read the roof for changes in its stability. They should also continue to sound the roof whenever they move about on it. If they must walk the ridge of a peaked roof, they should walk with one foot on either side of the ridge **(Figure 13.9)**.

Figure 13.9 Firefighters walking the ridge of a roof should place their feet on either side of the ridge.

Figure 13.10 If the structural integrity of the roof is in question, it is often best to ventilate from an aerial device.

Working on a Roof

In general, the strongest points of any roof are where the roof meets the outside walls, directly over roof supports, and at ridges or valleys. The weakest points are between the supports. Firefighters can reduce the risk of falling through a fire-weakened roof by walking only over roof supports.

In addition, fire-weakened roofs will sometimes fail under the weight of a heavy snow or rainwater accumulation. They may even fail under the weight of a single firefighter jumping from a ladder or parapet wall onto the surface because the firefighter's weight is concentrated at one point. Therefore, firefighters should never jump onto a roof, but should ease themselves onto the roof surface. However, they should also never use a roof ladder on a fire-weakened roof to spread their weight over a greater area. Roof ladders should only be used to give the firefighter more secure footing on pitched roofs.

The vent group leader must read the roof very carefully and inform the incident commander of his or her evaluation of the situation so that the risks and benefits of ordering firefighters onto the roof can be weighed. Whenever there is any doubt about the structural integrity of a roof, it may be prudent to limit vertical ventilation operations to those that can be done from an aerial device or other position of safety **(Figure 13.10)**.

Working with Protective Hoselines

Ideally, vertical ventilation operations are performed with the wind at the firefighters' backs. However, when the seat of the fire is at the windward end of a building, this may not be possible. In this situation, the wind may also push

> **WARNING!**
> Because roof supports almost always run perpendicular to the outside walls, firefighters should *never* walk diagonally across the roof of a burning building.

> **WARNING!**
> NEVER jump onto a roof or work on a roof that is known to be weakened.

Figure 13.11 Hoselines are often needed to support operations on large roofs.

flames and smoke toward the ventilation crew. In these instances, it may be necessary to have a charged hoseline on the roof with the ventilation crew for their protection. The need for a charged hoseline on a roof should be based on the need to protect the vent crew. Pertinent safety considerations are as follows:

- Wind direction and intensity
- Size of the roof **(Figure 13.11)**
- Type of roof covering
- Time needed to cut the ventilation exit opening
- Time needed to deploy the hoseline to the roof
- Additional firefighters needed to operate the hoseline

A hoseline may not be required on the roof of a single-family residence because firefighters can cut the hole and exit the roof quickly. However, a charged hoseline may be necessary to push heat and smoke away from the vent crew while they cut an exit opening on the roof of a large-area building. A protective hoseline can also be useful for extinguishing spot fires that may start on a roof with combustible coverings.

To prevent spot fires downwind of the burning building, a fire stream may also be used to cool the thermal column rising from the ventilation exit opening. When fire streams are used for this purpose, it is important that the stream be directed horizontally or at a slightly upward angle across the opening but *never* into the exit opening itself **(Figure 13.12)**. If a stream is directed into a ventilation exit opening, it will counteract the natural convection currents and push steam and smoke down into the building toward any firefighters working inside.

Opening a Roof

Once firefighters are on the roof, they should test the roof by gently bouncing on it while holding onto the ladder or parapet wall with one hand **(Figure 13.13)**. They should continue reading and sounding the roof as they walk on it. Firefighters should also stop frequently and bounce on the roof to see if the feel of it has changed. Any difference in the feel of the roof may indicate that they are standing on a weakened section of the roof.

> **CAUTION**
> While a charged hoseline may be useful and necessary on a roof during ventilation operations, firefighters must realize its limitations and not become overconfident and careless because it is close at hand.

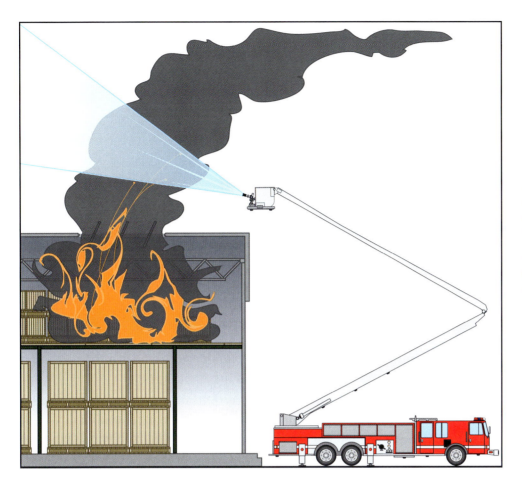

Figure 13.12 The master stream from an aerial device can be used to cool the smoke issuing from a ventilation opening; however, the stream should never be directed down into the opening.

Figure 13.13 Firefighters should test the roof while maintaining contact with the ladder prior to venturing out onto the roof.

The location for the ventilation exit opening will generally be determined by several factors such as the following:

- Layout of the building
- Coordination with interior operations
- Initial size-up of the fire situation
- Smoke coming from existing openings
- Smoke or fire coming through the roof covering
- Blisters in the roof covering
- Sagging roof

After determining the best place for the ventilation exit opening, firefighters can begin opening the roof. A key factor in opening roofs safely and efficiently is knowing the location and extent of the fire and the location and direction of the rafters. Most roof assemblies employ a parallel rafter system with rafters spaced from 12 to 24 inches (300 mm to 600 mm) on center, spanning the shortest distance between structural members or bearing walls. Exceptions to this rule are panelized roofs and specialty roofs using wooden or metal trusses or laminated beams. If a TIC is available, it can be used to reveal the location and direction of the rafters and other roof supports.

If a TIC is not available and all other signs indicate that the roof is stable, the roof should be sounded. If sounding does not reveal the location and direction of the rafters, a diagonal cut through the roof covering can be made with a chain saw or rotary saw at an angle of 45 degrees to any exterior wall **(Figure 13.14)**. The blade will usually encounter a rafter before the cut is 3 feet (1 m) long. If, after a rafter is located, its direction is still unknown, a cut parallel to a sidewall should be made, crossing the first cut **(Figure 13.15)**. This cut should be 2 to 3 feet (.6 m to 1 m) long. If no rafters are found, it can be assumed

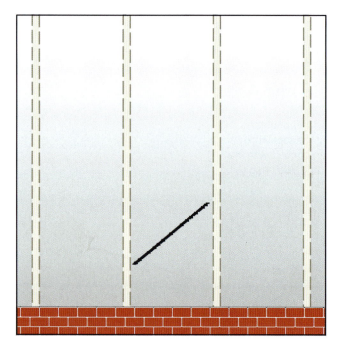

Figure 13.14 A diagonal cut is made until a roof support is located.

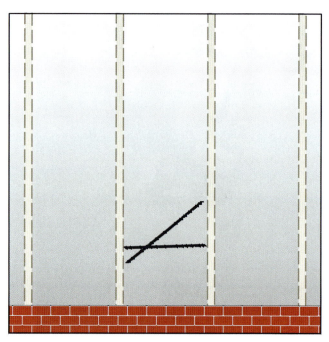

Figure 13.15 A second cut is made to determine the orientation of roof supports.

that the rafter direction is parallel to the second cut. A triangular hole, also known as an *inspection hole*, can be completed to determine spacing, roof thickness, and possible fire conditions in the attic **(Figure 13.16)**.

When firefighters reach the point where the ventilation opening is to be made, every cutting and pulling operation should allow them to continually work from the involved area back toward the uninvolved area. Once the first cut is made in the roof, the firefighters should avoid putting themselves between that first cut and the seat of the fire. The following precautions should be considered when ventilating any roof:

Figure 13.16 Inspection holes are useful for a number of purposes.

- Know the location of emergency escape routes and be ready to use them.
- When effective, use existing openings to limit damage to the roof.
- Maintain a safe distance between cutting tools in operation and other firefighters.
- Do not make the ventilation opening between firefighters and the escape routes or in the normal path of travel.
- Cut the roof covering and decking — not the rafters or other roof supports.
- Begin the ventilation opening on the *leeward* side and back toward the wind so that smoke and hot gases are blown away from the vent crew.
- Remove the ceiling below the roof if necessary to ensure maximum ventilation.
- Get off the roof as soon as the assignment is finished.

Vertical Ventilation Tools

Just as in the horizontal ventilation operations discussed in the preceding chapter, almost any forcible entry tool can also be used for vertical ventilation. However, some tools are better suited to this task than others. The specific applications of the tools most commonly used for vertical ventilation are discussed in the following sections.

Cutting Tools

Using any cutting tool is potentially dangerous, both for the operator and others nearby. Cutting tools can be especially hazardous in vertical ventilation operations because they must often be used on steeply pitched roofs, while working from roof ladders, and for cutting materials that resist being cut. One of the most important safety points to remember is that a safe distance should always be maintained between a firefighter using a cutting tool and other firefighters. While departmental SOPs must always be followed, it is recommended that a clear space of at least 10 feet (3 m) be maintained in all directions from anyone using a cutting tool in vertical ventilation. One exception to this rule is the use of a guide or backup when a power saw is being used. The guide watches where the operator is going, clears the path of obstructions, and provides safety and support during cutting operations. The most common cutting tools used for vertical ventilation are the rotary saw, chain saw, and the pick-head axe.

Rotary Saw

As with any gasoline-powered tool, the rotary saw should be started and run briefly at the ground or street level, and then shut off, before it is carried or hoisted aloft **(Figure 13.17)**. Also at the street level, the blade should be changed if the material to be cut requires something other than the multipurpose blade normally carried on these saws. When using this or any other power tool, the operator should wear full protective clothing (especially hearing and eye protection) **(Figure 13.18)**.

After determining the location for the ventilation opening, the operator places the saw flat on the roof surface, revs it up to cutting speed, and then slowly rocks the saw forward until the blade contacts and cuts the roof covering to the required depth **(Figure 13.19)**. The saw continues cutting as it is drawn back toward the operator. When the saw blade comes into contact with a rafter, the rotation of the blade may slow slightly and the sound of the motor may change. When that happens, the saw should be rocked back slightly to decrease the depth of cut until the blade is clear of the rafter **(Figure 13.20)**. The operator moves backward in a shuffle step — that is, both feet remain in contact with the roof surface at all times. The operator's rear foot slides backward and stops and the other foot slides back to meet the rear foot, and this process is repeated until the cut is completed.

> **CAUTION**
> Firefighters must be very careful to avoid cutting rafters and other structural members when using a rotary saw in vertical ventilation.

Figure 13.17 Saws should be started and run briefly at street level before being brought to the roof.

Figure 13.18 Proper PPE, including eye and hearing protection, should be used when operating power saws.

Figure 13.19 Care should be taken to ensure the proper cutting depth is maintained.

Figure 13.20 The saw should be rocked back slightly to reduce the cutting depth when a structural member is encountered.

Figure 13.21 Chainsaws are preferred by some firefighters for cutting roofs.

Chain Saw

All the safety precautions applicable to rotary saws also apply when using chain saws. Because of its versatility and safety when used by a well-trained operator, the chain saw is the preferred tool for many fireground cutting operations **(Figure 13.21)**. Chain saws used for forcible entry or ventilation are usually equipped with carbide-tipped chains to allow cutting through nails and light-gauge metal components. They may also be equipped with an adjustable depth gauge to reduce the chances of cutting rafters through roof decking or sheathing **(Figure 13.22)**.

The cutting procedure used with chain saws is very similar to that used with rotary saws. One difference is that the operator should first make sure that the chain oiler is working **(Figure 13.23)**. Then the chain speed is increased before engaging the material to be cut. Once contact is made with the material to be cut, the tip of the cutting bar is slowly pushed down into and through the roof covering and the decking or sheathing below.

Unlike the technique used when cutting structural members, which uses the area of the bar closest to the saw motor, roof cuts are made using only the last few inches (mm) at the tip of the cutting bar. Also, cutting is done using the bottom of the bar, not the top. To be most effective, a chain saw must be used with the bar at a right angle to the roof surface **(Figure 13.24, p. 358)**.

Figure 13.22 A depth gauge should be used to ensure the proper cutting depth.

Figure 13.23 The function of the chain oiler should be checked before cutting.

Figure 13.24 Chainsaws are most effective when they are at right angles to the material being cut.

Figure 13.25 Chain brakes are important features of chainsaws.

Some firefighters consider chain saws safer to use than rotary saws because they do not twist in the operator's hand when revved up as rotary saws tend to do. Chain saws are also equipped with a chain brake to instantly stop the movement of the chain if it jams and kicks back out of the material being cut **(Figure 13.25)**. Some firefighters also believe that the chain saw gives the operator a better *feel* for what is being cut, reducing the risk of accidentally cutting through joists or rafters. However, as with any cutting tool, careful and responsible operation by well-trained personnel is still the best safety device.

Pick-Head Axe

To keep both hands free for other work, some firefighters wear their axes in scabbards strapped around their waists **(Figure 13.26)**. One use of the pick-head axe is for scraping away pea gravel or slag from areas to be cut with a power saw. However, when power saws are unavailable or inoperative, a pick-head axe can be used effectively to open some types of roofs. Cutting a roof with an axe should be done as close to the rafters as possible to minimize the tendency of the roof surface to deflect when struck. Because of the flex in the roof between the rafters, an axe may simply bounce off the surface. Using a sharp axe also makes the job easier, but at best, opening a roof with a pick-head axe is a very physically demanding task. The safest way to cut a roof with an axe is to use short, controlled strokes, with the axe head cutting to the side of the firefighter's feet, not between them **(Figure 13.27)**. On roofs covered with shakes or shingles, it is usually more efficient for firefighters to scrape the roofing material with the axe rather than attempting to cut it **(Figure 13.28)**.

Figure 13.26 Scabbards are useful for keeping hands free while carrying an axe.

Figure 13.27 The cutting angle should be parallel with the firefighter's feet.

Figure 13.28 Axes are often used to strip shingles from the roof decking.

Stripping Tools

In some cases, once the roofing material has been cut around the perimeter of a ventilation exit opening, the roof covering may have to be stripped back to expose the sheathing. While some fire departments have designed their own special stripping tools, the most common ones are the pick-head axe, the pike pole, and the rubbish hook. A sledgehammer performs the equivalent function on tile or slate roofs if the tiles cannot be removed intact.

Pick-Head Axe

The pick-head axe can be used to strip the roof covering from the sheathing and then the sheathing from the rafters after the appropriate cuts have been made. A firefighter is first positioned on each side of the cuts. Facing leeward and working as a team, the firefighters insert the picks of their axes into the leeward crosscut and pull the roof covering toward them as they back away **(Figure 13.29)**. Then, they repeat the process to pull the sheathing.

Pike Pole

Pike poles can be used to strip roofing in much the same way as pick-head axes are used. The hook is inserted into the leeward crosscut, and the roofing is pulled back. Pike poles have longer handles than axes, and their length allows firefighters to position themselves farther away from the point where heat, smoke, and perhaps fire may be issuing. Also, if there is a ceiling below the roof, its removal may be necessary in order to release heat and smoke from the room below, and the handle of the pike pole is an excellent tool for this purpose.

Rubbish Hook

The rubbish hook is used in exactly the same way as the pike pole when stripping roofing. One further advantage of the rubbish hook is that it has two hooks instead of one, giving the tool twice the grip on the material being pulled **(Figure 13.30)**. Another advantage is the D-handle, which allows the operator a much more positive grip and therefore a stronger pull **(Figure 13.31)**. Finally, the width of the tool head makes pushing a ceiling down from above much more efficient than with a pike pole.

Figure 13.29 Roof decking can be pulled back with a pick-head axe once the cut has been made.

Figure 13.30 Rubbish hooks are versatile tools on the fireground.

Figure 13.31 The D-handle on rubbish hooks allows much better grip on the tool.

Sledgehammer

While not normally considered a stripping tool, the sledgehammer can be used on tile- or slate-covered roofs in much the same way that the pick-head axe is used with other roof coverings. Short, controlled blows with the sledgehammer will shatter the tiles without the head of the tool penetrating deeply enough to become lodged between the sheathing boards. If a sledgehammer is not available, a flat-head or pick-head axe can be used for this purpose.

Roof Construction

The extent to which firefighters are able to safely and efficiently ventilate a building through its roof will depend to some degree on their knowledge of roof construction. Construction practices and materials vary in different regions, so firefighters need to inspect buildings under construction in their response districts to become familiar with local construction materials and methods **(Figure 13.32)**. In most areas of North America, there are several types of pitched roofs, flat roofs, and arched roofs.

Figure 13.32 It is critical that firefighters tour buildings under construction in their response area to become familiar with construction features. *Courtesy of McKinney (TX) Fire Department.*

Pitched Roofs

In roof construction nomenclature, the angle or degree of slope is called the *pitch*. The slopes of pitched roofs often vary with climate and aesthetic considerations. The pitch is expressed in inches of fall per horizontal foot. A roof that decreases 5 inches (125 mm) vertically for each foot (300 mm) horizontally from the ridge would be described as a *five-in-twelve* roof, which is the most common pitch on residential roofs in areas with mild climates **(Figure 13.33)**. A roof designed to withstand a heavy snow load might have a twelve-in-twelve pitch (45-degree angle). Some roofs are even steeper. In addition, some homes and other buildings have sections of their roofs with different pitches than other sections.

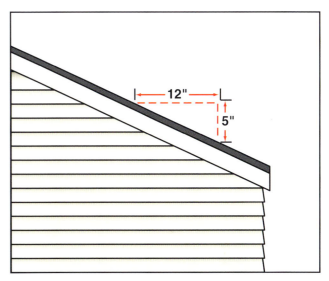

Figure 13.33 A typical 5-in-12 roof.

Pitched roofs are usually supported by wooden or metal rafters, laminated beams, or engineered trusses spanning the shortest distance between bearing walls. Where ceiling joists are used, they are fastened to the top plate of the walls and the rafters so that the entire assembly forms a series of triangles — the strongest of all geometric shapes **(Figure 13.34)**. In *post-and-beam* construction, the ceiling is often omitted and the rafters become part of the interior décor **(Figure 13.35, p. 362)**. The supporting structure carries the roof sheathing, which can be any of various materials

Figure 13.34 Truss assemblies form a series of triangles. *Courtesy of the McKinney (TX) Fire Department.*

such as plywood or oriented strand board (OSB), but is most often tongue-and-groove planking for aesthetic purposes. The sheathing is covered by some form of weather-resistant material such as shakes or shingles **(Figure 13.36)**.

In many structures with pitched roofs, the area between the underside of the roof and the ceiling forms an attic space, which may be vented by openings at the eaves, turbine vents, mushroom vents, eyebrow vents, or ridge vents. Attic spaces in some structures with gable roofs also have vents near the top of the end (gable) walls **(Figure 13.37)**. Structures with hip roofs have no gables so the attic spaces may have vents at the eaves, or one or more of the other types of roof vents just mentioned.

Access to attic spaces in residences and small office buildings can usually be gained through a small attic scuttle in the ceiling of a hallway or closet, or there may be a stairway or ladder leading into the space. Insulation material, which may or may not be combustible, is sometimes found between the framing members under the roof or on top of the ceiling. There may also be a considerable amount of ductwork in the attic, which can impede access.

Figure 13.35 An example of post-and-beam construction.

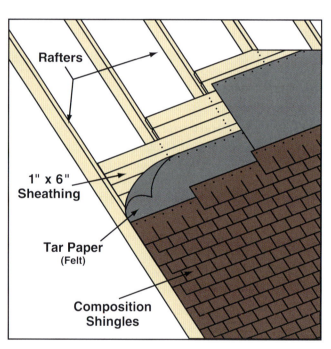

Figure 13.36 Features of a typical shingled roof.

Figure 13.37 A typical gable roof vent.

Types of Pitched Roofs

There are several types of pitched roofs commonly used on structures in North America. The most common examples of pitched roofs are the gable, hip, lantern, and shed styles. However, there are also bridge truss, mansard, modern mansard, gambrel, sawtooth, and butterfly styles.

Gable roof. The gable roof is one of the most common types of roof construction and can be found on many single-family residences and small commercial structures **(Figure 13.38)**. The pitch of this type of roof ranges from nearly flat to very steep, and the points where the rafters meet the outside walls and the ridge beam provide the most support. This A-frame configuration consists of rafters that run perpendicular to the ridge beam and down to and usually – but not always – beyond the outside walls. The ridge and rafters are often 2-×6-inch (50 mm by 150 mm) lumber or larger in *stick-built* roofs (those built on site), but in prefabricated roof trusses these components are commonly 2-× 4-inch (50 mm by 100 mm) depending upon the span.

Figure 13.38 A typical gable roof.

In both types of roof assemblies, the rafters are commonly spaced at 16 to 24 inches (400 mm to 600 mm) on center. The dimensions and spacing of the rafters will vary with the horizontal span. Additional support may be provided by collar beams and ceiling joists. Valley rafters are used where two roof assemblies intersect **(Figure 13.39)**. The trussed pitched roof is designed to cover a considerable span, and its rafters can be made of timber or metal. There may be local variations on these basic designs so firefighters must stay current on what is in their response districts.

Figure 13.39 A typical valley rafter.

Hip roof. The hip roof is similar to the gabled roof in every respect except that the ends of the roof terminate in a *hip* configuration rather than a gable. In other words, the roof slopes down to meet every outside wall **(Figure 13.40)**.

Hip roof construction consists of a ridge beam with conventional rafters running perpendicular to the ridge and hip rafters running from the ends of the ridge beam, at a compound angle of 45 degrees laterally and at some lesser vertical angle down to and beyond the outside walls at the corners **(Figure 13.41, p. 364)**. All rafters in hip roofs run perpendicular to the nearest outside wall. The dimensions and spacing of hip roof structural members follow the same engineering rules as those for gabled roof construction. The strongest parts of this roof system are the ridges, valleys, hips, and at the outside walls.

Figure 13.40 This house has a hip-type roof.

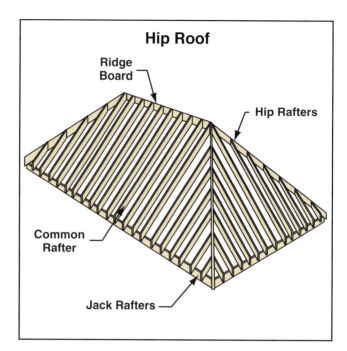

Figure 13.41 A hip roof assembly.

Lantern roof. The lantern roof consists of a high gabled roof with a vertical wall above a downward-pitched shed roof section on either side. This roof style is found on many barns, churches, and commercial buildings with rural-style construction **(Figure 13.42)**.

This roof may be difficult to ventilate without an aerial device because of the difficulty in gaining access to the upper roof from either lower roof. The peak of the upper roof may also be beyond the reach of available ground ladders.

Shed roof. The shed roof can be seen as half of a gable roof or as a slightly pitched flat roof sloped in one direction only — usually from the front of the building down to the back. This type of roof may be constructed with mono-pitch trusses, which employ only a single web member **(Figure 13.43)**. These trusses may be more prone to early collapse than other lightweight wooden trusses.

Figure 13.42 This restaurant incorporates a lantern roof for aesthetic purposes.

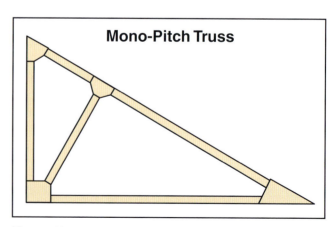

Figure 13.43 A mono-pitch truss.

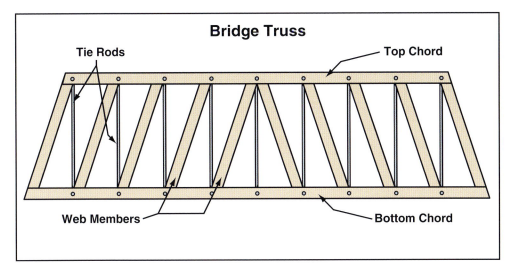

Figure 13.44 A bridge truss.

Bridge-truss roof. Bridge trusses are heavy-duty trusses with sloping ends **(Figure 13.44)**. The top chord is shorter than the bottom chord, and when installed, the bottom chord is supported by the outside walls. When constructed of wood, the trusses are often made from 2-×12-inch (50 mm by 300 mm) lumber, and vertical metal tie rods may be used for additional support. Joists are usually 2- × 6-inch (50 mm by 150 mm) or 2- × 8-inch (50 mm by 200 mm) lumber covered with 1- × 6-inch (25 mm by 150 mm) sheathing. Truss spacing may be as much as 16 to 20 feet (5 m to 6 m) on center. Composition roll roofing may be used throughout this type of roof, or the sloping sections may be shingled. Because of the shape of bridge trusses, they form a roof that is very similar to the modern mansard roof discussed later in this section.

The strongest areas of bridge-trussed roofs are at the perimeter of the building where the bottom chord of the trusses rest on the outside bearing walls. Trusses are in constant tension and compression and will fail under severe fire conditions, but the likelihood of roof collapse is dependent on a number of factors, including:

- The dimensions of the materials used
- The unsupported distance being spanned
- The live and dead loads being supported
- The duration of fire exposure

If vertical metal tie rods are used, early failure of the rods will also affect the stability of these trusses.

Figure 13.45 A true mansard roof.

Mansard roof. The mansard roof has a double slope on each of its four sides. In other words, instead of the roof pitch being a constant angle, there are two angles on each side. One angle forms a steep pitch running from the eaves to a certain height, and the other forms a flatter pitch to the ridge of the roof.

This style is similar to the gambrel roof (see gambrel roofs later in this section) in that the lower pitch is steeper than the upper pitch. The difference between the mansard and the modern mansard (see following paragraph) is the way in which the four sides meet in the middle. The true mansard forms a slight hipped peak or ridge **(Figure 13.45)**. On the other hand, the modern mansard has a flat central portion.

Modern mansard roof. The modern mansard roof includes characteristics of both flat and pitched roofs: four steeply sloped sides rise to meet a flat top called a *deck* **(Figure 13.46)**. This roof type may utilize bridge trusses or K-trusses as supporting members, both of which allow for the creation of an ample void or attic space between the roof and the ceiling, as well as a potential for early collapse under fire conditions. In addition, the modern mansard style roof may include overhangs that form concealed spaces through which fire and smoke can spread quickly (see *modern mansard roofs* under Types of Flat Roofs section).

Gambrel roof. A gambrel roof is most often found on barns and other outbuildings. This roof is essentially a gable type with two different slopes on each side of the peak and with the lower slope being steeper than the upper slope **(Figure 13.47)**. Such a design can make getting to the top of the roof difficult with ground and roof ladders, so an aerial device may be the preferred method of access. Because this roof design permits efficient use of the attic space under the roof, firefighters must consider that additional weight resulting from maximum interior attic storage could hasten the failure of the roof assembly during a fire.

Sawtooth roof. In the past, this type of roof was often used in industrial and institutional buildings to maximize natural light and ventilation but it is rarely seen in modern buildings. The sawtooth roof consists of a series of small pitched roofs similar in shape to the teeth of a saw **(Figure 13.48)**. The rafters are 2- × 8- inch (50 mm by 200 mm) lumber or larger and use wood or metal supports for bracing. The vertical walls include openable windows along their entire length, often containing panes of wired glass. The pitched roofs are sheathed with plywood, OSB, or planked sheathing and covered with roofing material.

Butterfly roof. The butterfly roof may be seen as two opposing shed roofs that meet at their lower edges in the middle of the building **(Figure 13.49)**. The same hazards and operational and safety considerations of all other pitched roofs also apply to butterfly roofs with one exception. A firefighter who slips and falls on a butterfly roof is not in as much danger of sliding off the edge of the roof as on other types of pitched roofs.

Figure 13.46 This building has a flat roof and a mansard fascia.

Figure 13.47 A typical gambrel roof.

Figure 13.48 This warehouse incorporates a sawtooth roof to make use of natural light.

Figure 13.49 A typical butterfly roof.

Hazards of Pitched Roofs

Pitched roofs are designed to shed rain and snow, so their main hazards are steepness and the lack of secure footing for firefighters working on them. These problems are increased when the roof is wet or covered with ice, snow, wet leaves, or moss. However, secure footing may even be a problem when these roofs are dry because of the loose granular texture of some roof coverings. Loose roof tiles, slate, or broken pieces can also be hazardous to firefighters working on the roof and those below. Loose tiles and broken shards may cause firefighters on the roof to slip, and the loose pieces can slide off the roof and fall on firefighters working at ground level.

In addition to the hazards presented by the pitch or slope of the roof and by falling debris, the growing use of lightweight roof trusses can present an equally serious hazard to firefighters. These assemblies are often held together only with metal gusset plates that can warp and pull out of the wood when exposed to direct flame impingement **(Figure 13.50)**. Therefore, these roof assemblies offer less fire resistance than stick-built types and can fail early in a fire, with little or no warning. Because of this possibility, it is SOP in some fire departments to track the elapsed time into a structure fire incident at 5-, 10-, 15-, and 20-minute intervals. This helps the IC decide if and when vent crews should be ordered off of a roof and interior crews ordered out of a burning building. For more information on metal gusset plates, see the discussion later in this chapter under Pitched Roof Trusses.

Figure 13.50 Metal gusset plates can often warp and fall away when exposed to fire. *Courtesy of the McKinney (TX) Fire Department.*

⚠️ While there are no established time criteria for the failure of lightweight trusses involved in fire, many departments start the elapsed-time clock when the fire is reported. SOPs vary on the point at which precautionary withdrawals are initiated.

Figure 13.51 The ventilation opening should be cut high on the roof near the ridge.

Figure 13.52 A pick head axe embedded in the decking can be used for additional footing.

Venting Pitched Roofs

As described in **Essentials**, pitched roofs should be vented at the highest point on the leeward side directly over the fire or as close to it as safely possible. The ventilation exit opening should be cut parallel to the rafters and perpendicular to the ridge **(Figure 13.51)**. In the absence of a thermal imaging camera (TIC), the first roof cut should be parallel to the ridge to help identify where the rafters are located. The ventilation exit opening should be at least 4×4 feet (1.2 m by 1.2 m), and in many cases may need to be larger. It is SOP in some departments to start with a much larger ventilation exit opening in commercial building fires. As a general rule, one large ventilation exit opening is better than several smaller ones.

In some cases, as with plank sheathing, it may be advantageous to strip the roof covering before cutting and pulling the sheathing. In other cases, especially when using the center-rafter technique on plywood or OSB decking, leaving the roof covering attached works well and saves time and effort. On metal-covered roofs it may be possible to remove an entire section at one time by cutting or prying along the edges, pulling screws or nails as necessary, and removing the panel.

Because of the steep pitch of some roofs, cutting a ventilation exit opening can be difficult and dangerous. Firefighters may need to use roof ladders to keep from sliding down the roof. When working from a roof ladder, firefighters will often need to reach as far as safely possible laterally from the ladder in order to cut the largest possible opening. To provide more secure footing and extend their reach, the points of a rubbish hook or the pick of an axe or Halligan can be embedded in the roof and the tool head used as a foothold **(Figure 13.52)**. Long pike poles or rubbish hooks may also be needed when ventilating this type of roof because the ceiling can be several feet (meters) below the roof level, and sections of the ceiling may have to be opened for complete ventilation **(Figure 13.53)**.

Flat Roofs

In many areas, flat roofs are more common on mercantile and industrial buildings, multiple dwellings, and apartment complexes than on single-family dwellings. This type of roof ordinarily has a slight slope of two-in-twelve pitch or less from the front toward the rear of the

Figure 13.53 Rubbish hooks are a good tool to use when punching out ceilings.

building to allow drainage **(Figure 13.54)**. Many flat roofs are penetrated by chimneys, vent pipes, shafts, scuttles, bulkheads, and skylights. These roofs may be surrounded by a mansard-type facade that overhangs the outside walls, or they may be surrounded and divided by parapet walls **(Figure 13.55)**. These roofs may also support water tanks, HVAC equipment, antenna masts, solar panels, billboards, and other dead loads that may interfere with tactical ventilation operations and increase the likelihood of roof collapse **(Figure 13.56)**. If firefighters observe new dead loads (HVAC, water tanks, etc.) on the roof of an old building, they should be aware of the increased collapse potential created by the additional weight.

Flat roofs are commonly supported by horizontal joists or rafters similar to the joists used in floor systems. The structural elements of flat roofs consist of a wooden, concrete, or metal substructure covered with sheathing **(Figure 13.57, p. 370)**. The sheathing is, in some cases, covered with a layer of dense foam insulation under the weatherproof finish layer. There is often a concealed space between a flat roof and the ceiling of the top floor below. This space is referred to as an *attic, cockloft, crawl space,* or *interstitial space.* The underside of the roof assembly is often unprotected and will be exposed to the effects of any fire in this concealed void, which may contribute to early roof failure.

Figure 13.54 Even roofs that appear flat have a slight slope to allow for water drainage.

Figure 13.55 Roofs are often surrounded and divided by parapet walls.

Figure 13.56 Heavy dead loads on roofs can significantly contribute to structural collapse.

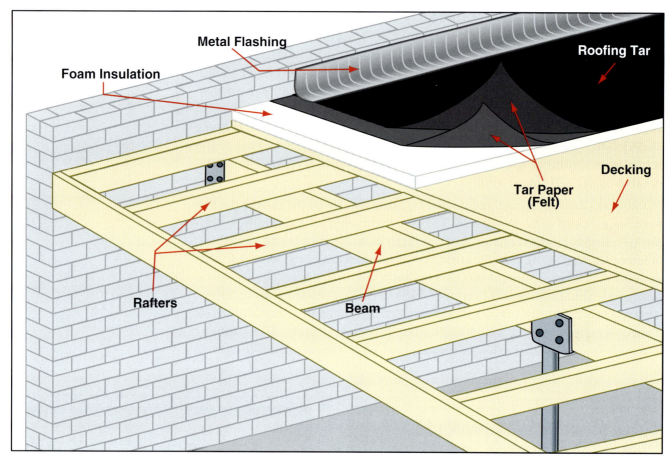

Figure 13.57 A common flat roof assembly.

Types of Flat Roofs

The general category of flat roofs includes several common styles and some that are less common. Sufficiently common to warrant discussion here are the inverted roof, rain roof, wooden deck roof, metal deck roof, concrete roof, poured gypsum roof, modern mansard roof, and panelized roof.

Inverted roof. Inverted roofs differ from conventional flat roofs primarily in the location of their main roof beams. In a conventional roof system the main joists are set at the final roof level, sheathing is attached to the tops of the joists, and a ceiling may be attached to the bottoms of the joists. More commonly, the ceiling is suspended below the joists, creating a concealed space. In the inverted roof, the main roof joists are set at the level of the ceiling, and a framework of 2- × 4-inch (50 mm by 100 mm) members is constructed above the main joists. The sheathing is attached to this framework, and the weatherproof covering is applied over the sheathing **(Figure 13.58)**. This is a fairly solid roof system that retains its structural integrity during a fire until the upright supports burn through.

From the outside, an inverted roof looks like any other flat roof, but the surface may feel *springy* or *spongy* to anyone walking on it. The design of the inverted roof often creates a concealed space several feet (meters) in height between the ceiling and the roof deck. The unprotected structural members within this concealed space are exposed on all four sides, so they are subject to severe damage from any fire within the space. Firefighters should familiarize themselves with any of these roofs in their districts by making thorough preincident planning surveys.

Rain roof. Very similar to an inverted roof is the so-called *rain roof*. While this can be found over any type of roof, it is most common on buildings with flat or arched roofs. The rain roof is built *over* an existing roof that has become so porous it does not keep out the rain or it sags sufficiently to allow rainwater to collect on the roof. The existing roof is left in place, and the new roof is built on a raised framework above the original roof **(Figure 13.59)**.

Rain roofs create several potential problems for firefighters. First, the void created between the two roofs may allow fire to burn undetected for some time and could result in an inaccurate size-up of the fire. Second, the existence of two separate roofs can seriously impede effective vertical ventilation or prevent it entirely. Finally, the original roof was not designed to support the additional weight, and therefore the entire roof assembly may be more susceptible to collapse.

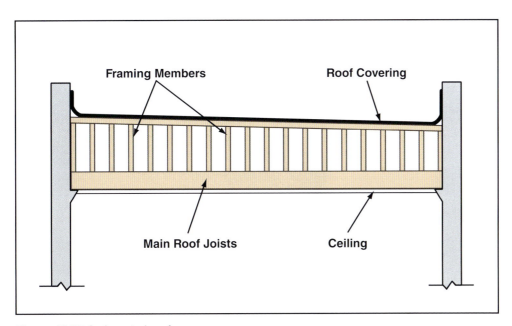

Figure 13.58 An inverted roof.

Figure 13.59 Rain roofs are built up over the original roof.

> **CAUTION**
>
> Some types of fire-resistant plywood delaminate and weaken over time, resulting in a deck that may not support the weight of a firefighter even if it has not been damaged by a fire. Identifying these hazardous roofs during preincident planning surveys is critical to firefighter safety.

Wooden deck roof. Wooden deck roofs may present a hazard if lightweight plywood or OSB decking is used. Panels of ⅜- to ⅝-inch (9 mm to 17 mm) thickness offer little fire resistance, but may be difficult to remove for tactical ventilation **(Figure 13.60)**.

Roofs sheathed with wooden planks are easier to strip but are more difficult in which to create louver vents or make trench cuts. The structural stability of the joists will vary depending on the span, the dimensions and spacing of the joists, and whether the joists are suspended by metal hangers.

Metal deck roof. Metal deck roofs consist of metal bar joists, which usually run across the narrow dimension of the building, over which metal decking is laid perpendicular to the joists **(Figure 13.61)**. In most cases, the metal decking is welded to the joists. Large-area metal deck roofs consist of large supporting beams that may run across the narrow dimension of the building or parallel to the long dimension, and bar joists that run perpendicular to the beams.

> **CAUTION**
>
> Unprotected metal deck roofs can be expected to fail within a few minutes of flame impingement. Because the heat of a fire will soften metal and make it more pliable, metal decking around roof vents and other openings may not support the weight of a firefighter.

Figure 13.60 Wooden decking has been installed prior to being covered by shingles. *Courtesy of the McKinney (TX) Fire Department.*

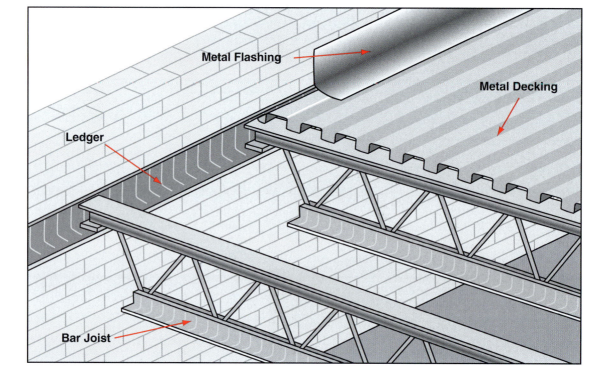

Figure 13.61 A typical metal deck roof assembly.

Concrete roof. Concrete roofs are constructed in a variety of ways. One of the most common is lightweight concrete poured over metal decking **(Figure 13.62)**. Another common concrete roof consists of precast Double-T panels **(Figure 13.63)**. Concrete roofs provide a smooth, hard surface that is structurally strong and highly resistant to fire, but it may be extremely difficult to breach for tactical ventilation. Opening these roofs may require special tools, such as jackhammers (concrete breakers), core drills, or burning bars, and will be a physically demanding and time-consuming operation. Because they are so difficult to breach, some concrete roofs have built-in knockout panels similar to those discussed in Chapter 9 regarding concrete walls. The presence of these roofs should be identified during preincident planning surveys.

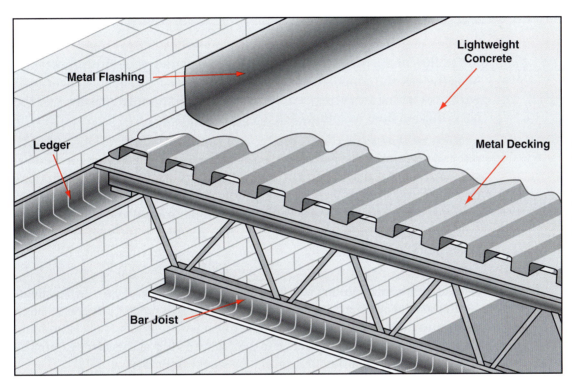

Figure 13.62 One type of concrete roof utilizes a lightweight concrete that is poured over the metal decking.

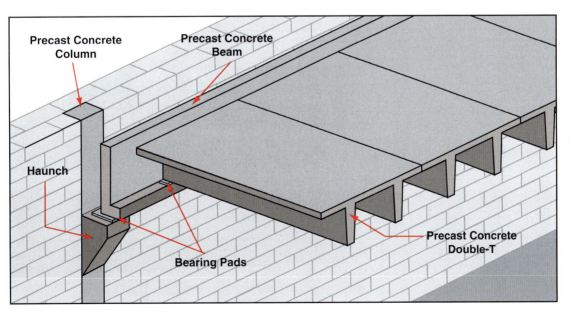

Figure 13.63 Another type of concrete roof uses precast concrete panels.

Lightweight concrete roofs may be cut using a rotary saw equipped with a masonry blade. Because it is difficult and time consuming to cut concrete roofs that are more than 4 inches (100 mm) thick, they are often designed with built-in access panels that can be lifted out in an emergency. Using existing openings, such as bulkheads, ventilators, scuttles, or skylights will certainly be the fastest way to ventilate these roofs and may be the only practical way. Once again, thorough preincident familiarization will greatly speed the process of ventilating these roofs.

Poured gypsum roof. Poured gypsum roofs consist of bar joists or I-beams with brackets welded to the joists. Gypsum board is placed on the brackets and is covered with a layer of gypsum cement up to 2½ inches (65 mm) thick to which wire mesh reinforcement is added. The gypsum board is then sealed with a weatherproof covering.

Because these roofs are constructed of materials that are highly resistant to fire, they retain their structural stability longer than some other roof types. Nonetheless, the supporting trusses can still fail early. The roof covering is easily cut with a power saw equipped with a metal-cutting blade, and the covering can then be rolled back to open the hole.

Modern mansard roof. This type of roof has characteristics of both pitched and flat roofs. As can be seen in the preceding section on modern mansard roofs, the perimeter of the roof consists of steeply pitched sections that surround a flat roof area in the middle. These roofs are most commonly supported by bridge trusses, and the same operational and safety considerations apply to these roofs as to any other pitched or flat roof — with two exceptions.

First, some modern mansard roofs are actually only facades, each consisting of a wall (with a triangular cross section) that has been added to the perimeter of a flat roof for aesthetic reasons **(Figure 13.64)**. This creates a depressed area in the middle of the roof that can range from a few feet to several feet (meters) deep. Unsuspecting firefighters can fall from the top of this facade onto the actual flat roof if visibility is obscured by smoke or darkness.

Second, in building these facade structures, an uninterrupted concealed space that extends around the entire perimeter of the roof may be created. This can allow fire to travel around the entire roof undetected.

> **WARNING!**
> The facades on modern mansard roofs are sometimes cantilevered beyond the exterior wall, creating an overhang that can collapse if fire weakens the bracing on the original roof.

Figure 13.64 A modern mansard roof.

Panelized roof. Many modern buildings have panelized flat roofs. These increasingly common roofs are discussed in the Lightweight Construction section later in this chapter.

Hazards of Flat Roofs

Firefighters preparing to ventilate a flat roof should quickly but carefully observe the roof before stepping onto it. They should look for signs of hot spots or sagging of the roof surface before and during ventilation operations. As noted earlier in this chapter, a sagging roof will often reveal itself when the vent pipes that penetrate the roof appear to be taller than usual. In addition, firefighters should always sound the roof before stepping onto it and continue to sound it when they are moving about on the roof.

> **WARNING!**
> Never step on any area of a flat roof that has not been sounded.

In some cases, hot spots can be identified by patches of melting snow and ice or heat waves rising from specific areas. Sagging of the roof's surface indicates damage to the substructure of the roof assembly. However, these observations are not always reliable so a thermal imaging camera (TIC) should be used, if available. A TIC may reveal both the hottest areas of the roof and the location and direction of roof supports. However, if the roof is heavily insulated, a TIC may not be as effective.

In the absence of a TIC, firefighters may have to cut one or more inspection holes to locate the direction and spacing of roof supports and the seat of the fire. Each of the signs just discussed indicates extreme heat directly below and suggests that the roof may be in danger of collapsing, either partially or totally. Crews working on flat roofs must exercise extreme caution if these signs exist or develop while work is in progress. In addition, firefighters should not congregate in any particular area because their weight will be concentrated on that section.

Some older buildings with flat roofs may have wooden or metal access ladders built onto the side of the structure **(Figure 13.65)**. These should generally not be used by firefighters because age and weathering may have made the ladders unsafe. If access from an adjacent roof is not possible, ground ladders or aerial devices should be used to gain roof access for tactical ventilation.

Inverted flat roofs create special hazards as well. This design also creates a concealed space, often several feet (meters) in height, which includes many unprotected wooden structural members. Heavy fire conditions can burn quickly through the 2- × 4-inch (50 mm by 100 mm) supporting members, causing the roof deck to collapse onto the roof joists. Likewise, roofs supported by unprotected steel members will often fail with relatively little direct fire exposure.

Other hazards that may be encountered on flat roofs include the security measures that some building owners have added to deter burglars from entering through skylights and other roof openings. Some have installed barbed wire or

Figure 13.65 Metal access ladders should not be used by firefighters.

razor ribbon around the perimeter of the roof **(Figure 13.66)**. Guard dogs can also be found on flat roofs of business and apartment buildings in high-crime areas. All of these security measures can injure firefighters or delay access to the roof for tactical ventilation.

Many buildings with flat roofs also have parapet walls that can be a help as well as a hazard to firefighters during ventilation operations. These walls may extend from a few inches (mm) to several feet (meters) above the roof surface. Properly constructed parapet walls can help prevent the spread of fire from building to building and can help prevent firefighters from accidentally falling or walking off the roof. However, high parapet walls create a potential fall hazard, and walls that are too low may cause firefighters to trip and fall over them **(Figure 13.67)**. Because the heights of parapet walls vary so much from building to building, firefighters must become familiar with those in their response districts through preincident planning surveys.

Before stepping off a parapet wall or ladder onto a flat roof, especially if the roof surface is obscured by smoke or darkness, firefighters should always sound the roof by striking it with the blunt end of an axe, rubbish hook, pike pole, or

Figure 13.66 Razor ribbon can be encountered on some rooftops.

Figure 13.67 Low parapet walls can allow firefighters to fall off the roof in poor visibility conditions.

other tool. This may give some indication of the condition of the roof, and it will reveal the vertical distance from the top of the wall to the roof. If firefighters must work on a roof when their vision is obscured, they should continually sound the roof as they shuffle-step on areas supported by structural members. Whenever these near zero-visibility conditions are encountered during an incident, this and any other significant information about conditions on the roof should be communicated to the IC.

Venting Flat Roofs

As with pitched roofs, flat roofs should be vented as close to directly over the seat of the fire as safely possible. Flat roofs may be vented by cutting a large square or rectangular ventilation hole, cutting a strip or trench vent, or by using existing roof openings such as ventilators, skylights, or monitors **(Figure 13.68)**. However, for a variety of reasons, existing roof openings must be used with discretion.

Existing roof openings may or may not be in the most desirable location. If not, opening them may draw fire, heat, and smoke to previously uninvolved areas of the building. This can threaten building occupants or interior fire attack crews, and it may cause additional sprinklers to open, which can reduce the efficiency of vertical ventilation. Also, existing openings may or may not be large enough to provide the needed ventilation. If not, they can be enlarged or used to supplement another opening cut in the roof.

Cutting holes in flat roofs. To create sufficiently large openings for the tactical ventilation of buildings with flat roofs, and to locate those openings where they will vent the fire without drawing it into uninvolved areas, cutting one large ventilation hole is usually the most effective method. Many flat roofs have a thick covering of tar and gravel or other material that may need to be removed or cut before cutting the sheathing. An axe can be used to cut the roof covering or to scrape away some of the gravel to facilitate cutting with a power saw. Thick tar coverings may gum up chain saws, so a rotary saw may be a better choice.

Figure 13.68 Flat roofs are ventilated in a similar manner to pitched roofs. *Courtesy of Matt Daly.*

Purlin — Horizontal member between trusses that supports the roof.

Ventilation holes in flat roofs should be cut parallel to the rafters and perpendicular to the outside walls of the building. Rafters or **purlins** can sometimes be located by sounding the roof. However, in many cases it will be necessary to make a diagonal cut in the roof until a structural member is found. Then, another cut is made to determine rafter direction as was previously described in the section entitled *Opening a Roof*. This process may also reveal the condition of the roof itself. If so, information about the roof's condition and stability should be communicated to the IC.

Once rafter location and direction have been determined, firefighters are ready to move to the desired location and begin cutting the ventilation opening. When cutting the ventilation opening, firefighters should work with the wind at their backs. They should start by making a cut across the leeward end so that the smoke will blow away from them as they continue to work. This should be followed by making parallel side cuts at least 4 feet (1.3 m) apart between the rafters **(Figure 13.69)**. These cuts should start at the ends of the first cut and be made as long as necessary to create an exit opening of the required size. The roof covering and the sheathing may then be pulled back, together or separately, with two pick-head axes, pike poles, or rubbish hooks **(Figure 13.70)**. If it is necessary to break out a section of ceiling below the exit opening, a rubbish hook or the butt of a pike pole will work.

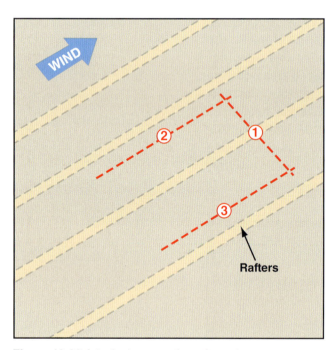

Figure 13.69 A typical *across-the-rafter* cut.

Figure 13.70 Rubbish hooks or other tools are used to pull back the roof covering.

Center-rafter or **louver cuts** may be performed in flat roofs in a manner similar to that just described but with an additional fourth cut connecting the other ends of the side cuts. Also, while a conventional square or rectangular ventilation opening may span several rafters, louver vents only leave one rafter in the center. If it is necessary to cut a strip or trench vent, the louver vents may simply be extended from one outer wall to the other across the full width of the building **(Figure 13.71)**.

Using existing openings. When smoke under pressure is issuing from a turbine vent, it may be more efficient to leave the vent alone. The ventilator is doing what it was designed to do; in most cases, it will expel smoke and heat more efficiently with the rotary vane in place than if it is removed. Removing the turbine takes time, does not increase the vent's efficiency, and can damage the vent pipe.

Roof monitors can also be used for vertical ventilation. To maximize their effect, at least two sides of the monitor housing should be opened or removed.

If bubble skylights are opened for tactical ventilation, the plastic bubble should be removed rather than broken. Likewise, the panes in wired glass skylights should be removed if possible, but they may have to be broken.

When glass skylights must be broken, firefighters should break a single pane first and pause before breaking out the remaining panes. The pause will give interior firefighters who may not have heard the warning an opportunity to move out of the way or to alert the vent crew of the need to delay breaking the remainder of the panes.

Louver Cut — Rectangular exit opening cut in a roof, allowing a section of roof deck (still nailed to a center rafter) to be tilted, thus creating an opening similar to a louver. Also called center rafter cut.

CAUTION
Interior crews should be warned before any glass skylights are broken.

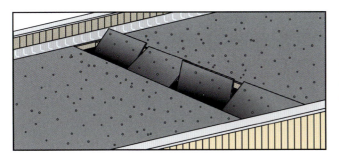

Figure 13.71 A trench cut extends from one side of the building to the other.

Arched Roofs

Arches are typically used to support roofs that must span large, open spaces unsupported by pillars or posts. Structures with this type of roof are typically convention centers, exhibition halls, sports arenas, and similar occupancies.

Arched roofs may be supported with bowstring trusses, or arches of steel, concrete, or laminated wood **(Figure 13.72, p. 380)**. Steel arches can be made from plate girders or trusses. Some wooden arches are laminated and glued under pressure at the factory. Others are constructed similar to trusses. Typically, arches are spaced at 16 to 20 foot (5 m to 6 m) centers.

Both horizontal and vertical forces continuously act on an arched roof. As the force of gravity bears down on the top of the arch, the resulting horizontal stresses attempt to force the ends of the arch apart. These forces are resisted by abutments or buttresses at the ends of the arch or by tension cables or tie rods between the ends of the arch **(Figure 13.73, p. 380)**. The presence of tie rods is often obvious from the metal star plates on the exterior of the building

Figure 13.72 An arched roof support.

Figure 13.74 Metal stars are often an indicator of the existence of tie rods.

Figure 13.73 Buttresses are used to counteract forces placed on the arch. *Courtesy of Ed Prendergast.*

(Figure 13.74). While buttresses are usually stable when exposed to fire, tension cables may lose their strength and integrity. Some arches may also contain hinges that permit some flexibility and allow for thermal expansion and contraction. These hinges can be found at the top of the arch or at the abutments.

Types of Arched Roofs

There are a variety of arched roof types. The three most common types are the bowstring arches, of which there are two major variations, and the trussless and lamella arches.

Bowstring truss roof. The bowstring truss roof, commonly found in older buildings housing a variety of commercial or industrial occupancies, uses an arch with a wooden or metal bottom chord. The top chords of these arches are usually laminated 2- × 12-inch (50 mm by 300 mm) or larger lumber **(Figure 13.75)**. The purlins (usually 2 × 10 inches [50 mm by 250 mm]) are covered by 1- × 6-inch (25 mm by 150 mm) or larger sheathing and composition roofing material. Under most fire conditions, this roof is quite strong because of the size of the lumber used in its construction. However, if the truss members burn away, the roof becomes vulnerable to collapse. The perimeter of the building and the arches are the strongest points.

Bowstring arch roof. These roofs incorporate the same or similar top chord as the truss roofs, but steel tie rods are used instead of bottom chords for lateral support with turnbuckles to maintain proper tension **(Figure 13.76)**.

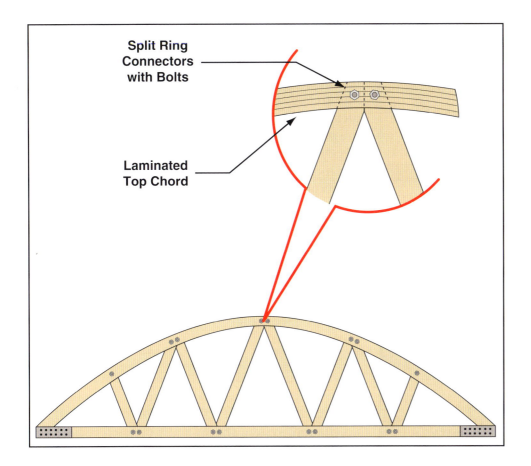

Figure 13.75 Components of the typical bowstring truss.

Figure 13.76 A bowstring arch roof.

The arches are easy to locate from the outside if the tie rods pass through the exterior wall to a plate or reinforcement star. Bowstring arches with steel tie rods have a history of early and sudden collapse when the tie rods are exposed to fire. Because the tie rods act to hold the outer walls together, these walls can be pushed outward when the tie rods fail, causing the entire building to collapse **(Figure 13.77, p. 382)**.

> **WARNING!**
> Because of the collapse potential, incident commanders must be extremely cautious about ordering crews inside or onto buildings using bowstring arch or truss construction and must carefully monitor elapsed time when deciding when to withdraw interior and roof crews.

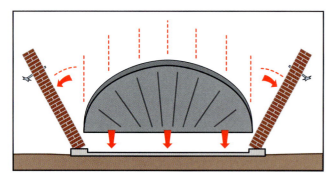

Figure 13.77 The roof collapses easily when tie rods fail.

Figure 13.78 A trussless arch roof.

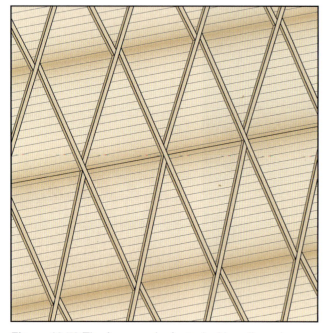

Figure 13.79 The framework of a typical lamella arch.

Trussless arch roof. The trussless arch roof uses massive arches of steel, concrete, or laminated wood buttressed into the ground at each end. These arches may be spaced between 16 and 20 feet (5 m to 6 m) apart. The arches are connected by purlins that run perpendicular to the trusses **(Figure 13.78)**. Rafters between the purlins support the roof decking. These roofs have large rafters and are covered by a layer of sheathing and roofing material. Over the arches are the strongest points on this type of roof.

Lamella arch roof. The lamella roof is another type of trussless arch made up of an interlocking geometric framework on which plank sheathing is laid **(Figure 13.79)**. The framework is usually constructed of dimensional lumber in which 2- × 12-inch (50 mm by 300 mm) wooden members are bolted together at the intersections with steel gusset plates. The roof sheathing is usually tongue-and-groove planking covered with composition roofing material.

Lateral support for lamella roofs is provided by exterior buttresses or internal tie rods with turnbuckles. The perimeter of the building is the strongest area. The lamella roof system shares many characteristics with the bowstring-type roofs, and the same operational and safety considerations apply. However, when 10 to 20 percent of a lamella roof burns away, sudden failure of the remainder of the roof is likely.

Hazards of Arched Roofs

Firefighters can estimate the hazards of some arched roofs by the size of the material and the span of the arches. In trussed arch roofs, the lower chord of the truss may be covered with a ceiling to form an enclosed cockloft or attic space. These concealed spaces are a definite impediment to effective tactical ventilation and may increase fire spread.

The single biggest hazard of arched roofs is the danger of sudden and total collapse, often without warning **(Figure 13.80)**. Because of this potential and because the rounded surface makes the use of roof ladders difficult, firefighters may have to work only from aerial devices when ventilating arched roofs. In addition, on roofs that have a tapered hip at one or both ends, failure of the main roof structure may cause these hip sections to push the end walls over.

Venting Arched Roofs

Arched roofs should be ventilated at the top of the arch directly over the fire or by a long, narrow strip vent along the centerline of the roof. A conventional square opening can be cut perpendicular to and between arches **(Figure**

13.81). A louver vent (which may be faster) can also be made. If a strip vent is to be cut along the centerline of the roof, a series of louver vents between the arches may be the best choice **(Figure 13.82)**.

Lightweight Roof Construction

Because of the rising costs of labor and building materials, lightweight roof construction has become much more common in recent years. In many modern buildings, heavy timber and plank sheathing have given way to laminated beams and 2- × 4-inch (50 mm by 100 mm) lumber covered by ½-inch (13 mm) plywood or OSB, regardless of building size. Because these lightweight materials are less fire resistive than traditional materials, firefighters have less time in which to ventilate before the roof becomes dangerously unstable. This section focuses on the three major types of lightweight roof construction: panelized roofs, trussed roofs, and those supported by wooden I-beams.

Panelized Roofs

Panelized roof construction consists of laminated beams of various sizes – commonly 6 × 36 inches (150 mm by 900 mm) – that span the length or width of the building. These beams are supported at their ends by **pilasters**, wooden

Pilaster — Rectangular masonry column built into a wall.

Figure 13.80 Arched roofs often collapse without warning. *Courtesy of Ed Prendergast.*

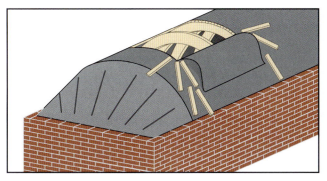

Figure 13.81 A conventional square opening can be cut in an arched roof.

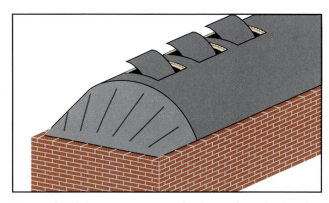

Figure 13.82 Louver vents can also be cut in arched roofs.

or steel posts, or saddles. Additional wooden or steel posts may provide support at intervals along the span. The beams may be bolted together to form lengths well in excess of 100 feet (30 m) and may be spaced between 12 feet (4 m) and 40 feet (12 m) apart. Wooden purlins, usually 4 × 12 inches (100 mm by 300 mm) with metal hangers are installed on 8-foot (2.4 m) centers between and perpendicular to the beams **(Figure 13.83)**. Wooden rafters or sub-purlins, usually 2 × 4 inches by 8 feet (50 mm by 100 mm by 2.4 m), are installed with metal hangers on 2-foot (.6 m) centers between and perpendicular to the purlins **(Figure 13.84)**. Sheets of plywood or OSB are nailed

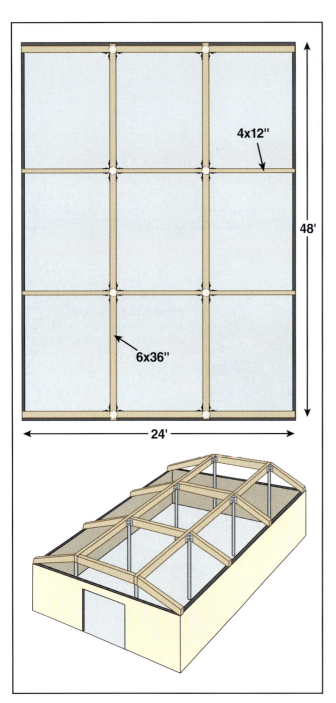

Figure 13.83 A basic panelized roof assembly.

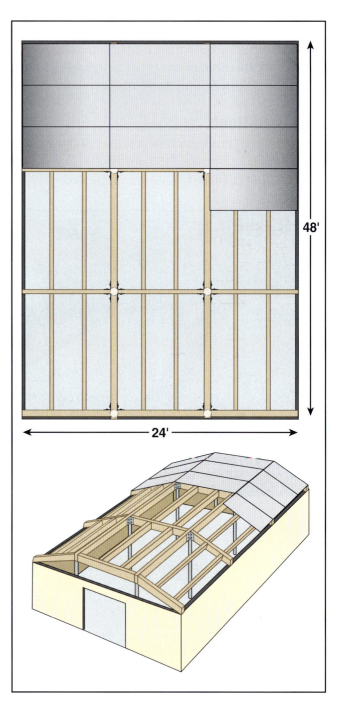

Figure 13.84 A partially sheathed panelized roof assembly.

over this framework and then covered with composition roofing material. The strongest parts of this construction are over the beams and around the perimeter of the building where the roof meets the exterior walls.

A three-layer, laminated insulation paper is sometimes used on the underside of panelized roof decking. This material offers little protection to the joists and decking panels because it consists of a tar-impregnated layer covered on either side by a layer of thin aluminum foil. When this insulation paper is subjected to fire, the foil peels away from the tar-impregnated paper and disintegrates, allowing the joists and decking to be exposed to fire.

Trussed Roofs

There are several common types of trusses used in roof construction, each with unique characteristics. However, all trusses have certain characteristics in common. Among their common characteristics are that all trusses, regardless of configuration or application, are designed as a series of triangles. All trusses also have a top chord and a bottom chord, connected by other components known as the *web*. Some trusses are designed as horizontal assemblies; others are designed with a pitch. The most common types of roof trusses are *parallel chord trusses* and *pitched roof trusses*.

Parallel Chord Trusses

Parallel chord trusses are constructed of metal or a combination of wood and metal. As the name implies, these trusses are designed with horizontal top and bottom chords that run parallel to each other. The top and bottom chords are connected by one or more web components. All parallel chord trusses are designed with web components that cause the space between the top and bottom chords to be mostly open. This design reduces the weight of the truss and allows easy penetration by ductwork, wiring, and plumbing. However, these open areas also allow for the rapid and unimpeded spread of heat, smoke, and fire.

The bridging effect of parallel chord trusses causes the top chord to always be in compression and the bottom chord in tension **(Figure 13.85)**. Because parallel chord trusses are capable of spanning large open spaces unsupported, they are used in a variety of applications and occupancies. The areas directly over the trusses and where they intersect with the outside bearing walls are the strongest points.

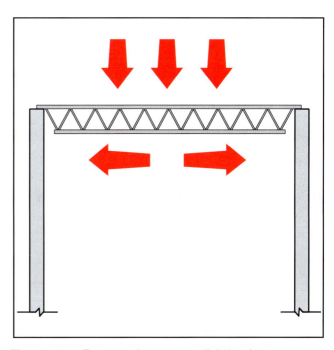

Figure 13.85 Forces acting on a parallel chord truss.

Wooden parallel chord trusses. Some parallel chord trusses are constructed of wooden components held together with sheet metal gusset plates, also known as **gang nails (Figure 13.86, p. 386)**. These gusset plates vary in size, thickness, and depth of penetration, but ⅜-inch (9 mm) prongs are common. Unless metal gusset plates are also corner-nailed, they can warp and pull out when exposed to fire. Like wooden I-beams (discussed later in this section), the bottom chords on wooden parallel chord trusses rest on and are supported by other beams or bearing walls **(Figure 13.87, p. 386)**.

Gang Nail — Form of gusset plate. These thin steel plates are punched with acutely V-shaped holes that form sharp prongs on one side that penetrate wooden members to fasten them together.

Figure 13.86 A wooden parallel chord truss with gang nails. *Courtesy of the McKinney (TX) Fire Department.*

Figure 13.87 Wooden parallel chord trusses that have been set in place.

Wooden/metal trusses. Other parallel chord trusses consist of wooden top and bottom chords that are cross-connected by web members made of steel tubing. The web members are usually made of 1-inch (25 mm) cold-rolled steel tubing with the ends pressed flat. Holes are punched in the flattened ends to receive connecting pins. These flattened ends are inserted into slots in the chords, and steel pins are driven through holes in the chord members and the web members, completing the assembly **(Figure 13.88)**. Normal spacing of these trusses is 2 feet (.6 m) on center. The areas directly over the trusses and where the roof meets the exterior walls are the strongest points. Like most other parallel chord trusses, only the top chord rests on and is supported by a beam or bearing wall, and the bottom chord is unsupported **(Figure 13.89)**.

Steel trusses. Still other parallel chord trusses are made entirely of steel components welded together. Also known as **bar joists**, these extremely strong assemblies often consist of top and bottom chords that are each made of two angle irons set in opposing directions. The web material may consist of

Bar Joist — Open web truss constructed entirely of steel, with steel bars used as the web members.

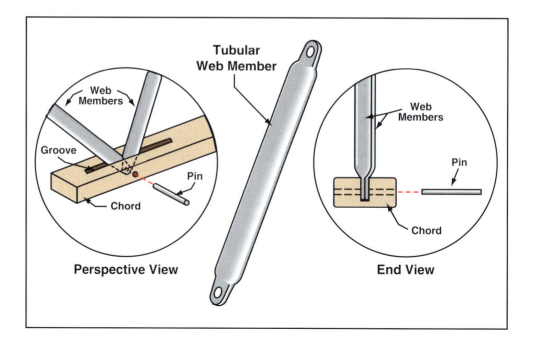

Figure 13.88 Some parallel chord trusses use both wood and metal.

individual members or a continuous strip of sheet stock formed into a zigzag pattern. In either case, the web material is sandwiched between the opposing pieces of angle iron and the entire assembly is welded together **(Figure 13.90)**. Bar joists are most often used to support a steel deck roof that is welded to the joists, and the joists may have significant spans.

Other steel trusses are made of angle iron components that are welded or bolted together. These massive trusses are most often found in large commercial or industrial occupancies.

> **WARNING!**
> Case studies indicate a potential for sudden collapse of fire-weakened parallel chord roof assemblies if interior crews inadvertently pull down on the bottom chord when opening ceilings.

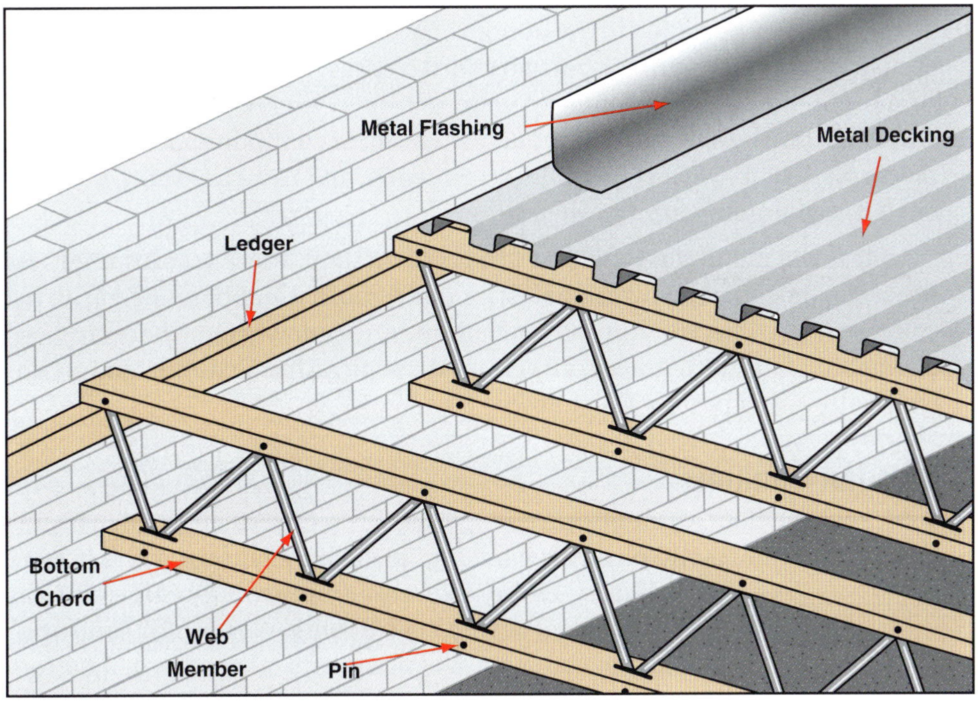

Figure 13.89 In these applications, the bottom chord is often unsupported.

Figure 13.90 Typical steel bar joists.

Pitched Roof Trusses

Pitched roof trusses are known by a variety of names depending upon their configuration and are made from a variety of materials. Common pitched roof truss configurations are the Howe, Pratt, and Fink trusses **(Figure 13.91, p. 388)**. Each of these trusses, and other less common ones, can be made of wood, metal, or a combination of the two. While each of these trusses has certain unique characteristics, they are all similar enough to be covered in the following discussion of pitched roof trusses. The pitched roof trusses used in residential construction are usually made of wood.

Like many parallel chord trusses, the most common pitched roof trusses are prefabricated of relatively small dimension wood, usually 2- × 4-inch (50 mm by 100 mm) lumber held together with metal gusset plates where the components intersect **(Figure 13.92)**. Pitched roof trusses are normally supported only by the outside bearing walls. In this type of construction, interior partition walls are essentially freestanding walls that do not actually support the truss at any point. However, to provide lateral support for partition walls, metal clips may be nailed to the bottom chord of the truss and to the top plate of a partition wall where the bottom chord crosses the wall. Even without the support of interior walls, spans of up to 55 feet (17 m) are possible using 2- × 4-inch (50 mm by 100 mm) components. The most common spacing between these trusses is 2 to 4 feet (.6 m to 1.2 m) on center, and ½-inch (13 mm) plywood or OSB is commonly used as sheathing.

Unless the metal gusset plates are corner-nailed, these trusses offer less fire resistance than conventional (stick built) roof assemblies, and early roof collapse is possible. In addition, roof failure can occur when the bottom chord or webbing fails, either from direct fire damage or from connected interior walls falling and pulling them down.

I-Beam — Steel or wooden structural member consisting of top and bottom flanges joined by a center web section so that the cross section resembles a capital I.

Wooden I-Beams

Some roof and floor assemblies are supported by prefabricated wooden beams that incorporate a solid piece of web material to connect the top and bottom chords. These assemblies are usually referred to as *engineered* or *wooden* **I-beams**. Wooden I-beams consist of three main components: a top chord, a bottom chord, and a solid ⅜-inch (9 mm) plywood or OSB web **(Figure 13.93)**. The web is connected to the top and bottom chords by a continuous, glued joint. The chords may be made of 2- × 3-inch (50 mm by 75 mm) lumber, 2- × 4-inch (50 mm by 100 mm) lumber, or a wooden

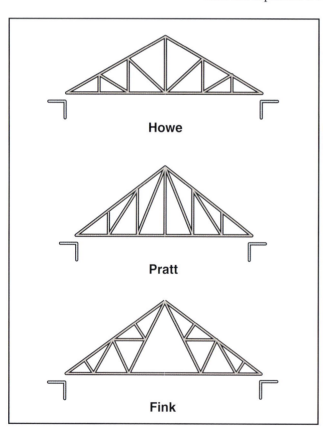

Figure 13.91 Howe, Pratt, and Fink trusses.

Figure 13.92 Typical pitched roof trusses.

laminate called *micro-lam*. Common spacing for this type of beam is 2 feet (.6 m) on center, and the area where the beams rest on the outside walls is the strongest point **(Figure 13.94)**.

Because the web in a wooden I-beam has relatively little mass and a large surface area for combustion, it can burn through and weaken quickly, causing collapse of the beam and the roof or floor assembly of which it is a part. If electrical conduits, plumbing, or heating and air conditioning ducts penetrate the web, some of the beam's strength is lost and an avenue for fire spread is created **(Figure 13.95)**. If the web remains intact during a fire, backdraft conditions may develop in the spaces between the I-beams. In a normal installation, the bottom chords on wooden I-beams are supported by other beams or by bearing walls.

Figure 13.93 The construction of a wooden I-beam.

Figure 13.94 Wooden I-beams that have been set in place.

Figure 13.95 Beams are sometimes penetrated for plumbing, electrical, and HVAC purposes.

Roof Coverings

Roof coverings are the weather-resistant materials applied over roof decking or sheathing. These coverings usually consist of one or more layers of underlayment (also called **substrate**) as a vapor barrier or insulation over which a waterproof covering is laid. The most common substrate is tar paper, also called *roofing felt*. Roof coverings may be combustible or noncombustible, depending on the application and local code requirements. Roof coverings are classified in NFPA® 203, *Guidelines on Roof Coverings and Roof Deck Construction*.

Substrate — Layer of material between a roof deck and the roof covering that may or may not be bonded to the roof covering. The most common substrate is roofing felt or tar paper.

The coverings most commonly used on pitched roofs are wooden shakes or shingles, composition shingles or roll roofing, ceramic or clay tile, slate, and light-gauge metal or fiberglass. On flat roofs, the most common coverings are tar and gravel, urethane/isocyanate foam, synthetic membrane, and metals in a variety of forms.

Wooden Shakes and Shingles

There are two main differences between wooden shakes and shingles. Shakes, which are much thicker than shingles, are split from large blocks of wood, so their shape and thickness are not uniform **(Figure 13.96)**. Because of their additional mass, shakes are somewhat less susceptible to ignition than shingles, but many jurisdictions still require them to be pressure-treated with fire retardant before installation. On the other hand, shingles are sawn from large rectangular blocks of wood, so they tend to be uniform in shape and thickness **(Figure 13.97)**.

Wooden shingles come in a variety of sizes and are made from a number of different woods. Cedar and redwood shingles are the most common because of their appearance and inherent durability. Because these wafer-thin, wooden slabs have so little mass, they tend to be highly combustible when dehydrated by time and weathering. Consequently, many jurisdictions allow wooden shingles to be used only if they have been pressure-treated with an approved fire retardant.

Shakes and shingles are usually nailed to wooden 1- × 4-inch (25 mm by 100 mm) or 1- × 6-inch (25 mm by 150 mm) plank **sheathing** with a space of about 1 inch (25 mm) between the planks. For obvious reasons, this form of sheathing is called spaced sheathing or skip sheathing **(Figure 13.98)**. There is usually a single layer of tar paper between the sheathing and the shakes or shingles.

For tactical ventilation, shakes or shingles can be quickly stripped from spaced sheathing by inserting the pick of an axe into the space between the planks and pulling the axe laterally in quick, short strokes. This alone may provide sufficient ventilation, but if not, the sheathing planks will have to be cut and stripped away as described earlier.

> **CAUTION**
> Wooden shakes and shingles can be very slippery when wet or covered by ice, snow, or moss. A roof ladder may be needed to provide safe footing during roof operations.

Sheathing — First layer of roof covering laid directly over the rafters or other roof supports. Sheathing may be plywood, chipboard sheets, or planks that are butted together or spaced about 1 inch (25 mm) apart. Also called Decking or Roof Decking.

Figure 13.96 Shakes are not uniform in size because they are split from large blocks of wood.

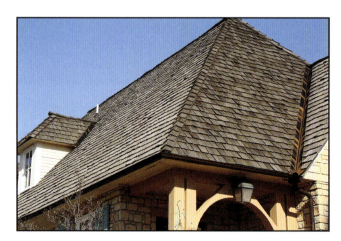

Figure 13.97 A wooden shingle roof.

Figure 13.98 Typical skip sheathing. *Courtesy of the McKinney (TX) Fire Department.*

Composition Roofing and Shingles

Composition roofing also comes in a variety of materials and shapes. The most common forms are shingles (in rectangular strips) and rolls of various widths **(Figure 13.99)**. As the name implies, they are usually made from a composite of an asphalt-base material and a granular mineral coating. The mineral coating provides weather resistance and acts as a fire retardant. Composition roofing containing fiberglass is also used in some areas.

Composition roof coverings are also usually installed over a layer of tar paper. The roof covering is nailed through the tar paper to solid plywood or OSB decking or butted plank sheathing.

While much less combustible than wooden roof coverings, composition roofing materials *will* burn. Once any part of this material has burned, the surrounding roof covering must be stripped far enough to expose unburned sheathing all around the burned area. This may require that the roof covering be stripped from the entire roof. A flat shovel works well for this operation. However, one of the most troublesome aspects of composition roofing for firefighters is that it is a common practice for a new layer of roofing to be applied over an existing one when a building is reroofed **(Figure 13.100)**. This process can continue over the life of a building, resulting in multiple layers of roofing accumulating on the roof.

Multiple layers can make the roofing much more difficult to cut for tactical ventilation because the thick asphaltic material tends to gum up the chains or blades of power saws. When multiple layers of roofing are found while ventilating a building during a fire, it indicates that the building is probably quite old and the added weight of the roofing materials, combined with the effects of the fire, may make the roof prone to early collapse.

Figure 13.99 A composition shingle roof.

Figure 13.100 It is often common to find multiple layers of shingles on a roof. These layers add significant weight to the roof.

Tar and Gravel

Tar and gravel roof coverings (also called *built-up roofs*) are very common on flat or nearly flat roofs. They are found on many types of buildings, ranging from single-family residences to large commercial or industrial buildings. During construction, melted roofing tar is *hot mopped* onto one or more layers of a tar paper substrate over plywood, OSB, or butted plank sheathing. Pea-sized gravel or crushed slag is commonly broadcast onto the melted tar to add durability and weather resistance **(Figure 13.101)**. This mineral material should be scraped away before the roof covering is cut with a power saw to protect the blade or chain. Because the tar is **thermoplastic**, it will soften and liquefy when exposed to the heat of a fire or that generated by a saw blade.

A single layer of tar and gravel roofing can be cut easily with a power saw or an axe, but this type of roofing is often found in multiple layers on the roofs of older buildings just as with the composition types of roof coverings. Older tar and gravel roofs may also be covered with a thick coating of foamed roofing (see following section), which often has a silver-colored finish layer. In either case, this type of roof covering can be cut and rolled back as a unit, or it may be louver cut.

> **Thermoplastic** — a petroleum-based product that softens with an increase of temperature and hardens with a decrease of temperature but does not undergo any chemical change.

Urethane/Isocyanate Foam

Urethane/isocyanate foams are applied to roofs in two forms. One is in the form of 4- × 8-foot (1.2 m by 2.4 m) sheets of foam insulation. The other form is called foamed-in-place applications. In either application, the foam is sealed by one or more layers of a weather-resistant covering **(Figure 13.102)**. While these foams may be applied to new roofs, they are often applied over older existing roof coverings. The latter may result in an unusually thick roof covering that slows cutting ventilation openings. These thick, heavily insulated roofs tend to hold heat longer than other roof coverings, which increases the likelihood of flashover or backdraft conditions developing. As always, firefighters should use their SCBA when ventilating these roofs due to the toxic products these products release when burned **(Figure 13.103)**.

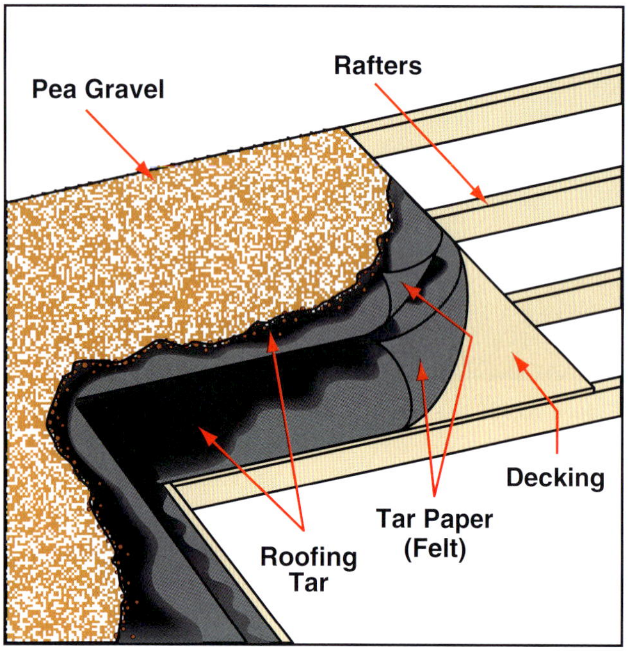

Figure 13.101 Gravel is often distributed on the roof while the tar is still hot to provide added protection.

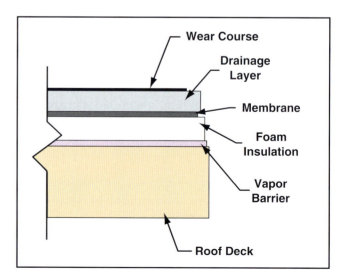

Figure 13.102 A cross section of a typical foam insulation roof.

Figure 13.103 Firefighters should always use SCBA when working in smoky conditions. *Courtesy of Matt Daly.*

Single-Ply/Synthetic Membrane

Several rubber-like liquid elastomers are applied to new roofs or over existing built-up roofs after the gravel has been removed. These coatings are then sealed with a single layer of any of a variety of approved flexible, water-resistant synthetic membranes (also known as *single-ply roofs*). These membranes are made of neoprene, polyvinyl chloride, chlorinated polyethylene, or bituminous sheets reinforced with polyester or fiberglass. The sheets are then sealed to the substrates below with an adhesive or by heating the underside of the sheet with an electric heat sealer gun or a propane torch. The seams in the membranes are overlapped and welded together by heating in the same way.

From a ventilation standpoint, these single-ply roof coverings can present serious problems for firefighters. While the membranes and their substrates are easily cut with common ventilation tools, they are highly combustible and liberate toxic products when they burn.

> **WARNING!**
> Single-ply/synthetic membrane roofing materials liberate highly toxic products of combustion when they burn. Firefighters must use their SCBA and people downwind of the fire may need to be evacuated.

Tile and Slate

Terra-cotta tile (sometimes called *Spanish* tile) roofs are common in some areas. They are made of either semicircular or S-shaped tiles that are *nested* together on the roof, usually over a single layer of tar paper on wooden sheathing **(Figure 13.104, p 394)**. Concrete, clay, or ceramic tile roofs use tiles that are usually flat, interlocking pieces that hook over 1- × 2-inch (25 mm by 50 mm) battens (sometimes called **furring strips**) nailed to the sheathing or directly to the rafters **(Figure 13.105, p. 394)**. Slate roofs are most common on churches and some larger, single-family dwellings. Slates are usually nailed directly to the roof sheathing.

Tile and slate roofs are somewhat fragile and often cannot be walked on without breaking the tiles. Firefighters walking on the roof may cause considerable damage while getting to the area to be ventilated. To reduce breakage, firefighters should step only on the lower half of the tiles, and they may spread their weight by working from roof ladders.

Furring Strips — Wood strips fastened to a wall, floor, or ceiling for the purpose of attaching a finish material.

Chapter 13 • Vertical Ventilation **393**

Figure 13.104 A typical Spanish tile roof.

Figure 13.105 A typical concrete tile roof.

CAUTION
Because tile or slate roofs cannot be sounded by traditional means, firefighters must remove tiles to identify where roof supports are located. To ensure that their weight is placed on roof supports, firefighters must remove tiles or slates ahead of them as they move about on these roofs.

Ideally, ventilating these roofs involves removing the individual tiles or slate. If possible, tiles should be removed and stacked, not broken. However, conditions may necessitate shattering the tiles or slate over the appropriate area. This is best accomplished with a sledgehammer, although a flat-head or pick-head axe can also be used. The sheathing can then be cut using an axe or power saw. Broken pieces of tile or slate may slide off the roof creating a safety hazard for anyone below; therefore, close coordination between ventilation crews and those working at ground level is critical. In addition, tile and slate roofs carry more weight per unit of surface area than any other roof style and may therefore be susceptible to early roof collapse. Also, when some buildings are remodeled, tile or slate is used to cover roof assemblies that were not designed to support the weight of these materials. Unless these existing roof assemblies are reinforced, the extra dead load makes these roofs susceptible to collapse.

Light-Gauge Metal or Fiberglass

This type of roof covering consists of aluminum, fiberglass, or 18- to 20-gauge steel panels over a wooden or metal substructure. The panels may be corrugated, ribbed, or shaped to simulate tiles or shakes **(Figure 13.106)**. Buildings with corrugated metal roofs often have plastic or fiberglass panels as skylights in shed and gable roof configurations **(Figure 13.107)**. If these panels are obscured by smoke, darkness, or snow, or if they have been painted over, firefighters stepping on the panels can fall through the roof. The ridge and the area where the roof crosses the outside bearing walls are the strongest points. Because these roof coverings are commonly used over the most lightweight substructures, this roof system has little fire resistance and is subject to early collapse. These roofing materials can be cut with an axe or a tin roof tool **(Figure 13.108)**. However, using a power saw with a metal-cutting blade or a chain saw is far more efficient.

Steel Clad

In an attempt to secure their property against entry through the roof, some property owners cover their roofs with steel grids or plates. The entire roof surface, including the steel components, is then resealed under a layer of tar. This seal coat sometimes makes the steel difficult to see and the roof very difficult to ventilate in a timely manner. Two types of these steel-clad roofs are common.

Figure 13.106 These metal roof panels are corrugated.

Figure 13.107 Plastic or fiberglass panels are often incorporated into metal roofs to allow natural light to enter.

Figure 13.108 Roof cutters are useful when cutting light-gauge metal roofs.

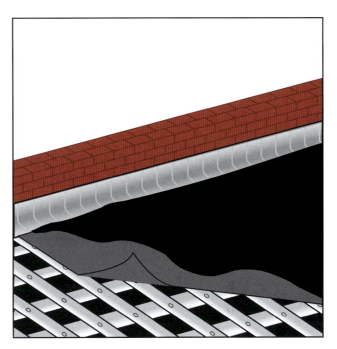

Figure 13.109 Steel straps are laid crossways and secured to the roof joists. Regular roofing materials such as tar are then laid over the straps.

The first type consists of ¼-inch (6 mm) thick by 2-inch (50 mm) wide steel straps laid out side-by-side on the roof. A second layer of straps crosses the first layer at right angles, and the straps are welded together at each intersection. The grid thus formed leaves small openings of from 6 to 8 inches (150 mm to 200 mm) square. The entire grid is lag-bolted through the roof to the joists below **(Figure 13.109)**. The roofing system is then covered with hot tar for weather resistance.

The second type consists of 4- × 8-foot (1.2 m by 2.4 m) sheets of steel, ranging from ⅛ to ¼ inch (3 mm to 6 mm) thick, being laid over the entire roof surface. The plates are then welded together to form a continuous layer of steel. Again, hot tar is applied for weather resistance.

Steel-clad roofs hold in heat and smoke, promote the development of flashover and backdraft conditions, impede ventilation efforts, and increase the chances of roof collapse due to the added weight. Because a ¼-inch (6 mm) steel plate weighs about 10 pounds per square foot (49 kg/m²), a 20- × 50-foot (6 m by 15 m) roof would have approximately 10,000 pounds (4 536 kg) added to it. The only effective way to prevent this type of construction from interfering with ventilation operations is to learn of its existence through preincident planning surveys and then to develop procedures for dealing with it.

The buildings most likely to have these measures will be high-value occupancies, although in high-crime areas they will also be found on ordinary commercial and industrial buildings. Because it may also discourage potential burglars, some building owners or occupants may be willing to post a prominent sign on the front of the building stating that the building has a steel-clad roof. This sign can alert firefighters during a fire so that the steel roof protection can be taken into account during size-up and planning.

Existing Roof Openings

Instead of having to cut through roof coverings and sheathing to create a ventilation exit opening, openings may already exist in the form of scuttle hatches, penthouses or bulkheads, skylights, monitors, turbine vents, light and/or ventilation shafts, ridge vents, and clerestory windows. With the exception of light and ventilation shafts, all such openings are likely to be covered and locked or secured in some manner against entry. Therefore, the covers on virtually all existing roof openings will have to be forced open or removed using whatever tools the vent team brought with them to the roof. All existing roof openings should be identified and evaluated during preincident planning surveys.

Scuttle Hatches

Scuttle hatches are normally square or rectangular metal-covered hatches that provide an exit from an attic or cockloft onto the roof and are often accessed from the top floor or the attic by a ladder **(Figure 13.110)**. If the scuttle hatch is forced open from the outside for tactical ventilation, any walls enclosing the scuttle access may need to be removed.

Penthouses (Bulkheads)

These structures usually enclose the tops of stairways that terminate on the roof, and they usually have a metal-clad exterior door of standard size **(Figure 13.111)**. Penthouse doors may be forced open in the same manner as other doors of a similar type. Once the door is opened, it should be blocked open to prevent it from closing and thereby disrupting the ventilation profile.

Skylights

Whether skylights are simply sources of natural light or coverings over large atria, they may be used effectively to ventilate heat and smoke **(Figure 13.112)**. In fact, some skylights are thermoplastic units that are designed to soften and fall out from the heat of a fire and thereby ventilate the building. Other types of skylights will have to be removed or broken out. They should be removed if possible. In many cases, the skylight can be lifted off if the flashings on all sides are pried loose. An alternative is to pry loose three sides and use the fourth side as a hinge **(Figure 13.113)**. Skylights equipped with thermoplastic panels or ordinary window glass can act as automatic vents because the temperature of a fire will melt the plastic or cause the glass to break and fall out. Even though skylights equipped with wired glass resist being broken, it may be faster to break the glass panels than to remove them for tactical ventilation.

Figure 13.110 A roof scuttle hatch.

Figure 13.111 Penthouses typically have metal clad exterior doors.

Figure 13.112 Atrium areas are often covered by a skylight.

Figure 13.113 Skylights can sometimes be hinged open.

In some buildings, especially those with corrugated metal roofs, translucent fiberglass panels may have been installed as an inexpensive form of skylight. If such a roof is covered by snow, or if visibility is reduced by smoke or darkness, firefighters can step on these panels and fall through the roof. In addition, these panels are highly flammable and may burn out quickly in a fire leaving an opening through which unwary firefighters might fall.

Monitors

Monitor vents are square or rectangular structures that penetrate the roofs of single-story buildings to provide additional natural light and/or ventilation. A monitor may have metal, glass, wired glass, or louvered roofs or sides **(Figure 13.114, p. 398)**. During a fire, monitors with ordinary glass panels provide ventilation when the glass breaks. If the fire has not yet generated enough heat to break the glass, the glass can be broken or removed by firefighters.

Turbine (Rotary Vane) Vents

Many commercial and residential structures have turbine vents on their roofs **(Figure 13.115, p. 398)**. In most cases, it is not necessary to remove the turbine for tactical ventilation — and removing it may even be counterproductive. Many fire fighting texts have recommended that turbine vents be removed

> **WARNING!**
> If visibility is obscured by smoke or darkness, skylights that have been opened or removed for tactical ventilation represent a potentially fatal fall hazard for firefighters working on the roof.

Figure 13.114 A typical roof monitor.

Figure 13.115 Turbine vents function more effectively when left intact.

to maximize ventilation efficiency. However, current practice in some of the busiest and most experienced truck companies in North America is to leave turbine vents alone. According to these firefighters, removing the turbines can actually reduce the ventilation efficiency of these openings. Turbines are designed to vent the spaces below them, and during a fire they should be allowed to do the work they were intended to do.

Light and Ventilation Shafts

Light and ventilation shafts in buildings can act as natural chimneys during a fire. This effect can cut off one possible means of egress for the occupants of the building. Except for the need to sometimes break windows within the shaft, light and/or ventilation shafts usually do not require opening or enlarging for tactical ventilation. To break the windows, an axe or other heavy tool can be lowered to the level of the window. The tool is then hoisted up far enough for it to be thrown outward from the wall, and then allowed to swing back and strike the window **(Figure 13.116)**.

If these shafts are not protected by a parapet wall or railing, they are a potentially fatal fall hazard to firefighters on the roof **(Figure 13.117)**. If vision is obscured by smoke or darkness, firefighters can fall into unprotected shafts — another reason why sounding a roof is especially important.

Figure 13.116 Tools can often be swung from above to break open windows.

Ridge Vents

Some newer residential buildings with pitched roofs have narrow, plastic attic vents that run the entire length of the ridge **(Figure 13.118)**. Because the vent opening is very narrow, these vents are almost invisible from the ground under normal circumstances. When there is smoke in an attic equipped with these vents, their presence is obvious because of the smoke issuing from the entire length of the ridge. However, simply pulling off the ridge vent will not provide an opening large enough to vent the fire below so a conventional ventilation exit opening will be needed.

Clerestory Windows

Some residential and small office buildings have a horizontal row of windows installed on a vertical wall between two offset roof sections **(Figure 13.119)**. These windows are designed to add natural light and ventilation. Under fire conditions, these windows can be opened or broken out faster than a vent hole can be cut in the roof and will be more economical to repair after the fire.

Figure 13.117 Firefighters may easily fall into roof lightwells in low visibility conditions.

Figure 13.118 Ridge vents typically run the entire length of the ridge.

Figure 13.119 Clerestory windows provide natural light and ventilation to structures.

Cutting the Ventilation Exit Opening

As previously discussed, before the ventilation exit opening is cut, the location of the fire should be determined and the opening made as close to the seat of the fire as safely possible. If a TIC is unavailable, firefighters may have to cut one or more inspection holes to locate the seat of the fire. Ideally, the ventilation exit opening should be made directly over the seat of the fire; however, this can be *extremely dangerous* if the roof has been weakened by the fire. The location of the ventilation exit opening must be based upon the type of roof construction, condition of the roof, fire conditions, available tools and equipment, and the experience, capabilities, and limitations of the vent crew.

> **WARNING!**
> If there is any doubt about the structural integrity of any part of a roof, firefighters should not be allowed in the questionable area. Ventilation operations in that area should be limited to those that can be performed from an aerial device.

When a ventilation exit opening is cut, it should be large enough to accomplish the purpose. The time required to enlarge an opening of inadequate size or to cut several smaller holes is greater than that required to make one large opening. One 8- × 8-foot (2.4 m by 2.4 m) opening is equal in area to four 4- × 4-foot (1.2 m by 1.2 m) holes **(Figure 13.120)**. When cutting through a roof, firefighters should make the opening square or rectangular and at right angles to the bearing walls to increase firefighter safety and to facilitate repairs after the fire.

Even though firefighters may use a power saw to cut the traditional large square opening, they may still have to contend with the nails in two or more rafters in order to pull the sheathing **(Figure 13.121)**. This can be a slow and very physically demanding process. On the other hand, rectangular, louver vents can be made very quickly and with much less effort **(Figure 13.122)**. If a larger opening is needed, the hole can be lengthened and used for trench ventilation (described later in this chapter), or a closely grouped series of holes can be cut.

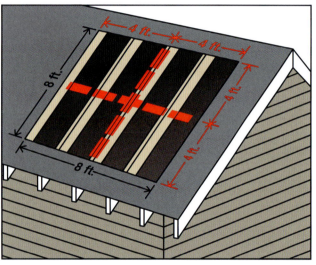

Figure 13.120 One 8- × 8-foot (2.4 m by 2.4 m) opening is equal in area to four 4- × 4-foot (1.2 m by 1.2 m) holes.

Figure 13.122 A rectangular louver vent.

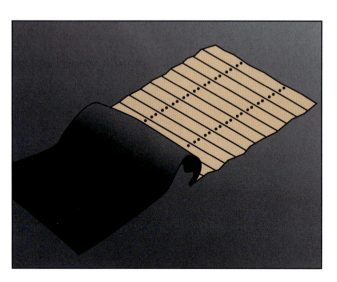

Figure 13.121 Sheathing can be difficult to pull if two or more rows of nails must be pulled as well.

Louver Vents

Cutting louver vents is often the fastest and most efficient way of opening a roof. Unlike large, square ventilation openings, in a louver vent there is always a rafter in the center of the sheathing being cut so that a constant reference point is maintained with the rafters. Knowing the location and direction of the rafters and the type of sheathing are critical to safe and efficient roof cutting operations **(Figure 13.123)**.

Basically, there are two methods that have proven effective for cutting louver vents in roofs. Both methods employ the center-rafter principle and take advantage of the roof's construction to facilitate opening the roof. In the first and most common method — the center-rafter cut, the longest cuts are made parallel to the rafters. In the other method — known as dicing — the longest cuts are made across the rafters.

Figure 13.123 It is important that firefighters practice ventilation operations regularly.

Center-Rafter Cut

The first of these methods involves cutting a long, rectangular center-rafter vent **(Figure 13.124)**. This method is sometimes referred to as *cutting with the rafters*. With a rafter spacing of 2 feet (.6 m) on center, the hole will be approximately 4 feet (1.2 m) wide and as long as is necessary.

The following steps outline the procedures for a center-rafter cut:

Step 1: Make the first cut parallel to rafter **A**, cutting 2 to 3 inches (50 mm to 75 mm) from the rafter to miss any metal joist hangers.

Step 2: If the roof is sheathed with plywood or OSB or if there are multiple layers of roof covering, make the second cut by starting near rafter **A**, rolling over rafter **B** without cutting it, and stopping just short of rafter **C**.

NOTE: If there is relatively thin roof covering over plank sheathing, it may not be necessary to make this end cut because there is a separation between each plank.

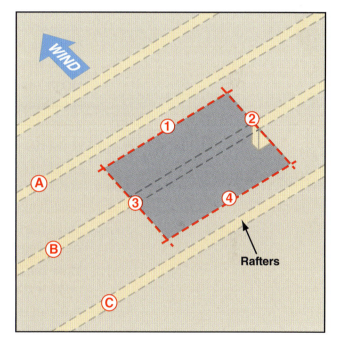

Figure 13.124 In a center-rafter cut, the longer cuts are made parallel to the rafter.

Step 3: Make the third cut (if necessary) by starting at rafter **A**, rolling over rafter **B** without cutting it, and stopping short of rafter **C**.

Step 4: Make the fourth and final cut parallel to rafter **C**, cutting as close to the rafter as possible without hitting any joist hangers.

Step 5: Push down on the near edge of the louver to expose the far edge, and then pull the far edge to fold back the sheathing and open the vent away from the crew.

> **NOTE:** If conditions require, plank sheathing can be stripped away with pike poles or rubbish hooks instead of being tilted into a louver vent.

Step 6: If it is necessary to enlarge the hole, repeat either Steps 1, 2, and 4 or Steps 1, 3, and 4 depending on whether the original opening is enlarged to the right or the left.

A center-rafter cut works equally well on pitched or flat roofs. This is particularly true in newer buildings with 2- × 4-inch (50 mm by 100 mm) trusses set on 24-inch (.6 m) centers.

Dicing

A second method of louver venting, sometimes called *rolling the rafters*, involves making the two longest cuts perpendicular to (across) the rafters. Subsequent cuts are made parallel to the rafters but in the center between the rafters instead of adjacent to them **(Figure 13.125)**.

The following steps outline the procedures for the dicing method:

Step 1: If the roof is sheathed with diagonal planks, plywood or OSB, or if there are multiple layers of roof covering, start the first cut centered between rafters *A* and *B*. Cut across rafters *B* and *C* without cutting them, stopping halfway between rafters *C* and *D*.

> **NOTE:** If the roof covering is thin and over perpendicular plank sheathing, it may not be necessary to make this cut because there is a separation between each plank.

Step 2: Make the second cut about 4 feet (1.2 m) long, centering it between rafters *A* and *B*.

Step 3: Make the third cut centered between rafters *B* and *C*, making it the same length as the second cut.

Step 4: Make the fourth cut centered between rafters *C* and *D*, making it the same length as the second and third cuts.

Step 5: Make the fifth and final cut in the same manner as the first cut, except make it at the opposite ends of the second, third, and fourth cuts.

Step 6: Once all the cuts are completed, tilt the sheathing between the cuts to open the louvers **(Figure 13.126)**.

> **NOTE:** Regardless of the cutting tool used, it is generally best to complete as many cuts as possible before pulling or folding back the roof covering and sheathing. This will help reduce the firefighters' exposure to heat and smoke during the cutting operations.

Step 7: To enlarge the opening, repeat either Steps 1-4 or Steps 2-5 to widen it, or repeat Steps 1, 2, 3, and 5 to lengthen it. In either case, repeat Step 6 to tilt the louvers.

Rolling Back Panelized Roofs

To quickly and efficiently create a large ventilation exit opening in a lightweight roof, firefighters can use a method some call *rolling back the roof*. This technique requires four firefighters – two with chain saws and two with rubbish hooks – working in unison. This method is possible because the decking on

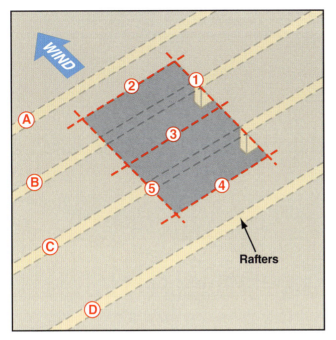

Figure 13.125 The pattern of cuts in a typical dicing operation.

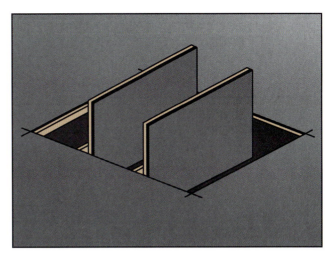

Figure 13.126 Diced sections are tilted up after the cuts are made.

these roofs is typically very thin compared to conventional roof decking. When finished, the opening will measure approximately 8 feet (2.5 m) wide times the distance between roof supports, which may be from 12 to 40 feet (4 m to 12 m).

NOTE: Unlike any other roof cut, this method REQUIRES that rafters or sub-purlins be cut.

The steps in rolling back a panelized roof are as follows:

Step 1: After sounding the roof to locate two adjacent roof beams, cut through the roof decking near the leeward end of the intended opening from one purlin to the next.

Step 2: Make two simultaneous side cuts starting from the ends of the first cut and perpendicular to it, cutting from the leeward end of the intended opening toward the windward end.

NOTE: The side cuts should be made a few inches (mm) from the adjacent purlin to avoid cutting into the joist hangers supporting the rafters or sub-purlins.

Step 3: As the saw operators continue cutting from the leeward end toward the windward –cutting through each rafter or sub-purlin as they go – the other two firefighters roll the roof decking back with their rubbish hooks.

Trench (Strip) Ventilation

Primarily a defensive maneuver, **trench ventilation** is sometimes referred to as *strip ventilation*. In some departments the term *strip vent* is used to describe a *louver vent*; however, the terms *strip* and *trench* are used interchangeably here to describe a ventilation exit opening that extends from one outside wall to the other, including the metal flashing at both ends **(Figure 13.127, p. 404)**. The term *trench* may be somewhat misleading. If firefighters assume they should

Trench Ventilation — Defensive tactic that involves cutting an exit opening in the roof of a burning building, extending from one outside wall to the other, to create an opening at which a spreading fire may be cut off. Also called Strip Vent.

Figure 13.127 Trench cuts extend from one outside wall to the other, including the metal flashing.

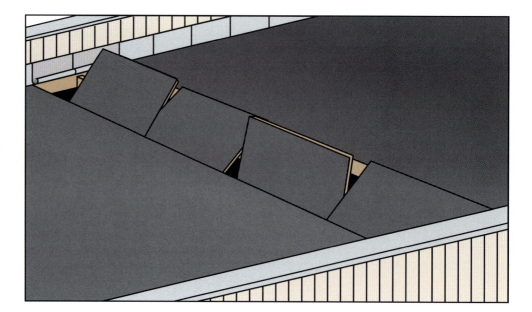

cut a long, deep hole and cut the rafters, purlins, or other supporting members, the roof system may be seriously weakened at that point. When creating an opening for trench ventilation, firefighters should cut only the roof covering and sheathing and not the members supporting the roof.

When done correctly, trench ventilation can help confine a fire to one section of a building by preventing the horizontal spread of heat, smoke, and fire beyond the opening. Trench ventilation has proven to be particularly effective in limiting the spread of attic fires in strip malls and other buildings that have long, narrow, common attics.

Trench ventilation is accomplished by cutting an opening in the roof, at least 4 feet (1.2 m) wide, across the entire width of the building. It is imperative that the vent extend fully from one outside wall to the other and any rain flashing is bent up out of the way. If any part of the roof within the vent opening is left intact, the fire can burn past the trench vent and involve the rest of the building. If the fire being cut off is not in the attic, the ceiling below must also be breached once the roof has been opened.

In most cases a center-rafter (louver) cut is fastest for making a trench vent. However, depending upon roof construction and rafter orientation, other methods may be more appropriate.

> **CAUTION**
> Because making a trench cut takes time, it is essential that it be started far enough ahead of the advancing fire to allow sufficient time to complete it before the fire reaches that point.

> **Vertical Ventilation Scenario:**
>
> On a rainy afternoon, you and your engine company arrive at the scene of a fire involving two rooms on the A side of the top floor of a large old two-story, wood-frame dwelling. You are ordered to open the roof to ventilate. The roof has a 6-in-12 pitch and is covered with weathered wooden shingles.
>
> - How would you determine where to ventilate the roof?
> - Where would you locate ground ladders?
> - What tools and equipment would you take to the roof?

- How would your tool selection change if the roof were covered by slate?
- Would your tool selection change if the roof were flat?
- What size ventilation opening would you cut?
- Where would you make the first cut?

Summary

Vertical ventilation offers a number of benefits to the overall fireground operation at structure fires. Properly done, vertical ventilation can influence the behavior of an interior structure fire to protect firefighters and other occupants by channeling heat and smoke away from them. Vertical ventilation can also reduce property damage by limiting the horizontal spread of a fire. Done at the right time, vertical ventilation can prevent both flashovers and backdrafts by allowing heat and smoke to vent harmlessly into the atmosphere.

However, vertical ventilation is also a potentially very dangerous operation. Even though the goal of ventilation crews is to perform their duties as quickly and efficiently as possible, whenever firefighters must operate on fire-weakened roofs that may collapse without warning, they may be in serious jeopardy. Firefighters may also fall from steeply pitched roofs that are slippery from rain, snow, or ice, and they may stumble over low parapets or into open light wells. Firefighters can be overcome by heat and fatigue while performing strenuous tasks on hot, wind-protected roofs surrounded by high parapet walls. Therefore, firefighters must protect themselves by learning as much as possible about the construction of the buildings within their response districts and devising plans for dealing with known hazards safely. They must know and apply the most efficient use of their ventilation tools and equipment. In every situation, they must function as a team and look out for each other. They must practice these skills so that they can get the job done quickly, thus reducing their exposure to risk. Finally, they must develop and maintain the physical and psychological strength and stamina required to perform vertical ventilation safely and effectively.

Review Questions

1. What are safety considerations for vertical ventilation operations?
2. What tools and equipment are commonly used for vertical ventilation?
3. What are the common types of roofs? What are the hazards associated with each?
4. What are the various types of lightweight roof construction?
5. What are the hazards associated with lightweight roof construction?
6. What are common types of roof coverings?
7. What existing roof openings may be used for vertical ventilation?

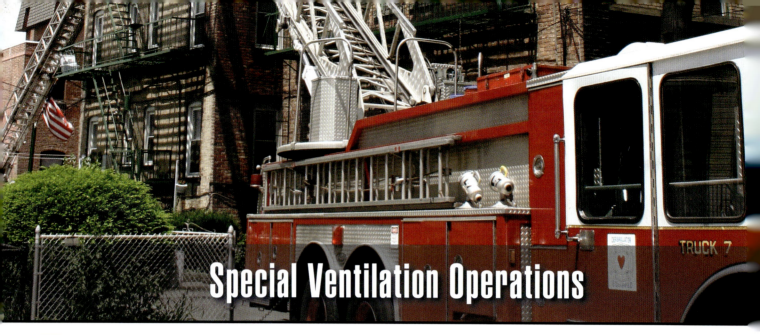

Special Ventilation Operations

Chapter Contents

CASE HISTORY ... 409	**HVAC and Smoke-Control Systems** ... 424
High-Rise Fire Operations ... 410	Built-In Ventilation Devices ... 425
Staffing ... 410	**Underground Structures** ... 428
Fire Attack ... 410	**Windowless Buildings** ... 429
Elevators ... 411	**Highly Secure Buildings** ... 429
Fire Behavior in High-Rise Buildings ... 412	**Remodeled Buildings** ... 430
High-Rise Ventilation ... 414	**Summary** ... 431
Vertical (Top) Ventilation ... 415	**Review Questions** ... 431
Channeling Smoke ... 417	
Ventilating Below the Fire ... 422	
Ventilating the Fire Floor ... 422	
Ventilating Above the Fire ... 423	

Divider page photo courtesy of Ron Jeffers.

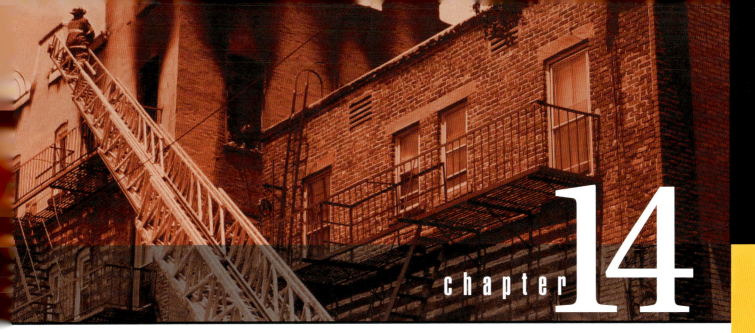

chapter 14

Key Terms

Atrium 425	Penthouse 417
Curtain Boards 425	Smoke Damper 424
Lobby Control 411	Stack Effect 412
Mushrooming 413	Stratification 413
Neutral Pressure Plane 418	

Special Ventilation Operations

Learning Objectives

After reading this chapter, students will be able to:

1. Summarize the challenges associated with high-rise fire operations.
2. Summarize fire behavior in high-rise buildings.
3. Describe three methods for ventilating high-rise buildings.
4. Describe the guidelines for using HVAC systems to control smoke movement in a building.
5. Summarize the considerations for ventilating an underground structure.
6. Summarize the considerations for ventilating a windowless building.
7. Summarize the considerations for ventilating a secured building.
8. Summarize the considerations for ventilating a remodeled building.

Safety Points

While reading this chapter, keep the following safety points in mind:

- Beware of falling glass and other debris in the collapse zone.
- No one should use elevators in a burning building unless the officer in charge on the fire floor determines that it is safe to do so.
- Beware of the potential stack effect when working in stairwells and other vertical shafts.
- Beware of light wells and other roof openings into which a firefighter might fall.

Chapter 14
Special Ventilation Operations

Case History

According to NIOSH Report F99-01, firefighters in New York state were called to a fire in a partially sprinklered ten-story apartment building in December of 1998. As responding units approached the rear of the building, an orange glow could be seen in the window of an apartment on the top floor. Upon arrival, firefighters received a report of an occupant trapped in the apartment next to the one that was burning.

While firefighters were struggling to connect attack lines to the stairwell standpipe on the ninth floor, a three-member search team crawled through heavy smoke on the tenth floor trying to locate the fire. When they reached the burning apartment and opened the door, wind blew fire and smoke out into the hallway and a flashover occurred. The crew was able to transmit a Mayday before succumbing to the intense heat. The three firefighters were quickly located but were unresponsive. They were treated at the scene and transported to a nearby hospital where they were pronounced dead of smoke inhalation and thermal burns.

The subsequent investigation revealed that the fire was not reported for 20 to 30 minutes after it was discovered because the elderly occupants had attempted to extinguish the fire with small pans of water. In addition, the sprinkler system that covered the hallways was inoperative because the control valves had been turned off.

As in many other case histories, investigators had to reconstruct what happened from the evidence available after the incident. This process sometimes leaves as many questions as answers. In this case, it is uncertain how the outcome would have been different if the sprinklers had been operational or the search team had waited for hoselines to be connected and charged before entering the hallway. Nor is it clear what would have happened if positive-pressure ventilation (PPV) had been used to pressurize the building before the door to the burning apartment was opened. What is clear is that the air flow into a burning building must be controlled if possible until attack lines are charged and ready.

Given the cost of land in urban areas throughout North America, high-rise structures continue to be built — even in suburban areas and rural communities. This type of development presents new challenges for many small fire

Figure 14.1 Smaller fire departments may be unprepared when high-rise structures are constructed in their areas.

departments that previously had to deal only with fires in one- and two-story buildings. Many fire departments now must perform rescues or fight fires well above the reach of their longest ladders **(Figure 14.1)**.

Many cities and towns have also seen the development of highly secure windowless and underground structures. To deal with these unusual occupancies, many fire departments have had to develop new strategies and tactics based upon the construction of new buildings and available resources. This chapter addresses the problems associated with tactical ventilation in high-rise buildings and other unusual structures such as those without windows and those underground, highly secure, and remodeled buildings.

High-Rise Fire Operations

High-rise fires present numerous challenges for firefighters. Some of these challenges include the following:

- Limited access
- Large numbers of offices or apartments
- Heavy occupant loads
- Falling glass and other debris
- Rapid smoke and fire spread through vertical shafts
- Locked interior doors
- Low water pressure
- Having to climb an extraordinary number of stairs to reach the fire

These are but a few examples of what firefighters can expect when fighting a high-rise fire. Crews may also have to deal with trapped occupants, unfamiliar floor layouts, complex elevator and HVAC systems, built-in fire protection equipment, and communications problems — each of which may complicate fireground operations.

Staffing

The staffing required for operations in this type of building may be several times greater than that required for similar fires in smaller structures. The problems of communication and coordination between attack and ventilation crews can be compounded as the number of involved personnel increases. In addition to the extra personnel required to handle the logistics of fighting a high-rise fire, the physical exertion required just to reach the fire floor or the roof may mean that crews will have less energy left to perform their assigned tasks. Consequently, crews may have to be relieved sooner than they normally would, and they may have to be rotated more frequently.

Fire Attack

As is true in other types of buildings, the greatest number of lives can often be saved in high-rise fires by an aggressive fire attack. It is SOP in many fire departments to attack high-rise fires from the floor below the fire and to concentrate relief crews and spare equipment on the staging floor, two floors below the fire floor. During a high-rise fire, truck company personnel should never enter the building empty-handed. If they do not have to carry forcible entry or ventilation tools and equipment, they should carry spare SCBA cylinders, hose, tools, lights, etc., to the staging area **(Figure 14.2)**. Moving massive amounts of tools and equipment is often coordinated by those assigned to **lobby control**.

Elevators

High-rise buildings often have a variety of elevators. These include the following types:

- *Low-rise elevators* — Serving the lower floors of the building. For example, they may serve floors 1 through 10.

- *Mid-rise elevators* — Serving only those floors between the low-rise and high-rise elevators. For example, they may serve floor 1 and floors 10 through 20.

- *High-rise elevators* — Serving only the upper floors. For example, they may serve floor 1 and floors 20 through 30.

- *Express elevators* — Usually serving only the ground floor and the uppermost floor of the building. For example, they may serve only floors 1 and 31 or whatever the highest floor happens to be.

- *Freight elevators* — Serving some or all floors.

Some departments allow their firefighters to use freight elevators to ascend partway to the fire floor and to transport additional equipment when it is deemed safe to do so by the Incident Commander. Departments that allow this do so because these elevators are usually not in blind shafts and the systems are designed to carry heavier loads than ordinary passenger elevators. A fully equipped firefighter, especially one wearing a full tool belt or carrying spare air tanks, can weigh more than 300 pounds (135 kg). Obviously, a half-dozen fully equipped firefighters and any spare equipment could weigh a ton (1 000 kg) or more **(Figure 14.3, p. 412)**. If possible, freight elevators should be used instead of passenger elevators due to these weight considerations. However, freight elevators should only be used when authorized by the officer in charge on the fire floor.

Figure 14.2 Firefighters should not go to the staging area empty handed.

Lobby Control — In high-rise fire fighting, the individual responsible for, and the process of, taking and maintaining control of the lobby and elevators in a high-rise fire fighting situation. Lobby control also includes establishing internal communications, coordinating the flow of personnel and equipment up the interior stairway(s) to upper levels, and coordinating with building engineering personnel.

Figure 14.3 Several fully-equipped firefighters can easily overload an elevator.

> **WARNING!**
> Elevators that serve the fire floor or above should not be used by occupants or firefighters unless the officer in charge on the fire floor has determined that it is safe to do so.

A danger in using elevators is that an elevator control malfunction could automatically call the elevator car to the fire floor, or a power failure could strand the elevator car above the fire or between floors. Therefore, those assigned to lobby control should bring all elevators to the ground floor and lock them there. Elevators that do not serve the fire floor or above and are equipped with manual fire department controls may then be used for evacuating occupants and for shuttling firefighters and equipment partway to the fire floor.

Fire Behavior in High-Rise Buildings

Because of structural characteristics that are unique to very tall buildings, fires may behave differently in these structures than in those of more modest dimensions. For example, fires in grain elevators or buildings with multistory stairwells or tall elevator shafts are subject to fire extension to a degree that shorter structures are not. Fire behavior in high-rise buildings is most affected by *stack effect* and *mushrooming*.

Stack Effect

As described in **Essentials**, **stack effect** is the natural vertical movement of heat and smoke (convection) in tall structures. Because of differences in the density of the air inside and outside of these buildings (due to temperature differences inside and outside the structure), heat and smoke rise as if in a smoke stack — thus, the name. The greater the difference between the inside and outside temperature and the greater the building height, the greater the stack effect will be **(Figure 14.4)**.

If a high-rise building is opened at the roof and at street level, the direction and intensity of airflow within the building depends primarily on the relative temperature differences. If it is hotter inside than outside, the airflow will be inward at the bottom and outward at the top. But if the outside air is hotter than the air inside, the flow will be reversed. This is known as reverse stack effect. If there is only a short distance between the upper and lower openings and if the inside and outside temperatures are equal, no natural airflow takes place.

Stack Effect — Phenomenon of a strong air draft moving from ground level to the roof level of a building. Affected by building height, configuration, and temperature differences between inside and outside air.

Mushrooming

Although referred to as *ceiling jets* in technical literature, firefighters have long called this phenomenon **mushrooming**; therefore, that is the term that will be used here. The mushrooming effect that commonly occurs at ceilings of the top floors of smaller buildings does not always occur in the same way in very tall buildings. Inside a building, heat and smoke rise through any vertical opening until they encounter a horizontal obstruction or until their temperature is reduced to the temperature of the surrounding air. As fire gases rise within a building, heat dissipates into the surrounding air and is absorbed by the structure itself.

If a fire generates insufficient heat to cause the smoke to rise to the top of the building, the temperature of the smoke will eventually equal that of the surrounding air. When this equalization of temperature occurs, the smoke loses its buoyancy, ceases to rise, and stratifies — forming layers of smoke within the building **(Figure 14.5)**. **Stratification** can occur near the top of the building or several floors below. Once stratification occurs, the smoke spreads laterally and downward until the building is either completely filled or it is ventilated.

Stratification of smoke can create a highly toxic atmosphere many floors above the fire, even where there is little heat. Ventilating this cooled, stratified smoke out of the building can be accomplished by using positive-pressure blowers

> **Mushrooming** — Tendency of heat, smoke, and other products of combustion to rise until they encounter a horizontal obstruction. At this point they will spread laterally until they encounter vertical obstructions and begin to bank downward.

> **Stratification** — Formation of smoke into layers as a result of differences in density with respect to height with low density layers on the top and high density layers on the bottom.

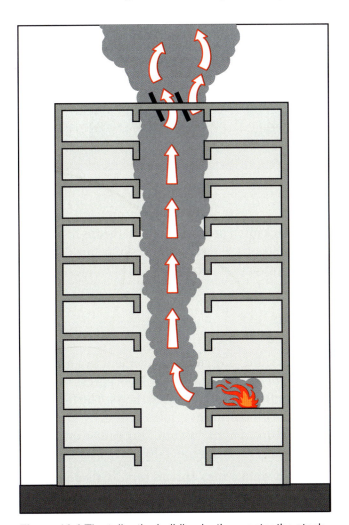

Figure 14.4 The taller the building is, the greater the stack effect.

Figure 14.5 Smoke will stratify at a certain level of a structure when its temperature decreases.

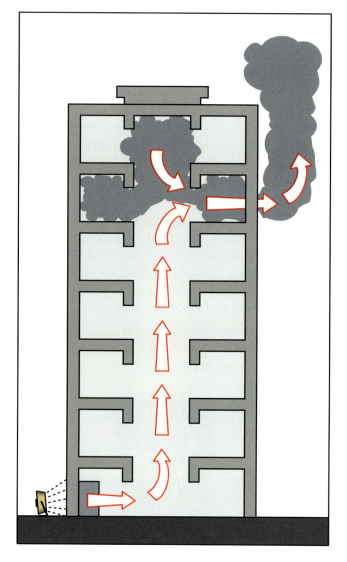

Figure 14.6 PPV can be used to vent cold smoke from a building.

to create a controlled flow of air up a stairwell and horizontally across the smoke-filled floors **(Figure 14.6)**. However, there are limits to the effectiveness of PPV in high-rise buildings. Most PPV blowers positioned at street level are effective up to about 22 floors. If ventilation is required above that level, additional blowers will have to be positioned at about the 22nd floor, smoke ejectors will have to be positioned at the highest level to be ventilated, or both may be required.

High-Rise Ventilation

Aggressive ventilation and fire attack often provides the best means of protecting the occupants of high-rise buildings. These buildings may be ventilated in several ways. The ventilation options available are:

- Vertical (top) ventilation
- Horizontal ventilation of the fire floor
- Horizontal ventilation above and below the fire floor

Because of the numerous factors affecting smoke movement in a high-rise building and the need to channel heat and smoke away from egress routes, it may be necessary to employ more than one of these methods. The following discussion of airflow within high-rise buildings relates primarily to natural ventilation. The natural airflow within a high-rise building can be enhanced or even reversed through mechanical means, especially when PPV is used.

In high-rise buildings, fire and smoke may spread rapidly through pipe shafts, stairways, elevator shafts, air-handling ducts, and other vertical channels because of convection. In some instances, ventilation must be done horizontally on the fire floor or on the floors immediately above the fire if they have become charged with smoke and heat. Despite the danger of the fire lapping into floors above the fire and the hazards of shards of broken glass falling onto those in the street below, horizontal ventilation may be the most efficient method in some situations. For example, if ventilating vertically would endanger occupants attempting to leave the building, horizontal ventilation may have to be used. In other situations, the fire can and should be vented vertically through stairwells or other vertical shafts, taking advantage of the stack effect described earlier.

Vertical (Top) Ventilation

During preincident planning, the potential for vertically ventilating serious fires in high-rise buildings should be considered. Top ventilation can prevent or reduce mushrooming on the upper floors and does not promote lapping, which is always a danger when horizontally venting multistory buildings below the top floor. A preincident survey of the roof will reveal the existence of any roof vents or other features that may lend themselves to the tactical ventilation process or any automatic smoke vents that may reduce or eliminate the need for additional top ventilation by firefighters.

Getting Firefighters to the Roof

One of the biggest challenges in top venting high-rise buildings is getting the vent crew and their equipment to the roof. The roofs of most high-rise and even some low-rise buildings are beyond the reach of the available aerial devices; therefore, some alternative means of getting to the roof must be found. The various ways of reaching the roof of a high-rise building may involve using an aerial device whenever possible, using a combination of elevators and interior stairways, and using helicopters. Each of these methods has certain advantages and disadvantages.

Aerial devices. When an aerial device is able to reach the roof of a high-rise building, using it is the preferred method of getting firefighters to the roof because it is the fastest, safest, and most direct route **(Figure 14.7)**. Using an aerial device to access the roof during a fire avoids the congestion of occupants exiting and firefighters and their equipment entering the interior stairways. However, in many cases aerial devices will not

> **CAUTION**
> Elevator shafts should not be used for ventilation because of the fall hazard created if shaft doors are left open and visibility is reduced by smoke or darkness.

Figure 14.7 Aerial devices are the preferred method of roof access in high-rise structures. *Courtesy of Ron Jeffers.*

> **WARNING!**
> Using a penthouse or bulkhead to ventilate the building could eliminate the firefighters' escape route.

reach the roof. In these situations they can be used as far as they will reach to access an exterior fire escape or to provide a platform from which entry can be forced into an upper floor of the building. The vent crew can then continue to the roof via the interior stairway.

Interior stairway. While many high-rise buildings have more than one interior stairway, few have more than one that terminates on the roof. In this context, references to the interior stairway assume that the stairway terminates on the roof. Preincident planning surveys of high-rise buildings will reveal which stairways lead to the roof, if they are smokeproof towers, if they can be pressurized from below, and if they are likely to be available for access during fire attack.

During a fire, an interior stairway may be relatively free of smoke but can be heavily congested with occupants, firefighters carrying equipment, and charged attack lines **(Figure 14.8)**. Therefore, dedicating one stairway for evacuation and another for fire attack is critical. The decision regarding which interior stairway to use for tactical ventilation must be made in coordination with interior attack operations.

Elevators. As mentioned earlier, any elevator that serves the fire floor or above should *not* be used by occupants or firefighters unless the officer in charge *on the fire floor* determines that it is safe to do so. If allowed by departmental SOP, elevators that do not reach the fire floor may be used to shuttle firefighters and equipment to the highest floor served by that elevator **(Figure 14.9)**. The vent group can then use an interior stairway to reach its destination. However, the vent group should assess heat and smoke conditions in the stairway before entering it.

Helicopters. One of the most direct means of moving personnel and equipment to the roof of a high-rise building when weather and smoke conditions permit is through the use of helicopters. To use helicopters safely and most effectively during a fire requires close

Figure 14.8 Interior stairways can quickly become congested during a fire.

Figure 14.9 Depending on departmental SOP, elevators can sometimes be used to shuttle firefighters and equipment.

Figure 14.10 A fire in an extremely tall building may necessitate the use of a helicopter to gain access to the roof.

coordination between fireground personnel and the helicopter crew. This level of coordination can only be achieved through preincident planning and realistic training exercises involving both groups **(Figure 14.10)**.

Procedures must be developed for identifying safe landing zones, for transporting firefighters to the roof, and for removing building occupants from the roof — some of whom may be injured. Once these procedures have been developed, they need to be tested in realistic exercises and revised as necessary. To maintain an adequate level of readiness, firefighters and helicopter crews need to train together on a regular basis.

Channeling Smoke

In buildings having only one stairwell that terminates on the roof, this natural *chimney* may be used to ventilate smoke, heat, and fire gases from various floors. The **penthouse** or *bulkhead* door on the roof must be blocked open before the stairway doors on the fire floors are opened. Blocking the bulkhead door open ensures that it cannot be closed accidentally, upsetting the ventilation profile and allowing the shaft to become filled with superheated gases.

The timing and coordination of ventilation with rescue and fire suppression operations is extremely important. Ventilation directed up the one stairwell that terminates on the roof must be delayed until all occupants above the fire floor have been either evacuated or moved to an area of refuge within the building. Firefighters should also be in positions of safety prior to executing the ventilation order. Once the ventilation operation has begun, the stairway may be untenable, even for firefighters in full protective clothing.

Penthouse — Structure on the roof of a building that may be used as a living space, to enclose mechanical equipment, or to provide roof access from an interior stairway. Also called a Bulkhead.

CAUTION
During fire fighting operations, firefighters should enter an interior stairway above the fire only when they are certain that it is safe to do so.

Pressure Transfer

Just as heat flows naturally from a hot object to a colder object until their temperatures are equal, pressure transfers from an area of higher pressure to another of lower pressure until they equalize. If two compartments are connected by an opening, and one of the compartments is pressurized such as when a fire starts inside it, air from the pressurized compartment moves into the other compartment, equalizing the pressure across both compartments **(Figure 14.11)**.

When gases within a compartment are heated, they expand and become less dense than the surrounding atmosphere. This buoyancy causes the gases to rise. If the gases are confined, the internal pressure of the compartment increases. However, if buoyancy forces are the only ones acting on the gases within a closed compartment, then in relation to atmospheric pressure, the pressure will be higher near the top of the compartment and lower near the bottom of the compartment **(Figure 14.12)**.

Neutral Pressure Plane

In a closed compartment, the point where the interior pressure is equal to the pressure outside the space is called the **neutral pressure plane**. This concept is important in understanding the stack effect discussed earlier. While the location of the neutral pressure plane can be precisely identified with instrumenta-

> **Neutral Pressure Plane —** The point within a building, especially a high-rise, where the interior pressure equals the atmospheric pressure outside. This plane will move up or down, depending on variables of temperature and wind.

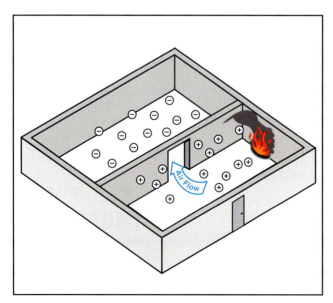

Figure 14.11 Pressure between connected compartments will eventually equalize.

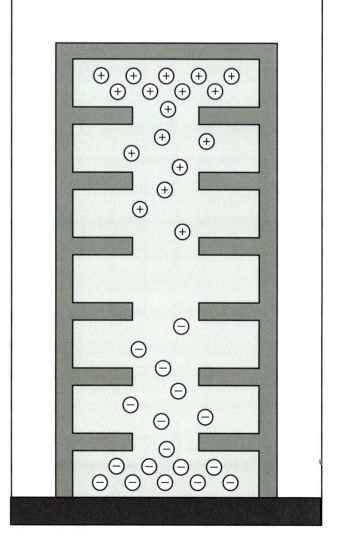

Figure 14.12 Atmospheric pressure is higher at the upper levels of a structure.

418 Chapter 14 • Special Ventilation Operations

tion, doing so on the fireground is neither practical nor necessary. Nonetheless, a basic understanding of pressure changes is needed to be able to understand certain ventilation practices, particularly those used in high-rise structures.

Assuming that the structure is closed, with little or no gases being vented to the atmosphere, a neutral pressure plane exists at the level of ambient atmospheric pressure (usually between 35 percent and 50 percent of the building height) **(Figure 14.13)**. As the distance away from this plane increases, the pressure difference also increases — positively above the plane and negatively below the plane. Because there is little or no movement of gases within a closed structure, upper areas are under positive pressure, and negative pressure (a vacuum) forms near the bottom of the structure.

These pressures have a pronounced effect on air movement within tall structures, such as high-rise buildings, where the distances from the top and bottom to the neutral pressure plane are extreme. If openings are made at the top and bottom of the structure, the escape of positive pressure from the upper end of the structure, and the inward pull of air at the bottom causes the entire structure to act as a chimney — the stack effect mentioned earlier **(Figure 14.14)**. The efficiency of the stack effect is even greater in situations

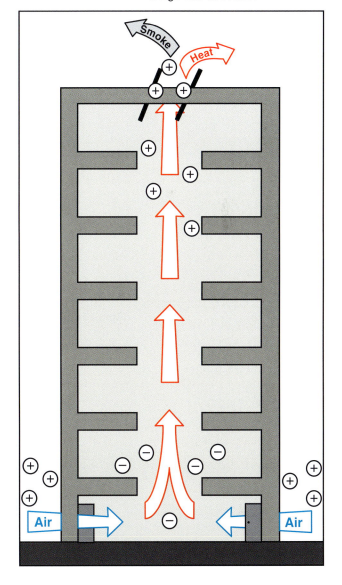

Figure 14.14 The stack effect in a high-rise structure.

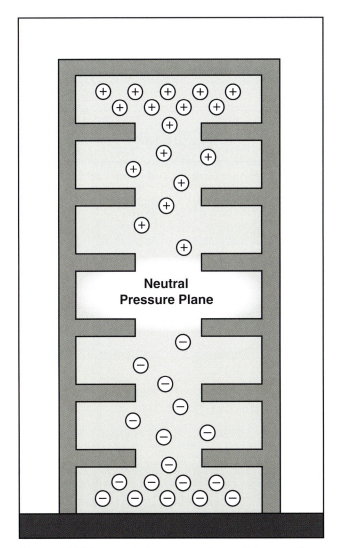

Figure 14.13 The neutral pressure plane will be near the vertical middle of the building.

where a significant difference in temperature exists between the inside and the outside of a building. Wind can also have a major influence on stack effect because of its ability to produce a positive pressure on the windward side of the building and a negative pressure on the leeward side.

Mechanical ventilation creates a pressure differential in the area being ventilated. When air is expelled, a low-pressure environment is created inside the structure, causing replacement air to enter. When air is blown in, a high-pressure environment is created inside the structure, causing air to move to the outside (an area of lower pressure). This difference in pressure is what enables firefighters to ventilate a structure.

Effects of Wind

Wind can raise or lower the neutral pressure plane within a building, which can have a major influence on the tactical ventilation of high-rise buildings. Wind produces a positive pressure on the windward side of the building (which tends to raise the neutral pressure plane) and a negative pressure on the leeward side of the building (which tends to lower the neutral pressure plane) **(Figure 14.15)**. Before venting the fire floor horizontally, it must be determined that air movement will be conducive to effective ventilation. For example, if the seat of the fire is located above the neutral pressure plane, ventilating on the leeward side of the building can make best use of the negative pressure condition created by the wind. However, ventilating on the windward side could work against effective ventilation and spread the fire into uninvolved areas.

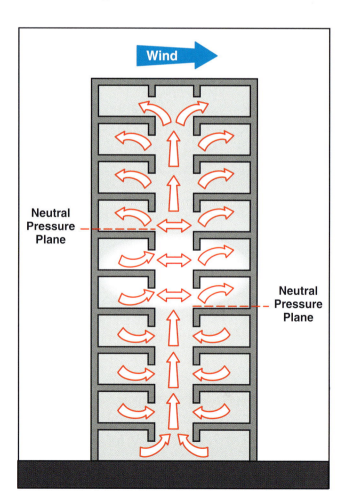

Figure 14.15 Effects of wind on the neutral pressure plane.

Wind can influence the stack effect in two ways. Wind blowing across the roof of a building can increase the stack effect if there is a ventilation opening in the roof **(Figure 14.16)**. And, as just discussed, wind also influences the stack effect by raising or lowering the neutral pressure plane. Positive wind pressure causes the neutral pressure plane to rise, and negative pressure causes it to fall. Opening a window below the neutral pressure plane may draw air into the building and increase the spread of smoke throughout the interior rather than ejecting it to the outside **(Figure 14.17)**. On the other hand, making an opening above the neutral pressure plane allows the smoke to escape to the outside **(Figure 14.18, p. 422)**. The closer that ventilation takes place to the neutral pressure plane, the less positive or negative effects wind will exert.

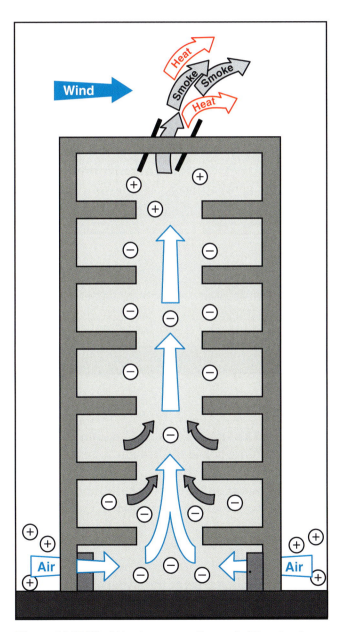

Figure 14.16 Wind blowing across the roof of the structure can greatly enhance the stack effect.

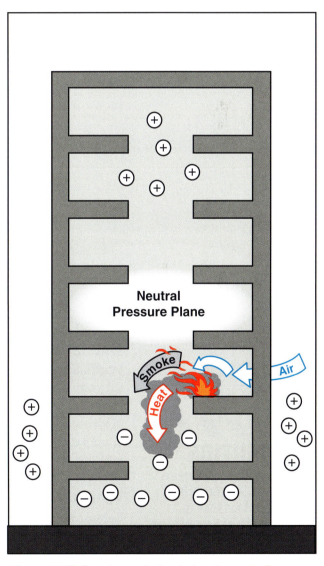

Figure 14.17 Opening a window below the neutral pressure plane may produce an unwanted effect.

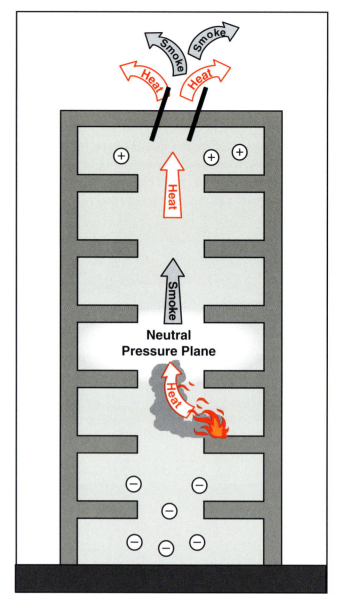

Figure 14.18 An opening above the neutral pressure plane allows proper ventilation to occur.

Ventilating Below the Fire

Ventilating below the fire floor is not a common practice but may be necessary when smoke has spread to the floors below the fire due to reverse stack effect or mushrooming. The most common technique, venting these floors horizontally, can be enhanced by pressurizing the entire building with blowers. As mentioned earlier, PPV may have to be supplemented if the fire floor is above the 22nd floor.

Ventilating the Fire Floor

Before attempting to ventilate the fire floor, knowing the layout of the building is extremely important. Trying to horizontally ventilate through a dead-end corridor or vertically through a stairwell that does not terminate on the roof can seriously delay fire control and increase both fire and smoke damage. Many modern high-rises are sealed buildings with windows designed to remain closed, so horizontal ventilation may necessitate breaking the windows.

CAUTION

Falling glass and other debris is potentially lethal to those in the street below. Permission must be obtained from Command, and clear warnings must be issued before such operations are begun.

Because this task is difficult, time-consuming, and potentially very dangerous to those in the street below, horizontal ventilation of the fire floor should be done only when there is no other choice.

To avoid the risks associated with horizontally ventilating sealed high-rise buildings, vertical ventilation should be used whenever possible. This can sometimes be accomplished by mechanically ventilating up a stairwell, across the smoke-filled fire floor, and out through the roof via another stairwell **(Figure 14.19)**.

Ventilating Above the Fire

Ventilating above the fire floor will be most effective if the process is started at the top of the building **(Figure 14.20)**. This provides a clear exit path for the smoke and heat when doors on the fire floor are opened. Starting at the fire floor and working upward is less efficient, may contribute to increased fire spread and smoke damage, and may put the vent crew in greater jeopardy.

Following fire control, when only cold smoke is left to be expelled, venting vertically eliminates the need for breaking windows for horizontal ventilation. Also, opening up floors near the neutral pressure plane only minimally affects smoke removal unless mechanical ventilation is added.

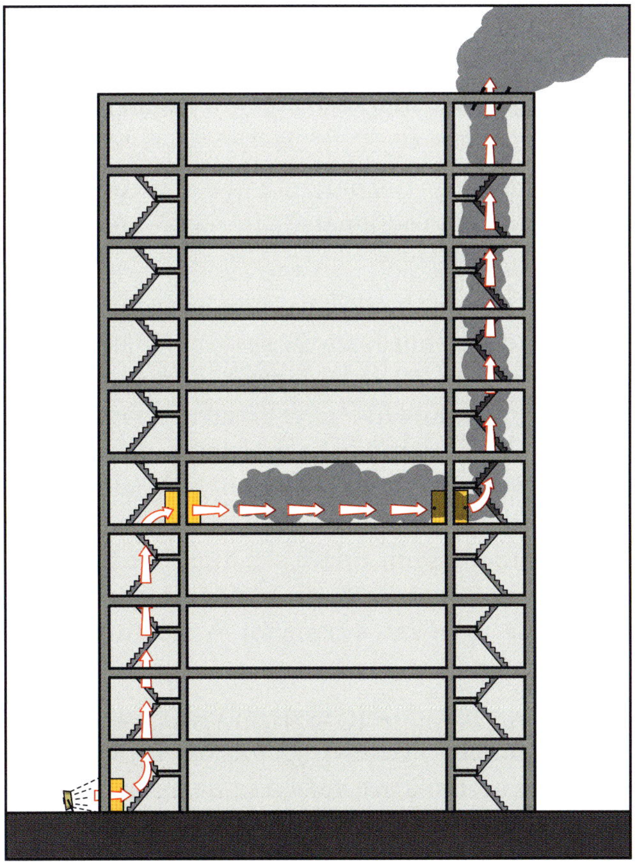

WARNING!
Because of the potential for fire extension or structural collapse, firefighters on the floor above a working fire are in a very dangerous location. They must have a sufficient number of protective hoselines and must always have an accessible means of egress.

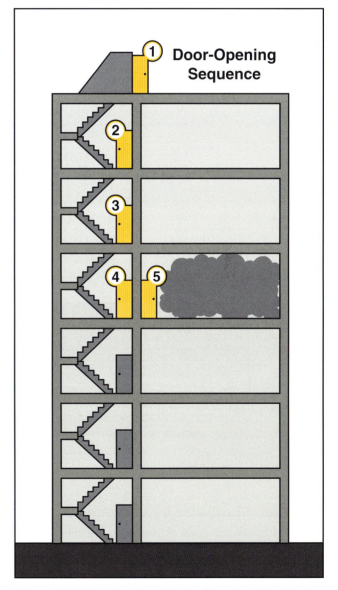

Figure 14.19 One way to mechanically ventilate a high-rise structure.

Figure 14.20 Venting above the fire floor should begin at the top of the building.

Chapter 14 • Special Ventilation Operations **423**

HVAC and Smoke-Control Systems

HVAC systems in very old buildings were designed around the demands of controlling the interior environment of high-rise structures under normal conditions. These early systems often contributed to the spread of smoke and fire throughout a building. Modern systems have many improvements including controllable **smoke dampers** that can be selectively opened and closed. With these features, HVAC systems are more easily adapted to also serve as smoke-control systems.

Correct and effective use of an HVAC system can limit the spread of smoke, fire, and heat, improve operating conditions for firefighters, and increase the likelihood of survival for building occupants. Although the actual manipulation of a high-rise HVAC system for smoke control should be left to the building engineer, firefighters should have an understanding of the system's capabilities and limitations. The building engineer should be included in preincident planning so that the system can be used to the best advantage during a fire. As part of the plan, the building engineer must remain available to the IC during a fire for consultation and for actual manipulation of the HVAC system under fire department direction.

To effectively use an HVAC system to control smoke movement, firefighters should use the following guidelines:

- The HVAC system should be operated by a qualified building engineer, not by firefighters.
- The HVAC system may be used to assist in locating the seat of the fire.
- The HVAC system should be used to limit the extension of fire and smoke to the smallest possible area.
- The HVAC system should not be allowed to spread the fire or smoke beyond the area of origin.
- The HVAC system should provide fresh, uncontaminated air to any occupants who are trapped or are located in a designated safe refuge area within the building.

> **Smoke Damper** — Device that restricts the flow of smoke through an air-handling system. Usually activated by the building's fire alarm signaling system.

> **CAUTION**
> Because elevators, stairwell pressurization fans, and other vital equipment require electricity to operate, the building's utilities should not be shut down arbitrarily when a fire is burning within the building.

The HVAC system should have dampers controlled by smoke detectors to shut down the system if smoke enters the ducts **(Figure 14.21)**. If the dampers do not shut down the system, smoke and fire may spread to several floors before the HVAC system can be shut down manually. To accomplish a manual shutdown with the least possible delay, the building engineer must be contacted as soon as fire department units arrive at a high-rise building. Under the direction of the IC, the building engineer may be able to use the HVAC system for exhausting smoke from the building.

Some heavy-duty HVAC systems can be of considerable assistance in removing cold smoke following a fire. These systems are varied in design and complexity, so firefighters should not attempt to manually control them.

Figure 14.21 Smoke dampers prevent smoke from spreading to other areas of the structure through the HVAC system.

Built-In Ventilation Devices

Roof vents and **curtain boards** are most common in large buildings having wide, undivided expanses of floor space. Some industrial or warehouse facilities have acres (hectares) of open floor space. If these structures are not properly vented or protected by other permanently installed systems for limiting fire spread, the entire contents are vulnerable to fire and smoke damage.

Roof vents and curtain boards have proven to be effective in limiting the spread of fire, releasing heated fire gases, and reducing smoke damage. The standard that provides guidelines for the design and installation of smoke and heat venting equipment, NFPA® 204, *Standard for Smoke and Heat Venting*, recommends using automatic heat-activated roof vents and curtain boards. The following is general information on various types of vents and curtain boards; however, firefighters need to become familiar with the specific types in use in their local areas.

Automatic Roof Vents

Automatic roof vents are intended to limit the spread of fire within a building by releasing heat and smoke to the outside before the fire mushrooms throughout the building. Because they work automatically, these vents may reduce or eliminate the need for additional vertical ventilation by firefighters.

Automatic roof vents take advantage of the fact that fire gases rise due to convection. Therefore, these vents are placed at the highest point of the roof. Although some are now activated by smoke detectors, most still operate through the use of fusible links connected to spring-loaded or counterweighted cover assemblies. When the fusible link reaches its designed melting temperature, it separates, allowing the vent covers to open. Automatic locking devices help to ensure that the covers remain open, even in gusty winds. Under some conditions, prevailing winds may prevent heat and smoke from exiting through automatic roof vents. When this occurs, closing the roof vents and using horizontal ventilation may be necessary.

Heat-activated roof vents may not open automatically when sprinklers discharge near them because the sprinklers may prevent the fire from developing enough heat to activate the vents. Attempting to force automatic roof vents open from the exterior can do extensive damage to their operating mechanisms, and spring-operated covers may be dangerous to firefighters. Therefore, firefighters should become familiar with the manual release mechanisms of automatic roof vents in their areas.

Atrium Vents

Many high-rise hotels and office buildings are constructed with an **atrium** in the center of the structure **(Figure 14.22, p. 426)**. These large, vertical shafts lend themselves to the stack effect. Therefore, building codes in most areas require that they be equipped with automatic vents. These automatic vents are usually designed to be activated by either smoke or heat. The potential consequences of a firefighter falling into an open vent over an atrium in a high-rise building are obvious, so the earlier caution about working on roofs in darkness and/or heavy smoke is especially important in these situations.

Curtain Boards — Vertical boards, fire-resistive half-walls, that extend down from the underside of the roof of some commercial buildings and are intended to limit the spread of fire, heat, smoke and fire gases.

CAUTION
In darkness or heavy smoke, firefighters must be extremely careful to avoid falling into automatic vents when working on roofs. Preincident familiarization is essential so that firefighters know that automatic vents are present.

Atrium — Open area in the center of a building, extending through two or more stories, similar to a courtyard but usually covered by a skylight, to allow natural light and ventilation to interior rooms.

Figure 14.22 It is common to find an atrium in many hotels and office buildings.

Monitor Vents

Monitor vents are usually square or rectangular structures that penetrate the roofs of single-story buildings, but may be found on older high-rise buildings as well **(Figure 14.23)**. Monitors are primarily intended to increase natural light inside these buildings, but may also provide some natural ventilation. Most monitors have ordinary window glass or wired glass panels sloping down from a center ridge. Monitor vents rely upon the glass breaking to provide ventilation in a fire. If the fire has not yet generated enough heat to break the glass, the glass can be removed by firefighters. Monitors with solid walls may have two opposite sides hinged at the bottom and held closed at the top with a fusible link that allows them to fall open by gravity in case of fire.

Skylights

As described in Chapter 13, Vertical Ventilation, skylights may be used to ventilate heat and smoke during a fire. Skylights equipped with thermoplastic panels or ordinary window glass can act as automatic vents because the heat of a fire melts the plastic or breaks the glass. In the absence of skylights with thermoplastic panels or those with automatic venting, firefighters will have to remove the skylight or break the glass panels for tactical ventilation. In skylights equipped with wired glass, the panes may have to be removed from their frames for ventilation purposes **(Figure 14.24)**.

Figure 14.23 Monitor vents can assist in ventilation.

Figure 14.24 Skylights may be removed or broken to allow for vertical ventilation.

Curtain Boards

Curtain boards, also known as *draft curtains*, are fire-resistive half-walls that extend down from the underside of the roof. They generally extend a distance equal to at least 20 percent of the vertical distance from the floor to the roof but not lower than 10 feet (3 m) above the floor. The areas encompassed by curtain boards will generally be those containing critical industrial processes or concentrations of flammable liquids or other hazardous materials with high fire potential.

The function of curtain boards is to limit the horizontal spread of heat and smoke by confining it to a relatively small area directly above its source. They also concentrate heat and smoke directly under automatic roof vents to accelerate their actuation. Curtain boards may also accelerate the activation of automatic sprinklers in the area, and this helps to get water onto the fire sooner. However, as mentioned earlier, operating sprinklers may also slow or prevent the actuation of automatic roof vents. If the roof vents do not open automatically, firefighters will have to open them manually.

> **WARNING!**
> Firefighters working below grade must wear SCBA because of the possibility of oxygen deficiency in addition to whatever toxic gases may be present.

Underground Structures

Because basements, utility vaults, tunnels, and other underground structures may not provide adequate natural ventilation during fires, forced ventilation may be required. In addition to the difficulties often encountered in gaining access for tactical ventilation below grade, there is a much greater likelihood of having to work in an IDLH atmosphere.

Because basements and cellars are the most common underground structures, this section deals primarily with ventilating these spaces. While they may be defined differently in different codes and other sources, in this context both basements and cellars have an interior access stairway. Some of these spaces also have an additional access from the exterior of the building — full access in those classified as daylight basements. Both basements and cellars may contain furnaces, boilers, heating oil tanks, and main electrical panels. Usually, but not always, cellars have no windows and basements have small windows between grade level and the first floor of the building.

Cellars are most often unfinished areas used for storage. Basements used for storage are often unfinished, and those used for habitation (game rooms, spare bedrooms, etc.) are usually finished. In general, the same ventilation problems that exist in basements and cellars exist in other underground structures, therefore; the same tactics and techniques apply as well.

While all basements and cellars can be accessed by an interior stairway, some also have openings for elevators, chutes, or dumbwaiters. As mentioned earlier, some of these access openings are inside the buildings and others are outside. Opening these access ways for tactical ventilation may be a slow and difficult process because they may be blocked or secured at the street level by iron gratings, steel shutters, security doors, or some combination of these. To quickly gain access into basements, cellars, and other underground structures, firefighters must be familiar with the access openings and any security measures employed so that they can bring the needed tools and equipment with them initially.

Building features, such as interior stairways, elevator shafts, pipe chases, laundry chutes, air-handling systems, and other vertical openings may contribute to the spread of fire and smoke from a basement to upper floors. Therefore, early and effective ventilation of below-grade fires is critically important to successful fireground operations.

To prevent or reduce the upward spread of smoke and fire from an involved basement or cellar, it must be ventilated as quickly as possible. If an opening of adequate size can be made opposite the interior point of entry into the space, the fastest way to ventilate the compartment may be to set up a positive-pressure blower at the entry point. This allows the vent crew to stay out of the compartment while still ventilating it effectively. However, the rest of the structure (especially those with balloon-frame construction) must be closely and continually monitored for signs of fire extension through walls or other vertical channels.

In some cases involving fires in cellars with no exterior access openings, it may be necessary to vent the cellar through the first floor of the building. In these cases, a ventilation exit opening is cut in the first floor near an exterior window. A smoke ejector is positioned in the window opening to facilitate the flow of heat and smoke to the outside **(Figure 14.25)**. This technique risks fire spread to the first floor area and should only be used when there is no other means available to vent the cellar.

Windowless Buildings

Many modern buildings have few windows, if any. These structures must use skylights and artificial lighting for interior illumination **(Figure 14.26)**. Some windowless buildings have various forms of translucent glass walls that admit light but are of little value for tactical ventilation. These walls may appear fragile, but they can be as resistant to being breached as are many masonry walls.

The absence of exterior openings severely limits the opportunities for horizontal ventilation and increases the likelihood of backdraft conditions developing within these structures. Both of these problems underscore the need for fast and effective vertical ventilation of fires in windowless buildings.

Highly Secure Buildings

In response to terrorist attacks such as the bombings of the federal office building in Oklahoma City and other buildings around the world, many public buildings (especially government buildings) have been retrofitted with a variety of security measures including barriers to keep vehicles a safe distance away. Unfortunately, these devices and barriers also keep emergency vehicles away and make it more difficult for firefighters to gain access into these buildings for tactical ventilation and other fireground operations **(Figure 14.27)**. Therefore, it is imperative that firefighters conduct preincident planning surveys of these buildings and develop effective operational plans for dealing

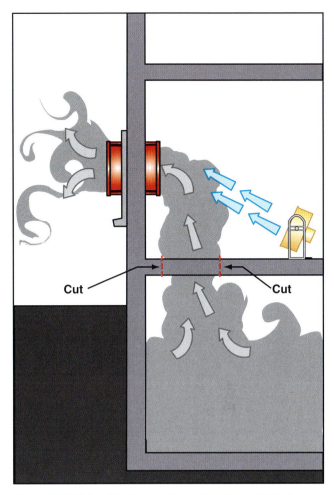

Figure 14.25 A cellar fire can be vented through the first floor and out a nearby window.

Figure 14.26 Windowless buildings are becoming more common for security reasons.

Figure 14.27 Jersey barriers and other similar barricades can prevent aerial apparatus from positioning in a desirable location.

with the identified obstructions. They must identify what the impediments to access are, what tools and equipment will be needed to overcome these impediments, and how to get those and other needed resources to the scene in a timely manner.

Government office buildings are not the only highly secure buildings that firefighters may have to ventilate during a fire. Jails, prisons, and other correctional facilities must necessarily be highly secure. As discussed in Chapter 9, Access into Structures, entry into and movement within these buildings is best done with the aid of staff members accompanying the firefighters. Because the firefighters may need to go into parts of the building that are charged with heat and smoke, the staff members need to be equipped with appropriate PPE including SCBA. Therefore, preincident planning and training with the institution's fire department or fire brigade are essential. Such cooperation and coordination allows fire operations to be conducted both safely and efficiently in these facilities.

Remodeled Buildings

Many older buildings have been remodeled numerous times over the years. These modifications are sometimes obvious from the outside of the building, sometimes not. As discussed in Chapter 9, some modifications are new sections added onto existing older buildings. Some modifications actually increase a building's structural stability and its fire resistance — others do quite the opposite. For example, modifications made to a Chinese food warehouse in Washington state made the floor more susceptible to collapse during a fire and that resulted in the loss of four firefighters.

Firefighters should pay attention to all construction projects in their response districts, especially large-scale remodeling projects. They should visit these sites as often as possible during the construction or remodeling process, and should observe and document changes that could affect access to or into the building. Firefighters should pay particular attention to changes in bearing walls, roof assemblies, floor assemblies, and any other structural elements that might increase or decrease the building's structural integrity. Finally, firefighters should familiarize themselves with the doors, windows, and roof coverings because these are the most likely points for tactical ventilation openings.

> **Special Ventilation Scenario:**
>
> On a hot Friday afternoon in summer, you and your truck company are ordered to ventilate a fire burning on the twelfth floor of a 20-story office building.
> - What precautions would you take as you approach the building?
> - With whom would you communicate as you decide where and how to ventilate?
> - What information do you need about conditions inside the building?
> - What tools and equipment would you bring to the lobby?
> - What tools and equipment would you take aloft?

- How would you reach the ventilation point?
- What would you do differently if the fire were in a large commercial basement?
- What would you do differently if the fire were in an underground utility corridor?

Summary

Firefighters must familiarize themselves with the various types of buildings and construction features that exist in their response districts. Of particular importance are high-rise buildings, windowless buildings, underground structures, highly secure buildings, and those that have undergone extensive remodeling. Once these structures have been identified, fire departments should develop operational plans for using horizontal or vertical ventilation techniques to ventilate these structures safely and effectively during any fire that might occur in them.

Review Questions

1. What are the challenges associated with high-rise fire operations?
2. What are the differences in fire behavior in a high-rise building compared to a common residential or commercial building?
3. What are three methods for ventilating high-rise buildings?
4. What are the guidelines for using HVAC systems to control smoke movement in a building?
5. What are the considerations for ventilating an underground structure?
6. What are the considerations for ventilating a windowless building?
7. What are the considerations for ventilating a secured building?
8. What are the considerations for ventilating a remodeled building?

Appendix

Contents

Appendix A
Coordinated Fireground Operations

Appendix A
Coordinated Fireground Operations

The activities of all personnel at an emergency scene must be carefully coordinated for both safety and efficiency. For example, if ventilation is performed before fire attack crews are ready and able to enter a burning structure, the fire can intensify, placing firefighters and trapped occupants in greater jeopardy, prolonging the incident, and significantly increasing primary damage. On the other hand, if a fire that has been burning for some time in a closed compartment is not properly vented first, firefighters can be injured or killed by a backdraft or by other extreme fire behavior when they open a door to enter. If the utilities in a burning building are not properly controlled, firefighters can be at risk for a variety of reasons. For example, firefighters could be injured by an explosion of accumulated natural gas or LP gas, electrocuted when they apply water to energized wiring or equipment, or buried in a structural collapse caused by water accumulating on upper floors. Any or all of these scenarios — and countless others — can result from lack of fireground coordination.

On the other hand, if firefighters have done adequate preincident planning on the building that is now burning, they know what forcible entry and ventilation tools and techniques are needed to quickly and efficiently perform their duties. They also know how the building is constructed, how old it is, and how a fire is likely to behave in it. Armed with this knowledge, their safety and effectiveness can be greatly increased. Familiarity with the burning building and its contents can assist truck company personnel in doing their main job — helping to implement the incident action plan (IAP).

Safely and efficiently implementing the IAP requires the coordination of a variety of fireground resources and functions. The majority of the resources that must be coordinated on the fireground are personnel and equipment. The major functions that must be coordinated are search and rescue, fire attack, and support activities. Therefore, this chapter discusses the coordination of all these resources and functions.

Coordinated Fireground Operations

Even when adequate numbers and types of resources are immediately available to handle an incident of the nature and scope presented by a burning building, the most effective use of those resources requires coordination. Effective coordination translates into the safest, quickest, and least costly means of achieving all three of the universal priorities in structure fires. However, the amount and type of coordination needed will vary with the situation. While all structure fires require the coordination of fire attack and support operations, some structure fires require more coordination than others.

To effectively control on-scene resources, fire departments must use an incident management system. In 2003, Homeland Security Presidential Directive-5, *Management of Domestic Incidents*, was issued. HSPD-5 directed the U.S. Secretary of Homeland Security to develop and administer a National Response Plan, later renamed the *National Response Framework*. A major part of that framework is the National Incident Management System (NIMS). In the U.S., NIMS is the mechanism by which large numbers of fire companies and larger units are organized and managed during emergency incidents. While there are other systems, the most commonly used command/management system is the NIMS-compliant Incident Command System, or NIMS-ICS. However, firefighters must use whatever incident management system that their department has adopted.

Command Options

In all incident management systems, the first-arriving fire officer or firefighter assumes initial command of the incident. Because fires vary in size and complexity, some departments allow the initial IC some flexibility in how to size up the fire, develop an IAP, and implement it. In these departments, the first-arriving officer can use any of three possible command modes: *investigation*, *fast attack*, or *command*.

Investigation Mode

When the nature and extent of a structure fire is not obvious on arrival, the first-in officer will need to investigate as part of the size-up. In these cases, the officer assumes initial command of the incident while investigating. The IC transmits *nothing showing* or *investigating* over the radio. In some departments, the IC also advises other incoming units to reduce their response mode to one in which lights, sirens, and other warning devices are turned off and all traffic laws are observed. In other departments, the IC advises other incoming units to stage. In staging, other incoming units continue to respond using all warning devices but stop (stage) at an adjacent location (such as the last intersection) in their normal route of travel before reaching the reported incident location. Units that are staging stand by at their locations. Once the investigation (size-up) has been completed, the IC can deploy the other units as needed or release them to return to their districts. Staging in this way allows for maximum deployment flexibility.

Fast Attack Mode (Also Known as Quick Attack)

In situations that require immediate action by the first-arriving company, some departments allow the officer in charge of that company to simultaneously take command, direct the actions of the company, and participate in those actions as needed. Some examples of situations in which a fast attack command might be needed are as follows:

- Fires in which immediate action could save lives
- Relatively small fires with potential for spread
- When adjacent structures are uninvolved but seriously threatened

In the fast attack mode, the officer maintains command by communicating over a portable radio. There must be adequate resources on scene to meet two in/two out requirements. The fast attack mode should not last for more than a few minutes, and it ends with either of the following:

— The incident is stabilized.

— The incident has not been stabilized, but the officer must withdraw to the exterior to establish a Command Post. The officer must then decide whether to withdraw the remainder of the crew. This decision is based on the number of personnel, the crew's capabilities and experience, their safety, and the likelihood of their being able to contribute to incident stabilization. The crew must not be left inside without radio communications capability.

Command is transferred to another officer. The new IC must decide whether to have the former IC rejoin his or her crew or be reassigned to a role on the Command Staff.

Command Mode

If a structure fire is of such size and complexity or has such spread potential that it is unlikely that the on-scene crew can bring it under control, the first-arriving officer should assume command of the incident. The IC assumes command by announcing the following items over the radio:

- Incident name
- A brief report on conditions (including actions taken)
- Location of command post
- Additional resources needed
- Location of Staging or Base

In addition, the IC must decide how to use the balance of the crew. There are normally three options:

- Appoint one member as crew leader and assign the leader a tactical objective.
- Assign the crew to work under the supervision of another company officer.
- Use the crew members to perform staff functions in support of command.

Transfer of command. When there is a need for the IC to transfer command of the incident to another officer, the transfer must be done correctly. Otherwise, there can be confusion about who is really in command of the incident. The officer relinquishing command must communicate directly with the officer assuming command by radio or face-to-face — with face-to-face being strongly preferred. *Command cannot be transferred to someone who is not on the scene.* When transferring command, the officer relinquishing command should brief the new IC on the following:

- Name of the incident
- Incident status (fire conditions, number of victims, etc.)
- Safety considerations
- Action plan for the incident
- Progress toward completion of tactical objectives
- Deployment and location of assigned resources
- The need for additional resources

Structure Fire Scenarios

In the following section, the coordination of typical fireground resources in three common structure fire scenarios is discussed. These scenarios are *initial attack*, *sustained attack*, and *extended attack* fires.

Initial Attack

In this context, an initial attack fire is defined as one that can be handled by a single unit or the resources in the initial (first-alarm) response. Unless requested by the IC, no additional resources will be dispatched to this incident. Depending upon the size, age, construction, and configuration of the building and the nature of its contents, the number and types of resources included in the initial alarm may vary considerably. In general, an initial attack structure fire is probably not beyond what is commonly called a *room-and-contents* fire. In other words, the fire is confined to a very small structure or a single room or other small portion of a larger building. These fires typically involve only the contents of the building and have not yet spread to the structural supporting elements.

A typical initial attack fire in a single-family dwelling may be confined to the following:

- Wastebasket
- Clothes dryer
- Oven or range top
- Car in the garage
- Contents of a room
- Attic

Typically, at least two engines (perhaps more if there is no truck company), a truck company (if one exists), and one or more chief officers are initially dispatched to such a fire. Some departments have increased the number of engines included in the first-alarm response to reported structure fires to provide enough firefighters to comply with the OSHA two-in/two-out rule. Other departments include a heavy rescue unit, especially if they do not have a truck company. In some departments, every engine is a *quint* (pump, water tank, hose, ground ladders, and an aerial device), thereby reducing the need for a separate ladder company except on fires in high-rise buildings. In areas with a minimal public water supply system, or none at all, a mobile water supply unit (water tender) may also be included in the initial alarm assignment. Assuming that there is an officer and two or more firefighters on each unit, there may be from fifteen to twenty personnel in the initial alarm assignment.

If the fire is in a large residential, commercial, institutional, or other structure with a potentially heavy occupant load or fire load, the number of units and firefighters in the initial alarm assignment may be much higher. Even though there may be more units and many more firefighters than on a typical initial alarm response to a single-family residence, it remains an initial attack fire unless and until the IC begins to request additional resources.

On relatively small initial attack fires, the IC must also fulfill the role of Incident Safety Officer (ISO). On larger initial attack fires, the IC is likely to delegate this authority by appointing an ISO. The ISO is responsible for enforcing departmental safety-related SOPs regarding the use of PPE (including SCBA), personnel accountability, search and rescue (including two-in/two-out), rapid intervention, fire attack, firefighter rehabilitation (Rehab), and in all other fireground operations. The ISO is also responsible for ensuring that all fireground operations are conducted according to the requirements of any applicable state, provincial, or federal safety regulations, such as those from OSHA, or locally adopted NFPA® standards.

Once life safety has been provided for, the IC must make one of the most critical initial decisions — are the resources at the scene and en route sufficient to handle this incident? If the answer to that question is *no*, or even *maybe*, the IC should *immediately* request any additional resources that may be needed. The sooner these additional resources are requested, the sooner they will arrive on scene where they are needed. If there is doubt about the need for any specific resource, they should be requested so that they can start to respond toward the scene as soon as possible. Any of these additional resources that prove to be unnecessary can be released to return to service while still enroute or after arriving at the scene. Additional resources that arrive, but for which there is no immediate assignment are directed to specified locations for staging where they are held in reserve until needed.

The next critical decision that the IC must make is which operational mode is most appropriate at this point in the incident. As discussed earlier, the options are offensive, defensive, or rescue modes. This decision is based upon the current situation, what is likely to happen in the next few minutes, and the capabilities and limitations of the on-scene resources. The initial mode chosen may or may not be used throughout the incident. As the situation changes — for better or worse — the IC may find it necessary or desirable to switch from one mode of operation to another. As also mentioned earlier, any change in the operational mode must be clearly communicated and closely coordinated.

Once the initial operational mode has been chosen, the IC must do a quick risk/benefit analysis of the available deployment options. This and all the other considerations previously discussed are then combined into the initial IAP. Based on this plan, the on-scene resources must then be deployed in the safest and most effective way possible. Initially, resources must be assigned to the following:

- Building access (forcible entry)
- Search and rescue
- Fire attack
- Ventilation
- Utilities control

As soon as the fire situation and the available resources allow, salvage operations must be conducted. However, everyone in the fireground organization should keep loss control in mind as they carry out their assignments. After fire control has been achieved, the fire cause has been investigated, and any critical evidence has been protected, overhaul must also be conducted.

Sustained Attack

There are no universally accepted timelines that differentiate an initial attack fire from a more sustained one. However, for purposes of this discussion, once a structure fire has progressed to the point where the IC decides that the first-alarm resources need to be supplemented, the incident moves into the category of a sustained attack fire. When this happens, a number of additional concerns are added to the coordination of fireground operations. It is important that a dedicated ISO be assigned to incidents of this magnitude. If a Rehab unit has not been established, one should be because firefighter fatigue needs to be managed. Managing firefighter fatigue may also necessitate calling in additional companies for crew rotation or relief.

In fires of this size, the IC will most likely assign resources to divisions or groups. If span of control dictates, an Operations Chief can be appointed. Under the ICS, the Operations Chief is responsible for designating the locations for staging areas, in addition to other fireground responsibilities. The Operations Chief also appoints a manager for the staging area. This allows the additional resources to be managed efficiently as they arrive in the area of the fire and helps to avoid the congestion that could otherwise result. Companies that are staging must be ready to respond within three minutes of being called. In high-rise fires, additional companies and spare equipment are usually staged two floors below the fire floor and their apparatus parked about a block away.

Extended Attack

When a structure fire is such that it continues burning beyond the original operational period, it is considered to be an extended attack fire. An operational period may be 12 hours from the time of alarm, the point at which the on-duty crews are scheduled to be relieved, or some other arbitrary point in time. A new IAP is created for each operational period and disseminated to all assigned units.

Extended attack fires frequently involve mutual aid companies, strike teams, task forces, or other outside assistance. These outside resources may be used to staff vacated fire stations within the district, provide technical assistance at the fire scene, or play a tactical role on the fireground. Personnel from outside the district may not be familiar with the district's layout and topography. If they are to be used to respond to emergency calls in place of local units that are assigned to the fire, they may require detailed maps or a member of the host department to help them find their way around. If personnel from outside the district are responding to the scene, they may need to rendezvous with a local representative at some well-known landmark and be escorted to the scene from that point. When mutual aid personnel are to be used on the fireground, they must be briefed on the current IAP, and their operational capabilities and limitations must be determined. Unless they are capable of communicating on the assigned fireground radio frequencies, mutual aid personnel must be supplied with portable radios that will allow them to do so.

If outside resources are to be used on the fireground, they must be used selectively and with discretion. Before any outside resource can be relied upon for a tactical assignment, that resource must be carefully evaluated. The capabilities and limitations of the apparatus, equipment, and personnel must be verified. Outmoded or poorly maintained apparatus and equipment may not meet the minimum requirements for safe and effective operation. If the apparatus, equipment, or outside personnel do not meet the minimum requirements, they should be used either in support functions or not at all.

Extended attack fires may also involve other considerations that fires of shorter duration do not. Some of these considerations are as follows:

- Apparatus on scene need to be refueled and perhaps repaired.
- On-scene personnel and outside agency personnel staffing fire stations may need to be supplied with food. A nearby restaurant or fast-food outlet may be contracted to fill this need.
- Sanitary facilities for on-scene personnel must be provided in addition to the services provided by one or more Rehab units. Portable toilets may have to be brought to the scene if facilities in nearby buildings are insufficient or unavailable.
- Sleeping bags or other bedding and folding cots may be needed. Gymnasiums or other large buildings may be used as improvised dormitories when outside resources are to be committed beyond their initial operational period.
- Large spaces may also be needed as improvised morgues.

Supplying the resources just described will probably require establishing a Logistics Section. Obviously, the fireground organization must expand if the fire continues to grow in size and complexity.

Finally, fires of this magnitude may require different strategies and tactics than those used in smaller fires. For example, in large strip malls and other commercial or industrial complexes, there may be more reliance on trench or strip ventilation to help contain the fire. Also, there may be a need to apply massive quantities of foam or other chemical agents to extinguish the fire. However, the vast majority of extended attack fires are controlled and extinguished by conventional fire attack methods.

Extraordinary control measures may be necessary in *group fires* (those involving large-scale building-to-building spread) that may involve an entire city block, and *conflagrations* (huge fires that cross streets, highways, rivers, or other natural fire breaks) that may engulf entire neighborhoods. In these extremely rare situations, it may be necessary to perform such functions as demolishing buildings in the path of the fire to deny it more fuel.

Glossary

Glossary

A

All Clear — Signal given to the incident commander that a specific area has been checked for victims and none have been found or all found victims have been extricated from an entrapment.

Atrium — Open area in the center of a building, extending through two or more stories, similar to a courtyard but usually covered by a skylight, to allow natural light and ventilation to interior rooms.

Autoignition — Ignition that occurs when a substance in air, whether solid, liquid, or gaseous, is heated sufficiently to initiate or cause self-sustained combustion without an external ignition source.

Autoignition Temperature — The temperature at which autoignition occurs through the spontaneous ignition of the gases or vapor given off by a heated material.

B

Backdraft — Instantaneous explosion or rapid burning of superheated gases that occurs when oxygen is introduced into an oxygen-depleted confined space. The stalled combustion resumes with explosive force. It may occur because of inadequate or improper ventilation procedures. Very rapid, often explosive burning of hot gases that occurs when oxygen is introduced into an oxygen-depleted confined space. It may occur because of inadequate or improper ventilation procedures.

Balloon-Frame Construction — Type of structural framing used in some single-story and multistory wood frame buildings wherein the studs are continuous from the foundation to the roof. There may be no fire stops between the studs.

Bar Joist — Open web truss constructed entirely of steel, with steel bars used as the web members.

Boiling Liquid Expanding Vapor Explosion (BLEVE) — Rapid vaporization of a liquid stored under pressure upon release to the atmosphere following major failure of its containing vessel; failure is the result of over-pressurization caused by an external heat source, which causes the vessel to explode into two or more pieces when the temperature of the liquid is well above its boiling point at normal atmospheric pressure.

Bowstring Truss — Lightweight truss design noted by the bow shape, or curve of the top chord.

British Thermal Unit (Btu) — Amount of heat energy required to raise the temperature of one pound of water one degree Fahrenheit. One Btu = 1.055 kilo joules (kJ).

Buddy System — Safety procedure used in rescue work. When rescuers work in a hazardous area at least two rescuers must remain in contact with each other at all times.

Butt —Heel (lower end) of a ladder.

C

Carabiner — A steel or aluminum D-shaped snap link device for attaching components of rope rescue systems together.

Carcinogen — Cancer-producing substance.

Celsius Scale — Temperature scale on which the freezing point is 0 degrees and the boiling point at sea level is 100 degrees. Also known as Centigrade scale.

Churning —Movement of smoke being blown out of a ventilation opening only to be drawn back inside by the negative pressure created by the ejector because the open area around the ejector has not been sealed. Also called recirculation.

Cockloft — Concealed space between the top floor and the roof of a structure.

Combustible Gas Indicator (CGI) — Device that indicates the explosive levels of combustible gases.

Combustion — An exothermic chemical reaction that is a self-sustaining process of rapid oxidation of a fuel, that produces heat and light.

Compartmentalization — The systematic venting of a structure by controlling which windows and doors are opened at any given time.

Compressed Air Foam System (CAFS) — Generic term used to describe a high-energy foam-generation system consisting of an air compressor (or other air source), a water pump, and foam solution that injects air into the foam solution before it enters a hoseline.

Conduction — Physical flow or transfer of heat energy from one body to another through direct contact or an intervening medium from the point where the heat is produced to another location or from a region of high temperature to a region of low temperature.

Control Zone — System of barriers surrounding designated areas at emergency scenes intended to limit the number of persons exposed to the hazard and to facilitate its mitigation. At a major incident there will be three zones — restricted (hot), limited access (warm), and support (cold).

Convection — Transfer of heat by the movement of heated fluids or gases, usually in an upward direction.

Course — Horizontal layer of individual masonry units.

Curtain Boards — Vertical boards; fire-resistive half-walls that extend down from the underside of the roof of some commercial buildings and are intended to limit the spread of fire, heat, smoke and fire gases.

D

Deadbolt — Movable part of a deadbolt lock that extends from the lock mechanism into the door frame to secure the door in a locked position.

Dead Load — Weight of the structure, structural members, building components, and any other feature permanently attached to the building that is constant and immobile. Load on a structure due to its own weight and other fixed weights.

E

Emergency Escape Breathing Support System (EEBSS) — Safety system on an SCBA that allows two units to be hooked together in the event that one fails.

F

Fahrenheit Scale — Temperature scale on which the freezing point is 32°F (0°C) and the boiling point at sea level is 212°F (100°C) at normal atmospheric pressure.

Fire Door — A specially constructed, tested, and approved fire-rated door assembly designed and installed to prevent fire spread by automatically closing and covering a doorway in a fire wall during a fire to block the spread of fire through the door opening.

Fire Tetrahedron — Model of the four elements/conditions required to have a fire. The four sides of the tetrahedron represent fuel, heat, oxygen, and chemical chain reaction.

Fire Triangle — Plane geometric figure of an equilateral triangle that is used to explain the conditions necessary for fire. The sides of the triangle represent heat, oxygen, and fuel. The fire triangle was used prior to the general adaptation of the fire tetrahedron that includes a chemical chain reaction.

Fire Wall — Fire rated wall with a specified degree of fire resistance, built of fire-resistive materials and usually extending from the foundation up to and through the roof of a building, that is designed to limit the spread of a fire within a structure or between adjacent structures.

Flashover — Stage of a fire at which all surfaces and objects within a space have been heated to their ignition temperature and flame breaks out almost at once over the surface of all objects in the space.

Fly Section — Extendable section of ground extension or aerial ladder.

Fog Stream — Water stream of finely divided particles used for fire control.

Forcible Entry — Techniques used by fire personnel to gain entry into buildings, vehicles, aircraft, or other areas of confinement when normal means of entry are locked or blocked.

Furring Strips — Wood strips fastened to a wall, floor, or ceiling for the purpose of attaching a finish material.

G

Gang Nail — Form of gusset plate. These thin steel plates are punched with acutely V-shaped holes that form sharp prongs on one side that penetrate wooden members to fasten them together.

Gypsum Wallboard — Widely used interior finish material. Consists of a core of calcined gypsum, starch, water, and other additives that are sandwiched between two paper faces. Also known as gypsum wallboard, plasterboard, and drywall.

H

Hasp — Fastening device consisting of a loop, eye, or staple and a slotted hinge or bar; commonly used with a padlock.

Header Course — Course of bricks with the ends of the bricks facing outward.

Heat Flux — Scientific measurement of how much heat is available for transfer to human skin (or any other surface).

Heat of Combustion — Total amount of thermal energy (heat) that could be generated by the combustion (oxidation) reaction if a fuel were completely burned. The heat of combustion is measured in British Thermal Units (Btu) per pound or calories per gram.

Heat Release Rate (HRR) — Total amount of heat produced or released to the atmosphere from the convective-lift fire phase of a fire per unit mass of fuel consumed per unit time.

Hydrocarbon Fuel — Petroleum-based organic compound that contains only hydrogen and carbon.

I

I-Beam — Steel or wooden structural member consisting of top and bottom flanges joined by a center web section so that the cross section resembles a capital I.

Immediately Dangerous to Life and Health (IDLH) — Any atmosphere that poses an immediate hazard to life or produces immediate irreversible, debilitating effects on health. A companion measurement to the permissible exposure limit (PEL), IDLH concentrations represent concentrations above which respiratory protection should be required. IDLH is expressed in ppm or mg/m3.

Incident Action Plan (IAP) — Written or unwritten plan for the disposition of an incident. The IAP contains the overall strategic goals, tactical objectives, and support requirements for a given operational period during an incident.

Incident Command System (ICS) — System by which facilities, equipment, personnel, procedures, and communications are organized to operate within a common organizational structure designed to aid in the management of resources at emergency incidents.

Incident Management System — System described in NFPA® 1561, *Standard on Fire Department Incident Management System*, that defines the roles, responsibilities, and standard operating procedures used to manage emergency operations. Such systems may also be referred to as Incident Command Systems (ICS).

Incipient Stage Fire — Fire that is in the initial or beginning stage and that can be controlled or extinguished by portable fire extinguishers or small hoselines.

Index Gas — Any commonly encountered gas, such as carbon monoxide in fires, whose concentration can be measured. In the absence of devices capable of measuring the concentrations of other gases present, the CO measurement may be assumed to indicate their concentrations as well.

Intrinsically Safe Equipment — Equipment designed and approved for use in flammable atmospheres that is incapable of releasing sufficient electrical energy to cause the ignition of a flammable atmospheric mixture.

J

Joule (J) — Unit of work or energy in the International System of Units; the energy (or work) when unit force (1 newton) moves a body through a unit distance (1 meter); takes the place of calorie for heat measurement (1 calorie = 4.19 J).

K

Kinetic Energy — The energy possessed by a moving object.

L

Laminated Glass — A type of glass consisting of two layers of glass with a transparent layer of vinyl bonded into the center.

Lapping — Means by which fire spreads vertically from floor to floor in a multistory building. Fire issuing from a window laps up the outside of the building and enters the floor(s) above, usually through the windows.

Leeward — Protected side; the direction opposite from which the wind is blowing.

Lexan® — Polycarbonate plastic used for windows. It has one-half the weight of an equivalent-sized piece of glass, yet is 30 times stronger than safety glass and 250 times stronger than ordinary glass. It cannot be broken using standard forcible entry techniques.

Liquefied Petroleum Gas (LPG) — Any of several petroleum products, such as propane or butane, stored under pressure as a liquid.

Litter — Portable device that allows two or more persons to carry the sick or injured while keeping the patient immobile.

Lobby Control — In high-rise fire fighting, the individual responsible for, and the process of, taking and maintaining control of the lobby and elevators in a high-rise fire fighting situation. Lobby control also includes establishing internal communications, coordinating the flow of personnel and equipment up the interior stairway(s) to upper levels, and coordinating with building engineering personnel.

Loss Control — The practice of minimizing damage and providing customer service through effective mitigation and recovery efforts before, during, and after an incident.

Louver Cut — Rectangular exit opening cut in a roof, allowing a section of roof deck (still nailed to a center rafter) to be tilted, thus creating an opening similar to a louver. Also called center rafter cut.

Lower Explosive Limit (LEL) — Lowest percentage of fuel/oxygen mixture required to support combustion. Any mixture with a lower percentage would be considered *too lean* to burn.

M

Mayday — International distress signal broadcast by voice.

Mechanical Ventilation — Any means other than natural ventilation. This type of ventilation may involve the use of fans, blowers, smoke ejectors, and fire streams.

Mullion — Vertical division between multiple windows or a double door opening.

Mushrooming — Tendency of heat, smoke, and other products of combustion to rise until they encounter a horizontal obstruction. At this point they will spread laterally until they encounter vertical obstructions and begin to bank downward.

N

Natural Ventilation — Techniques that use the wind, convection currents, and other natural phenomena to ventilate a structure without the use of fans, blowers, or other mechanical devices.

Negative Pressure Ventilation (NPV) — Technique using smoke ejectors to develop artificial circulation and to pull smoke out of a structure. Smoke ejectors are placed in windows, doors, or roof vent holes to pull the smoke, heat, and gases from inside the building and eject them to the exterior.

Neutral Pressure Plane — The point within a building, especially a high-rise, where the interior pressure equals the atmospheric pressure outside. This plane will move up or down, depending on variables of temperature and wind.

O

Oriented Strand Board (OSB) — Construction material made of many small wooden pieces (strands) bonded together to form sheets, similar to plywood.

Overhaul — Those operations conducted once the main body of fire has been extinguished that consist of searching for and extinguishing hidden or remaining fire, placing the building and its contents in a safe condition, determining the cause of the fire, and recognizing and preserving evidence of arson.

P

Panic Hardware — Hardware mounted on exit doors in public buildings that unlocks from the inside and enables doors to be opened when pressure is applied to the release mechanism.

Penthouse — Structure on the roof of a building that may be used as a living space, to enclose mechanical equipment, or to provide roof access from an interior stairway. Also called a Bulkhead.

Personnel Accountability Report (PAR) — A roll call of all units (crews, teams, groups, companies, sectors) assigned to an incident. Usually by radio, the supervisor of each unit reports the status of the personnel within the unit at that time. A PAR may be required by SOP at specific intervals during an incident, or may be requested at any time by the IC or the ISO.

Piercing Nozzle — Nozzle with an angled, case-hardened steel tip that can be driven through a wall, roof, or ceiling to extinguish hidden fire.

Pilaster — Rectangular masonry column built into a wall.

Pole Ladder — Large extension ladder that requires tormentor poles to steady the ladder as it is raised and lowered. Also called Bangor Ladder.

Positive Pressure Ventilation (PPV) — Method of ventilating a confined space by mechanically blowing fresh air into the space in sufficient volume to create a slight positive pressure within and thereby forcing the contaminated air out the exit opening.

Potential Energy — Stored energy possessed by an object that can be released in the future to perform work once released.

Primary Damage — Damage caused by a fire itself and not by actions taken to fight the fire.

Purlin — Horizontal member between trusses that supports the roof.

Pyrolysis — Thermal or chemical decomposition of fuel (matter) because of heat that generally results in the lowered ignition temperature of the material.

R

Rabbet — Groove cut in the surface or on the edge of a board to receive another member.

Radiation — The transmission or transfer of heat energy from one body to another body at a lower temperature through intervening space by electromagnetic waves such as infrared thermal waves, radio waves, or X rays.

Rain Roof — A second roof constructed over an existing roof.

Rapid Intervention Crew (RIC) — Two or more fully equipped and immediately available firefighters designated to stand by outside the hazard zone to enter and effect rescue of firefighters inside, if necessary. Also known as Rapid Intervention Team.

Razor Ribbon — Coil of lightweight, flexible metallic ribbon with extremely sharp edges; often installed on parapet walls and on fence tops to discourage trespassers.

Rebar — Steel bars that are placed inside concrete structural elements to reinforce and strengthen the element.

Rehab — Term for a rehabilitation station at a fire or other incident where personnel can rest, rehydrate, and recover from the stresses of the incident.

Rekindle — Reignition of a fire because of latent heat, sparks, or smoldering embers; can be prevented by proper overhaul.

Rollover — Condition in which the unburned combustible gases released in a confined space (such as a room or aircraft cabin) during the incipient or early steady-state phase accumulate at the ceiling level. These superheated gases are pushed, under pressure, away from the fire area and into uninvolved areas where they mix with oxygen. When their flammable range is reached and additional oxygen is supplied by opening doors and/or applying fog streams, they ignite and a fire front develops, expanding very rapidly in a rolling action across the ceiling.

S

Salvage — Methods and operating procedures associated with fire fighting by which firefighters attempt to save property and reduce further damage from water, smoke, heat, and exposure during or immediately after a fire by removing property from a fire area, by covering it, or other means.

Secondary Damage — Damage caused by or resulting from those actions taken to fight a fire and leaving the property unprotected.

Sheathing — First layer of roof covering laid directly over the rafters or other roof supports. Sheathing may be plywood, chipboard sheets, or planks that are butted together or spaced about 1 inch (2.5 cm) apart. Also called Decking or Roof Decking.

Shelter in Place — Having occupants remaining in a structure or vehicle in order to provide protection from a rapidly approaching hazard (fire, hazardous gas cloud, etc.).

Short Circuit — An abnormal, low-resistance path between conductors that allows a high current flow that normally leads to an overcurrent condition.

Size-Up — Ongoing mental evaluation process performed by the operational officer in charge of an incident that enables him or her to determine and evaluate all existing influencing factors that are used to develop objectives, strategy, and tactics for fire suppression before committing personnel and equipment to a course of action.

Smoke Damper — Device that restricts the flow of smoke through an air-handling system. Usually activated by the building's fire alarm signaling system.

Solid-Core Door — Door whose entire core is filled with solid material.

Spurs — Metal points at the end of a ladder or staypoles.

Stack Effect — Phenomenon of a strong air draft moving from ground level to the roof level of a building. Affected by building height, configuration, and temperature differences between inside and outside air.

Staypoles — Poles attached to long extension ladders to assist in raising and steadying the ladder. Some poles are permanently attached, and some are removable. Also called Tormentor Poles.

Stratification — Formation of smoke into layers as a result of differences in density with respect to height with low density layers on the top and high density layers on the bottom.

Substrate — Layer of material between a roof deck and the roof covering that may or may not be bonded to the roof covering. The most common substrate is roofing felt or tar paper.

T

Tactical Ventilation - A methodical, thought-out approach to changing the ventilation profile of a structure.

Target Hazard — Facility in which there is a great potential likelihood of life or property loss in the event of an attack or natural disaster.

Tempered Glass — Type of glass specially treated to become harder and more break-resistant than plate glass or a single sheet of laminated glass. Tempered glass is most commonly used in side windows and some rear windows.

Thermal Layering — Outcome of combustion in a confined space in which gases tend to form into layers, according to temperature, with the hottest gases found at the ceiling and the coolest gases at floor level. Also called Thermal Balance or Heat Stratification.

Thermoplastic — a petroleum based product that softens with an increase of temperature and hardens with a decrease of temperature but does not undergo any chemical change.

Triangular Cut — Triangular opening cut in a roll-up or tilt-slab door to provide access into the building or a means of egress for those inside.

Truck Company (Ladder Company) — Group of firefighters assigned to a fire department aerial apparatus who are primarily responsible for search and rescue, ventilation, salvage and overhaul, forcible entry, and other fireground support functions.

Topography — Physical configuration of the land or terrain.

Trench Ventilation — Defensive tactic that involves cutting an exit opening in the roof of a burning building, extending from one outside wall to the other, to create an opening at which a spreading fire may be cut off. Also called Strip Vent.

U

Unprotected Openings — Openings in floors, walls, or partitions that are not protected against the passage of smoke, flame, and heat; generally used to refer to such openings in fire walls.

V

Vaporization — Process of evolution that changes a liquid into a gaseous state. The rate of vaporization depends on the substance involved, heat, and pressure.

Veneer — Surface layer of attractive material laid over a base of common material.

Ventilation — Systematic removal of heated air, smoke, gases or other airborne contaminants from a structure and replacing them with cooler and/or fresher air to reduce damage and to facilitate fire fighting operations.

W

Windward — Unprotected side; the direction from which the wind is blowing.

Wired Glass — Flat sheet glass containing a wire mesh that is embedded in it during manufacture, which increases resistance to breakage and penetration.

Index

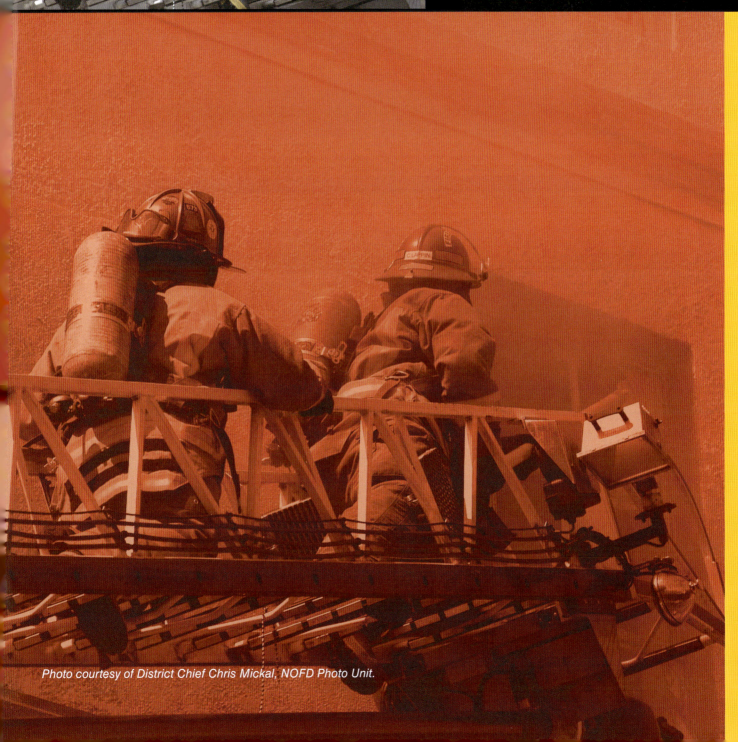

Photo courtesy of District Chief Chris Mickal, NOFD Photo Unit.

Index

A

Access into structures
    doors, 222–235
    forcible entry tools, 220–222
    overview, 12, 219–220
    using ground ladders, 136–138
    walls, 242–248
    windows, 235–242
    barricades, 206
    building placement on lots, 204–205
    fences, 209–211
    aerial devices, 348, 415–416
    gates, 206–209
    landscaping, 203–206
    overview, 12
    security measures, 212–214
    site obstacles, overcoming, 206
    topography, 203–206
Acrolein, 104
Aerial devices for roof access, 348, 415–416
Air chisel, 248
Air management, situational awareness, 76
Airflow, 40-42
AIT (autoignition temperature), 23
All clear, 254
Alternating current detectors, 194–195
Ambient conditions, 35
Apparatus positioning, 68
Arched roof
    construction, 161, 379–380
    hazards, 382
    venting, 382–383
Area of refuge, 271
Area of rescue and assistance, 271
Asbestos, 157
Atrium, 425
Atrium vents, 425
Attack methods. See Method of attack
Attic
    fire characteristics, 164–165
    in flat roofs, 369
Autoignition, 23
Autoignition temperature (AIT), 23
Automatic roof vents, 425
Automatic sprinkler systems, 296. *See also* Sprinkler systems
Awning windows, 318

B

Backdraft
    defined, 51
    development, 51–52
    flashover vs., 53–54
    influencing factors, 55
    recognition of, 8
    smoke explosion vs., 54

Balloon-frame construction
    attic fire characteristics, 164–165
    basement fire characteristics, 165
    defined, 160
    in old wood frame buildings, 160
    in Victorian-style houses, 166
Bar joist, 386–387
Barbed wire, 212, 375–376
Barium, strontium, titanium (BST) technology, 260
Barricades, 206
Basements
    cellars, 198, 428–429
    fire characteristics, 165
    flooding, 114
    underground structures, 410, 428–429
    ventilation, 428–429
Battering ram, 226, 246–247
Bifold doors, 230
BLEVE. See Boiling liquid expanding vapor explosion (BLEVE)
Blowers
    mechanical horizontal ventilation, 333–334
    smoke blowers, 313
Blowout panels, 246
Boiling liquid expanding vapor explosion (BLEVE)
    defined, 181
    fuel oil, 184
    LPG tank explosions, 181
Bolt cutters, 312
Booby traps, 214
Bowstring arch roof, 380–381
Bowstring truss roof, 161, 380
Bridge-truss roof, 365
Bridging, 142–143
British Thermal Unit (Btu), 22
Buddy breathing, 83, 278
Buddy system, 260
Building
    codes, 295
    configuration, impact on fire development, 31
    contents, impact on fire development, 31
    thermal characteristics, 35, 37–38
    type, for search size-up, 255
Building construction
    arched roofs, 161. *See also* Arched roof
    built-in fire suppression systems, 296
    elevator shafts, 298–299
    fuel load impact on fire development, 31
    horizontal ventilation, 316–327
        doors, 320–324
        walls, 324–327
        windows, 316–320
    Lamella roof, 161
    newer buildings, 295
    occupancy-related features, 299

Index **453**

Building construction *(continued)*
    older buildings, 293–295
    planters and landscaping, 299
    remodeling (renovations), 162–163, 294–295, 430
    security systems, 299
    self-closing fire doors, 296
    size-up considerations, 160–168, 292–299
        age of building, 160–161, 293–295
        attics, 164–165
        basements, 165
        fire characteristics, 164–168
        large dwellings, 167
        modifications, 162–163
        negative construction features, 298–299
        office buildings, 168
        positive construction features, 295–298
        townhouses, 165–166
        type of construction, 161–162, 293–295
        Victorians, 166
        warehouses, 167–168
    steel framing members, 296
    synthetic materials, 295, 299
    upsetting established ventilation, 338
Building materials
    insulation, 36
    masonry, 35
    metal, 35
    modern fire environment, 36
    Type I construction, 37
    Type II construction, 37
    Type III construction, 37
    Type IV construction, 37
    Type V construction, 37
Built-up roofs, 392
Bulkheads, 396, 417
Butterfly roof, 366

C

Carabiner, 268
Carbon dioxide, 104
Carbon monoxide (CO), 102
Carcinogen, 191
Casement windows, 318
Ceilings
    false ceilings, 162
    height, impact on fire development, 33, 40
    pulling ceilings for access, 106–107
Cellars. *See also* Basements
    ventilation operations, 428–429
    water leaks without fire, 198
Celsius scale, 22
Center-rafter cut, 401–402
Chain saw, 246, 357–358
Chain-link fences, 209–210
Chemical composition of fuel, 36
Chemical energy, 21
Churning, 333
Class A foam, 112
Claw tool, 226
Clerestory windows, 399
Cockloft, 164, 369
Collapse. *See* Structural collapse

Collapse zones, 68, 69
Combustible gas indicator (CGI), 185, 186
Combustion, 20–21
    defined, 20
    fire tetrahedron, 21
    fire triangle, 20
    flaming, 21
    nonflaming, 20
    products of combustion and toxic effects, 74
    smoldering, 20
Communications
    distress calls, 78
    for fireground safety, 78
    public address system, 271
    reporting identified hazards, 79
    two-in/two-out rule, 78
Compartment
    fire development, 24–36
        changing conditions, 35–36
        conduction, 24
        convection, 24
        factors affecting development, 30–35
        modern fire environment, 36
        radiation, 24
        stages of fire development, 24–30
    fire development factors, 30–35
        additional fuel, 31–32
        ambient conditions, 35
        compartment geometry, 32–33
        fuel type, 31
        thermal properties of the enclosure, 35
        ventilation, 34–35
    stages of fire development, 24–30
        decay stage, 29–30, 289
        fully developed stage, 29, 289
        growth stage, 26–28, 289
        incipient stage, 26, 289
Compartmentalization, 296
Composition roofing and shingles, 391
Compressed air foam systems (CAFS), 112
Concertina wire, 212
Concrete. *See also* Masonry
    breaching concrete walls, 246–247
    exterior walls, 326
    knockout (blowout) panels, 246
    rebar, 247
    reinforced, 170
    roofs, 373–374
    veneer walls, 327
Conduction, 24
Construction of buildings. *See* Building construction
Contents of buildings
    content removal, 110–112
    protection of, 110–112
    upsetting established ventilation, 338
Control zone
    defined, 185
    electricity control, 192–195
    gas leaks without fire, 185
    purpose of, 186
Convection, 24
Counseling for victims, 116

Courses of masonry, 246
Crawl space, 369
Crew Resource Management (CRM), 64-65
Curtain boards, 425, 427

D
Dead load
    collapse potential, 70, 255
    defined, 255
Deadbolt, 234
Decay stage fire
    backdraft, 30
    self-extinguishment, 29
    ventilation size-up, 289
    ventilation-induced flashover, 30
Deck roof, 372
Decorative metal fences, 211
Deployment mode, 280
Dicing, 402
Distress calls, 78
Doors
    access into structures, 222–235
        industrial/institutional, 228–234
        residential/commercial, 224–228
        security systems, 234–235
        size-up, 222–224
    deadbolts, 234
    decay stage fire, 29
    door opening tools, 224, 226
    egress through, 83–86
    fire behavior and door openings, 223
    fire door, 296, 321
    fire gas ignition, 54–55
    forcible entry, 105–106, 222–235, 331
    guarding the line of retreat, 264
    for horizontal ventilation, 320–324
        natural ventilation, 331
        overhead-type doors, 323
        roll-up doors, 323
        sliding doors, 321–323
        swinging doors, 321
        telescoping doors, 323–324, 323–224
    industrial/institutional
        bifold doors, 230
        forcible entry, 230–234
        horizontal sliding doors, 230
        sectional doors, 228
        service doors, 228
        sheet-curtain door, 228–229
        steel roll-up door, 228
        telescoping door, 230, 233, 323–324
    kicking in of inward-opening door, 264
    latch straps, 266–267
    locating for emergency egress, 83–84
    lockbox, 223, 235
    padlocks, 235
    panic hardware, 224, 234
    rabbet, 224
    roll-up doors
        construction, 228–229
        forcible entry, 231–233
        for horizontal ventilation, 323
    security barriers, 233–234
    security systems, 234–235
    self-closing fire doors, 296
    sheet-curtain door
        construction, 228–229
        forcible entry, 231–233
    sidelight, 223
    single-piece slab doors, 226–227
    size-up, 222–224
    sliding doors, 321–323
    softening the building, 228, 279–280
    solid-core, 224
    swinging doors, 321
    tempered glass, 224
    triangular cut (tepee cut), 231
Double-hung windows, 317
Draft curtains, 427
Ducts, flexible, for ventilation, 313–316
Dwellings
    electricity control in structure fires, 188–190
    large dwellings, 167
    sprinkler systems, 197
    townhouses, 165–166
    water supply, 197
Dynamic Risk Assessment, 63–64, 74

E
Economic loss control, 114–116
EEBSS (Emergency Escape Breathing Support System), 83
Egress. *See* Emergency egress
Electricity control, 188–195
    commercial occupancies, 190
    downed wires, 191–192, 193
    hazard identification, 194–195
    industrial occupancies, 190–191
    perimeter control, 192–195
    residential occupancies, 188–190
    in structure fires, 188–191
Elevator shafts, 298–299
Elevators, 411–412, 416
Emergency egress, 82–87
    door egress, 85–86
    firefighter lost, 82
    firefighter trapped, 82–83
    secondary egress using ground ladders, 137–138
    using emergency escape techniques, 82
    wall breach, 86–87
    window and door locations, 83–84
    window egress, 84–85
Emergency Escape Breathing Support System (EEBSS), 83
Energy
    chemical energy, 21
    conversion, 23
    defined, 21
    energy-efficient (thermal) windows, 319–320
    heat energy, 21
    kinetic energy, 21
    potential energy, 21
Entry mode, 280
Environmental Protection Agency (EPA), 114, 191
Evacuation, 272
Evidence preservation, 101

Explosions
    BLEVE, 181, 184
    lower explosive limit (LEL), 186
    natural gas explosion prevention, 181
Exposures, ventilation size-up considerations, 303-304
Exterior walls, 325-327
Extreme fire behavior, 46-55
    backdraft, 51-54
    fire gas ignition, 54-55
    flashover, 46-51
    ignition source, 55
    increased heat, 55
    increased ventilation, 55
    smoke explosion, 54

F

Factory windows, 319
Fahrenheit scale, 22
Fans for ventilation, 313
Fences, 209-211
    fence spikes, 213
    field fence, 209
    hog wire, 209
    razor ribbon, 210
    types of, 209-211
Fiberglass roof covering, 394
Film-coated glass, 242
Fink roof truss, 387
Fire behavior
    burning regime, 289-290
    defined, 19
    door opening and, 223
    extreme fire behavior, 46-55, 289-290
    in high-rise buildings, 412-414
    indicators, 36-46
    overview, 9
    reading the fire, 290
    size-up considerations, 157-160
    smoke behavior, 290-292
    stages, 289
Fire characteristics for size-up, 164-168
    attics, 164-165
    basements, 165
    large dwellings, 167
    office buildings, 168
    townhouses, 165-166
    Victorians, 166
    warehouses, 167-168
Fire door, 296, 321
Fire gas
    fire gas ignition, defined, 54
    ignition development, 54-55
    listing and sources, 104
    smoke explosion, 54
Fire science
    backdraft, 51-54
        defined, 51
        flashover vs., 53-54
    combustion, 20-21
    compartment fire development, 24-36
        changing conditions, 35-36
        factors affecting development, 30-35

        modern fire environment, 36
        stages of fire development, 24-30
    fire development factors, 30-35
        additional fuel, 31-32
        ambient conditions, 35
        compartment geometry, 32-33
        fuel type, 31
        thermal properties of the enclosure, 35
        ventilation, 34-35
    fire gas ignition, 54-55
    flashover, 46-51
        backdraft vs., 53-54
        misconceptions, 50-51
        radiation-induced, 47-48
        ventilation-induced, 48-49
    heat and temperature, 21-23
    heat of combustion, 23-24
    heat release rate, 24
    initiating events, 55
    smoke explosion, 54
    stages of fire development, 24-30
        changing conditions, 35-36
        decay stage, 29-30, 289
        factors affecting development, 30-35
        fully developed stage, 29, 289
        growth stage, 26-28, 289
        incipient stage, 26, 289
        modern fire environment, 36
Fire stream, 338
Fire suppression systems, 296
Fire tetrahedron, 21
Fire triangle, 20
Fire wall, 165-166
Firefighter safety and survival
    Crew Resource Management, 64-65
    Dynamic Risk Assessment, 63-64, 74
    emergency egress, 82-87
        door egress, 85-86
        firefighter lost, 82
        firefighter trapped, 82-83
        using emergency escape techniques, 82
        wall breach, 86-87
        window and door locations, 83-84
        window egress, 84-85
    fireground safety
        elements, 71-82
        emergency egress, 82-87
        routine calls, 66-67
        self-vented fires, 67-68
        structural collapse, 68-71
    IFSTA *Principles of Risk Management*, 63
    key safety behaviors, 65-66
    life safety priority, 62
    during overhaul, 102-103
    overview, 10, 61-62
Fireground safety
    communications, 78
    company discipline, 77
    elements, 71-82
    emergency egress, 82-87
        door egress, 85-86
        firefighter lost, 82

456 Index

firefighter trapped, 82–83
  using emergency escape techniques, 82
  wall breach, 86–87
  window and door locations, 83–84
  window egress, 84–85
emergency escape techniques, 82
Incident Action Plan, 72
Incident Management System, 71
personnel accountability system, 72–73
PPE and respiratory protection, 74
Rapid Intervention Crew, 79–80
Rehab unit, 80–82
reporting identified hazards, 79
risk/benefit analysis, 75
routine calls, 66–67
self-vented fires, 67–68
situational awareness, 75–77
size-up, 74–75
standard operating procedures, 79
strategy and tactics, 79
structural collapse, 68–71
team integrity, 77
Fire-resistive construction (Type II), 37
Five-in-twelve roof, 361
Fixed windows, 317
Flame
  fire behavior indicators, 43
  ghosting, 43
Flashover
  backdraft vs., 53–54
  defined, 28
  development, 46–47
  factors in development, 29
  indicators, 49
  influencing factors, 55
  misconceptions, 50–51
  radiation-induced, 47–48
  ventilation-induced, 30, 48–49
Flat roofs
  concrete roof, 373–374
  coverings, 390
  hazards, 375–377
  inverted roof, 370–371, 375
  louver cuts, 379
  metal deck roof, 372
  modern mansard roof, 374
  panelized, 375
  poured gypsum roof, 374
  purlins, 378
  rain roof, 371
  security, 375–376
  venting, 377–379
  wooden deck roof, 372
Flexible ducts, 313–316
Floors
  hall runners, 110
  protection of, 110
Fly section, 128
Fog stream, 334, 336
Forced ventilation, 287. *See also* Mechanical ventilation

Forcible entry
  concrete walls, 246–247
  defined, 220
  doors, 105–106, 230–234, 331
  residential/commercial doors, 224–228
  RIC tools, 277
  roll-up doors, 231–233
  sheet-curtain door, 231–233
  tools, 220–222
  walls, 242–248
    concrete, 246–247
    masonry, 245–246
    metal, 248
    wood-frame, 243–245
  windows, 105, 237–238, 332
Fuel
  control in structure fires, 178–184
    fuel oil, 183–184
    liquefied petroleum gas, 181–183
    natural gas, 179–181
    situational differences, 179–184
  fire development factors, 31
  fuel controlled fire, 27
  unburned fuel as smoke, 38, 157
Fully developed stage, 29, 289
Furring strips, 393

G

Gable roof, 363
Gambrel roof, 366
Gang nails, 385
Gas leaks without fire, 185–188
  approach, 185
  combustible gas indicator, 185
  hazard assessment, 186–187
  hazard mitigation, 187–188
  perimeter control, 185–186
Gates, 206–209
  automated, 206–208
  hasps, 207
  lockboxes, 208–209
  manually operated, 207
  padlocks, 207
  scissor gate, 235
Ghosting, 43
Ground ladders
  access uses, 136–138
    to buildings, 136–137
    roof access, 137–138
    secondary egress, 138
    into structures, 137
  handling, 126–127
  nonstandard uses for, 139–143
    bridging, 142–143
    mechanical advantage systems, 140
    positioning intake strainers, 140
    water removal, 141–142
  pole ladder
    defined, 128
    raises, 128–134
    staypoles, 128, 129

Ground ladders *(continued)*
    positioning, 135–136
    preincident planning for, 123
    raises, 127–134
    for rescue, 138
    selection, 125–126
        butt placement, 126
        effective length, 125–126
    tactical use, 136–139
    uses for, 123
    for ventilation, 138–139
Growth stage fire, 26–28, 289
Guard dogs, 214
Gypsum roof, poured, 374

H
Hall runners, 110
Halligan, 226
Hasp, 207
Hazards
    arched roofs, 382
    communication of, 79
    electricity, 194–195
    flat roofs, 375–377
    flying guillotine hazard, 237
    gas leaks without fire, 186–188
    hazardous materials size-up considerations, 171
    life hazard identification, 263, 347
    pitched roofs, 367
    products of combustion, 74
    structural collapse, 68
    target hazards, 324
    toxic substances. *See* Toxic substances
    water contamination, 114
Header course, 246
Heat
    extreme fire behavior and, 55
    fire science, 21–23
    heat energy, 21
    heat flux, 28, 48
    heat of combustion, 23–24, 36
    infrared heat sensors, 42
    stratification, 26
    tactile effects, 42–43
    ventilation for removal of, 108
Heating, ventilation, and air conditioning (HVAC)
    smoke-control systems, 424–427
        atrium vents, 425
        automatic roof vents, 425
        built-in ventilation devices, 425–427
        curtain boards, 425, 427
        monitor vents, 426
        skylights, 426
        smoke dampers, 424
    ventilation of fire, 34
    ventilation-induced flashover, 49
Heating oil
    control in structure fires, 183–184
    white ghost, 184
Heat release rate (HRR)
        chemical composition of fuel, 36
        defined, 23
        measurement, 24

Heavy timber construction (Type IV), 37
Helicopters, 416–417
Hidden fires, 103
High-rise buildings
    electricity control, 189–190
    fire behavior, 412–414, 421
    fire department challenges, 409–410
    fire operations, 410–414
        elevators, 411–412
        fire attack, 410–411
        fire behavior, 412
        lobby control, 411
        mushrooming, 413–414
        stack effect, 412, 421
        staffing, 410
    fire walls, 165–166
    firefighters to the roof, 415–417
    searches, 273–274
    townhouses, 165–166
    ventilation, 415–423
        above the fire, 423
        below the fire, 422
        channeling smoke, 417–421
        on the fire floor, 422–423
        opening location, 302
        vertical ventilation, 415–417
Hip roof, 363
Hopper windows, 319
Horizontal sliding doors, 230
Horizontal ventilation
    doors, 320–324, 331
    establishing and supporting of, 329
        location of fire, 329
        opening locations, 329
        wind direction and speed, 329
    mechanical ventilation, 333–336
        blowers, 333–334
        nozzles (hydraulic ventilation), 334, 336
        smoke ejectors, 313, 315–316, 333
    natural ventilation, 330–332
    overview, 13, 311–312
    upsetting established ventilation, 337–339
        building construction, 338
        exit openings, 337–338
        fire streams, 338
        implementation errors, 337
        salvaged contents placement, 338
        wind, 339
    uses for ladders, 138–139
    ventilation equipment, 312–316
        fans, 313
        flexible ducts, 313–316
    ventilation tools, 312
    vertical ventilation vs., 302
    walls, 324–327
    windows, 316–320, 332
Horizontal-sliding windows, 318
Hoselines, 351–352
Hot gas layer, 40
Howe roof truss, 387

Humidity
    fire development factors, 35
    smoke color and, 40
HVAC. *See* Heating, ventilation, and air conditioning (HVAC)
Hydraulic ventilation, 334, 336
Hydrocarbon fuels, 291

I

IAP. See Incident Action Plan (IAP)
I-beam, 388–389
ICS. *See* Incident Command System (ICS)
IDLH. *See* Immediately Dangerous to Life and Health (IDLH)
IFSTA *Principles of Risk Management*, 63, 75
Immediately Dangerous to Life and Health (IDLH)
    defined, 72
    entering buildings, 234
    personnel accountability system, 72
    two-in/two-out rule, 78, 274
Incident Action Plan (IAP)
    access into structures, 219
    defined, 72
    size-up and, 99
Incident Command System (ICS)
    company discipline, 77
    defined, 71
Incident Commander (IC), 155, 220
Incident Management System, defined, 71
Incipient stage fire, 26, 289
Index gas, 272
Industrial occupancy electricity control during structure fires, 190–191
Infrared heat sensors, 42
Initiating events, 55
Insulation
    modern fire environment, 36
    pulling ceilings for access, 106
    thermal properties, 35
Intake strainer positioning, 140
Interior finishes, 31–32
Interstitial space, 369
Intrinsically safe equipment, 316
Inverted flat roof, 370–371, 375
Isocyanate foam roofing, 392

J

Jails, 233–234, 430
Jalousie windows, 319
Joists, bar, 386–387
Joule (J), 22

K

Kilowatts (kW), 24
Kinetic energy, defined, 21
Knockout panels, 246

L

Ladder company, 8
Ladders. *See* Ground ladders
Lamella arch roof, 161, 293, 382
Laminated glass, 241

Landscaping
    access to structures, 203–206
    in building construction, 299
Lantern roof, 364
Lapping, 108
Large-area search, 268–270
Latch straps, 266–267
Leeward, 332
LEL. *See* Lower explosive limit
Lexan, 239, 240, 320
Life safety, 62, 170, 286–287
Light shafts, 398
Lighting
    chemical light sticks, 277
    illuminated ropes, 277
    personal illumination equipment, 277
Liquefied petroleum gas (LPG)
    BLEVE, 181
    CGI readings, 186–187
    controlling in structure fires, 11, 181–183
    defined, 178
    gas leaks without fire, 182–183
    ignition sources, 187–188
    leak control, 187–188
    tank fires, 182
Litters, 278–279
Live loads, 70
Lobby control, 411
Lockboxes, 208–209, 223, 235
Loss control
    defined, 93
    economic loss control, 114–116
    incident loss control operations, 98
    overview, 10
    post-incident operations, 114–117
Louver cuts, 379
Louver vents, 401–402
Lower explosive limit (LEL), 186
LPG. *See* Liquefied petroleum gas (LPG)

M

Mansard roof, 365–366, 374
Masonry. *See also* Concrete
    courses, 246
    exterior walls, 326
    fences, 211
    header course, 246
    thermal properties, 35
    Type III construction, 37
    unreinforced, 245–246, 293
    veneer walls, 327
    walls, 211, 245–246
"Mayday" distress call
    communication of, 78
    defined, 276
    emergency egress, 82, 83
    RIC deployment, 280
    RIC response, 276
Mechanical advantage systems, 140
Mechanical ventilation
    defined, 287

Mechanical ventilation *(continued)*
    horizontal ventilation, 333–336
        using blowers, 333–334
        using nozzles (hydraulic ventilation), 334, 336
        using smoke ejectors, 333
    natural ventilation vs., 302–303
    situations requiring, 303
Megawatts (MW), 24
Method of attack
    high-rise fire operations, 410–411
    primary loss control, 99–100
Microbolometer technology, 260
Micro-lam, 388–389
Modern mansard roof, 366, 374
Monitor vents, 397, 426
Mono-pitch truss, 364
Mule kick, 226
Mullion, 318
Multistory buildings. *See* High-rise buildings
Mushrooming, 413–414

N

National Incident Management System (NIMS), 71
National Incident Management System-Incident Command System (NIMS-ICS), 78
National Institute of Standards and Technology (NIST), 48
Natural gas
    controlling in structure fires, 11, 179–181
    explosion prevention, 181
    ignition source elimination, 187–188
    leak control, 187–188
    lighter than air characteristic, 181
Natural ventilation
    defined, 286
    horizontal ventilation, 330–332
    mechanical ventilation vs., 302–303
Negative pressure ventilation (NPV), 313
Neutral pressure plane, 418–420
Nitrogen oxides, 104
Non-combustible construction (Type I), 37
Nozzles (hydraulic ventilation), 334, 336

O

Occupancy type, 170–171
Opacity of smoke, 40
Opening a roof, 352, 354–355
Optical density of smoke, 40
Oriented strand board (OSB), 243
Overhaul and loss control, 100–104
    evidence preservation, 101
    firefighter safety, 102–103
    hidden fire, 103
    overhaul, defined, 100
    psychological loss control, 116
    rekindle, 101
    toxic products of combustion, 103–104
Overhead-type doors, 323

P

Padlocks, 235
Panelized roof
    construction, 383–385
    flat roofs, 375
    pilasters, 383–384
    rolling back the roof, 402–403
Panic hardware, 224, 234
PAR. *See* Personnel accountability report (PAR)
Parallel chord trusses, 385–387
Parapet walls, 376
PASS device, 82–83
Passport, 72
Penthouses, 396, 417
Perimeter control
    electricity control, 192–195
    gas leaks without fire, 185–186
Personal protective equipment (PPE)
    for firefighter safety, 103
    for fireground safety, 74
    heat retention, 81
    rapid intervention crew use, 276
Personnel accountability report (PAR)
    defined, 72
    elapsed time in the building, 71
    uses for, 72–73
Personnel accountability system, 72
Phosgene, 104
Physical density of smoke, 40
Pick-head axe, 358–360
Piercing nozzle, 109
Pike pole, 360
Pilaster, 383–384
Pitched roofs, 361–368
    bridge-truss, 365
    butterfly, 366
    construction, 361
    coverings, 390
    five-in-twelve roof, 361
    gable, 363
    gambrel, 366
    hazards, 367
    hip roof, 363
    lantern roof, 364
    mansard, 365–366
    post-and-beam, 361–362
    sawtooth, 366
    shed roof, 364
    trusses, 387–388
    venting, 368
Planters, 299
Plexiglas, 240–241
Pole ladder
    defined, 128
    raises, 128–134
    staypoles, 128, 129
Polychlorinated biphenyls (PCBs), 191
Positive-pressure ventilation (PPV), 108, 313, 409
Post-and-beam construction, 361–362
Potential energy, 21
Poured gypsum roof, 374
PPE. *See* Personal protective equipment (PPE)

Pratt roof truss, 387
Preincident planning
    access through doors, 222
    door security systems, 234–235
    evacuation, 272
    gas meter location, 179–181
    ground ladders, 123
    life hazard identification, 263
    loss control, 94–98
        overview, 94–95
        plans development, 97–98
        purpose of, 94
        risk evaluation, 96–97
        risk identification, 95–96
    preincident size-up, 150
    survey, reading the building, 37
    wall breaching, 242–243
Pressure transfer for channeling smoke, 418
Primary loss control
    defined, 93
    effective strategy, 99
    method of attack, 99–100
    on-scene resources, 99
    overhaul, 100–104
    size-up, 98–99
    ventilation, 100
Primary search, 259–266
    buddy system, 260
    methods, 263–266
    perimeter search, 265
    priorities, 259–260
    tools, 260–263
    victim shelter from fire, 265
Prisons, 233–234, 430
Projected windows, 319
Propane. *See* Liquefied petroleum gas (LPG)
Property conservation, 287
Psychological loss control, 116–117
Purlin, 378
Pyrolysis, 23

R
Rabbet, 224
Radiation, 24
Radiation-induced flashover, 47–48
Rain roof, 162, 294, 371
Rapid Intervention Crew (RIC)
    defined, 71
    fire situation, 257
    for fireground safety, 79–80
    formation, 275
    limitation on effectiveness, 275
    NFPA® requirements, 274
    operational modes, 279–280
        entry or deployment mode, 280
        stand-by mode, 79–80, 279–280
    tools and equipment, 275–279
    two-in/two-out rule, 78
Razor ribbon, 210, 212, 375–376
Reading a roof, 348–350
Rebar, 247
Recirculation, 333

Rehab units, 80–82
    location of, 82
    purpose of, 80–81
Reinforcing stars or plates, 163
Rekindle of fire, 101
Relief agencies, 116–117
Remodeled (renovated) buildings, 162–163, 294–295, 430
Rescue. *See also* Search and rescue
    above-grade ladder rescues, 138
    below-grade ladder rescues, 138
    evacuation, 272
    sheltering in place, 271
    uses for ladders, 138
    ventilation size-up coordination with, 299–303
Rescue saw, 221–222, 226. *See also* Rotary saw
Residences. *See* Dwellings
RIC. *See* Rapid Intervention Crew (RIC)
Ridge vents, 398–399
Risk/benefit analysis, 75
Rolling back the roof, 402–403
Rollover, 28
Roll-up doors
    construction, 228–229
    forcible entry, 231–233
    for horizontal ventilation, 323
Roof coverings
    composition, 391
    fiberglass, 394
    metal, 394
    reading a roof, 349
    roofing felt, 389
    sheathing, 390
    single-ply, 393
    sounding a roof, 350
    steel clad, 394–396
    substrate, 389
    synthetic membrane, 393
    tar and gravel, 392
    tile and slate, 393–394
    urethane/isocyanate foam, 392
    wooden shakes and shingles, 390
Roofs
    access using ground ladders, 137–138, 416
    arched roof
        bowstring arch, 380–381
        bowstring truss, 380
        construction, 161, 293, 379–380
        hazards, 382
        lamella arch, 161, 293, 382
        trussless arch, 382
        venting, 382–383
    automatic roof vents, 425
    bowstring truss, 161, 293
    built-up roofs, 392
    construction, 368–369
    flat roofs, 368–379
    gusset plates, 367
    lamella, 161, 293
    newer construction, 295
    openings, 396–399
        clerestory windows, 399
        light and ventilation shafts, 398

Roofs *(continued)*
   openings, 396–399 *(continued)*
      monitors, 397
      penthouses (bulkheads), 396, 417
      procedure for, 352, 354–355
      ridge vents, 398–399
      scuttle hatches, 396
      skylights, 396–397
      turbine (rotary vane) vents, 397–398
   panelized
      construction, 383–385
      flat roofs, 375
      pilasters, 383–384
      rolling back the roof, 402–403
   pitched roofs, 361–368
   rain roof, 162, 294, 371
   reading a roof, 348–350
   rolling back the roof, 402–403
   skylights, 379, 396–397
   sounding a roof, 350
   trussed roofs, 385–388
   valley rafters, 363
   ventilation size-up consideration, 305
   vertical ventilation. *See* Vertical ventilation
   working on a roof, 351
Ropes
   illuminated ropes, 277
   rescue ropes, 278
Rotary saw
   breaching concrete walls, 246–247
   breaching metal walls, 248
   cutting into doors, 235
   forcing residential/commercial doors, 224, 226
   masonry cutting, 327
   uses for, 221–222
   for ventilation, 312
   for vertical ventilation, 356
Rotary vane vents, 397–398
Rubbish hook, 360

S
Safe person, 63–64
Safe place, 63
Safe zoning, 263
Safety behaviors of firefighters, 62–66
   Crew Resource Management, 64–65
   Dynamic Risk Assessment, 63–64, 74
   IFSTA *Principles of Risk Management*, 63
   key safety behaviors, 65–66
   life safety, 62
Salvage
   defined, 109
   exposed contents, 110–112
   floor protection, 110
   salvaged content placement, 338
   starting, 109
   water control, 112
   water removal, 113–114
Sawtooth roof, 366
SCBA. *See* Self-contained breathing apparatus (SCBA)
Scissor gate, 235
Scuttle hatches, 396

Search and rescue
   all clear signal, 254
   conducting a search, 258–273
      building safety, 258–259
      large-area search, 268–270
      marking systems, 266–267
      primary search, 259–266
      rescue, 270–272
      search objectives, 258
      secondary search, 272–273
      vent, enter, search (VES), 266
   Lead team member, 268
   multistory building search, 273–274
   Navigator, 268–270
   operational modes, 279–280
   overview, 12
   primary search, 259–266
   rapid intervention, 274–280
   rescue, 270–272
   rescue tools and equipment
      communications equipment, 276
      forcible entry tools, 277
      personal illumination equipment, 277
      PPE and SCBA, 276
      rescue air supply, 277–278
      rescue litters, 278–279
      rescue ropes, 278
      thermal imaging cameras, 276
   search line, 268–270
   search size-up, 254–258
Seat of the fire
   thermal imaging cameras for locating, 301
   ventilation considerations, 329
   working with protective hoselines, 351
Secondary loss control, 104–114
   ceilings, pulling, 106–107
   forcible entry, 105–106
   heat removal, 108
   salvage, 109–114
   secondary damage, defined, 93
   smoke control, 107–108
   ventilation, 107–108
   walls, opening, 107
   water control, 112
   water removal, 113–114
Secondary search, 272–273
Sectional doors, 228
Security
   barbed wire, 212, 375–376
   building modifications, 163
   door barriers, 233–234
   door security systems, 234–235
   economic loss control, 114–116
   flat roofs, 375–376
   highly secure buildings, 429–430
   measures. *See* Security measures
   razor ribbon, 375–376
   release document, 116
   ventilation size-up, 299
   windowless structures, 410
   windows, 238–242, 320

Self-contained breathing apparatus (SCBA)
    air management situational awareness, 76
    EEBSS, 83
    firefighter trapped, 83
    for fireground safety, 74, 103
    rapid intervention crew use, 276, 277–278
    temperature-sensing device, 42–43
    for toxic products of combustion, 102
Self-rescue, 82
Self-vented fires, 8, 67–68
Service doors, 228
Shakes, wooden, 390
Sheathing, 390
Shed roof, 364
Sheet-curtain door
    construction, 228–229
    forcible entry, 231–233
Shelter in place, 271
Shingles. *See* Roof coverings
Short circuit, 195
Shuttered windows, 242
Single-hung windows, 317
Single-ply roof, 393
Site obstacles, access to structures, 206
Situational awareness
    air management, 76
    defined, 75
    fire effects on the building, 76–77
    for fireground safety, 75–77
    reading the fire, 36
Size-up
    access into structures, 220
    defined, 98
    door, 222–224
    factors, 152–155
    for fireground safety, 74–75
    Incident Action Plan, 99
    primary loss control, 98–99
    reading the fire, 46
    search, 254–258
    ventilation, 290–292
        air flow (pressure), 292
        building construction, 292–299
        coordination with rescue and fire attack, 299–303
        exposures, 303–304
        fire behavior, 289–292
        method of ventilation, 302–303
        opening location, 300–302
        overview, 12, 287–289
        smoke color and density, 291
        smoke volume, 290
        timing, 300
        weather, 304–305
    windows, 237
Size-up for truck company operations
    on arrival, 155
    building construction, 160–168
        age of building, 160–161
        attics, 164–165
        basements, 165
        fire characteristics, 164–168
        large dwellings, 167
        modifications, 162–163
        office buildings, 168
        townhouses, 165–166
        type of construction, 161–162
        Victorians, 166
        warehouses, 167–168
    dispatch and response, 152–155
        factors, 152
        season of the year, 153–154
        time of day, 152
        time of week, 153
        weather, 154–155
    fire behavior, 157–160
    importance of accuracy, 149, 155–156
    initial size-up considerations, 155–156
    NIOSH model, 156–157
    occupancy type, 170–171
        hazardous materials, 171
        life safety, 170
    ongoing, 155–156
    overview, 11
    preincident size-up, 150
    smoke, 157–160
        air flow (pressure), 159–160
        color and density, 158
        reading smoke, 158–160
        size-up, 157
        volume, 158
    structural collapse, 168–170
Skylights, 379, 396–397, 426
Slate roof, 393–394
Sledgehammer, 246–247, 361
Sliding doors, 321–323
Smoke
    air flow (pressure), 159–160, 292
    automatic smoke vents, 298
    behavior in high-rise buildings, 290–292
    channeling in high-rise buildings, 417–421
    churning, 333
    color, 38, 40, 158, 291
    density, 158, 291
    fire behavior and, 157–160
    hot gas layer, 40
    HVAC smoke-control systems, 424–427
    hydrocarbons, 291
    life-threatening environment, 7–8
    optical density and opacity, 40, 291
    physical density, 40, 291
    size-up considerations, 157–160
    smoke explosion, 54, 55
    toxic substances in, 157
    unburned fuel, 38, 157
    volume, 158, 290
Softening the building, 228, 279–280
Solid-core door, 224
Sounding a roof, 350
Spanish tile, 393
Spray stream, 334, 336
Sprinkler systems, 162-163, 196–197, 296
Spurs on ladders, 129
Stack effect, 412, 421
Stairways for roof access, 416

Standard operating procedures (SOP), 78-79
Stand-by mode, 279-280
Staypoles, 128
Steel clad roof, 394-396
Stem walls, 325
Stratification, 413-414
Strip ventilation, 403-404
Stripping tools, 359-361
Structural collapse
    collapse indicators, 70
    collapse potential size-up, 169-170
    collapse zones, 68, 69
    dead loads, 70
    live loads, 70
    size-up considerations, 168-170
Substrate, 389
Swinging doors, 321
Synthetic building materials, 295, 299
Synthetic membrane roof, 393

T
Tactical ventilation, 286-287
Tag line, 260, 264-265
Tar and gravel roofs, 392
Target hazards, 324
Telescoping doors
    construction, 230
    features, 323-324
    forcible entry, 233
Temperature
    British Thermal Unit (Btu), 22
    Celsius scale, 22
    Fahrenheit scale, 22
    fire development factors, 35
    Joule (J), 22
    smoke color and, 40
    ventilation size-up consideration, 305
Tempered glass door, 224
Tepee cut, 231
Terra-cotta tile, 393
Thermal balance, 26
Thermal imaging camera (TIC)
    advantages of use, 262-263
    BST technology, 260
    downed electrical wire detection, 195
    interior fire detection, 42
    limitations of use, 261-262
    for locating the seat of the fire, 301
    microbolometer technology, 260
    for opening a roof, 354
    primary search visibility issues, 265
    rapid intervention crew use, 276
    search tools, 260-262
    small room search, 266
    venting pitched roofs, 368
    whiteout, 262
Thermal layering, 26
Thermal properties of enclosures, 35
Thermal windows, 35, 320
Thermoplastic
    defined, 392
    roof, 392
    windows, 240-241

TIC. *See* Thermal imaging camera (TIC)
Tile roof, 393-394
Time available for escape (TAE), 219
Time of day, size-up factor, 152
Time period for search size-up, 255-256
Tools. *See also* Equipment
    battering ram, 226, 246-247
    bolt cutters, 312
    chain saw, 246, 357-358
    claw tool, 226
    cutting torch, 226
    door opening, 224, 226
    Halligan, 226
    nonstandard uses, 140
    primary search, 260-263
    rapid intervention crew, 275-279
        forcible entry tools, 277
        litters, 278-279
        personal illumination equipment, 277
        PPE and SCBA, 276
        rescue air supply, 277-278
        rescue ropes, 278
        thermal imaging cameras, 276
    rotary saw. *See* Rotary saw
    search rope (tag line), 260, 264-265
    sledgehammer, 246-247, 361
    stripping tools, 359-361
    thermal imaging cameras, 260-262
    ventilation, 312
    vertical ventilation, 355-361
Topography
    access to structures, 203-206
    defined, 203
Tormentor poles, 128
Townhouse fire characteristics, 165-166
Toxic substances
    asbestos, 157
    fire gases, 104
    firefighter risks, 102-103
    products of combustion and toxic effects, 74
    toxic products of combustion, overhaul, 103-104
Trench ventilation, 403-404
Triangular cut, 231
Trusses
    bowstring truss, 161, 380
    bridge truss, 365
    Fink roof truss, 387
    gusset plates, 367
    Howe roof truss, 387
    mono-pitch truss, 364
    Pratt roof truss, 387
    trussed roofs, 385-388
        parallel chord trusses, 385-387
        pitched roof trusses, 387-388
        steel trusses, 386-387
        wooden parallel chord trusses, 385
        wooden/metal trusses, 386
    trussless arch roof, 382
Tunnel vision, 76
Turbine vents, 397-398

Two-in/two-out rule
  communications during IDLH, 78
  exception, 257, 274
  OSHA regulations, 274
Type I construction (non-combustible), 37
Type II construction (fire-resistive), 37
Type III construction (masonry and wood), 37
Type IV construction (heavy timber), 37
Type V construction (wood frame), 37

U

Underground structures, 410, 428–429. *See also* Basements; Cellars
Unprotected openings, 325
Unreinforced masonry, 245–246, 293
Urethane roofing, 392
Utility and building system control
  electricity, 188–195
    alternating current detectors, 194–195
    commercial occupancies, 190
    downed wires, 191–192, 193
    hazard identification, 194–195
    industrial occupancies, 190–191
    perimeter control, 192–195
    residential occupancies, 188–190
    short circuit, 195
    sources of, 188
    in structure fires, 188–191
    thermal imaging cameras for hidden wire detection, 195
  fuel control, 178–184
    fuel oil, 183–184
    LPG, 181–183
    natural gas, 179–181
    situational differences, 179–184
  fuel oil, 183–184
  gas leaks without fire, 185–188
    approach, 185
    hazard assessment, 186–187
    hazard mitigation, 187–188
    perimeter control, 185–186
  importance of, 177–178
  liquefied petroleum gas
    controlling, 181–183
    hazard mitigation, 187–188
    overview, 11
  natural gas
    controlling, 179–181
    hazard mitigation, 187–188
    overview, 11
  overview, 11
  water control, 195–198
    basements or cellars, 198
    short circuit, 195
    sprinklered buildings, 196–197
    unsprinklered buildings, 197
    water leaks without fire, 198

V

Valley rafters, 363
Vaporization, 23
Veneer walls, 244
Veneer-over-frame walls, 326–327
Vent, Enter, Search (VES), 266
Vent-as-you-go, 108
Ventilation
  building features, 37
  built-in devices, 424–427
    atrium vents, 425
    automatic roof vents, 425
    curtain boards, 425, 427
    monitor vents, 426
    skylights, 426
    smoke dampers, 424
  defined, 285
  fire development impact, 34–35
  forced, 287
  heat removal, 108
  high-rise buildings, 415–423
    above the fire, 423
    below the fire, 422
    channeling smoke, 417–421
    on the fire floor, 422–423
    opening location, 302
    vertical ventilation, 415–417
  horizontal. *See* Horizontal ventilation
  hydraulic, 334, 336
  for loss control, 107–108
  mechanical. *See* Mechanical ventilation
  natural, 286, 302–303
  negative pressure, 313
  overview, 285–287
  positive-pressure ventilation, 108, 313, 409
  primary loss control, 100
  size-up
    air flow (pressure), 292
    building construction, 292–299
    coordination with rescue and fire attack, 299–303
    exposures, 303–304
    fire behavior, 289–292
    method of ventilation, 302–303
    opening location, 300–302
    overview, 12, 287–289
    smoke behavior, 290–292
    smoke color and density, 291
    smoke volume, 290
    timing, 300
    weather, 304–305
  smoke control, 107–108
  special operations
    highly secure buildings, 429–430
    high-rise buildings, 410–423
    HVAC and smoke-control systems, 424–427
    overview, 14, 409–410
    remodeled buildings, 430
    underground structures, 428–429
    windowless buildings, 429
  tactical ventilation, 286–287
    horizontal ventilation, 311
    incident stabilization, 287
    life safety, 286–287
    property conservation, 287
  underground structures, 428–429
  uses for ladders, 138–139

Ventilation *(continued)*
    vent-as-you-go, 108
    ventilation controlled fire, 27
    ventilation-induced flashover, 30, 48–49
    vertical. *See* Vertical ventilation
Vertical ventilation
    establishing and supporting of, 346–355
        opening a roof, 352–355
        safety, 347–352
    functions, 346
    high-rise buildings, 415–417
    horizontal ventilation vs., 302
    overview, 14, 345–346
    rolling back the roof, 402–403
    roof construction, 361–389
    roof coverings, 389–396
    roof openings, 396–399
    safety, 346–355
        firefighters to the roof, 348
        hazard identification, 347
        protective hoselines, 351–352
        reading a roof, 348–350
        sounding a roof, 350
        working on a roof, 351
    tools, 355–361
        chain saw, 357–358
        cutting tools, 355–359
        pick-head axe, 358–360
        pike pole, 360
        rotary saw, 356
        rubbish hook, 360
        sledgehammer, 361
        stripping tools, 359–361
    uses for ladders, 139
    ventilation exit opening, 399–404
        louver vents, 401–402
        panelized roofs, rolling back, 402–403
        trench (strip) ventilation, 403–404
Vinyl fences, 211

W

Walls
    access into structures, 242–248
    breach for emergency egress, 86–87
    concrete, 246–247
    double-course brick, 245
    fire wall, 165–166
    forcible entry, 242–248
    gypsum wallboard, 244
    for horizontal ventilation, 324–327
        exterior walls, 325–327
        interior firewalls, 325
        masonry and concrete, 326
        metal, 327
        stem walls, 325
        veneer-over-frame, 326–327
    masonry, 211, 245–246
    metal, 248, 327
    opening for access, 107
    oriented strand board, 243
    parapet walls, 376
    security measures, 213
    veneer, 244, 326–327
    wall ties, 327
    wall tops, 213
    water damage, 112
    wood-frame, 243–245
Warehouse fire characteristics, 167–168
Water
    in basements or cellars, 198
    contamination hazards, 114
    control in structure fires, 196–197
        sprinklered buildings, 196–197
        unsprinklered buildings, 197
    leaks without fire, 198
    removal techniques, 113–114
    secondary loss control, 112, 113–114
    short circuits in basements, 195
    supply, size up of, 157
    using ladders for removal of, 141–142
    water chutes, 114, 142
Weather
    size-up factors, 154–155
    ventilation size-up considerations, 304–305
    wind
        fire development factors, 35
        horizontal ventilation consideration, 329
        leeward, 332
        neutral pressure plane effects, 420
        size-up factor, 154
        stack effect and, 421
        upsetting established ventilation, 339
        ventilation size-up consideration, 304
        windward, 332
        working with protective hoselines, 351–352
White ghost, 184
Whiteout, 262
Wildland fires
    extreme fire behavior, 46
    situational awareness, 76
Wind
    fire development factors, 35
    horizontal ventilation consideration, 329
    leeward, 332
    neutral pressure plane effects, 420
    size-up factor, 154
    stack effect and, 421
    upsetting established ventilation, 339
    ventilation size-up consideration, 304
    windward, 332
    working with protective hoselines, 351–352
Windowless buildings, 410, 429
Windows
    breaking, 237–238, 332
    clerestory windows, 399
    decay stage fire, 29
    egress through, 83–85
    film-coated glass, 242
    fire gas ignition, 54
    for fire ventilation, 34
    flying guillotine hazard, 237
    forcible entry, 105, 237–238, 332
    horizontal ventilation, 316–320
    for horizontal ventilation, 332

horizontal ventilation
    awning windows, 318
    casement windows, 318
    double-hung windows, 317
    energy-efficient (thermal) windows, 319–320
    fixed windows, 317
    hopper windows, 319
    horizontal-sliding windows, 318
    jalousie windows, 319
    projected (factory) windows, 319
    single-hung windows, 317
industrial/institutional, 238
laminated glass, 241
lapping, 108
Lexan, 239, 240, 320
locating for emergency egress, 83–84
mechanical advantage systems, 140
Plexiglas, 240–241
    reflective film, 37–38
    residential/commercial, 238
    security systems, 238–242, 320
    shuttered, 242
    size-up, 237
    thermal, 35, 320
    thermoplastic, 240–241
    types, 237
    ventilation from, 312
    windowless structures, 410, 429
    wired-glass, 241
Wired-glass windows, 241
Wood construction (Type III), 37
Wood frame construction (Type V), 37
Wooden deck roof, 372
Wooden fences, 211

Indexed by Nancy Kopper